THE OSAGE AND THE INVISIBLE WORLD

THE CIVILIZATION OF THE AMERICAN INDIAN SERIES

# The Osage
# and the Invisible World

FROM THE WORKS OF FRANCIS LA FLESCHE

INTRODUCED AND EDITED BY
## Garrick A. Bailey

UNIVERSITY OF OKLAHOMA PRESS : NORMAN AND LONDON

This book is published with the generous assistance of Edith Gaylord Harper.

**Library of Congress Cataloging-in-Publication Data**

La Flesche, Francis, d. 1932.
    The Osage and the invisible world : from the works of Francis La Flesche / introduction and edited by Garrick A. Bailey.
        p.  cm. — (Civilization of the American Indian series ; v. 217)
    Includes bibliographical references (p. 307) and index.
    ISBN: 0-8061-2743-0 (alk. paper)
    1. Osage Indians—Rites and ceremonies.  2. Osage Indians—Religion.  I. Bailey, Garrick Alan.  II. Title.  III. Series.
E99.O8L18  1995
299'.7852—dc20                                                    95–17999
                                                                      CIP

*The Osage and the Invisible World: From the Works of Francis La Flesche* is Volume 217 in The Civilization of the American Indian Series.

Book design by Bill Cason

1 2 3 4 5 6 7 8 9 10

*In Memory of*

Leroy Logan (Isolated Earth clan)
Louise Gray Red Corn (Deer clan)
Harold Red Corn (Gentle Sky clan)
Josephine Claremore Walker (Gentle Sky clan)

# Contents

List of Illustrations and Tables     ix
Preface     xi
Acknowledgments     xiii
CHAPTER 1. Introduction     3
CHAPTER 2. Francis La Flesche     10
CHAPTER 3. Osage Cosmology and Tribal Organization     27
CHAPTER 4. The Purpose and Meaning of Ritual     61
CHAPTER 5. Songs of the Wa-xo'-be     76
CHAPTER 6. Rite of the Chiefs     222
CHAPTER 7. Conclusion     277
Notes     287
References Cited     307
Index     315

# Illustrations and Tables

MAP

3.1 Osage territory in about 1690      28

PHOTOGRAPHS

1.1 Francis La Flesche      8
2.1 Saucy Calf      20
2.2 Charles Wah-hre-she      22
2.3 Shunkahmolah      24
2.4 Bacon Rind      25
3.1 Clan bundle      51
5.1 Face painting of the priests      93
5.2 Painting and dress of the Sho'-ka      109
5.3 Painting and dress of the Xo'-ka      113

FIGURES

3.1 Structure of the Osage cosmos      33
3.2 Osage clan structure      41
3.3 Traditional Osage village arrangement      43
3.4 Traditional Osage ritual structure      46
3.5 The House of Mystery      59
5.1 Cutting of the symbolic moccasins      105
5.2 Organization of the House of Mystery      128
5.3 Painted buffalo robe      178

TABLES

3.1 Clan names and life symbols      36
3.2 Traditional Osage religious structure      48
7.1 Two religious patterns defined by Hultkrantz      283

# *Preface*

No discipline has so consciously and vigorously fought to free itself of the constraints of ethnocentrism and cultural bias as anthropology. Although anthropologists have been far more successful than their colleagues in other disciplines in overcoming these cultural barriers, serious questions remain concerning the objectivity of anthropological research. Anthropology was a product of colonialism; the vast majority of anthropologists were and are European in their cultural heritage. Anthropologists, like other human beings, are products and carriers of cultural traditions and beliefs. Each brings with him or her into the discipline certain explicit and implicit beliefs about the nature of other peoples. The explicit beliefs, because they are concise and voiced, present little difficulty in overcoming. The problem lies in anthropologists' implicit beliefs about others. It was these implicit concepts that most concerned Francis La Flesche, the first Native American anthropologist and one of the earliest anthropologists from a non-Western cultural background.

Anthropologists have long held that all peoples have the same cognitive abilities and basic intelligence. Indeed, anthropologists were asserting this point when most Western scholars still believed that American Indians, Africans, Asians, and other non-Europeans were intellectually inferior. At the same time, anthropologists recognized that non-Western people, particularly "tribal" or "primitive" people, structured the world conceptually in a very different manner from Europeans. This recognition raised a question that is still with us: whether these conceptual differences were logical alternatives derived from a common base, or whether they represented discrete and logically incompatible systems of reasoning.

No true consensus has been reached concerning this question. In the early part of the twentieth century, Lucian Levy-Bruhl argued that "natives" were "prelogical," and thus Europeans could not truly comprehend their thoughts and behavior.[1] More recently, C. R. Hallpike defined "primitive" mental processes as "preoperative." Although they may be adults, the reasoning abilities of "primitives" reach only the level of a seven-year-old Western child.[2] Few contemporary scholars fully accept the ideas of Levy-Bruhl or Hallpike, but many still feel that there is a major conceptual difference between the thinking of "tribal" peoples and that of "civilized" peoples.

Whether one views "tribal" thought as prelogical, preoperative, or merely different from that of "modern" peoples, the implications are the same. These cultures are relics not merely of an earlier human way of life but also of an earlier, antiquated process of thought. Thus they are of interest to "civilized" peoples not for their intellectual content, because by implication they have none, but only for their historical significance and exotic character.

It was these ideas that Francis La Flesche wished to challenge through his writings on Osage religion. "We are told . . . that it [Native America] has no contribution to the world's thought or the world's pleasure, nothing to articulate with Eastern [Old World] lines of culture, nothing to gladden the heart of man and cause it to thrill under the unifying touch of a common nature. Never-the-less . . . the folk were here, living their story and singing their song."[3]

GARRICK A. BAILEY

*Tulsa, Oklahoma*

# *Acknowledgments*

THIS book is but one product of my long-term research on Osage culture. Over the past thirty years, numerous members of the Osage community have assisted me in one way or another. To these people I owe a tremendous debt of gratitude, and I would like to thank all of them collectively for their help, encouragement, hospitality, and friendship. In my next book on the Osages I am going to acknowledge many of these individuals personally. For this book, however, I must limit my acknowledgments to a few people who were particularly important, either directly or indirectly, to this study.

Harold and Louise Red Corn were my primary sources of support and encouragement while I was a graduate student researching Osage culture. If it had not been for them I doubt that I would ever have finished my dissertation. Had it not been for the encouragement of Leroy Logan and Josephine Walker, I never would have studied the Osage peyote religion. At the time, neither they nor I realized how much I was learning about traditional Osage religion as well. To these four I owe my greatest debt. In addition, I would like to thank Morris Lookout, Carl Ponca, Charles Pratt, James Red Corn, Sean Standing-Bear, and Robert Walker. The discussions I have had with them over the past few years concerning Francis La Flesche's studies have added immeasurably to my understanding of Osage culture and thus to my understanding and interpretation of traditional Osage religious beliefs.

Over the past twenty-five years, the University of Tulsa has on several occasions, through faculty research grants, supported my research on the Osages. Much of this research was relevant to this project. In 1987–88 I received a fellowship from the National Endowment for the Humanities and a supplemental grant from the University of Tulsa to research Osage culture change. It was during this period that the initial research for this study was accomplished and I first realized the true value and importance of La Flesche's studies.

Most of the research specifically for this book took place while I was a senior fellow in anthropology at the Smithsonian Institution from January to August 1992. During that time I had the opportunity to study La Flesche's papers in the National Anthropological Archives. I would like to thank all the members and staff of the department of anthropology at the Smithsonian for making my residence so productive and enjoyable. I especially thank William Sturtevant, who acted as my sponsor. His advice and comments were invaluable. In addition, I thank Jo Allyn Archambault, Ives Goddard, Candice Green, Donald Ortner, Dan Rogers, Gus Van Beek, John Ewers, Jim Griffin, Tom Kavanagh, and Ceasar Marino for their hospitality and for making my time at the Smithsonian such an intellectually rewarding experience; Robert Laughlin, for the use of his office, an ideal environment; and the staff of the anthropology department—Carole Lee Kin, Karen Moran, Joyce Sommers, and Lawan Tyson—for their assistance in guiding me through the intricacies of Smithsonian life. Among the staff of the National Anthropological Archives, I would like to thank Mary Ruwell, Kathleen Baxter, and Paula Fleming.

Our stay in Washington was made all the more enjoyable thanks to Charles and Mary Winters, who kindly allowed my wife and me to occupy their house in Maryland.

Dale Phelps, secretary of the anthropology department at the University of Tulsa, helped to prepare the manuscript, and Jane Kepp copy edited the final version. Finally, I would like to thank my wife, Roberta, for all her help, encouragement, and patience, and for her copy editing of the initial draft of the manuscript.

G.A.B.

THE OSAGE AND THE INVISIBLE WORLD

CHAPTER 1 *Introduction*

THE potential importance of Francis La Flesche's studies of Osage religion has long been recognized by anthropologists familiar with his writings. In quantity and quality of data presented, there are few studies of any Native American group that equal La Flesche's work on the Osages. All together, his publications on the Osages exceed two thousand pages. An Omaha Indian, La Flesche spoke as his native language a language mutually intelligible with Osage. He collected information about ritual in Osage and translated it himself. The men who gave him this information were among the most knowledgeable Osage religious leaders of their day.

What distinguishes La Flesche's studies from other studies of American Indian religion is what he attempted to show through his research and through the religious tradition these men represented. La Flesche was not interested merely in describing Osage ritual; his primary objective was to explain Osage ideas, beliefs, and concepts. He wanted his readers to see the world of the Osages for what it was in reality—not the world of simple "children of nature" but a highly complex world reflecting an intellectual tradition as sophisticated and imaginative as that of any Old World people.

The men whose knowledge he recorded were the remaining priests in what had been the last functioning Mississippian priesthood. The basic religious practices, ideas, and concepts of the traditional Osages were derived from those of the earlier "Mississippian peoples"—the horticultural peoples of the Mississippi Valley and adjacent regions who, in the centuries prior to European contact, had constructed the great mound complexes at Cahokia, Aztalan, and elsewhere. In terms of both the types of cultural data he recorded and the religious tradition they represent, La Flesche's studies of Osage religion constitute a unique, critically important, and irreplaceable record.

Francis La Flesche died in 1932. In his obituary, Hartley Alexander wrote, concerning his Osage studies, that these "texts and translations, accompanied by full exposition . . . collectively form what is certainly the most complete single record of the ceremonies of a North American Indian people."[1] Yet for the past sixty years, La Flesche's studies of the Osages have languished with little recognition. Today, many anthropologists are unfamiliar with his name, let alone his work. Even in studies of American Indian religion, mention is seldom made of either La Flesche or the Osages.

There are two reasons why La Flesche's monumental studies of Osage religion have faded into obscurity. First, the Osage religious practices and concepts he recorded contrast sharply both with Euro-American stereotypes of American Indian religion and with the religious beliefs and practices recorded for more western and northern tribes. In the Osage world, for example, there were no named "culture heroes," no "sacred places," and no exotic "mystic beings" who wandered the land. Second, La Flesche's style of presentation rendered the data almost incomprehensible. Alfred Kroeber hit the crux of the problem when he wrote, "The Osage are . . . difficult to place. Thanks to La Flesche, we know several of their rituals in detail, but these give relatively few indications of the type of the culture as a whole."[2]

La Flesche was fifty-three when he began his Osage research and sixty-four when the first of his major Osage studies was published. There is little doubt that he planned a comprehensive study of Osage religion.[3] He discovered, however, that Osage ritual structure was far more complex and elaborate than he had originally imagined. As a result, he never reached the point of analyzing or integrating his Osage studies, which are little more than his published field notes—a series of lengthy but disarticulated fragments of Osage ritual knowledge. They do not lend themselves to ready comprehension by the casual reader.

My interest has not been in Osage religion per se; I first became acquainted with La Flesche's work as a graduate student researching Osage social organization. But because the social, political, and religious aspects of Osage organization were components of a highly integrated, unified system, it is impossible to speak of or understand one without reference to the others. Initially I studied La Flesche's writings in search of information about the basic structural features of Osage social institutions. His works proved to be an invaluable source of information, but on the whole I found La Flesche's Osage publications confusing and ignored most of their information on cosmology and ritual.

Although I finished my dissertation in 1970, there was one problem in Osage culture history that I could not adequately resolve. At the beginning of the twentieth century, the peyote religion was introduced to the Osages, and within ten to fifteen years the vast majority of Osage full-bloods had converted. The peyotists demanded total abandonment of traditional Osage religious beliefs and practices. Within a decade or so, most of the sacred bundles had been sold, buried, or burned. Older Osages turned their backs on the old religion and refused to discuss the past even with their children. Traditional religious practices continued in only a few families. The last initiated member of the old priesthood died in 1971. For most families, the break with the past was sharp and decisive. Children born after their families converted to peyotism grew up with little, if any, knowledge about the old religion. When I began my research in the mid-1960s, the Osages used the term "traditional" to refer to either the peyote church or the I'n-lon-schka dance, a dance that had been adopted from the Kaws and Poncas in the 1880s.

What puzzled me was the absence of any readily definable continuity between the traditional Osage world described by La Flesche and the Osage world of the 1960s and early 1970s. I knew that continuity had to exist, because the Osages still maintained a distinctive culture, but I could not define the nature of that continuity. During the early and mid-1970s, I continued my research on contemporary Osage social and cultural institutions. With the encouragement of Leroy Logan, a close friend and peyotist, I began to study the peyote church. Since I strongly believe that religion and religious worship are private matters, I initially turned down invitations to attend meetings. It was Josephine Walker who finally said that I could never understand the peyote church merely by talking about it. As she told me, you have to take part, because it "shows you." I was also continuing to collect data on the I'n-lon-schka dance, and I was surprised at how many people kept mentioning that the dance "teaches you." At the time I did not fully understand what Josephine Walker was talking about, nor did I understand what people meant when they said that the dance "teaches."

In the late 1970s I become involved in studying the Navajos, and my Navajo research ended up occupying the better part of ten years. But all along my intention was someday to return to the Osages and finish that study. I had become fixated on what appeared to be a hiatus in their cultural continuity. I knew that something was wrong in the way I was viewing the question. Osage culture had changed drastically, but there was still a readily definable Osage culture.

In 1987–88 I received a fellowship from the National Endowment for the Humanities to finish my study of Osage culture change. One of the first tasks I undertook was a rereading and analysis of La Flesche's studies. I was particularly interested in the cosmology they described. One day, during the course of this research, an Osage friend and I were discussing historic changes in the I'n-lon-schka dance. In the middle of the conversation, my friend, Morris Lookout, suddenly interjected that although the history of the dance was interesting, what truly concerned him was what the dance was like today and what it would be like in the future. Instantly I recalled one of the basic teachings of the ancient priests: "Nothing in the cosmos moves backward." Contrary to popular conceptions about American Indians, the traditional Osages were, and the contemporary Osages continue to be, strongly future oriented.

For the first time I began to see the nature of the continuity that linked the contemporary Osages with their ancestors. Continuity in Osage culture was not to be found in formal institutions but rather in ideas, concepts, and beliefs. In my conversations with Osage friends over the weeks and months that followed, I heard La Flesche's ancient priests speak to me time and time again through the mouths of their descendants. The basic social norms and values, as well as the general concepts of the world expressed in the teaching of the old priests, were alive and well in the collective minds of members of the contemporary Osage community.

Now I realized what people had meant when they told me that participation in the peyote church or the I'n-lon-schka dance "shows" or "teaches" one. Rituals were the means by which a people, particularly a nonliterate society, preserved and transmitted knowledge. This knowledge was transmitted not just in words but also through the formal structuring of the physical behavior of individuals and through the use of a variety of material symbols. Any formal institution could be made "Osage." The particular social norms, values, and concepts and how they were transferred from one set of formal institutions to another is the subject of another book. I did, however, realize that the key to understanding the culture history of the Osages was to be found in a more complete understanding of Osage traditional religion—in other words, in La Flesche's studies.

In 1992 I was a senior fellow in anthropology at the Smithsonian Institution. This fellowship allowed me to study La Flesche's notes in the National Anthropological Archives, as well as his published studies, with the ultimate objective of producing an introduction to Osage cosmology and ritual.

The purpose of this book is to provide an introduction to La Flesche's studies of Osage religious rituals. Because his work cannot be fully appreciated or understood without some knowledge of the man himself, I offer a short biography of La Flesche in chapter 2. Francis La Flesche (photo 1.1) was a unique scholar. His objective in his Osage writings was not the same as that of his anthropological colleagues. La Flesche wanted to demonstrate to the academic world the true intellectual achievements of the American Indian. His descriptions of Osage rituals were merely the means by which he wanted to demonstrate those achievements.

Chapter 3 provides a general overview of Osage culture, with emphasis on cosmology, religious organization, and ritual structure. Whenever possible, I quote directly from La Flesche. When direct quotation is impossible, I try to keep the wording and ideas as close to La Flesche's as possible. I must warn you, however, that gaps exist in the data and some of the material presented cannot be adequately explained. There are also factual contradictions in La Flesche's works, and I was forced to make judgments about the correct interpretations. I may not always be right.

In chapters 4, 5, and 6, I introduce and provide highly edited versions of two rituals recorded by La Flesche: the Songs of the Wa-xo'-be initiation rite and the Rite of the Chiefs. Neither of these rituals was completely described in La Flesche's published versions. In order to make them as complete as possible, I have integrated information presented in his discussions of other rituals. The sources of this additional information are indicated in the footnotes. Moreover, to save space as well as to make the text more comprehensible, I have deleted much of the material he presented. For example, La Flesche included musical scores and the Osage words to songs and, at the end of each of his volumes, an Osage transcription of every song and recitation as well as a literal English translation. Because these data are of primary interest to relatively few scholars, and because they are readily available in most major libraries, I have omitted them. La Flesche also frequently inserted lengthy discussions of comparative or related information into the text. Although they are informative, these passages break up the natural flow of the ritual being described. In some cases I have deleted these passages altogether; in other instances I have extracted them as endnotes; and in still other instances I have moved them to another part of the text.

I have also restructured some of La Flesche's presentation by inserting new topic headings, removing some of his topic headings, collaps-

PHOTO 1.1. Francis La Flesche (1857–1932). Courtesy National Anthropological Archives, Smithsonian Institution, 4804.

ing many of his short paragraphs into single, longer paragraphs, and occasionally reordering the sequence in which the data are presented. For the sake of clarity, I have deleted many of the Osage terms included in the original text and used only their English translations. As important and interesting as these terms may be, La Flesche used them so extensively that their effect was to make a complex subject even more difficult to understand. I have also modified La Flesche's manner of transcribing Osage terms. For example, nasalized vowels are now indicated by an *n* following the vowel.

I have changed some of La Flesche's translations, too. For example, La Flesche went to great lengths to emphasize that Wa-kon-da ("God") was a single unified force that manifested itself in various ways in all living, moving things. Osage rituals frequently appealed to certain qualities of Wa-kon-da as expressed in particular living, moving things. Thus, in a ritual the Osages might appeal to Wa-kon-da *hon'-ba-don*. La Flesche usually translated this term as "the god of day." The difficulty with this translation is that it creates in the reader's mind the image of a distinct deity that was not present in the minds of the Osages. To try to create in the reader's mind an image closer to the Osage one, I have changed such translations from "god" to either "force" or "power."

With this brief introduction, let us now look at La Flesche and the world of the Osages. I think you will discover an Indian world you never imagined.

## CHAPTER 2

*Francis La Flesche*

THE last three decades of the nineteenth century and the first two of the twentieth were among the most chaotic and traumatic in American Indian history. During the early years of that half-century, the western tribes suffered their final military defeats, along with the near extinction of the bison herds. Most tribes had hardly settled on their new reservations before the government instituted a policy of forced acculturation and assimilation. Imbued with the myth of the "vanishing Indian" and the idea that nothing Indian was of any value, government officials instituted programs deliberately designed to destroy Indian cultural institutions. Indian children were separated from their families and placed in boarding schools where they were taught not only English and Christianity but also contempt for Indian cultural traditions. Courts of Indian Offenses were established on the reservations to eliminate objectionable Indian religious and social practices. In 1887, passage of the Dawes Act, or General Indian Allotment Act, began the destruction of the reservation system by allotting land to individual Indians and opening unallotted lands to white settlement. The prevailing attitude of government officials was well expressed by Captain Richard Pratt, founder of Carlisle Indian School, in his philosophy of "destroying the Indian to save the man."[1]

With their economic independence gone and their lives controlled and manipulated by government officials, most tribes experienced the collapse of their traditional economic, social, political, and religious institutions. Because physical resistance was no longer possible, many Indians turned to religious movements—the Ghost Dance and later the peyote religion.

Until the late nineteenth century, there had been only a handful of Native American writers.[2] Owing in large part to the government's vigorous Indian education program, the number of Indian writers and scholars increased steadily during the late nineteenth century. By the early twentieth century, a small but growing literature on American

Indians written by American Indians was emerging. Among these scholars and writers were Charles Eastman (Sioux), William Jones (Sac and Fox), James Murie (Pawnee), and Arthur Parker (Seneca), to name only some. The most prolific was Francis La Flesche. A trained linguist and ethnographer for the Bureau of American Ethnology of the Smithsonian Institution, La Flesche wrote or coauthored more than three thousand pages on the Omahas, Osages, and American Indians in general.

All of these men had been born in a time of tremendous cultural and social upheaval, and most had witnessed the cultural and social disintegration of their people. All of them realized that the Indian peoples would have to adjust to white domination, but few Native Americans of La Flesche's generation understood as clearly as he the misconceptions Euro-Americans held about Indians. As a government bureaucrat, professional anthropologist, and Indian activist who spent most of his adult life in Washington, D.C., La Flesche came to realize that whether they were government officials, missionaries, scholars, or average people in the street—and whether they were "pro" or "anti" Indian in sentiment—the vast majority of Euro-Americans saw and judged Indians in the same basic terms. He understood that these misconceptions had far-reaching, deleterious effects on almost every aspect of Indian life—social, economic, political, and religious.

La Flesche took on as one of the primary objectives of his writing and research the goal of changing white Americans' conception of the Indians. To accomplish this end, he had to challenge the basic, implicit assumptions about Indians that not only permeated American popular culture but also gave focus and direction to most academic studies. Although his overall objective was never stated in his academic writing, he expressed this goal elsewhere. In the introduction to his popular autobiographical account, *The Middle Five: Indian Boys at School,* he wrote that "the object of this book is to reveal the true nature and character of the Indian boy . . . [and it is hoped that] it may help these little Indians be judged, as are other boys, by what they say and what they do."[3] Another time he criticized the "pro-Indian" Lake Mohonk Conference and government officials for acting as if "the Indians were not capable of thinking for themselves, [or] of having sentiments like other human beings . . . [and for not having Indians] consulted or allowed a voice in the management of their personal affairs."[4]

La Flesche most clearly stated his position in a published lecture he gave in Philadelphia in 1903. In it, he attacked both the American public and the academic community for their lack of understanding:

The real character of peoples is never fully known until there has been obtained some knowledge of their religious ideas and their conception of the Unseen Power that animates all life. It is not generally credited by the white race that the tribes of this continent did not differ from the other people of the earth, in the effort to understand the meaning of life in all its infinite variety of forms and relation of these forms to the great, mysterious Power that animates all life. It is true, however, that the natives of this land had given these themes much thought and had formulated their ideas concerning them long before the European set foot upon this soil.

The lack of intelligence as to this fact has been in part due to the absence of a written literature among the tribes living within the area of the United States, while such records as did exist have suffered grave misapprehension and mistreatment on the part of the observers. Moreover, the idea commonly entertained by the white race that they alone possess the knowledge of a God, has influenced the minds of all those of that race who have come in contact with the Indians. We find that most of the missionaries who have labored among the Indians did not stop to inquire if the people had any idea of a Power that made and controlled all things. These well-meaning and zealous men seem to have taken for granted that savages were not capable by their own effort of conceiving the thought of such a Power. . . . It was not possible therefore for the white people to gain, through the medium of these teachers, any definite knowledge of the real thoughts of the Indian concerning the supreme Being.

Nor has the Indian fared much better at the hands of those who have undertaken to study him as an object of ethnological interest. The myths, the rituals, and the legends of the race have been frequently recorded in such a manner as to obscure their true meaning and to make them appear as childish or as foolish. This has been in a large measure due to linguistic difficulties. The Indian tongues differ widely from the English language, not only in the construction of sentences but in general literary form. Moreover, the imagery of the Indian speech conveys a very different meaning to the mind of the Indian from that which it conveys to the mind of the white man. The Indian looks upon nature, upon all natural forms, animate and inanimate, from a different standpoint and he draws from them different lessons than does one of the white race. So when scholars give a literal translation to an Indian story, both its spirit and its form are lost to the English reader. Or when the myth is interpreted by an Indian who has picked up a scanty and colloquial knowledge of English, even if by chance he has himself a comprehension of the meaning of the myth he translates, his rendition will be one that no intelligent Indian can accept as a true presentation of the mythic story. It is from translations such as these that the mental capacity of the Indian has been judged and conclusions drawn as to his conception of the Supreme Being and the relation of that Being to man and all other things, animate and inanimate.[5]

It is important to realize that La Flesche's ideas were not unique to him. He was not the only American Indian writer of the time to assert that Native American religious beliefs and practices were being misconstrued by non-Indians. In a similar vein, Charles Eastman wrote in his book *The Soul of the Indian:*

The religion of the Indian is the last thing about him that the man of another race will ever understand. . . . Even if he [the Indian] can be induced to speak, the racial and religious prejudice of the other [the white] stands in the way of his sympathetic comprehension. . . . Practically all existing studies on this subject have been made during the transition period, when the original beliefs and philosophy of the native American were already undergoing rapid disintegration. There are to be found here and there superficial accounts of strange customs and ceremonies, of which the symbolism or inner meaning was largely hidden from the observer.[6]

Eastman wrote *The Soul of the Indian* in an attempt to correct the misconceptions the white world had concerning Indian religion. He noted, however, that his "little book does not pretend to be a scientific treatise."[7] Instead, he wrote it for a general audience.

Whereas Eastman chose to address the problem as a popular writer for the general public, La Flesche chose to write as a scholar for an academic audience. Instead of writing about Indian religion in a general sense, he chose to explain and describe Osage religion and ritual in detail.

La Flesche saw religion as the intellectual core of a people's culture, and he believed that a people's mental capacities and intellectual achievements found their greatest expression in their religion. By focusing on Osage religion, he hoped to correct some of the whites' misconceptions about Indians and to demonstrate the Indians' true mental and intellectual capabilities. One may well ask why La Flesche did not openly state this objective in his academic writings. I can only speculate that as an Indian he may have felt that he was in no position to challenge directly the prevailing notions of the white world. He probably feared that his work would be dismissed as subjective and unscientific if he blatantly challenged his colleagues. So without comment, he presented his data, perhaps hoping that the material would speak for itself.

Was La Flesche's appraisal of his academic colleagues unfair? Those same colleagues had at one time elected him president of the Anthropological Society of Washington.[8] Didn't he think they fully accepted him as a professional scholar? Although Hartley Alexander's obituary of La Flesche in *American Anthropologist* praised his Osage studies, it also referred to them as a "sentimental account." In compiling La Flesche's list of publications, Alexander included only those articles and works for which he was sole author, omitting the numerous publications he had coauthored with Alice Fletcher, a Euro-American anthropologist. Was this omission intended to convey that these were really her works, not truly his? Finally, although photographs of La Flesche almost invariably show him formally dressed in a shirt, tie, and coat, his obituary was accompanied by a photograph of a bare-chested La Flesche clad only in a buffalo robe. The original photograph had been retouched to remove the shirt and tie he was actually wearing under the robe.[9] In death La Flesche was treated by other anthropologists not as a professional colleague but as a native informant. His wariness about the academic community seems to have been well founded.

La Flesche was a remarkable man from an exceptional family.[10] Born on the Omaha reservation in Nebraska Territory in 1857, he was the son of Joseph La Flesche and his second wife. His older sister, Susette La Flesche Tibbles (1854–1903), also known as Bright Eyes, was one of the best-known Indian political activists and lecturers of the late nineteenth century. His younger sister, Susan La Flesche Picotte (1865–1915), graduated from Hampton Institute and then attended the Women's Medical College in Philadelphia. She was the first American Indian woman to become a physician.

The achievements of the La Flesche children reflected their father's attitude toward the changing world of the Indians. Joseph La Flesche, or Iron Eye, was the son of a French trader and a Ponca Indian woman. When he was still a small boy, his mother left his father to live with the closely related Omahas. Eventually Iron Eye was adopted by Big Elk, the principal chief of the Omahas. When Big Elk died in 1853, Iron Eye succeeded him as chief.

Iron Eye realized that the Indian world was rapidly changing and that the Indians had to adjust to the ever-increasing numbers of white settlers. Following the creation of the Omaha reservation in 1854, Iron Eye encouraged the Omahas to emulate the whites. Although opposed by many Omahas, Iron Eye and some of his followers established a new village in which they built houses instead of the traditional earth lodges, and in which fields were plowed and fenced in a Euro-American manner. More traditional Omahas came to refer to this village as the "Make Believe White Man's Village." Iron Eye also believed that education was important for the survival of the tribe. At his request, the Presbyterian church established a mission school on the reservation and continued to operate it until 1869, when the Indian Service took it over. Francis, Susette, and Susan, as well as the other La Flesche children, attended this school.

Although the world of the Omahas was changing rapidly, their traditions were still very much alive when Francis La Flesche was a boy.

A majority of the Omahas continued to live in earth-lodge villages and make biannual treks onto the Great Plains, where they camped in tipis and hunted bison. Most people practiced the traditional religion and religious rituals. The La Flesche family lived in a house and fenced and plowed their fields, but they accompanied the tribe on bison hunts. Iron Eye spoke English and all his children attended boarding school, but Omaha was the language they spoke at home. And although Iron Eye was a Christian, he had two wives and allowed his children to take active roles in traditional religious rituals. Thus young Francis grew up exposed to both the white world and that of the traditional Omahas. In the Presbyterian boarding school, he studied English, received training in Christian teachings, and learned of the white world beyond Nebraska. As a child he filled the ceremonial role of the Sacred Child in the tribal Wawan or Pipe ritual, and as a teenager he served as one of the runners during the bison hunt.

The event that most strongly affected the course of La Flesche's life was the famous trial of the Ponca leader Standing Bear.[11] Not only had the Poncas lived near the Omahas, but the two peoples also spoke mutually intelligible languages, and their social relations were close. In the summer of 1877, the Poncas were forcibly removed from their reservation in Nebraska and sent south under military guard to Oklahoma (then Indian Territory). Many Poncas died during removal and in the year that followed—among them, the son of Standing Bear. In the winter of 1878–79, Standing Bear and a small group of followers left for Nebraska in order to bury the body of his son in their old home. The Omahas welcomed back their Ponca friends, giving them shelter and food.

Once back in Nebraska, Standing Bear asked the government to allow him and his followers to remain there. In response, federal officials had them arrested and imprisoned and made plans to return them to Oklahoma. These arrests outraged not only the Omahas but many local whites as well. With the help of sympathetic white attorneys, the case was taken to federal court. Susette La Flesche acted as Standing Bear's interpreter. A young newspaper editor named Henry Tibbles publicized the trial in a series of sensational articles carried in newspapers throughout the country. Standing Bear, Susette La Flesche, and Henry Tibbles became national celebrities. The court ordered that Standing Bear be freed. The federal judge ruled that an Indian had the same rights as a white man and allowed him and his followers to remain in Nebraska.

After the trial, Indian rights groups organized an eastern lecture tour for Standing Bear, Susette La Flesche, and Henry Tibbles. Young Francis, called Frank, accompanied them on this tour, which included Washington, D.C., and other eastern cities. In 1882, Susette married the widowed Henry Tibbles and then spent the rest of her life fighting for Indian rights. Attractive and articulate, she became a popular lecturer, traveling not only in the United States but in Europe as well.

Following the tour of 1879–80, La Flesche returned to Nebraska, but he did not stay long. In 1881 he secured a job as a copyist for the Indian Service and moved to Washington. Although he returned frequently to Nebraska to visit his relatives, he actually lived in Washington until 1929, three years before his death. Several factors may have prompted him to leave Nebraska and live most of his life in Washington. First, La Flesche was a socially marginal person. He was half Omaha, through his mother, but the Omahas were a patrilineal society; his father, Iron Eye, was recognized by some as an Omaha chief, yet he was still half Ponca and half French. To many traditional Omahas, Iron Eye and his children were at best Ponca and at worst French. There can be no doubt that the members of the La Flesche family felt their social ambiguity.[12]

A second factor may have been La Flesche's divorce. About the time of the tour he had married an Omaha woman. They separated shortly before he took the job in Washington, although they did not divorce until 1884. A third factor may have been the marriage of his sister Susette to Henry Tibbles. The two lived with the La Flesche family, and Francis detested his brother-in-law.[13] The main reason he chose to live in Washington, however, may have been the close relationship he quickly developed with Alice Fletcher. Almost twenty years his senior, Fletcher was one of the earliest women anthropologists. The relationship between Fletcher and La Flesche was the subject of rumor at the time. For most of his life in Washington the two shared a house, and on her death Fletcher willed her property to La Flesche.[14]

In Washington, La Flesche quickly developed ties with members of the local anthropological community, especially Alice Fletcher and James Dorsey. He had originally met them on the tour of 1879–80. Both were deeply involved in the study of American Indians in general and the Siouan tribes, such as the Omahas, in particular. La Flesche studied linguistics with Dorsey, but it was Fletcher who would prove the stronger influence. Although he remained an employee of the Indian Service, he soon began to work with Fletcher on her research, initially as her informant and interpreter. It is difficult to pinpoint when he emerged as a professional anthropologist in his own right. In 1885 he published his first professional paper,[15] but for the next twenty years he also continued to collaborate with Fletcher on her Omaha research. This research produced a number of coauthored academic papers and culminated in the monumental study *The Omaha Tribe*,[16] which was completed in January 1909 but not published by the Bureau of American Ethnology until 1911.

While collaborating with Fletcher, La Flesche was developing his own distinct professional identity. Anthropology was not yet an academic discipline within universities, so La Flesche chose to study law. In 1891 he received his LL.B. from the National University in Washington, D.C., and in 1893 he was awarded an LL.M. from the same institution.[17] In 1900, he published *The Middle Five*, a book about his life at the Presbyterian boarding school. This widely read book established La Flesche as a major, if not the major, Indian writer of the period.

In 1910 La Flesche left the Indian Service to take a position as ethnographer for the Bureau of American Ethnology in order to produce a study of the Osages that would be comparable to what he and Fletcher had written about the Omahas. La Flesche's career as an anthropologist falls into two distinct periods. The first was his period of collaborative research with Fletcher, when he learned anthropology and when his research reflected the overriding interest of the anthropologists of his day—the desire to record general descriptions of tribal cultures. He learned this approach well, and his coauthored study of the Omahas has been called one of the best descriptions of a tribal people ever written.[18]

The second period in his career began in 1910 with his studies of the Osages. By this time Fletcher was seventy-two years old. Although she contributed to the Osage studies by transcribing the music to many of the Osage songs recorded by La Flesche, this was not a collaborative project. The focus of his Osage research was markedly different from that of his earlier Omaha research. Independent of Fletcher, La Flesche focused his research efforts narrowly on the study of Osage religious beliefs and rituals, with an emphasis on explanation and meaning rather than on mere description.

Noting the different orientations of the Omaha and Osage studies, Joan Mark has suggested that the Omaha project was "for anthropologists and the public, to help them understand the Indians."[19] On the other hand, she feels that La Flesche wrote the Osage study "not for anthropologists, but for future generations of Indians."[20] I think she is only partially correct about La Flesche's intent. He certainly did publish his Osage studies for the benefit of future generations of Indians, but the academic community was also one of his intended audiences.

His Osage studies were meant to show the academic world how poorly it understood the American Indian.

La Flesche had several advantages in his studies of the Osages. His native Omaha language was mutually intelligible with Osage, so he was able to discuss religious concepts with Osage religious leaders with total fluency in their own language. Omaha religious beliefs and rituals, though different in many particulars, were basically the same as Osage beliefs and rituals, which minimized the problem of misinterpretation. But the most important factor was one over which neither La Flesche nor anyone else had control—timing.

La Flesche could not have arrived among the Osages at a more opportune time to study traditional religion and ritual. Had he arrived ten years earlier, no one of importance would have spoken to him about these matters. Had he arrived ten years later, most of the men who helped him would have been dead. Important Osage ritual knowledge was limited to men who had been formally initiated into one of the priesthoods. Osage priests would not, under normal conditions, have allowed an uninitiated outsider like La Flesche to record their most sacred and secret religious knowledge. The times were far from normal, however. Following the Osages' removal to Oklahoma in 1872, their population declined precipitously, from almost 3,700 full-bloods to only 1,000 twenty years later.[21] Many of the older priests died without passing on critical ritual knowledge. By the early 1880s, the Osage ritual cycle had collapsed. Many of the major rituals were extinct, having died with the last priests who had the knowledge and authority to perform them.

Thus a vacuum had developed within the Osage religious structure. In 1884 and 1885, the various Osage bands adopted the I'n-lon-schka dance from the Kaws and Poncas. Originally a military society dance, the I'n-lon-schka dance had evolved into a religious movement by the 1870s and 1880s.[22] The I'n-lon-schka soon emerged as the major socioreligious ritual for the Osages.

In 1891, Sitting Bull, the Arapaho, brought the Ghost Dance to the Big Hill band of Osages. Few Osages participated, and even fewer were converted. It was never danced again.[23] In 1894 or 1895, the Otoe prophet William Faw Faw introduced his new dance to the Osages. Although it attracted more Osage adherents than the Ghost Dance, Old Man Faw Faw's dance, as the Osages called it, did not gain wide acceptance.[24]

In 1898, John Wilson, a Caddo/Delaware, introduced the Osages to the new peyote religion.[25] By the time La Flesche arrived in 1910, the traditional religion was virtually gone, replaced by peyotism. In 1911, a mourning dance was held at Gray Horse;[26] it would prove to be the last performance of a major, traditional Osage public ritual. After 1911, only minor rites and initiation rituals were performed. Some families continued to have traditional naming rites for their children, and some young men were still initiated into the clan priesthoods. La Flesche attended an initiation in 1919,[27] and a few were held as late as the 1930s.[28] The majority of full-blooded Osages, however, including most of the surviving traditional priests, had been converted to the peyote church. Osage peyotism called for the abandonment of traditional religious practices.[29] The earlier restrictions on ritual knowledge were no longer in effect, and it was among the former priests who had become peyote church leaders that La Flesche found his most willing informants.

La Flesche's contacts with individual Osages dated back at least to the mid-1890s. Alice Fletcher had an interest in Osage culture, and she and La Flesche had entertained and interviewed Osage delegations visiting Washington. In their Omaha book they included a short comparative segment on the Osages based on these interviews.[30] When La Flesche arrived in Pawhuska, Oklahoma, in September 1910, he was already well acquainted with a number of Osage leaders and appears to have had his closest relationships with Black Dog and Saucy Calf.

Black Dog (Shon-ton-ca-be) was one of the major leaders of the Osage full-bloods and had served as principal chief of the tribe. Among the earliest Osage converts to the new peyote religion, he was one of four men authorized by John Wilson to lead the church after his death. La Flesche had known Black Dog since at least 1896, and Black Dog had been the source of much of the comparative material on the Osages published in *The Omaha Tribe*.[31] Unfortunately, Black Dog died about a month after La Flesche's arrival.[32]

After Black Dog's death, La Flesche's closest friend and main source of information about the Osages became Saucy Calf (Tse-zhin'-ga-wa-da-in-ga; photo 2.1). The two had met in Washington shortly before La Flesche began his Osage research. A very warm, father-son relationship quickly developed between them. Saucy Calf was a priest of the Buffalo Bull clan.[33] Although he had become a peyotist, he was not a major figure in the new religion, and his commitment to the peyote church was lukewarm. Seeing the disintegration of the traditional religion, Saucy Calf wanted to leave a written record of his knowledge for future Osages. He provided La Flesche with the first ritual he recorded— the Buffalo Bull clan version of the Songs of the Wa-xo'-be.

PHOTO 2.1. Saucy Calf (?–1912) Reproduced from La Flesche (1939:Plate 11).

But Saucy Calf worked with La Flesche only for a little more than a year and gave him the text of just this one ritual before dying mysteriously in a fire at his home in February 1912.[34] Although he was an elderly man, Saucy Calf was a widower with an eye for women. Following his death, a rumor circulated that Saucy Calf's white girlfriend had had him murdered and his house burned to make it look like an accident. Whether the rumor was true or not, many Osages were convinced that Saucy Calf had brought this tragedy on himself by "giving" his songs to La Flesche.[35]

Saucy Calf's death was a blow to La Flesche's research, depriving him not only of his closest Osage friend and strongest supporter but also of his main source of information. Thanks to Saucy Calf, by this time La Flesche had gained a clear understanding of the magnitude of his research problem. The Osage religious structure was far more complex than he had anticipated.[36] Ritual knowledge and authority were divided among twenty-four clan priesthoods. Each clan priesthood was in turn divided into seven degrees, each degree associated with a specific segment of the clan's ritual knowledge and authority. In addition, there were three tribal priesthoods, each with its own ritual knowledge and authority. Two of these tribal priesthoods had their own initiation rituals. The core of Osage religious knowledge was found not in public ceremonies but in the 170 clan and tribal priesthood initiation rituals—each of which was lengthy. Saucy Calf's description of the Buffalo Bull clan version of the Songs of the Wa-xo'-be initiation rite covered 140 pages. By 1910, complete knowledge of many, if not most, of these initiation rituals had already been lost. La Flesche decided to concentrate on recording a sample of Osage initiation rituals. In the course of his research he would also record some public rituals: the war ceremony, the mourning dance, the peace ceremony, the new year rite, and two versions of the child naming rite.

To conduct his planned research successfully, La Flesche had to gain the cooperation and support of a number of the former priests. Unlike other tribes during the early twentieth century, the Osages were not a poor and impoverished people. In 1910, with oil exploration just starting, they were already the "richest people per capita in the world," and they were getting even richer with every passing year.[37] La Flesche could not "buy" the cooperation of the Osages. He had to find men who would willingly give him the information. Eventually he won the confidence of several important former priests.

Charley Wah-hre-she (Wa-xthi'-zhi) was a remarkable man (photo 2.2). A priest of the Puma clan, he was the son of Wa-thu-tse-ga-zhi

PHOTO 2.2. Charles Wah-hre-she (?–1923). Reproduced from La Flesche (1921: Plate 15).

(Never Fails), the last of the tribal priests and keeper of one of the "great bundles."[38] Wah-hre-she had acted as his father's assistant in some of the rituals associated with the great bundle. According to La Flesche, he was "a man of an inquiring mind. He did not hesitate to ask . . . the meaning of the parts of the rituals which he did not fully understand."[39] An early convert to peyotism, he first joined Black Dog and served as "fireman" in his church. Later he broke off from Black Dog and set up a separate church.[40] Rejecting the old religion, Wah-hre-she had his father's tribal bundle buried with him when he died in 1910.[41]

Wah-hre-she was strongly opposed to assimilation and the influence of the Euro-Americans on the Osages. In 1910 he traveled to Mexico and secured an agreement with the Mexican government to allow the Osages to buy a reservation in the mountains of Chihuahua. In this isolated region Wah-hre-she thought the Osages could live undisturbed. But he found few members of the tribe willing to follow him to Chihuahua, and the project failed. Later he proposed that the Osages pool their money and purchase Vermejo Park, a large ranch in northern New Mexico, for a new "reservation." This plan failed, too.[42]

Wah-hre-she proved to be La Flesche's major source of ritual data. Before his death in 1923,[43] he gave La Flesche the texts of the Puma clan's versions of the child naming rite, the rite of vigil, and the "Sayings of the Ancient Men," as well as texts of the rite of the chiefs, the peace ceremony, the war ceremony, the new year rite, and the mourning dance.

Shunkahmolah (Shon'-ge-mon-in) was a priest of the Gentle Sky clan (photo 2.3). As a young man he had won war honors in the attack on Confederate forces in Kansas in 1863. At the time of his death in 1919,[44] he was one of only three living men who had earned all thirteen o-don' (war honors). Only a man who had earned all thirteen war honors could act as wa-don'-be (guardian), a key ritual position in clan initiations.[45] An early convert to peyotism, he took an active role in Black Dog's church.[46] Shunkahmolah gave La Flesche the Gentle Sky clan's versions of the child naming rite and the rite of vigil, as well as the ritual segment performed by the wa-don'-be in initiations.

Born in 1860,[47] Bacon Rind (Wa-tse-mon-in) was one of the best-known Osage leaders of the early twentieth century (photo 2.4). The grandson of the great Osage prophet Wa-tian-kah,[48] he had been initiated as a priest of the Bear clan before converting to peyotism. Bacon Rind's adherence to the new religion was not complete. In 1919 he acted as Xo'-ka (sponsor) at William Pryor's initiation into the Bear

PHOTO 2.3. Shunkah-molah (?–1919).

clan priesthood.[49] Although he was knowledgeable about Osage religion, Bacon Rind preferred the life of a politician to that of a religious leader.[50] Elected chief in 1912,[51] he remained active in Osage public affairs until his death in 1932.[52] Bacon Rind believed that younger Osages needed to know their past and was the first to suggest the creation of museums for the tribe's "relics."[53] Bacon Rind gave La Flesche information on the Bear clan's version of the Sayings of the Ancient Men, along with information on a number of other rituals.

Other priests also helped La Flesche. Xuth-tha'-wa-ton-in (clan unknown), Mon-zhon-a'-ki-da (Gentle Sky clan), Wa-sho-she (Eagle clan), Pa-thin-wa-we-xta (Elder clan), Wa-thu-xa-ge (Gentle Sky clan), and Pe-dse-mon-i (Night clan) all gave him fragments of ritual knowledge.

PHOTO 2.4. Bacon Rind (1860–1932). The lines on his chest are tatoos. Courtesy National Anthropological Archives, Smithsonian Institution, 4130-A.

A number of other Osages assisted La Flesche by providing information on Osage culture in general. Although few of their names appear in his published works, they do appear in his field notes. Among these people were Arthur Bonnicastle (Osage hero of the Boxer Rebellion, peyote roadman, and chief, 1920–22), Fred Lookout (peyote roadman and chief, 1916–18 and 1924–49), Julia Lookout (wife of Fred Lookout), Roman Logan (one of the four principal peyote church leaders), and Paul Red Eagle (peyote roadman and chief, 1923–24).

Although there was opposition to La Flesche's research, particularly from leaders of the Big Hill (Gray Horse) band,[54] the men who gave him the accounts of rituals were not socially marginal individuals. Counted among La Flesche's informants and supporters were major surviving priests of the old religion, major leaders of the new peyote church, and major tribal political leaders. Despite the many gaps and questions to be found in La Flesche's published works, the information he presented was given to him by men who were among the most knowledgeable Osage religious leaders of their time and whose authority to give him this information was beyond question.

Although he maintained his contacts with individual Osages until his death, La Flesche's active field research ended in the summer of 1923.[55] By this time most of the older priests on whom he depended had died. In April 1923, his close friend and companion, Alice Fletcher, died. Now in his mid-sixties, La Flesche stopped his fieldwork and devoted the remainder of his life to publishing his studies of the Osages. Between 1921 and 1930, his four major studies of Osage rituals were published in the annual reports of the Bureau of American Ethnology. In poor health, La Flesche retired from the Bureau of American Ethnology in 1929 and returned home to Nebraska to live with his younger brother. He died in 1932. That same year the Bureau of American Ethnology published La Flesche's *A Dictionary of the Osage Language,* and in 1939, seven years after his death, it published *War Ceremony and Peace Ceremony of the Osage Indians.*

CHAPTER 3   *Osage Cosmology and Tribal Organization*


$T$HE Osages are one of the Dhegiha Siouan tribes, a linguistic grouping of peoples that also includes the Omahas, Kaws, Poncas, and Quapaws. At the time of contact with Europeans in 1673, the Osage villages were located along the Osage River in what is today southwestern Missouri (map 3.1). In their general life-style, the Osages were typical of the native peoples who occupied the prairies and woodlands of what is now the midwestern United States. They lived in permanent villages of mat-covered wigwams along streams or rivers. Economically, they depended upon both horticulture and foraging. Women tended crops of corn, beans, and squash; men hunted bison, elk, deer, bear, and smaller game animals. Seasonally the Osages collected a wide variety of wild plant foods, including roots, berries, fruits, nuts, and tubers. The most important of these foods were water lily roots and persimmons. It was not until the eighteenth century, after they acquired horses, that the Osages began making their long summer and fall treks to the Great Plains in search of bison.[1]

Osage history before the arrival of the French is poorly known. Osage legends, as well as the legends of other Dhegiha-speaking peoples, tell of an eastern origin. These traditions say that in the past these peoples formed a single tribe that lived in the Ohio River valley. As they migrated westward, they began to separate. When they reached the junction of the Mississippi and Ohio rivers, the Quapaws turned south, eventually settling on the lower Arkansas River. The other Dhegiha peoples moved north and west, up the Mississippi and out the Des Moines and Missouri rivers. At the mouth of the Osage River, the people who were to become the Osages moved south, up the tributary. Eventually the Kaws settled along the Kaw River, while the Omahas and Poncas settled farther up the Missouri.[2] Ar-

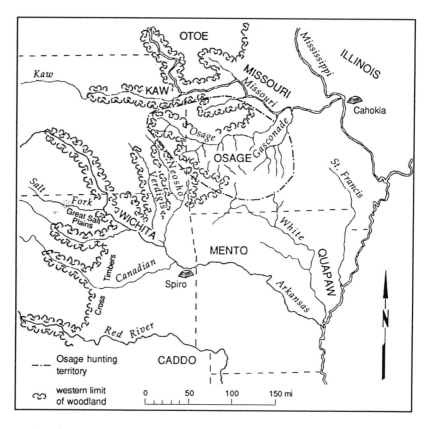

MAP 3.1. Osage territory in about 1690.

chaeological evidence has yet to confirm or date this legendary migration.[3]

The Dhegiha Siouan peoples, the Chiwere Siouans (the Otoes, Missouris, Ioways, and Winnebagos), and the Central Algonkian tribes (the Illini, Sac, Fox, Miamis, Kickapoos, and Shawnees) are frequently grouped together as the Prairie tribes. These peoples were similar not only in their general life-style but also in their basic cultural institutions. All of them had similar patrilineal clan structures, formalized priesthoods, and religious rituals. Clan medicine bundles and the calumet, or pipe, dance are but two examples of the common elements in their rituals. The known similarities in the core social and religious institutions of the Dhegiha Siouans, Chiwere Siouans, and Central

Algonkian peoples are so striking that there can be little doubt that these institutions were derived historically from a common source. The history of the Prairie tribes since European contact has also been basically similar. Old World diseases such as malaria, smallpox, measles, and cholera repeatedly swept the region during the seventeenth, eighteenth, and nineteenth centuries, destroying much, if not most, of the native population. European trade—initially the exchange of guns and metal tools for slaves, furs, and hides—rapidly transformed the Prairie peoples' lives. Competition for slaves, land, and resources dramatically increased the level and intensity of warfare, both among the native peoples and between them and the Europeans. European settlers eventually evicted most of the tribes from their territories, the richest farmlands of North America, and pushed them west onto the plains. Greatly reduced in numbers, some of the Prairie tribes vanished; their survivors were absorbed by other groups. By the late nineteenth century, the once-numerous Prairie tribes had been reduced to only about twelve thousand people living in small, widely scattered communities from Wisconsin to northern Mexico.

Although the Osages experienced the same general problems as the other Prairie peoples, they suffered neither as sharp a population decline nor as severe a geographical displacement.[4] Geography played a decisive role in Osage history. Located away from the major rivers— the Missouri, Mississippi, and Ohio—the Osages were better able to maintain their population and actually prospered during the first century of European contact. By the late eighteenth century, they had emerged as the most powerful tribe in what was then Spanish Louisiana. As a result, their cultural institutions were not disrupted as early as those of the other tribes.[5] Although their population declined after contact, as late as 1872 there were still almost 3,700 full-blooded Osages.[6] Although their economy, political organization, and material culture had changed, their basic social and religious institutions were still functioning. It was not until the 1880s that these institutions disintegrated. Thus the men from whom La Flesche collected his data had grown to adulthood before the collapse of the traditional Osage social and religious institutions.

## THE STRUCTURE OF THE COSMOS

Traditional Osage social, political, and religious institutions were so highly integrated that they constituted a single unified system. Osage institutional structure was consciously created as a model of the cosmos and was conceived of as symbolically representing the mirror image of the cosmos. Consequently, any discussion of Osage institutional structure has to begin with their concept of the cosmos. The Osages saw the cosmos as a highly integrated and unified system in which humans were only one factor. They also thought that the cosmos was knowable through observation and reasoning. This is not to say that they thought humans could fully understand the cosmos in all its variety and dimensions. They did believe, however, that humans could and should strive constantly to increase their knowledge about the cosmos.[7] To the Osages, knowledge was the key to human survival.

In the early part of the life of the Osage, according to tradition, they kept together for protection and moved about without tribal or clan organization, a condition which they termed "ga-ni'-tha," which may be freely translated as, without law or order.

It was in those days that a group of men fell into the habit of gathering together . . . to exchange ideas concerning the actions of the sun, moon, and stars which they observed move within the sky with marvelous precision, each in its own given path. They also noticed, in the course of their observations, that the [celestial bodies] in the upper world move from one side of the sky to the other without making any disturbances in their relative positions, and that with the great movements four changes take in the vegetal life of the earth, which they agreed was affected by the actions of some of the heavenly travelers. These seasonal changes they named Be, Do-ge', Ton, and Ba'-the (Spring, Summer, Autumn and Winter).[8]

They further noticed that this same pattern of birth, maturity, old age, and death was repeated over and over again. They saw it in the life cycle of humans and animals. They observed it daily in the succession from sunrise to midday, sunset, and night. The cosmos was in constant motion and consisted of unending, varied cycles of birth, maturity, old age, death, and rebirth. These temporal cycles could not be stopped or reversed, for "nothing in the cosmos moved backward."[9]

The delving into the mysteries of the universe by this group of men was primarily for the purpose of finding, if possible, the place from which comes all life.[10]

The seasonal changes upon the earth which appear to accompany the movements of the sun and other cosmic bodies suggested to these men the existence between sky and earth of a procreative relationship, an idea which fixed itself firmly in their minds. It fitted their notion that the earth was related to and influenced by all of the great bodies that move around within the sky. However, they were not satisfied that these celestial bodies move without guidance of some governing power, and they continued their search and their discussions. Then, in the course of time, there crept into the minds of the men . . . the thought that a silent, invisible creative power pervades the sun, moon and stars and the earth, gives to them life, and keeps them eternally in motion and perfect order. This creative power, which to their minds was the source of life, they named Wa-kon-da, Mysterious Power, and sometimes E-a'-wa-won a-ka, the Causer of Our Being.[11]

The Osages believed "that this great power [Wa-kon-da] resides in the air, the blue sky, the clouds, the stars, the sun, the moon, and the earth [as well as in all living and moving things]. . . . Sometimes the Osage speak of a tree, a rock or a prominent hill as Wa-kon-da, but when asked if his people had a great number of Wa-kon-das he would reply, 'Not so; there is but one God and His presence is in all things and is everywhere. We say a tree is Wa-kon-da because in it also Wa-kon-da resides.'"[12]

Although all pervasive, Wa-kon-da was invisible. "No living man has seen him. No living man ever will."[13] The Osages came to see the cosmos as having both visible and invisible components. The invisible universe was the realm of Wa-kon-da, and was in fact Wa-kon-da. The visible universe was the world of the living, the world in which the Osages dwelled. Every quality and characteristic of Wa-kon-da was thought to have its expression or counterpart in the world of the living. The visible world was the mirror reflection of Wa-kon-da, and so to understand the visible world was to understand the essence of Wa-kon-da.[14] As a result, Osage religious leaders worked to gain an ever-increasing understanding of the visible world in which they lived, of its patterned regularities, of the structural relationship between the various life forms and moving things, and of the almost infinite array of qualities and characteristics of its life forms.[15]

In their study of the cosmos, the Osages had come to see sky and earth as the two main divisions. As they put it, "life is conceived in the sky and descends to earth to take material form."[16] Life was the product of the interaction between the sky, which they came to call father, and the earth, which they called mother.[17] Humans and other living things existed on the surface of the earth, the space between earth and sky. This space they called the *ho'-e-ga,* or snare of life, referring to a snare or trap "into which all life comes through birth and departs therefrom by death."[18] They further noted that the earth portion of the cosmos was divided between land and water. Associated with each of these major divisions was a wide range of life forms—animals, birds, plants, celestial bodies, and other moving, changing things. The Osages recognized these spatial divisions along with the temporal divisions present in the universe: the unending cycles of birth, maturity, old age, and death. These temporal divisions took the form of the light of day and life and the dark of night and death, which followed a relentless path from east to west.

Thus the Osage defined the four major divisions of the universe: sky and earth, day and night. The direction of the sky was up, and it formed the symbolic "left side" of the universe. The sky was also a masculine force that for some unexplained reason was associated with the sacred number six. The direction of the earth was down, and it formed the symbolic "right side" of the universe. The earth was a feminine force that for some unexplained reason was associated with the sacred number seven. The light of day and the sun were seen as the most powerful of life-giving forces. The light of day was associated with the east, the direction of the sunrise, and with red, the color of the rising sun. The night and the moon were seen as the most powerful of the forces of death. The night was associated with the west, the direction of the setting sun, and with black, the color of the night. Daily this cycle of day and night repeated itself as the sun traveled from east to west across the surface of the earth (fig. 3.1).[19]

All living and moving things were reflections of one or another force of Wa-kon-da. The very fact that something existed in the visible universe meant that it had a meaning and a purpose, whether the Osages as humans could understand it or not. Everything that existed had its own unique set of qualities or characteristics that gave it real or potential value to humans. Therefore the Osages also studied intensely the secondary forces of the visible world. They noticed that some of these secondary forces were life sustaining while others were destructive of life. There were life forms, both plant and animal, that provided food and nourishment, such as buffalo, deer, corn, and water lilies.[20] There were other plants, such as the "man medicine" plant, that cured illness.[21] In contrast, they saw destructive forces in birds of prey, particularly hawks and eagles, and in animals such as the puma, the bear, and the wolf.[22] Although many life forms fell readily into one or the other of these opposing dimensions of Wa-kon-da, some life forms could be both. Fire, for example, one of the most powerful of forces, was the most beneficial of life-giving and life-sustaining forces when under the control of humans. Uncontrolled fire, however, as in a prairie fire, could be one of the most powerful, deadly, and destructive of forces.[23]

Every life form had certain qualities or characteristics that either exceeded those of humans or were lacking in humans altogether. Many of these qualities, if humans possessed them, could aid them in their lives. For example, hawks, bears, pumas, and deer surpassed humans

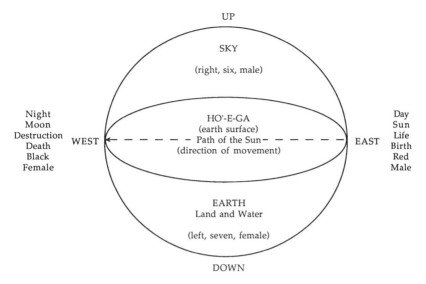

FIG. 3.1. The structure of the Osage cosmos.

in courage, a quality that humans at times needed for survival.[24] Otters and beavers had great swimming abilities, which humans sometimes needed.[25] Freshwater mussels and pelicans lived much longer than other life forms, a quality that humans desired.[26] The Osages studied and classified each life form in terms of its behavioral qualities and characteristics, with particular interest in those traits that would help the tribe in its unending struggle to survive in the visible world.

The wa-kon-da-gi ("men of mystery")—the name sometimes given by the Osages to the ancient priests[27]—also gave considerable thought to the place of humans in the universe. In contrast to other living things, "when [humans] . . . emerged from the unseen world they appeared with a perfect physical structure, with the additional capabilities of thinking and of bringing to pass, capabilities not possible to the animals."[28] Humans were "brought into existence, endowed with . . . [the] power of reason and speech,"[29] and only humans had the power of wa-thi'-gethon, the ability to search with the mind and thus learn.[30] Endowed with this unique ability among living things, humans were "sent forth to travel the earth as though it . . . [was their] own to occupy."[31]

Within the visible world, the world of the living, humans were dominant. The Osages did not see humans locked in a struggle for survival with nonhuman life forms. Rather, the competition for survival in the visible world was between human groups. As individuals, the Osages did not see themselves as superior to other human beings. The "enemy had the same powers of action, thought, and expression."[32] Although Wa-kon-da's assistance was sought in this struggle between humans, Wa-kon-da placed the primary burden for survival on the people themselves.[33] Given this unending struggle between human groups for survival, war, not surprisingly, was a major focus of their lives. Among the Osages, "war was regarded . . . as a necessary evil, but necessary only for self-preservation."[34] Regretfully they saw that "the best of their young men must go and kill and be killed in order that the individual and tribal life might continue."[35]

The Osages believed the cosmos was not stable but consisted of an indeterminate number of cycles of birth, growth, maturity, and death. All things that are born will eventually die.[36] This generalization applied to individual living things, both human and nonhuman, and to all groups of living things, both human and nonhuman. Just as every individual Osage born would someday die, so at some time in the future the Osages as a people would die.[37] The same was true of all other humans and groups of humans. There was no answer as to why this was true; it just was. Everything moved from east to west, from birth to death. There was no discernible reason why some groups of living things died when they did and other groups survived longer. Wa-kon-da was the source of all life. Fertility and children were the greatest of Wa-kon-da's blessings because they demonstrated that Wa-kon-da desired one's continued existence.[38] The Osages believed that to secure Wa-kon-da's blessings, particularly children, they had to show their respect and reverence for Wa-kon-da constantly.

The survival of a people depended upon two factors: their collective ability to defend themselves against other humans and the continued blessing of Wa-kon-da. The Osages emphasized the long-term survival of the group and not the survival of individuals in their own right. The most basic requirement for the survival of a people was the raising of children to adulthood, or, as they repeatedly expressed it, an "endless line of descendants."[39] In order to survive as a people, they needed Wa-kon-da's blessing in the form of children and health, along with nourishment and protection from their human enemies. Individuals and families acting separately would eventually be destroyed. To enhance their chances of survival, people had to act in concert. The Osage view was that "in order to meet and successfully overcome the enemies that beset life's pathway there must be a complete unity of purpose and of action . . . and all the people must share alike in the fortunes and misfortunes of the common defense."[40]

Since human actions in themselves were insufficient, Wa-kon-da's blessing and assistance had to be sought in all of life's endeavors. The Osages felt that the people had to act as one in regard to both Wa-kon-da and the world of the living. To achieve this unity, the ancient priests determined that the Osages must organize the tribe as a mirror image of the universe—the image of Wa-kon-da, the perfect unified structure. This organizational model served the dual purposes of, first, showing respect for Wa-kon-da and thus asking Wa-kon-da's blessing and, second, simultaneously organizing the people in such a manner as to allow them to act with a singleness of purpose toward their human enemies.[41]

## THE CLAN SYSTEM

The basic structural units of the tribe were its twenty-four patrilineal clans, called *ton-won-gthon*[42] or *u-dse'-the* ("fireplaces")[43] by the Osages. Clans were both social and religious units. Every clan had a set of *zho'-i-the,* or "life symbols,"[44] which included animals, plants, celestial bodies, and natural occurrences such as storms and thunder (Table 3.1). Although in this book I will call each clan by a single specific name, my assigning of names is only for the sake of clarity. Osage clans did not have specific names as such, but could be referred to by direct or metaphorical reference to any of their life symbols. As a result, there were multiple terms of reference or "names" for every clan. The question of clan names becomes even more complex when one realizes that a particular life symbol was not necessarily the exclusive property of one clan; frequently, several clans shared a particular life symbol. The bear, for example, was a life symbol for three different clans, those I call Bear, Puma, and Night. The word *wa-ca-be,* "bear," could be used to refer to the members of any of these three clans.

The relationship between clan members and the clan life symbols has often been misunderstood. Clan members usually had some taboos concerning their treatment of the living manifestations of their life symbols. In rituals, clan members spoke of having "taken for their body" these symbols. By this phrase they meant that "from him they shall receive the means by which to sustain and prolong life."[45] Some clan myths spoke of these life symbols as ancestors, and members often referred to their life symbols as grandfather or grandmother. These kinship terms were terms of respect, not of biological ancestry.[46] One Osage summarized this relationship by saying, "We do not be-

TABLE 3.1
**Clan Names and Life Symbols**

| Clan | Life Symbol |
|---|---|
| EARTH PEOPLE | |
| *Land (Hon'-ga) Phratry* | |
| 1. Eagle | |
| Hon'-ga A-hius-ton, "Winged Earth" | Golden eagle |
| Hi-ca-da, "Eagle Leg" | Sacred eagle |
| ?Hon'-ga Gthe-zhe, "Golden Eagle" | Immature golden eagle |
| 2. Bear | |
| Wa-ca-be-ton, "Black Bear" | Black bear |
| Wa'-tse-ga-we, "Radiant Star" | White swan |
| Wa-ca-be Cka, "White Bear"* | Black water beetle |
| | Moon |
| | Swallow |
| 3. Puma | |
| In-ghton-ga, "Puma" | Great red boulder |
| Hin-wa Wa-ge, "Porcupine"* | Sun |
| | White boulder |
| | Puma |
| | Black boulder |
| | Swan |
| | Black bear |
| | Morning star (male star) |
| 4. Metal Bunched | |
| Mon'-ce Ba-tse, ?"Metal Bunched" | |
| 5. Elk | |
| O'-pon, "Elk" | Elk |
| Ta-he'-sha-be, "Dark Horned Deer"* | Puma |
| ?I-ba-tse, "Wind"* | Entire earth |
| Mon-zhon-ga-xe, "Earth Maker" | ?Immature golden eagle |
| 6. Crawfish | |
| Mon'-shkon, "Crawfish" | Crawfish |
| Mon-in-ka-zhin-ga, "Little Clay" | Blue, red, yellow, and black clay |
| 7. Wind | |
| I'-ba-tse Tad-dse, "Wind People" | Great spotted eagle |
| Hon'-ga Zhin-ga, "Little Sacred Thing" | Corn |

TABLE 3.1 (*continued*)
## Clan Names and Life Symbols

| Clan | Life Symbol |
|------|-------------|
| Hon'-ga We-ha-ge, "Youngest Earth"<br>Hon'-ga U-thu-he-ge, "Last Earth"<br>?Hon'-ga Gthe-zhe, "Sacred Spotted Eagle" | |
| *Isolated Earth Phratry* | |
| 1. Hon'-ga U-ta-non-dsi, "Isolated Earth" | Spider<br>Buffalo bull<br>Bull snake<br>Spreading adder<br>Black snake<br>Rattlesnake<br>Red boulder |
| *Water (Wa-zha-zhe) Phratry* | |
| 1. Elder Water<br>Wa-zha'-zhe Wa-non, "Elder Water"<br>Ke'-kin, "Carrier of the Turtle"<br>Ba'-k'in Zho-i-ga-the,<br>    "Cottonwood Tree People"* | Snapping turtle<br>Little pipe |
| 2. White Water<br>Wa-zha'-zhe Cka, "White Water"<br>    (referred to mussel shell)<br>In-gthon'-ga Ni Mon-tse,<br>    "Puma in the Water"* | Mussel shell<br><br>Sun |
| 3. Gentle Ponca<br>Pon-ka Wa-shta-ge, "Gentle Ponca"<br>Wa-tse-tsi, "Meteor"<br>Wa-tse-tsi Wa-shta-ge, "Gentle Meteor"<br>Xu-tha' Pa-con Zho-i-ga-the,<br>    "Bald Eagle People"* | Female cedar<br>Red cedar<br>Sedge grass<br><br>Water |
| 4. Deer<br>Ta' I-ni-ka-shi-ga, "Deer People"<br>Non-pon-da, "Deer"<br>Ta-tha-xin, "Deer's Lungs"<br>Ta-cin'-dse-cka, "White-tailed Deer"<br>Wa-dsu-ta Zhin-ga, "Small Animals"* | Water<br>Deer or little animals<br>Oak trees |

TABLE 3.1 (*continued*)
**Clan Names and Life Symbols**

| Clan | Life Symbol |
|---|---|
| 5. Cattail | |
| Mi-ke'-the'-stse'-dse, "Cattail" | Cattail |
| Mi-ke'-stse-dse, "Cattail" | |
| Wa-ke'-the-stse-dse, "Cattail" | |
| Wa-ke'-stse-dse, "Cattail" | |
| Ka'-xe Wa-hu-ge, "Youngest Brother"* | |
| 6. Clear the Way | |
| Ga-Tsiu' | |
| O-cu-ga-ze, "They Who Make the Way Clear" | |
| Mon-sho'-dse Mon-in, | |
| "Travelers in the Mist"* | |
| 7. Bow | |
| Ho' I'ni-ka-shin-ga, "Fish People" | Right and left side of river |
| E-non Min-dse-ton, | |
| "Sole Owners of the Bow"* | Red fish and black fish |
| | Otter |
| | Beaver |
| | Willow |
| | Bow |
| SKY (TSI-ZHU) PEOPLE | |
| *Sky (Tsi-zhu) Phratry* | |
| 1. Elder Sky | |
| Tsi-zhu Wa-non, "Elder Sky" | Sun |
| Wa-kon-da Non-pa-bi, "God Feared by All" | |
| (reference to the sun) | Sun's rays |
| Wa-ba'xi, "Awakeners"* | Morning and evening stars |
| Tsi-zhu, "Sky" | Pileated woodpecker |
| | Nighthawk |
| | Moon |
| | Double star |
| | Pleiades |
| | Orion's Belt |
| | Pole Star (Red Star) |
| | Canis Major (Dog Star) |
| | Dipper |

TABLE 3.1 (*continued*)
**Clan Names and Life Symbols**

| Clan | Life Symbol |
|------|-------------|
| 2. Buffalo-Face | |
| Tse-do'-ga In-dse, "Buffalo Face People" | Nighthawk |
| Tse Thon-ka, "Buffalo Back" | Buffalo back |
| Tse-a'-kon, "Buffalo Back" | |
| Thon-ka, "Buffalo Back" | |
| 3. Gentle Sky | |
| Tsi-zhu Wa-shte-ge, "Gentle Sky" | Earth and overreaching sky |
| Ba-po, "Elderberry Tree"* | Red eagle |
| Tsi-u-ckon-cka, "House in Center"* | Peace pipe |
| Mon-ca-hi, "Arrow Tree"* | Red, blue, yellow, and speckled corn |
| Zhon-con, "Sycamore"* | Cornflower (yellow flower) |
| Tsi-u-thu-ha-ge, "Last Houses"* | Elderberry |
| Pe-ton Ton-ga Zho-i-ga-the, "Great Crane" | Great crane |
| ?Hon-ba Tha-gthi, "Peaceful Day"* | Swallow |
| ?Xu-tha Zhu-dse, "Red Eagle"* | Cloudless day |
| ?U'-Xthi- Rhin-ge, "No Anger"* | Red oak tree |
| Tsi-zhu Wa-bin I-ta-zhi, "Touch No Blood" | Sun and moon |
| | Morning and evening stars |
| | Ursa Major |
| | Pleiades |
| | Orion's Belt (Three Deer) |
| | Double Star |
| 4. Wolf | |
| Cin-dse-a-gthe, "Weavers of the Symbolic Locks" | Canis Major (Dog or Wolf Star) |
| Shon-ge Zho-i-ga-the, "Wolf or Dog People" | Sun |
| | Buffalo tail |
| 5. Sun Carrier | |
| Mi-k'in Wa-non, "Elder Sun Carrier" | Sun and moon |
| Mi-k'in, "Sun Carrier" | Male star |
| | Evening star |
| | Six rays of sun |
| | Great dragonfly |

TABLE 3.1 (*continued*)
## Clan Names and Life Symbols

| Clan | Life Symbol |
| --- | --- |
| 6. Night | |
| Hon I-ni-ka-shi-ga, "Night People" | (Red) black bear |
| Hon Zho'-i-ga-the, "Night People" | Night |
| Ta-pa Zho-i-ga-the, | |
| "Deerhead or Pleiades People"* | ?Pleiades |
| 7. Last Sky | |
| Tsi-zhu We-ha-ge, "Last Sky" | |
| Tsi-zhu U-thu-ha-ge, "Last Sky" | |
| *Last to Come (Tsi' Ha-shi) Phratry* | |
| 1. Men of Mystery | |
| Ni'-ka Wa-kon-da-gi, "Men of Mystery" | Red, black, yellow, and rough metal |
| Gthon' I-ni-ka-shi-ga, "Thunder People" | Flint corn |
| Xon-dse Wa-tse, ?"Cedar Star"* | Hailstones |
| Ba-ci, "Hailstone" | Cloud region of sky |
| 2. Buffalo Bull | |
| Tho-xe, "Buffalo Bull" | Buffalo |
| Tho-xe Pa-thi-ho, "Buffalo Lift-Your-Heads" | Various colored corn |
| | Squash |
| | Medicine plants |
| | Blazing star flower |

*Subclan.

lieve that our ancestors were really animals, birds, etc., as told in the traditions. These things are only wa-we'-ku-ska-ye, 'symbols' of something higher. On saying this he pointed to the sky."[47] The relationship between clan members and clan life symbols was merely symbolic. Each clan symbolically represented that portion of the universe associated with its life symbols, and collectively all twenty-four clans, through their life symbols, symbolically represented the cosmos in all its diversity.

Just as the cosmos was divided between sky and earth, so the clans were divided into two groups, or moieties (fig. 3.2). Nine clans were grouped as the Sky People, and fifteen clans were grouped as the Earth People. Together the nine clans of the Sky People symbolically represented all of the forces of the sky, whereas the fifteen Earth clans symbolically represented all of the forces of the earth. These moieties

| CLAN | PHRATRY | MOIETY |
|------|---------|--------|

FIG. 3.2. The Osage clan structure.

were further divided into phratries. The clans of the Sky moiety were divided into one group of seven clans called the Sky and another group of two clans called the Tsi-ha-shi, or "Those Who Came Last." Just as the earth was divided into land and water, so too the Earth People were divided. One group of seven clans symbolically represented all the life forms of the Land, while another group of seven clans symbolically represented the various forces associated with the Water regions of the earth. One of the fifteen clans of the Earth People belonged to neither Land nor Water, but stood alone as the Isolated Earth clan.[48]

Each clan was divided into a number of subclans, each in turn associated with some particular life symbol of the clan and called by reference to this life symbol. In some instances, it is impossible to determine whether a particular reference is to the clan as a whole or only to a particular subclan. There was some ranking of subclans, and subclans frequently differed in their ritual significance. One subclan in each clan was designated as the Sho'-ka subclan, whose members acted as the official ceremonial messengers for the clan.[49]

Clan membership was of great social significance. An individual was Osage by virtue of membership in a clan. Each clan had its own set of personal names—usually, but not always, metaphorical allusions to one of the clan's life symbols.[50] Each clan had its own formal naming rite in which a clan name was given to an individual.[51]

Clan membership also regulated marriage. Moieties were exogamous, which meant that a person had to marry a member of the other, or opposing, moiety. A member of one of the nine Sky clans had to marry a member of one of the fifteen Earth clans, and vice versa. Just as all life was the product of the interaction between the sky and earth, so every Osage child was the product of a union of the Sky People and the Earth People.[52]

## VILLAGE AND POLITICAL STRUCTURE

Osage villages also were organized as mirror images of the cosmos (fig. 3.3). They were divided in half by an east-west street that symbolized the surface of the earth—the ho'-e-ga—and the path of the sun on its daily journey. Each clan had its own section of the village. Families of the Sky People were arranged by clan groupings in precise locations along the north side of the street. Similarly, families of the Earth People were arranged in clan order along the south side.[53]

During most of the historic period, the Osages were divided into five permanent, named villages. These villages were primarily economic and residential units that had, in themselves, only limited social significance and virtually no religious significance. Each village had complete representation of all twenty-four clans and was symbolically the mirror image of the others.[54] Secular political structure existed only at the village level. Within each village were two ga-hi'-ge, or chiefs. There was a Sky chief (tsi-zhu ga-hi'-ge), who was chosen from the Gentle Sky clan of the Sky People, and an Earth chief (hon-ga ga-hi'-ge), who was chosen from the Gentle Ponca clan, one of the Earth People clans. The chiefs did not live in their clan's segment of the village but had their dwellings in the very center of the village, across the street from one another; the house of the Sky chief was on the north side, and the house of the Earth chief, on the south. The chiefs chose ten men to act as their a'-ki-da, or "soldiers," and provide assistance. These men located their houses next to those of the chiefs, so their houses were not in clan order either.[55]

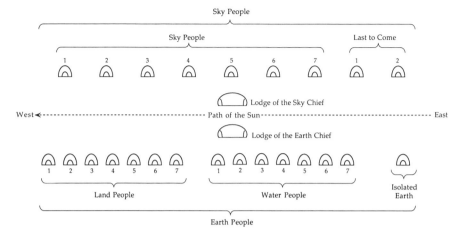

FIG. 3.3. Traditional Osage village arrangements (normal clan order).

Although a chief was chosen from each moiety, these men were not the leaders of their respective moieties. Instead, the village was a single, unified political unit with two heads. The chiefs had essentially identical authority over all members of the village and acted in concert. Their main function was to see to the internal harmony and well-being of the village. As secular leaders, they settled quarrels and disagreements and even had the authority to expel troublemakers from the village. Their houses were sanctuaries where no one could be harmed. If an enemy warrior fled to the house of one of the chiefs, he would be protected. The houses of the chiefs were sacred because they symbolically represented the

two life giving powers—the Earth and the Sun [sky]. The house stands for the earth and must have two doors, one opening toward the rising sun and the other toward the setting sun. The fire that is placed midway between the two doors represents the sun, whose pathway symbolizes endless life, and thus passes through the middle of the house that stands for the earth. The fireplace was also consecrated and the fire taken therefrom by the people to start their home fires was thought of as holy and as having the power to give life and health to those who use it.[56]

Since the villages functioned primarily as economic units, it is not surprising that the chiefs played a major role in many collective economic activities. The two chiefs acted as leaders of the summer and fall buffalo hunts, alternating daily as leaders of the hunting party. They chose the route to be taken and controlled the hunters so that everyone had an equal opportunity.[57] Although they were not religious leaders, they were responsible for the well-being of the village. It was the chiefs who formally requested that the priests perform the new year rite, various hunting rituals, and rituals relating to weather control.[58]

The authority of the chiefs, then, was limited to things directly associated with the daily, internal lives of village members. Greater authority rested in the collective hands of priests who controlled the relationship between the Osages and the external world, both visible and invisible. In matters of both war and peace, they were the ultimate authority.

The village priests gathered daily in what constituted a council.

From the earliest times there was among the Osage a "house" or place of gathering called the Non-hon-zhin-ga Wa-thin Tsi, House of the Priests. At this house the priests met almost every morning, sometimes officially but more often in an informal way. At the informal gathering the conversation frequently turned to matters of importance to the tribe, such as any practices among the people that seemed to be injurious in their effects or liable to become a menace to the internal peace of the tribe. Some means would then be sought by which to overcome these evils. On the other hand, any acts that tended to promote a feeling of friendliness or kindliness among the people found hearty expressions of approval in the sacred "house."

No "house" was purposely established and maintained by the priests for their gatherings. They selected for their home the house of a man (who might belong to any other of the various clans of the tribe), but he was always one who, by his valor, generosity, and hospitality, had won the esteem and affection of all the people. The title given the man at whose house the priests made their home was Non-hon-zhin-ga Wa-thin, Keeper of the Priests. The selection of a man's house for the home of the priests was regarded as conferring an honor of the highest character upon the owner.[59]

Although most meetings of the priests were informal gatherings, formal meetings would be called in times of crisis. If enemy raiders were seen or attacked the tribe, the Keeper of the Priests would send a messenger to summon the priests to meet. At these meetings the Keeper of the Priests presided, but decisions were reached collectively by the assembled priests.[60]

Together the priests were the ultimate power and authority within the tribe. Every major and most minor decisions and actions required a ritual and the formal sanction of the priests. It was they alone who determined policies of war and peace. Only the priests could authorize a war party or award war honors. Only the priests could perform the necessary farming, hunting, and other rituals. As we will see in chapter 4, the whole tribal structure and even the offices of the chiefs were creations of the priests. Ritual and the concurrent authority of the priests permeated every aspect of Osage life.

## RELIGIOUS ORGANIZATION

The Osages were an extraordinarily religious people. Even members of closely related neighboring tribes were frequently surprised by the overtly religious nature of the Osages. An Omaha Indian once noted:

My father and I visited them when they had moved to their reservation [the 1870s]. Before sunrise in the morning following the first night of our visit, I was awakened by the noise of a great wailing. I arose and went out. As far as I could see men, women, and children were standing in front of the doors of their houses weeping. My parents explained to me that it was the custom of the [Osage] people to cry to Wa-kon-da morning, noon and evening. When I understood the meaning of the cry I soon learned not to be startled by the noise.[61]

This ritualized praying, called the rite of vigil, was repeated at noon and again at sunset.

From sunrise to sunset, from birth to death, in all endeavors—war, peace, hunting, farming, child rearing—Osage life was one continuous flow of rituals. Although some, such as the rite of vigil, were personal acts, most rituals were performed and controlled by four interlocking, formal priesthoods collectively called the *ni'-ka xo'-be,* "holy men" (fig. 3.4).[62]

Each priesthood was associated with a particular *wa-xo'-be,* or sacred object, from which the priests derived their ritual knowledge and their authority to initiate and perform a particular set of ceremonies. The priesthoods were divided into clan priesthoods and tribal priesthoods. The *non-hon'-zhin-ga,* or "little-old-men," were the clan priests and custodians of the clan sacred objects or bundles called the *wa-xo'-be zhin-ga* ("little sacred objects").[63] The three other priesthoods were tribal-level priesthoods: (1) the *ni'-ka don-he,* or "good men," who were custodians of the *wa-wathon,* or peace ceremony pipes;[64] (2) the *ton'-won a-don-be,* "village guardians," who were custodians of the *wa-xo'-be ton-ga,* the "great sacred object,"[65] and (3) a priesthood whose name was not recorded but whose members were custodians of the *mon-kon ton-ga wa-xo'-be,* or "great medicine sacred object." There were very few tribal priests at any one time, and thus the vast majority of priests were clan priests.

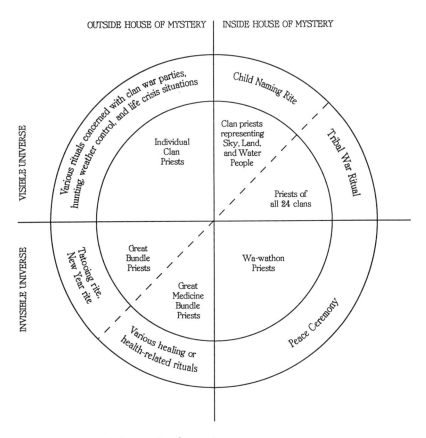

OUTSIDE HOUSE OF MYSTERY | INSIDE HOUSE OF MYSTERY

VISIBLE UNIVERSE

INVISIBLE UNIVERSE

Various rituals concerned with clan war parties, hunting, weather control, and life crisis situations

Child Naming Rite

Tatooing rite, New Year rite

Various healing or health-related rituals

Tribal War Ritual

Peace Ceremony

Individual Clan Priests

Clan priests representing Sky, Land, and Water People

Priests of all 24 clans

Great Bundle Priests

Great Medicine Bundle Priests

Wa-wathon Priests

FIG. 3.4. Traditional Osage ritual structure.

## The Wa-xo'-be

Because the authority and knowledge of a priesthood was associated with its wa-xo'-be, it is best to begin by discussing these sacred objects.

The term *wa-xo'-be* refers to something "made sacred"—in other words, objects consecrated for religious use.[66] Sometimes the term *wa-kon-da-gi*, referring to someone or something that was "mysterious," was also used in speaking of these objects.[67] A wide range of ritual items was or could be wa-xo'-be: clan bundles, tribal bundles, pipes, rattles, war clubs, war standards, tally sticks, charcoal, and so forth. Wa-xo'-be actually fell into two unnamed classes: primary wa-xo'-be and secondary wa-xo'-be.[68]

Primary wa-xo'-be were sacred objects from which ritual authority was derived. There were only four categories of primary wa-xo'-be: (1) the wa-xo'-be zhin-ga, which I will call the clan bundles, (2) the wa-wathon, which I will call the peace pipes, (3) the wa-xo'-be ton-ga, which I will call the great bundles, and (4) the mon-kon ton-ga wa-xo'-be, which I will call the great medicine bundles. Each priesthood was associated with a particular primary wa-xo'-be (Table 3.2).

In addition to the priests who were custodians of the knowledge and rituals derived from the primary wa-xo'-be, each category of wa-xo'-be had a clan or clan group designated as its symbolic keeper. The Men of Mystery and Buffalo Bull clans were the symbolic keepers of all the clan bundles.[69] The symbolic keeper of the great bundles was the Gentle Ponca clan,[70] and the Gentle Sky clan was the symbolic keeper of the great medicine bundles.[71] The Elder Water clan was the symbolic keeper of the peace pipes.[72] The ritual significance and function of these symbolic keepers is not clear.

In addition to the primary wa-xo'-be, there were many different types of secondary wa-xo'-be: war standards, rattles, war clubs, sacred bows and arrows, charcoal, and other things. These wa-xo'-be appear to have been associated with one or another of the primary wa-xo'-be. Like primary wa-xo'-be, each had a clan that served as its symbolic keeper. With secondary wa-xo'-be, however, the ritual significance is clearer. The clan priests of the symbolic keepers usually made the item for use in ritual.

Not all ritual objects were considered wa-xo'-be. In rituals the Osages often made use of still another category of objects—the *wa-zha-wa a-thin-bi-kshe*, which means "those carried to excite enthusiasm."[73] These objects were identical in construction to one of the secondary wa-xo'-be, but not being consecrated, they were not real wa-xo'-be.[74]

It is important to realize that many Osages misunderstood the true significance of the wa-xo'-be.

The [men] who formulated these intricate rites, and many of the men of the succeeding generations through whom these rites were transmitted, knew that the various articles dedicated for ceremonial use [the wa-xo'-be], together with their prescribed forms, were intended to be employed as aids in conveying certain fundamental ideas that could not be adequately expressed by words alone. They also knew that there resided in the articles thus dedicated no mystical power to excite fear or to be adored. There were, however, men and women, initiated as well as uninitiated, who drifted hopelessly into a literal belief that articles declared by the "Holy Men" to be sacred and to be treated with reverent regard had thereby become possessed of a mystical power which the articles themselves could exercise for good or for evil.[75]

TABLE 3.2
**Traditional Osage Religious Structure**

| Priesthood | Wa-xo'-be | Initiation Rite | Ritual Authority |
|---|---|---|---|
| Clan priests, or *non-hon-zhin-ga*, "little-old-men" | *Wa-xo'-be zhin-ga* (clan bundles; each clan had its own bundles) | 1. *Wa-xo'-be a-wa-thon* (Songs of the Wa-xo'-be)<br>2. *Ca tha-dse ga-xe* (Rush Mat Shrine)<br>3. *Mon-sha-kon u-gthon* (Sacred Burden Strap)<br>4. *Non'-zhin-zhon wa-thon* (Rite of Vigil)<br>5. *Wa-zhin-ga-o* (Shooting of a Bird)<br>6. *Wa-do-ka we-ko* (Distribution of Scalps)<br>7. *Ni'-ki wa-thon* (Sayings of the Ancient Men)<br>(Each clan had its own version of each rite.) | Collective:<br>*Wa-sha'-be a-thin* (war ceremony)<br><br>Individual:<br>Child naming rites<br>Clan war rites<br>Hunting rites<br>Weather control rites |
| *Wa-wathon* priests, or *ni'-ka don-he*, "Good Men" | *Wa-wathon* pipes | None (initiate sponsored four *wa-wathon* ceremonies) | *Wa-wathon* (peace ceremony) |
| Great bundle priest, or *ton'-won a-don-be*, "village guardian" | *Wa-xo'-be ton-ga* (great bundle) | *Ga-hi-ge o-k'on* (Rite of the Chiefs) | Spring or new year rite<br>Tattooing rite |
| Great medicine bundle priest | *Mon-kon ton-ga wa-xo'-be* (great medicine bundle) | Unknown | Healing rites(?) |

Among the adherents of the Osage religion, as among adherents of many religions in the world, there were both those who looked upon the rituals and ritual objects as symbolic and something to be interpreted and those who accepted them in a literal sense.

### Clan Priesthoods and Clan Bundles

Just as the cosmos was divided into the visible world of the living and the invisible realm of Wa-kon-da, so ritual authority and responsibility was divided. The clan priests were concerned with and responsible for rituals directed toward the visible world. The most important of these were the war and hunting rituals, but a wide range of other rituals also fell under their authority.

There were twenty-four clan priesthoods—one for each of the clans. Each clan symbolically represented part of the cosmos, and its priests were entrusted only with the ritual knowledge and authority associated with that portion of the cosmos. In other words, the ritual knowledge and authority of the tribe, relative to the visible world, was divided into twenty-four separate parts, and each part was controlled by the priesthood of a particular clan. As we will see, some rituals required the representation and participation of priests from all twenty-four clans. Others, depending upon which portions of the visible world were being addressed, required the priests of only one particular clan.

Every clan priesthood was in turn divided into seven degrees or stages. To become a clan priest, a man had to be formally accepted and initiated into one of the seven degrees of the priesthood of his clan. Although theoretically any man could become a priest, only a small minority of men actually did so.[76] Becoming a priest was costly. Gifts had to be collected for presentation to all the participating priests, and food had to be found to feed the visiting priests and their families during the three- to seven-day initiation rite. The expense of initiation varied with the degree taken. Although each clan appears to have had its own names and order for these degrees, they were basically the same. In the Buffalo Bull clan priesthood these degrees were called

1. Wa-xo'-be A-wa-thon, "the Songs of the Wa-xo'-be"
2. Ca Tha-dse Ga-xe, "Making of the Rush Mat Shrine"
3. Mon-sha-kon U-gthon, "The Sacred Burden Strap"
4. Non'-zhin-zhon Wa-thon, "Songs of the Rite of Vigil"
5. Wa-zhin-ga-o, "Rite of the Shooting of a Bird"
6. Wa-do'-ka We-ko, "Ceremonial Distribution of Scalps"
7. Ni'-ki Wa-thon, "Sayings of the Ancient Men"[77]

Each of these degrees conferred on the initiate particular ritual prerogatives and authority. Exactly which prerogatives and authority went with each degree is not clear. Although individuals could and sometimes did take more than one degree, the seventh degree—the Sayings of the Ancient Men—conferred on the initiate all the ritual prerogatives and authority bestowed by the other six degrees.[78] Thus the men holding the seventh degree were the leaders of their clan's priesthood. Associated with each of the seven degrees was also a segment of the clan's ritual knowledge, which was expressed in the initiation ritual for that degree. All together, then, knowledge of and ritual responsibility for the visible world was divided into 168 parts.

Regardless of the clan of the priest or the degree taken by him, all the wa-xo'-be used were identical in physical form and symbolic meaning. There was only one form of clan bundle. For reasons that will become apparent, these clan bundles were frequently called "hawks" or "hawk bundles." Each of the twenty-four clans possessed a number of these bundles.

Every clan bundle consisted of eight main articles, each with its own symbolic meaning. These articles were (1) the hawk (actually a hawk skin), (2) the woven mat bag, (3) the deerskin bag, (4) the woven buffalo hair bag, (5) the buffalo hide rope for the mat bag, (6) the eagle leg, (7) the scalp, and (8) the buffalo hide rope for the hanging strap. The hawk was kept inside the woven mat bag, which was tied with the buffalo hide rope. The mat bag was placed inside the deerskin bag, which was put inside the buffalo hair bag. This bundle was tied with the hanging strap, with the scalp and eagle leg attached to this strap (photo 3.1) In addition to these eight articles, each bag had a pipe and/or a war club associated with it. These two items, although of ritual importance, do not appear to have been considered technically part of the actual clan bundle.

Great symbolism was attached to the bundles as well as to their various parts. The hawk skin, painted blue, was the primary sacred object in the bundle. At every initiation ritual, the hawk was reconsecrated by a priest of the Men of Mystery clan. This reconsecration will be described in chapter 4. The hawk skin

symbolized the courage of the warriors of each fireplace [clan]. The choice of the hawk to symbolize the courage and combative nature of the warrior proved satisfactory to all of the people, for the courage of the hawk was considered as equal to that of the eagle, while the swift and decisive manner in which the smaller bird always attacked its prey ever excited the admiration of the warrior.[79]

In battle, the leader of a war party carried one of the clan bundles.

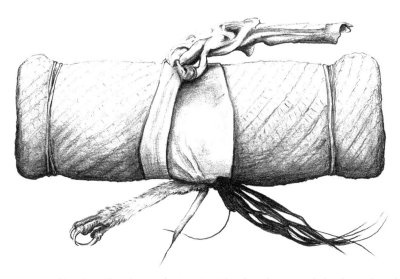

PHOTO 3.1. Clan bundle (drawn from a La Flesche photograph by Sean StandingBear).

The rush mat bag in which the hawk was placed was the most sacred of the three coverings. This bag, ritually constructed out of rush and nettle weed, symbolically represented the universe: the earth, the sky, and the life forms.[80] The bag

was woven in one piece, but divided by the symbolic designs into two equal parts, one part representing the sky, the other part the earth. The two parts also represented night and day. The part that represented the earth and the sky had conventional designs woven into the matting and symbolized the clouds that move between the sky and the earth. The portion of the matting that symbolized the day is left undyed and is of a very light color. Across the entire width of this portion of the mat are woven, equidistant, narrow dark lines that represent night. The pocket in which were to be placed the hawk and other sacred articles was made by doubling that part of the matting having on it the symbols representing the sky and earth, and it was fastened at the ends with cords. The space within the pocket symbolized the expanse between the earth and the sky into which all life comes through birth and departs therefrom by death (the Ho'-e-ga or snare). The knots fastening the ends of the pocket of the shrine were not without significance. Seven knots were tied to the end of the shrine that points, when in ceremonial position, to the Earth moiety . . . that the knots may correspond to the seven songs that are accredited to that division, and six knots were tied at the end of the pocket that will point to the Sky moiety . . . so as to correspond in number to the six songs belonging to the Sky division.[81]

The six songs and seven songs will be discussed in chapter 5.

The rush mat, along with the ritual used in making it, were the symbolic property of the Water People. The office of providing the materials—the rush and nettle weed—for the making of the bag belonged to the Elder Water and Cattail clans.[82]

When the hawk was put into the pocket of the shrine, its head was placed toward the end having the seven fastenings and its feet toward the end having six. After the hawk and other sacred articles had been put into the pocket, the flap that represents day and night was drawn over the upper part of the shrine and a ceremonial rope then wound around the middle. This buffalo hide rope was symbolic of the ropes carried by warriors to tie the hands of the captives which they took. The hide for the making of these straps was supplied by the Buffalo Face clan.[83]

The closed mat bag was placed inside the deerskin bag. The hide for making this bag was furnished by the Deer clan.[84] The deerskin bag and its contents were then placed inside a bag made of woven buffalo hair. The buffalo hair used for the weaving of this bag was supplied by the Buffalo Bull clan.

In the manner of procuring this requisite material the people are again reminded of the importance of a unity of purpose and of action by the people of the two great divisions in all tribal matters, for when performing the duty of gathering the material the hair must be plucked from the right shoulder of the buffalo when the shrine is to be made for a clan of the Earth People and from the left shoulder when the shrine is to be made for a clan of the Sky People. This prescribed rule for gathering the materials for the case also teaches that when hunting the buffalo, a food animal, the people must arrive at their decisions as with one mind and act as with a single body in order that each member of the tribe may have a chance of securing his share in the common herd.[85]

A wide strap of buffalo hide was wrapped around the middle of the bundle so that it could be hung. If the priest was a member of one of the Sky People clans, it was hung on the left side of the doorway. If the priest was a member of one of the Earth People clans, it was hung on the right side. The hide for making this strap was furnished by the Elder Sky and Wolf (Dog Star) clans.[86] Attached to the hanging strap was a scalp provided by the Bear and Puma clans and an eagle leg supplied by the Winged Hon-ga clan.[87]

*Tribal Priesthoods and Tribal Wa-xo'-be*

The tribal priests had authority over and responsibility for rituals that directly addressed the invisible world, the realm of Wa-kon-da. There were three tribal priesthoods: the wa-wathon (pipe) priests, the great bundle priests, and the great medicine bundle priests. Each priesthood had authority over a different ritual or set of rituals. The wa-wathon priests controlled the peace ceremony. The great bundle priests had responsibility for rituals associated with fertility and long life. The great medicine bundle priests were responsible for health and healing-related rituals.

Any man, regardless of clan or moiety affiliation, could be initiated as a member of any of these priesthoods. Unlike the clan priesthoods, however, for which men proposed themselves as candidates, candidacy for the tribal priesthoods was by invitation from tribal priests. Initiations into these priesthoods were far more costly in terms of gifts and food than were initiations into the clan priesthoods, but the prestige and honor were also far greater.[88]

*Wa-wathon Priests:* The wa-wathon priests were the men responsible for the wa-wathon or peace ceremony. The primary wa-xo'-be used in this ceremony were two wa-wathon, or peace pipes.

There are many ambiguities concerning the wa-wathon pipes. Pipes were a critical part of Osage ritual. Virtually every ritual required the use of one or more pipes because every ritual required that an offering be presented to Wa-kon-da. Tobacco smoke was the offering, and the pipe was the means of its transmission. The "pipe was to symbolize a man, conscious of his own limitations and seeking the aid of the All-Powerful."[89] The pipe represented not only the man but also the unity of the people in their prayers and requests to Wa-kon-da for help.[90] Considering the extensive ritual use of pipes, it should not be surprising that the Osages defined several different types of them. Pipes were sent with ceremonial messengers as symbols of the sacred nature of their visits.[91] Each clan bundle had its own pipe.[92] There was also a special war pipe or pipes entrusted to the care of the Elder Water clan and used only in the war ceremony.[93] All these pipes were or could be wa-xo'-be, but only the wa-wathon pipes were considered primary wa-xo'-be.

It was said that there were seven sacred pipes.[94] It appears, however, that both the number and the pipes themselves were purely symbolic. The symbolic relationship between the seven sacred pipes and the pipes used in the peace ceremony is unclear. There were no actual pipes permanently consecrated for use in the peace ceremony. Instead, the ceremony required two pipes, which were constructed as part of the ceremony itself. The sponsor of the ceremony supplied the materials needed to make the pipe stems: (1) skins of the heads of ivory-billed woodpeckers, (2) tail feathers of the golden eagle, (3) large downy feathers from the undertail of an eagle, (4) a forked stick, (5) fat taken from the back of a buffalo, (6) large downy feathers from the undertail of a yellow-tailed hawk, (7) straight sticks for the pipestems, or "arrow shafts," and (8) owl feathers. Apparently, any pipe bowl could be used; it was only the pipe stem that was of ritual significance. At the opening of the ceremony, priests from the Elder Sky, Eagle, Gentle Sky, Crawfish, Buffalo Bull, Isolated Earth, Cattail, Bow, and Deer clans ritually assembled the pipes from the materials supplied.[95]

The symbolic keepers of the pipes were the Water People, but it is not clear whether they included the entire Water phratry or only the Elder Water clan. The Elder Water clan was the keeper of the war pipes,[96] and the clan may have served as keeper of the peace pipes as well. Regardless of who the symbolic keeper was, the wa-wathon was a tribal wa-xo'-be. In contrast to the procedure for initiating a clan priest, there was no initiation ritual for a wa-wathon priest. The candidate hosted a peace ceremony under the sponsorship of a priest for four consecutive years; then he assumed the title *ni'-ka don-he* and the authority to sponsor new priests and ceremonies.[97]

*Great Bundle Priests:* The wa-xo'-be ton-ga, or great bundles, were also tribal bundles. La Flesche was able to record the physical existence of five great bundles.[98] All five appear to have been basically identical in their form and usage. They were actually composite bundles; each combined two closely related wa-xo'-be—the cormorant or tattooing bundle and the pelican or old age bundle. Tattooing was considered a prayer for long life and fertility. Men had themselves, their wives, and their children tattooed in the hope of gaining an unbroken line of descendants.[99] The pelican lived longer than other birds and so came to symbolize the reaching of old age.

The outer case, like those of the clan bundles, was made of woven buffalo hair. The inner case, within which are kept the pelican and cormorant wa-xo'-be and other sacred articles, was made of woven rush, with symbolic designs similar to those on the rush case of the clan bundles.

The two wa-xo'-be were folded one inside of the other, so as to make one roll. The tattooing wa-xo'-be, which is the skin of a cormorant, is split down the entire length of the back. Around the base of the tail is wound a string of scalp locks, 10 or 12 in number, that hang down like a skirt. Within the body of the skin are placed eight tattooing instruments, the points toward the head and the tops toward the tail. The shafts of some of the instruments are flat, others round, and about the length of a lead pencil. To the lower ends of the shafts are fastened steel needles, some in straight rows and others in bunches. To the tops of some of the shafts are fastened small rattles made of pelican and eagle quills. The needle parts of the shafts are covered with buffalo hair to protect them against rust. The skin of the cormorant was folded over the tattooing instruments, the neck of the bird doubled over the back and tied down. The skin of a pelican, split down the back, is wrapped around the cormorant and tied around the middle with a band of woven fiber. . . .

Within the woven rush case, placed without any particular order, are seven weasel skins; one tobacco pouch made of a buffalo heart-sack; bits of braided sweet-grass; half of the shell of a fresh-water mussel for holding the coloring matter; four tubes, one bamboo and three of tin, worn by the operator on his fingers as guides for the instruments when he is at work; two bunches of the wing-feathers of small birds used in applying the coloring matte; an old burden-strap; four wing-bones of a pelican or an eagle, tied together with a twisted cord of wood or nettle fiber; two rabbits' feet, used for brushing the skin of the parts that have been gone over with the instruments when the subject becomes nervous by the irritation of the wounds; and a large brass ring worn by the operator around his neck as part of his symbolic paraphernalia.[100]

The Gentle Ponca clan acted as the symbolic keeper of this bundle. It was, nevertheless, a tribal bundle, and its priests could belong to any of the twenty-four clans. Unlike clan bundles, great bundles were rarely transferred. Only when the priest of one of these bundles became too elderly or too blind to perform the tattooing ritual would he ask another man to assume his bundle and ritual responsibilities. The initiation rite for a new priest of a great bundle was called the rite of the chiefs, and on assuming one of these great bundles, the man became the ton'-won a-don-be, or guardian of the village.

*Great Medicine Bundle Priests:* Very little is known about the mon-kon ton-ga wa-xo'-be. None were in existence in the early twentieth century, and Osages at that time could recall the existence of only one such bundle.[101] The main elements in this wa-xo'-be were two herbs or roots, that of the *mon-kon ni-ka-shi-ga,* or "man medicine," and its female counterpart. Both roots cured bodily ailments. The Gentle Sky clan served as the symbolic keeper of this bundle, but, like the great bundle, this was a tribal bundle and its priests could be from any clan. Nothing specific is known about the initiation ritual or the other rituals associated with this bundle.[102]

## RITUALS

Formal rituals were part of almost every aspect of Osage life. They fell into two main categories: initiation rituals used by the priesthoods, and public rituals performed by the priests for individual Osages or for the tribe as a whole.

Initiation rituals were used to initiate candidates into one or another of the priesthoods. Although there were some public segments to initiation rituals, most of the rites took place with only the priests present. Each of the twenty-four clan priesthoods had its own distinct initiation ritual for each of its seven degrees. Thus there were, all together, 168 different initiation rituals for the clan priesthoods. Although there was no distinct initiation ritual for the wa-wathon priests, there were initiation rituals for both the great bundle priests and the great medicine bundle priests. Counting these two tribal initiation rituals, there were in all 170 initiation rituals.

Initiation rituals served two purposes: they were supplicatory and explanatory. Like all Osage rituals, initiations were requests for Wa-kon-da's blessing. But their primary purpose was explanatory, telling of the ritual authority conferred on the initiate over a portion of the clan's or the tribe's sacred knowledge. The initiation ceremony explained that portion of the sacred knowledge that had been entrusted to the clan, and only the priests of that clan had the right to make ritual use of that knowledge. In turn, each clan divided its sacred knowledge into seven parts, or degrees. The songs and other elements of the ritual spoke of the universe and of those portions of the clan's ritual knowledge associated with the degree being taken. Some sacred knowledge had been entrusted to the tribe as a whole rather than to the individual clans. This tribal sacred knowledge and its associated rituals were the subjects of the initiation rites into the great bundle and great medicine bundle priesthoods.

In contrast, public rituals were primarily supplicatory, with only a limited presentation of sacred knowledge. Sacred knowledge was not to be entrusted to everyone. The sacred knowledge presented in these rituals was basic, superficial, and limited to what the priests thought the general public needed to know.

In his research, La Flesche concentrated on recording the initiation rituals. He wanted to explain Osage religious beliefs, and the explanations were found in the initiation rites, not in the public ceremonies. All together, he published lengthy descriptions of six of the 168 clan priesthood initiation rituals and a description of the great bundle priesthood initiation. Although he also published descriptions of six public ceremonies, he took little interest in those ceremonies per se and made no attempt to present a complete picture of Osage public rituals and how they were associated with the various priesthoods.

The Osages performed crisis rituals as well as rituals undertaken as part of a ritual calendar. Crisis rituals, performed only when the need

arose, included war rituals, peace rituals, burial rituals, naming ceremonies, healing ceremonies, and so forth. Five of the six public rituals
La Flesche described were crisis rituals. The Osages also had a calendar of rituals performed at specific times or seasons of the year for the
benefit of the tribe as a whole. La Flesche published a description of
only one annual ritual: the new year or spring ritual. From scattered
comments in La Flesche's published works and field notes, however, as
well as from comments by other early observers, we know that the
Osages had a rich calendar of annual hunting, farming, and seasonal
ceremonies. Lack of information about these annual ceremonies consti-
tutes a major gap in our knowledge of Osage ritual life.

From the fragmentary information available, it is possible to define
the main categories of Osage public rituals and the way authority and
responsibility for them were divided among the various priesthoods
(see Table 3.2, fig. 3.4). Public rituals were grouped on the basis of
whether they were concerned with the visible or the invisible world
and whether they did or did not require the creation of a symbolic *tsi'*
*wa-kon-da-gi,* or "House of Mystery."[103]

The visible world was the world of living things—of other humans,
animals, plants, and weather. Thus there were sets of rituals concerned
with the relationships between the Osages and other living things.
Many of these rituals were concerned with war, but others dealt with
hunting, farming, weather control, and naming, a ritual by which a
living thing became an Osage. The visible world was the responsibility
of the clan priests, and so the clan priests, through the rituals they
controlled, addressed issues of the world of the living.[104]

The invisible world was the realm of Wa-kon-da. Fertility, health,
long life, and the general well-being of the people were the direct gifts
of Wa-kon-da. Thus there were sets of ceremonies that addressed the
continuing relationship, both individual and collective, between the
Osages and Wa-kon-da. These rituals—the peace ceremony, the new
year rite, the tattooing ritual, and the various healing rites—which
appealed directly to Wa-kon-da, were placed under the authority of
the tribal priests: the wa-wathon priests, the great bundle priests, and
the great medicine bundle priests.[105]

Further distinguishing the public rituals was whether or not a House
of Mystery—a symbolic representation of the universe—was part of
the ritual.[106] A ritual was symbolically either "inside the House of
Mystery" or "outside the House of Mystery." A symbolic universe was
ritually created by bringing together clan priests, each representing a
portion of the universe, and physically placing them in their proper

symbolic relationships to one another. The term *house* is misleading, because an actual dwelling was not always used or required. In most cases the priests were seated outside in their symbolic positions.

There were at least four different possible forms of the House of Mystery. It could have either a full or an abbreviated representation of clans and could "face" either east or west. Some rituals required full representation of priests from all twenty-four clans; others required only the representation of the Sky, Water, and Land portions of the universe. In these rituals a single priest from any one of the seven clans of the Sky, Water, or Land People could represent that region of the universe in its entirety.

A House of Mystery was oriented to "face" either east or west (fig. 3.5). The priests were seated along an east-west axis facing each other across an open space that separated the two groups. The priests of the Sky clan(s) would be seated together on either the north side or the south side. The priests of the Earth clans would be seated together on the opposite side. The open space separating the two lines of priests symbolized the earth's surface and the path of the sun. The Sky People represented the "left side" of the universe, and the Earth People the "right side" of the universe. Thus, if the priests of the Sky clans were seated on the north side, the universe would symbolically face east, just as a human being standing with his or her left shoulder pointing north would be facing east. East was the direction of the sun and of all life-giving and life-sustaining forces. If, on the other hand, the priests of the Sky clans were seated on the south side, the universe would symbolically face west, the direction of night and of those forces destructive of life.

The seating arrangement and symbolism in an east-facing House of Mystery was similar to, but not identical with, the arrangement of dwellings within a village. For the House of Mystery, the Isolated Earth clan's position was moved from the east end of the line of Earth People to the center, between the Land People and Water People. The seven clans of both the Land and Water also shifted their relative positions.' The arrangement was turned around so that the clan that had occupied the westernmost position now occupied the easternmost position, and vice versa. A similar shift took place among the clans of the Sky People. The two Those-Who-Came-Last clans shifted from the east end of the line to the west end of the line. The positions of the seven clans of the Sky phratry were also reversed. The symbolic significance of these slightly different arrangements of clans is not known.

In a west-facing House of Mystery, the priests of the Sky People

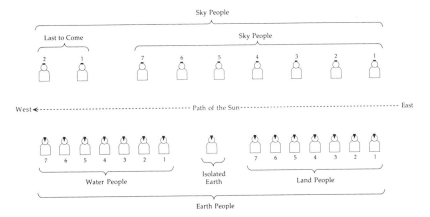

FIG. 3.5. The House of Mystery (seating of clan priests for a house "facing" east).

clans were seated on the south, and the priests of the Earth People clans on the north. There is no information, however, about the precise seating locations of particular clans and clan groupings in this form of the House of Mystery.

An east-facing House of Mystery with full representation of all twenty-four clans was required for all clan and tribal priesthood initiation rituals, as well as the peace ceremony. An abbreviated form of the east-facing House of Mystery was used in the child naming rite and probably in some other public rituals as well.

A west-facing House of Mystery with full representation of all twenty-four clans was required for the war ceremony. A west-facing House of Mystery was associated with death and war, and, although none was reported by La Flesche, there may have been an abbreviated form used for some war rituals.

The Bear clan was the symbolic keeper of the House of Mystery used in the war ceremony,[107] while the Isolated Earth clan acted as the symbolic keeper of the House of Mystery used in the child naming rite.[108] La Flesche does not mention any symbolic keeper for the House of Mystery used in the peace ceremony or in the priesthood initiation rites. Nor does he provide information about the actual functions of these symbolic keepers.

Rituals that utilized either a full or an abbreviated form of the House of Mystery were rituals that addressed *all* the forces or elements of the visible or invisible world. Rituals that were "outside the House of

Mystery" addressed only a limited range of the forces or elements of the visible or invisible world. Most rituals performed by clan priests and by the great bundle and great medicine bundle priests were public rituals performed outside the House of Mystery. Although La Flesche provided very little information about this form of public ritual, there is little doubt that a wide range of public rituals concerning hunting, farming, weather, healing, and other things were performed by priests outside the House of Mystery for both individual Osages and for the tribe.

## CHAPTER 4

*The Purpose and Meaning of Ritual*

O SAGE rituals served two pur-
poses. First, according to La Flesche, the "songs with their . . . symbols
and dramatic action are supplicatory in character: they are expressions
of a craving for divine aid toward the perpetuity of the tribal existence
and the continuity of the life of the individual by an unbroken lineage."[1] Second, and more importantly, they were for the Osages the
"means . . . by which to transmit to their posterity something of what
they had learned" of the nature of the universe.[2]

Saucy Calf told La Flesche: "Our ancestors knew not the art of
writing, but they put into ritual form the thoughts they deemed worthy of perpetuation."[3]

The ancient priests have handed down to us, in songs, wi'-gi-e [recitations],
ceremonial forms, symbols, and many things, [what] they [had] learned of the
mysteries that surround us on all sides. All these things they learned through
their power of wa-thi'-gethon, the power to search with the mind. They [the
rituals] speak of the mysteries of the light of day by which the earth and all
living things that dwell thereon are influenced; of the mysteries of the darkness
of night that reveal to us all the great bodies of the upper world, each of which
forever travels in a circle upon its own path, unimpeded by the others. They
searched, for a long period of time, for the source of life and at last came to the
thought that it issues from an invisible creative power to which they applied
the name Wa-kon-da.[4]

Rituals were the means by which the Osages consciously preserved
and transmitted knowledge; they were, in effect, the "books" of a
nonliterate people.

The priests also realized that not all people were equally respectful
of sacred knowledge. As Saucy Calf explained: "There are some things
that are not spoken of by the priests in the rituals they made, things

that are not confided to the thoughtless and irreverent, but are discussed only by men who are serious minded and who treasure the thoughts that are sacred and mysterious."[5]

Although all Osage rituals preserved and imparted portions of the collective knowledge of the tribe, public rituals and priesthood initiation rituals differed in both content and purpose.

The pedagogical purpose of public rituals and of the public portions of the priesthood initiation rituals was to convey certain basic concepts and ideas to the populace as a whole. The priests realized that most people had little intellectual curiosity or interest. The main thrust of the public rituals was to impress on the minds of the people the basic social paradigm created by the priests. Through words, actions, and symbols, the priests communicated the idea that no individual could act alone, that they were dependent upon others. People had to act together in a unified and organized manner for the common good. The priests also seem to have realized that most people adhered to society's socioreligious norms out of unquestioned faith in, or fear of, what they did not understand. Substantive explanations in public rituals were limited and simple. The structure of the tribe and of families, clans, phratries, and moieties was the mirror image of the invisible world of Wa-kon-da, and thus was sacred or divine. There was power in the various wa-xo'-be that could be used for good or evil and so was dangerous. Only the priests had the knowledge necessary to control and use this power. Thus, the ultimate authority of the priests rested on the control of knowledge that uninitiated Osages lacked.

Because the priests' authority rested on the control of knowledge, the most important parts of the initiation rituals, unsurprisingly, were conducted in seclusion and secrecy, and the uninitiated were allowed no knowledge of these teachings. In the initiation rituals, the true collective knowledge of the Osages was recorded. In words, symbols, and actions, these rituals described the nature of the cosmos and the development of the Osage people. In essence, these rites recorded Osage history, theology, and philosophy while defining the socioreligious organization in highly metaphorical terms. Osage priests had to learn more than the words, symbols, and actions used in the rituals; they had to study them for underlying meanings as well. It was in these teachings, the rituals, that the true intellectual achievements of the Osages found their expression.

Each of the 170 different priesthood initiation rituals addressed different issues and presented a different set of knowledge, but all of them revolved either directly or indirectly around a central theme or story. This story did not exist as a single narrative but was presented in fragments scattered throughout the rituals. By piecing together these fragments, La Flesche was able to construct what he called the "allegorical story of the tribe." This narrative—which is, in effect, the Osage origin myth—creates the basic framework for the information and concepts presented in the rituals. The following account of the allegorical story was originally given as an introduction to La Flesche's description of the rite of the chiefs.[6]

## THE ALLEGORICAL STORY OF THE TRIBE

In the beginning the peoples of the Water, the Land, and the Sky came from the sky to the earth. After these three groups of people had descended they started forth to wander over the earth, observing, as they marched, the sequence in which they had reached the earth: first the Water, then the Land, and last the Sky. One day, after they had wandered for a great length of time, the Water People suddenly halted, and the leader looked back over his shoulder to his followers, who had also halted, and in an undertone said: "We have come to the village of a strange people." The leader of the Land People looked back over his shoulder and in the same manner passed the word to the Sky People.

Overhearing the words cautiously spoken by the Water leader and his followers, the people of the village sent a messenger to inquire who these strangers were and what was their mission. On the invitation of the messenger, the Water People alone entered the village, for the Land and the Sky peoples declined to follow because they had noticed with revulsion that the bones of animals and of men lay scattered and bleaching around the village. It was the village of death to which they had come, when they had been seeking for life.

The leader of the Water People was conducted to the house of the leader of the strange people and there the two men exchanged words in friendly terms. The Water leader presented a ceremonial pipe to the leader of this strange village, who in turn gave a pipe to the leader of the Water People, and then the two leaders conversed freely about the life and customs of their peoples. In the course of their conversation the Water leader said that he belonged to a people who called themselves the Earth, whereupon the stranger said: "I also am Earth." He then told the Water leader the manner in which his people destroyed life wherever it appeared on the earth, using for their weapons the four winds, and that whichever way the people turned the winds, the animals and men stricken by them fell and died. It was at this point that the Water leader made known to his host that the Land and the

Sky peoples desired to dwell with him and his people, but did not like their habit of destroying life. The Water leader then suggested that his host and his people move to a new country, where the land was pure and free from the signs of death. The Isolated Earth People, as the Water [People] called these strange people, willingly accepted the invitation and moved with the Water People to a "new country," where they joined the Land and the Sky.

All the four groups, the Water, the Land, the Sky, and the Isolated Earth, thereupon moved to a new country, where the land was undefiled by decaying carcasses and where there were no visible signs of death. There they united themselves in friendship, each pledging to the other its strength and support in resisting the dangers that might beset them in the course of their united tribal life.

It was at this time that the following dramatic incident took place between the Water and the Land peoples. The Water People offered to the Land People a symbolic pipe, but before accepting it the Land asked, "Who are you?" The Water replied:

I am a person who has verily made of a pipe his body.
When you also make of the pipe your body,
You shall be free from all causes of death, O Land.

The Land People took the pipe and said in response:

I am a person who has made of the red boulder his body.
When you also make of it your body,
The malevolent forces in their destructive course
Shall pass by and leave you unharmed, O Water.

The expression of the Water, "I am a person who has made of a pipe his body," is figurative and means that the pipe is the life symbol of his people, the medium through which they approach Wa-kon-da with their supplications. The words used by the Land in his response, "I am a person who has made of the red boulder his body," are also figurative and mean that the red boulder is the life symbol of the Land People. The red boulder has a dual symbolism; it is the symbol of endurance and is also a symbol of the sun, the emblem of neverending life.

It was thus that the two groups, the Water and the Land, pledged support to one another in times of danger so long as tribal life should last. The words of the Water People and those of the Land People were put in the wi'-gi-e form and are embodied in the rite called Ni'-ki-e, the Words of the Ancient Men.[7] These two wi'-gi-es are also used in a certain part of the Wa-sha'-be A-thin, a war ceremony, where it is intimated that the Water People also presented a ceremonial pipe to the Sky People.[8] The narrator of the foregoing paraphrase offered no information concerning the part of the Sky People in this council of alliance, as he was not a member of that division.

At the time of this council the people of the three groups gave to the Isolated Earth People a house which they called Tsi' Wa-kon-da-gi, House of Mysteries. Both the house and its fireplace they consecrated to ceremonial uses and made them to represent the life-giving earth. To this House of Mysteries were to be brought all the infants of the four groups to be ceremonially fed upon the sacred foods of life that they might arrive safely at the age of maturity, and the children were here to be given their clan names in order to take their established places in the tribal organization.

The council at this time also established another house, Tsi' Wa-kon-da-gi, House of Mysteries, which they called Earth Tsi, and placed it in the keeping of the Bear clan of the Land People. In this house were to be performed the ceremonies that pertain to war. Within its fireplace, which was called ho'-e-ga, Snare, were placed four stones, arranged at the cardinal points, one for each of the four winds. Upon these four stones was placed the Tse'-xe Ni-ka-po, a cauldron for the boiling of certain plants that represented certain persons belonging to enemy tribes.

When the Tsi' Wa-kon-da-gi of the Bear clan and its fireplace had been consecrated, each of the clans of the four groups placed within the house its life symbol. This statement is not meant to be understood in a literal sense, as some of the clan life symbols are of the great objects in nature, such as the sun, moon, stars, earth, while there are others that are intangible, as the day, the night, and the sky. Therefore the act of placing the sacred life symbols in the House of Mysteries was represented by the reciting of the wi'-gi-es that relate to these various sacred life symbols. [These wi'-gi-e will be given in chapter 6.—Ed.]

These four warrior groups conducted both the war and hunting movements of the people, and no one group could act independently of the others. A war party thus ceremonially organized by all of these four groups was called Do-don'-hin-ton-ga, War Party in Great Numbers.

After living for a long period of time under this form of government, the people were again seized with a desire to "move to a new country" (a term expressive of a slow movement that preceded a change in the government of the tribe). It was while the tribe was in the "new country" that the people made the Wa-xo'-be Zhin-ga, the Little Wa-xo'-be, one for each of the seven fireplaces of the Sky great division; one for each of the seven fireplaces [clans] of the Land subdivision; and one for each of the seven fireplaces of the Water subdivision of the Earth People.[9]

These wa-xo'-be were made of hawk skins and symbolized the courage of the warriors of each fireplace. The choice of the hawk to symbolize the courage and combative nature of the warrior proved satisfactory to all the people, for the courage of the hawk was considered as equal to that of the eagle, while the swift and decisive manner in which the smaller bird always attacks its prey ever excited the admiration of the warrior.

From the story relating to the adoption of the hawk as the warrior symbol, given in wi'-gi-e form by a member of the Puma clan and by a member of the Buffalo Bull clan in a paraphrase of the wi'-gi-e, it would appear that the ceremonies of the formal adoption and the acts of preparing the hawk skin for preservation were accompanied by dramatic action.

In the version of the Puma, a clan belonging to the Earth People, the principal characters of the drama are left vague as to identity. But in the version of the Buffalo Bull, a clan belonging to the Sky People that symbolizes the sky, it becomes clear that the warrior whom the hawk typifies is a child born of the forces of day and of night. [Because these bundles fused day and night, they were symbolic of both life-giving and life-destroying forces.] In this version the principal characters are four brothers (stars), their sister (the moon), and the sun.

The supernatural birth of the wa-xo'-be, the symbolic hawk, is referred to in the words of three songs belonging to the ritual of the Songs of the Wa-xo'-be degree of the Buffalo Bull clan. The three songs bear in common the title "Little Songs of the Sun."

Song 1

1

I go to the call of those who are assembled,
To the call of those who are gathered around the hawk.

2

I go to the call of those who are assembled,
To the call of those who are gathered around the black bird.

3

I go to the call of those who are assembled,
To the call of those who are gathered around the One of the Night.

### 4

I go to the call of those who are assembled,
To the call of those who are gathered around the One of the Day.

### Song 2

#### 1

He is born! He is born!
Behold, the hawk, he is born,
They have said. They have said,
He is born!

#### 2

He is born! He is born!
Behold, the black bird, he is born,
They have said. They have said,
He is born!

#### 3

He is born! He is born!
Behold, he is born of the One of the Night,
They have said. They have said,
He is born!

#### 4

He is born! He is born!
Behold, he is born of the One of the Day,
They have said. They have said,
He is born!

### Song 3

#### 1

Lo, it has come to pass,
Behold, the hawk that lies outstretched
Is now born they proclaim. Is now born they
proclaim.
Welcome! be it said. Lo, it has come to pass.

#### 2

Lo, it has come to pass,
Behold, it is of the One who is of the Day,
He is born they proclaim. He is born they proclaim.
Welcome! be it said. Lo, it has come to pass.

#### 3

Lo, it has come to pass,
Behold, the black bird that lies outstretched

Is now born they proclaim. Is now born they proclaim.
Welcome! be it said. Lo, it has come to pass.

4

Lo, it has come to pass,
Behold, it is of the One who is of the Night,
He is born they proclaim. He is born they proclaim.
Welcome! be it said. Lo, it has come to pass.

The priests sat within their long house as they worked on the wa-xo'-be. Their heads were still bent over the last one when they were startled by the angry bellowing of an animal. All eyes turned upon the servant, who hastened to the door and quickly threw aside the flap. There stood an angry buffalo with his head lowered and his tail trembling in the air, pawing the earth and throwing clouds of dust toward the sky. Stricken with fear, the servant asked with unsteady voice, "Who are you?" The bull answered, "I am Buffalo Bull, lift ye your heads!" At that moment there came a crash of thunder that seemed to issue from the end of the ridgepole of the house. In an excited manner the priests gathered up all the wa-xo'-be and threw them toward the bull, who at once lowered his tail, ceased pawing the earth, and became friendly.

These two angry visitors, the bull and the thunder, were representatives of the Buffalo Bull and the Men of Mystery clans. It was in this dramatic manner that these two clans were jointly given the office of caring for the wa-xo'-be. At an initiation of a member of one of the various clans into the mysteries of the war rite, the hereditary caretaker of the wa-xo'-be, who belongs to the Men of Mystery clan, is given the bird to redecorate, an act equivalent to its reconsecration for the benefit of the initiate. If the hereditary caretaker happens to be absent from the initiation, this duty is performed by the second official caretaker, who belongs to the Buffalo Bull clan. It is said that all the wa-xo'-be belong to these two clans because the priests had given them to the two clans through fear; also that the Buffalo Bull and the Men of Mystery had originally brought the birds from the sky and given them to the people.

The Buffalo Bull and the Men of Mystery were also spoken of as the Tsi Ha-shi, Those Last to Come—that is, those of the clans who were last to take part in the formulating of the war rite.

From the foregoing story it appears that the military branch of the tribal government in the course of its development passed through two stages, each one of which was spoken of as a "departure to a new country." The introductory statement that the peoples of the Water, the Land, and the Sky came from the sky to the earth expresses the conception that all life descends from the sky to the earth. The story that immediately follows has a historical basis and indicates the point of departure from a chaotic to an orderly state of tribal existence.

It also appears that at the beginning the affairs of the tribe were under the control of the Isolated Earth, a division representing the earth. During this period the tribe was in a continual state of confusion from external and internal disturbances. In order to preserve the tribal existence, a movement toward reorganization became necessary, and in time such a movement was initiated by the Water People, a subdivision of the Earth People.

In this reorganization certain offices were established and distributed as follows: To the Isolated Earth was given the priestly office of keeping the house wherein the children of all the people were initiated into the tribal life and given their clan personal names. To the Land People, a subdivision of the Earth People, was given the office of keeping the house wherein the ceremonies pertaining to war were to be conducted. This house was placed in the direct keeping of the Bear clan and the Puma clan, which were related clans. The authority for the initiation of all war movements was conferred upon these four tribal divisions: Bear, Water, Sky, Isolated Earth, each having an eagle for its war symbol. The authority with which they were vested included the management of the tribal hunting expeditions. Such was the first stage of the development of the military branch of the tribal government.

The reorganized government proved effective in the maintenance of peace and order within the tribe and in upholding the dignity of the people as an organized body, but it was burdened with ceremonial forms which did not admit of the prompt action often necessary for moving against aggressive and troublesome enemies.

The priests, becoming conscious of this defect, again made a "move to a new country" to bring their organization to final completion. In this second move, the various clans of the tribe were empowered to organize war parties in three classes, as follows:

1. A war party composed of the warriors from [all?] the clans of one of the two great divisions.
2. A war party made up of two or more of the clans of one of the two great divisions.
3. A war party organized by one clan.

War parties of the first two classes were called Tsi'-ga-xa Do-don; Tsi'-ga-xa probably meaning "Outside of the House of Mystery"; Do-don, War Party—i. e., war party organized outside of the House of Mystery. War parties of the third class were called Wa-xo'-be U-kon-dsi; Wa-xo'-be, the Sacred Hawk; U-kon-dsi, Isolated; An Isolated Wa-xo'-be. War parties of these three classes were not required to observe the tedious ceremonial forms prescribed for the war parties organized under the rule of the four divisions. Under this new movement each clan of the tribe was given a hawk wa-xo'-be for ceremonial purposes. This was the second stage in the development of the military branch of the tribal government.

For the perpetuation of the memory of these events, as well as for the guidance of the people in organizing their forces for defensive or aggressive warfare, the priests formulated rites and ceremonial acts which were memorized by men capable of such a task and handed down by them to the successive generations.

In the progress of time the priests made a third "move to a new country." At this time the civil branch of the tribal government was instituted. It was then agreed that the people should be governed by two men, one for each of the two great tribal divisions, who should bear the official title of Ga-hi'-ge, Chief. The duties assigned to these two chiefs were as follows:

1. When two men quarrel, come to blows, and threaten to kill each other, the chief shall compel them to cease fighting.
2. When a murder is committed and a relative of the person slain threatens to take the life of the murderer in revenge, the chief shall compel the relative to keep the peace.
3. If the relative persists in his effort to take the life of the slayer, the chief shall expel him from the tribe.
4. If the relative takes the life of the slayer when the chief had already offered him the sacred pipe to smoke, the chief shall give the order for him to be put to death.
5. The chief shall require the murderer to bring gifts to the relatives of the man he has slain as an offering of peace.
6. If the murderer refuses to do this, the chief may call upon the people to make the peace offering and then expel the murderer from the tribe.
7. If a man's life is threatened by another and he flees to the house of the chief, he shall protect the fleeing man.
8. If a murderer pursued by the relatives of the slain man flees into the house of the chief, he shall protect the man.
9. If a stranger, although he be from an enemy tribe, enters the house of the chief for safety, the chief shall protect him.

10. When a war party comes home with captives, the chief shall give them their lives and have them adopted into the tribe.

When the tribe goes out for the annual buffalo hunt it shall be the duty of the chief to designate the route to be taken and the site in which the camp is to be pitched, and the order shall be proclaimed by a crier. The two chiefs shall take turns each day in conducting the journey, both when going forth and when returning to the home village.

For the enforcement of their orders the two chiefs shall be empowered to select and appoint ten officers, one from each of the following clans: on the Earth side: Bear or Puma; Deer; Elk; Winged Earth (Eagle); Isolated Earth; on the Sky side: Men of Mystery; Buffalo Bull; Elder Sky; Sun Carrier; Buffalo Face.

These officers shall bear the title A'-ki-da, Soldier, and shall be chosen because of the military honors that they had won as well as for their personal friendship for the chief. The chief, in selecting his officers, shall not be restricted to his own division, but he may, according to his own preference, choose his officers from any of the designated clans of the opposite division. These officers shall have their houses close to that of the chief.

The officers selected from three of these designated clans were honored with special titles, which afterwards became in these clans personal names. These titles, and later the names, were: A'-ki-da Ton-ga, Great Soldier, for the officer chosen from the Bear clan or the related Puma clan; A'-ki-da Zhin-ga, Little Soldier, for the one chosen from the Deer clan; and A'-ki-da Ga-hi'-ge, Chief Soldier, for the one from the Men of Mystery clan.

It was agreed at this time that the office of the chief shall descend to the lineal male heirs. In case the heir is disqualified for the office owing to mental infirmity or indifference to the customs held sacred by the people, the Soldiers in council shall determine who of the nearest kin to the former chief shall succeed to the office.

The clans from which the two chiefs were chosen were the Ponca clan, of the Water subdivision of the Earth People; and the Sky clan[10] of the Sky People. The title Wa-shta'-ge, Gentle, was at that time added to the names of these two clans, so that in speaking of them both the name and title were mentioned, as the Gentle Ponca and the Gentle Sky. This clan was sometimes called the Tsi-zhu Wa-bin' I-ta-zhi, the Sky people who do not touch blood, because the people of that clan are supposed to refrain from the shedding of blood. The rule that required the chief to protect a man fleeing to his house for refuge applied to all the families of this clan.

It was also agreed that the house of the chief should be held as sacred as it represents two life-giving powers, the Earth and the Sun. The house stands for the earth and must have two doors, one opening toward the rising sun and the other toward the setting sun. The fire that is placed midway between the two doors represents the sun, whose pathway symbolizes endless life, and thus passes through the middle of the house that stands for the earth. The fireplace was also consecrated, and the fire taken therefrom by the people to start their home fires was thought of as holy and as having power to give life and health to those who use it. It was also declared that the two doors, which represent the continual flow of life, shall be closed to the man who approaches them when contemplating murder. The ceremonial position of the chief's house in the village was also established at this time.

Sometime after the creation of the office of chief for each of the two great divisions, and the men chosen had been inducted into their offices, the two chiefs went out separately to seek for some sign of approval from the Supernatural. For seven days and six nights the men fasted and cried to Wa-kon-da.

As the darkness of evening spread over the land, on the sixth day of his vigil, the Gentle Sky chief removed from his face the sign of vigil and sat down to rest for the night. While he was yet awake and in deep thought he heard approaching footsteps, and as he looked up he beheld a man standing before him, as though in the light of day. The stranger spoke, saying: "I have heard your cry. I am a person who can heal all the pains and the bodily ailments of your people. When the little ones make of me their bodies they shall always live to see old age. In the morning when the mists have cleared away, go to yonder river, follow its course until you come to a bend and there, in the middle of its bank, you will see me standing in the midst of the winds."

When morning came the chief followed the course of the river, as the stranger bade him, until he came to a sharp bend, where the waters had washed away the earth, leaving a high bank. The chief looked up and there, in the middle of the bank, he saw the stranger, who was Mon-kon Ni-ka-shi-ga, the Man Medicine (Cucurbita perennis). The chief removed from its place the strange man-shaped root, being careful not to break any part of it. As this was the seventh and the last day of his fast, the chief then started toward his home, following the course of the river. He had not gone far when he came to another bend of the stream where there was a high bank. In the middle of it he beheld another root which he examined and found to be of the female sex. The chief carried home these two roots, which afterwards were used to cure bodily ailments. For ceremonial purposes a portable shrine was made for these two roots and wi'-gi-e relating to their revelation, but as they did not belong to the clan of the narrator, he declined to give further details of the ceremonies.

The story of the vigil of the Gentle Ponca chief [the second of the two chiefs] is given in three wi'-gi-e. On the evening of the sixth day of his vigil the Gentle Ponca chief removed from his face the sign of vigil and sat down to rest for the night. While he was yet awake there appeared before him a very aged man, who spoke to him, saying, "I have heard your cry and have come to give myself to your people. I am Old Age. When the little ones make of me their bodies they shall always live to see old age. When morning comes, go to yonder river, and in a bend where the water, sheltered by a high bank, lies placid you will find me. Take from my right wing seven feathers. Let your people make of them their bodies and they shall always live to see old age."

In the dawn of the morning which was the seventh day of his vigil the chief arose and again put upon his face the sign of vigil. He went to the river, and in a bend where the water was sheltered from the winds by a high bank he saw, on the water's edge, a white pelican so old that he could not move. In this bird the chief recognized his visitor of the night before. From the right wing of the bird the chief plucked seven feathers and started for home. As he was approaching a brook he met an eagle, who gave him a downy feather as a symbol of old age. When he was nearing home he beheld lying on the ground a piece of black metal, which he also took as a symbol of old age.

From these stories it would seem that the two chiefs directed their efforts toward the understanding of bodily ailments and the finding of suitable remedies. The chiefs thus sought, by combating disease, to maintain the numerical strength of the tribe. The people on their part put faith and confidence in the healing powers of the chiefs, which led to the adoption of "Wa-stse'-e-don," the Good Doctor, by the two Gentle clans for a clan personal name.

On his return to the village the chief assembled the people of both great divisions, to whom he told the story of his vigil. The people were well pleased and formally consecrated the pelican to be thenceforth their sacred symbol of old age, and it thus became wa-xo'-be. The portable shrine which held the sacred symbols and the symbols themselves are spoken of collectively as wa-xo'-be.

## EDITOR'S SUMMARY

From this allegorical story, the evolution of Osage tribal structure becomes clear. This structure developed in three distinct stages. The sacred pipes existed before the tribe came into existence, and it was the Water People who had the pipes. The sacred pipes, the symbol of unity, were initially the only wa-xo'-be. The first stage of tribal organization was the unifying of the Land, Water, Sky, and Isolated Earth People, achieved under the sacred pipes. At the same time, the people established the House of Mystery for the naming of children, which they placed under the custodianship of the Isolated Earth clan, and the House of Mystery for war, which they put under the custodianship of the Bear clan of the Land People. Under this form of organization, they had to act with total unity in all things. The only type of war party that was allowed was a tribal war party (a "War Party in Great Numbers"). Later the people realized that this organization was not adequate to meet their needs, and the tribe was reorganized.

In the second stage of development, the priests decided that the clans had to have the authority to act independently in war. Thus the priests created a new form of wa-xo'-be, the little wa-xo'-be, or clan bundle. A wa-xo'-be was made for each of the clans, which gave them the authority to initiate war independently. It was at this time that the Buffalo Bull and Men of Mystery clans joined the Osages, completing the clan structure. These two clans were made keepers of all the clan wa-xo'-be. Eventually the priests realized that even this new structure was not sufficient, and so for a third time they reorganized the tribe.

In the third stage of development, the priests created a secular branch to their organization: the two chiefs who would manage the internal daily problems of village life. These two chiefs undertook vision quests and had knowledge revealed to them. On their return, the Gentle Ponca chief created the great bundle, while the Gentle Sky chief created the great medicine bundle. Each bundle was dedicated to the life-giving forces that had been revealed.

The clan priesthoods and the clan wa-xo'-be were associated with the first two stages of tribal development. Thus the knowledge conferred in the initiation rituals of the clan priests addresses only issues concerned with these early stages. Although basic knowledge was shared by the twenty-four clan priesthoods, each clan also had exclusive control over parts of this knowledge. Their ritual authority was derived from control this knowledge. In turn, the knowledge of every clan was divided into seven parts, each associated with one of the seven degrees of its priesthood. As a result, any initiation ritual presented only a small portion of the total knowledge controlled by the clan priests as a whole.

During the third and last stage of tribal development, two of the tribal wa-xo'-be came into existence: the great bundle and the great medicine bundle. The initiation rituals for the two tribal priesthoods associated with these wa-xo'-be tell of this final stage of tribal development.

La Flesche recorded relatively complete descriptions of seven initiation rituals. Six of these descriptions were of initiation rituals for the clan priesthoods: the Buffalo Bull clan version of the Songs of the Wa-xo'-be, the Puma clan and Gentle Sky clan versions of the rite of vigil, the Gentle Sky clan version of the Shrine degree, and the Puma clan and Bear clan versions of the Words of the Ancient Men. In addition, he recorded the rite of the chief, the initiation rite for the great bundle priests.

In the next two chapters I present as complete descriptions as possible of two initiation rituals: the Buffalo Bull clan version of the Songs of the Wa-xo'-be, and the rite of the chiefs. I chose these two rituals on the basis of the knowledge they confer and their structural forms. The Songs of the Wa-xo'-be was concerned with the structure of the universe and the first two stages of tribal development, with particular emphasis on the organization and conduct of tribal and clan war parties. A four-day ritual, the Songs of the Wa-xo'-be communicates its information through the elaborate use of human and nonhuman symbols, songs, wi'-gi-e (recitations), and we'-ga-xe (dramatic acts). In contrast, the rite of the chiefs is much less complex in form, relying primarily on the reciting of long wi'-gi-e to communicate its message. In these wi'-gi-e, the story of the vigil of the Gentle Ponca chief is told and the main life symbols of the different clans are defined.

CHAPTER 5  *Songs of the Wa-xo'-be*

THE name "Songs of the Wa-xo'-be" refers both to a degree in the clan priesthoods and to the initiation rite into that degree. Although not the most important of the degrees, the Songs of the Wa-xo'-be was one of the more important of the initiation rites because only it and the rite of vigil included the use of the full set of "the seven songs" and "the six songs."[1] The seven songs and the six songs were concerned with the early tribal organization: the creation of tribal war parties and the creation of the clan bundles and their associated clan war parties. As an initiation ritual, the Songs of the Wa-xo'-be was a grand theatrical production that occupied most of a four-day period. It involved a sizable number of participants, many of whom symbolically represented various cosmic forces. It demanded the use of a variety of ritual objects, each with its own symbolic significance, and took shape through a large of number of songs, recitations, and dramatic acts involving particular participants and ritual items. In many respects this ritual was analogous, in terms of production, to a Western-style opera—although the ritual was far more complex in both form and meaning.

Before presenting La Flesche's description of the ritual, I will briefly discuss its symbolism and basic structure. The Osages made great use of symbols to communicate ideas. The symbolism found in the Songs of the Wa-xo'-be is rich and complex. Within the ritual are different levels of symbolic meanings as well as features that have multiple symbolic meanings. Human participants, ritual objects, and songs have both individual and collective meanings. I will begin with the general symbolic nature of the ritual and will then turn to the specific symbolic significance of each of its major elements.

INTRODUCTION TO THE RITUAL

For the Songs of the Wa-xo'-be, an east-facing House of Mystery was created by using the priests of all twenty-four clans to symbolically represent portions of the universe. No actual structure was required for this ritual; the priests usually just sat on the ground in a large open area. Other participants and ritual items were used to symbolically represent particular elements of the universe.[2] As La Flesche wrote, "the rite as a whole was of cosmic character; . . . it was a dramatization of the movements of certain cosmic forces whose combined power brought forth material life upon the earth and set it in perpetual motion."[3] Thus, to understand the meaning of the ritual, one must first understand which element of the universe a particular individual or ritual item symbolically represented.

### The Participants

Nine individuals or groups of individuals took part in this ritual: (1) the candidate/Singer, (2) the Xo'-ka, (3) the Assisting Xo'-ka, (4) the priests of all twenty-four clans, (5) the Wa-don'-be, (6) the Sho'-ka, (7) the widows of former priests, (8) the wife of the candidate/Singer, and (9) the assisting singers. Some, but not all, of these participants had symbolic significance.

The candidate/Singer. The candidate, or Singer, was the man who was being initiated into this degree of the clan priesthood. There was no Osage term for this person at the beginning of the ceremony, so I have used the English term "candidate." On the third night of the ceremony, after taking part in the Night Singing, he received the title "Singer" (wa-thon a-ka) and was called by this title throughout the remainder of the ceremony.[4] At the end of the ritual, the wa-xo'-be used in the ritual was physically transferred to him for his keeping.[5] Although this ritual was his initiation, he actually played a minor role in the ceremony. Most of the time he sat or stood quietly. In the ritual, he represented "not only human life but all other forms of life that move apace with the sun on its endless journey."[6]

The Xo'-ka. The Xo'-ka was the sponsor of the candidate/Singer. A member of the candidate/Singer's clan, he held the degree that was being conferred, and it was under his authority as a priest that the initiation was conducted.[7] It was the wa-xo'-be in his possesion that would be transferred to the candidate/Singer at the end of the ceremony. The Xo'-ka was the central focus of the ceremony and its main symbolic actor. The Xo'-ka was a highly complex symbolic figure whose main representation was that of the sun, the most powerful force in the cosmos.[8] The Xo'-ka's ritual attire, which will be described later, was indicative of this role. The Xo'-ka did not, however, represent in the sun in its totality. The particular elements of the sun that were symbolically represented by the Xo'-ka varied with the type of initiation ritual. Because the Songs of the Wa-xo'-be was concerned with war and the preservation of life through the destruction of others, the Xo'-ka wore a puma skin robe, a symbol of destruction.[9] In some other initiation rituals, the Xo'-ka wore a buffalo robe as a symbol of sustaining life.[10] In the rite of the chiefs (chapter 6), the Xo'-ka wore a bearskin robe, but its symbolic significance is unclear.[11]

At some stages in the ritual, the role of the Xo'-ka shifted from that of the symbolic sun to that of the "symbolic man."[12] The symbolic man was conceptualized as "a man, perfect in physical form, possessed of mental powers and the ability to express thought,"[13] who combined the forces of the sky and earth. In other words, the symbolic man was the embodiment of the tribe and of tribal life. It is not always clear in La Flesche's description of the Songs of the Wa-xo'-be whether the Xo'-ka is representing the sun or the symbolic man. Although the Xo'-ka says nothing during the ceremony, it is his physical actions, particularly in relationship to the wa-xo'-be, on which everything focuses.

*The Assisting Xo'-ka (a'-ki-hon xo'-ka).* The Assisting Xo'-ka was the man who actually directed and performed most of the ritual. La Flesche sometimes referred to him as the "master of ceremonies." He sang the songs and recited most of the long wi'-gi-e (recitations). He also directed the other participants in their actions and timing.[14] Because a man held a particular degree in the clan priesthood did not necessarily mean that he knew all the songs and recitations associated with the degree. Only a few of the more serious-minded priests studied and learned the songs and recitations.[15] So although any holder of a degree had the authority to act as Xo'-ka, only a minority of priests had the requisite knowledge to act as the Assisting Xo'-ka.[16] The Assisting Xo'-ka's role appears to have been purely functional and not symbolic.

*The Sho'-ka.* The Sho'-ka was the official ceremonial messenger. One of the subclans within each clan was designated as the Sho'-ka subclan, and the Sho'-ka was chosen from the men of this clan. A Sho'-ka carried with him a little pipe and a bag of tobacco as emblems of his office. He served as the go-between for the participants in the ceremony.[17] The Sho'-ka symbolized a captive and a servant.[18]

*The Wa-don'-be.* The Wa-don'-be symbolized the warriors of the tribe as well as the collective courage of the people. To be a Wa-don'-be, a man had to have earned all of the thirteen o-don', or war honors, a man could acquire.[19] Since one of these honors was awarded for having served as a Sacred Warrior (the leader of a tribal war party), this requirement meant that the Wa-don'-be also had to be a priest, because only a priest could serve as a Sacred Warrior.[20]

*The clan priests.* For this initiation, or for any initiation into the priesthood, a symbolic House of Mystery had to be created. For the Songs of the Wa-xo'-be, a full representation of the priests of all twenty-four clans was required. The priest or priests of each clan symbolically represented that portion of the cosmos associated with their clan. During the ceremony, the priests were seated in clan order, with the priests of the Sky People to the north and those of the Earth People to the south.[21] The one exception to this rule was that the priests of the initiating clan—in this case the Buffalo Bull clan—sat at the east end, behind the Singer and the Xo'-ka. Only priests who had been initiated into the degree of the priesthood being taken by the candidate or priests who had been initiated in the Sayings of the Ancient Men degree—the seventh and all-encompassing degree—could take part in an initiation.[22]

*The widows of priests.* Although women were not initiated into the priesthoods, a highly respected widow of a former priest might be given honorary membership in the clan priesthood of her deceased husband.[23] Seated behind the clan priests, the widows would, during portions of the ritual, "wail in sympathy with the candidate as an appeal to the priests that they will perform their part without reserve or prejudice."[24]

*The wife of the Singer.* The role of women in Osage society was considered to be as important as the role of men. The initiation ritual emphasized the role of the male warrior as the protector of the people and the destroyer of their enemies. In one part of the ceremony, however, the wife of the Singer was brought into the House of Mystery and a special segment called "Instructions to the Wife of the Initiate" was performed, in which the role of the wife as the life-giving mother was the theme.[25]

*The assisting singer(s).* The Assisting Xo'-ka usually had one or two other priests to assist him in the singing.[26] Although nothing is said about who these singers were, it seems reasonable to assume that they were also priests of the initiate's clan, because only priests of his clan would know these songs and have the right to sing them.

### Ritual Items

A wide range of ritual items was used in the ceremony: (1) the wa-xo'-be zhin-ga, or clan bundle, (2) the tally sticks, (3) the seven animal skins, (4) the rattle, (5) o-don' counting sticks, (6) the war standard,

(7) the war club, (8) the sacred bow and arrows, and (9) the little pipe. Each of these items had its own significance.

*The wa-xo'-be zhin-ga (little sacred objects).* The wa-xo'-be zhin-ga or clan bundle used in the ceremony was the bundle that was being transferred to the Singer.[27] During the ritual, the bundle would be opened and the hawk displayed and reconsecrated. The component elements and the symbolism of the clan bundle were discussed in chapter 3.

*The tally sticks (zhon'-xa wa-zhu).* Tally sticks were the means by which the Assisting Xo'-ka kept count of the songs. These were sticks with small notches cut to represent each song. The notches were clustered in groups of varying numbers, representing the number of songs in a particular song group. Tally sticks were consecrated and so were considered sacred. The sticks themselves were of willow, a symbol of everlasting life and the life symbol of the Water People.[28]

*The seven animal skins (pe-thon-ba tse).* As part of his preparations for his initiation, the candidate had to acquire the skins of seven specified animals: the lynx, the gray wolf, the male puma, the male black bear, the buffalo, the elk, and the deer. These animals were admired for their courage, and so they were used as symbols of courage.[29] Although La Flesche's statements are vague, it appears that the candidate himself had to collect these skins.[30] The first major preliminary ritual was the smoking of these skins, which was a way of consecrating them for ceremonial use. In the main ceremony, the skins hung on racks in the center of the House of Mystery.[31]

*The rattle (pe'-xe).* The only musical instrument used in the initiation ceremonies was a simple gourd rattle. It possessed dual symbolism related to the head. In one form, the rattle represented the head of a puma and symbolized the relentless fire. In another form, it represented the head of a man who was head of the Isolated Earth clan. When used in the initiation of priests of the Earth People, the "seeds" (stones) inside the gourd were said symbolically to be the teeth from the right jaw of a puma or man, and the wooden handle was said to be the right forearm of a puma or man. In the initiation of priests of the Sky People, the symbolism was opposite: the teeth were of the left jaw, and the handle was the left forearm. Although the rattle was used by all clans in their initiations, it was the symbolic property of the Isolated Earth clan.[32] In the text of the seven songs, the Rattle wi'-gi-e as recited by a priest of the Sky People will be given.

*The o-don' counting sticks (we'-tha-wa).* Thirteen willow branches were used for the counting of the o-don', or war honors. These sticks were divided into a bundle of seven, representing the seven Earth war honors, and a bundle of six, representing the six Sky war honors. During one part of the seven songs, the Wa-don'-be used these branches to count his war honors, dropping a branch every time he recounted one.[33]

*The war standard (wa-xthe'-xthe).* The war standard was a wooden staff about six feet long with a crooked top, the so-called shepherd's staff. It was encased in a deerskin and then wrapped in one long strip of swanskin. Twelve eagle feathers in four bunches of three each were attached along the staff. Finally, a deerskin was tied to the top of the staff. The staff was made jointly by the priests of the Bow and Black Bear clans. The deerskin was furnished by the Deer clan. For the war ceremony, two standards were made, one for the Sky People and another for the Earth People.[34] In the seven songs, only one standard was used, and it appears that this standard was not a sacred object but was only representational.[35]

*The war club (i'-tsin).* The war club was a plain, heavy wooden stick that was slightly curved at the head. This symbolic war club was in the keeping of the Elder Sky clan.[36] It symbolized indestructible life and the desire to maintain tribal existence,[37] as well as the striking of an enemy.[38] Many of the clan bundles had a war club associated with them. If the bundle being transferred did not have its own war club to use in the ritual, then the Sho'-ka would substitute a stick to symbolically represent the club.[39]

*The sacred bow and arrows.* A special bow and two arrows were made by the Bow clan for initiation rituals. The bow was a standard, simple self-bow. The breast of the bow was painted red, which symbolized the recurrent day, while the back was black, symbolizing the night. The two arrows were standard arrows in form, but one was painted red to represent the day, the other black to represent the night.[40] The shooting of the symbolic arrows was a common feature of many of the initiation ceremonies.

*The little pipe.* The Osages had several classifications of ritual pipes. The only type of pipe used in initiation ceremonies was the *non-ni'-on-ba zhin-ga* or "little pipe." These pipes "belonged" to the Elder Water clan.[41] It appears that the pipe used in these ceremonies was the pipe the candidate gave to the Sho'-ka—in other words, the candidate's pipe. This pipe and the tobacco pouch were the emblems of office for the Sho'-ka, showing that he was on a sacred mission. Most of the clan bundles had a pipe that went with them, but it is not known when or under which ritual conditions they were used. For the Osages, "the pipe was a symbol of unity of purposes and . . . a symbolic prayer to Wa-kon-da for compassion and help."[42]

## The Structure of the Ritual

Each ritual was divided into a number of named song groups represented by clusters of notches on the tally sticks. La Flesche recorded no Osage term for song group; the Osages seem to have referred to them as *wa-thon*, which meant "a song" or "songs." Song groups, however, included more than just songs. Along with one to twelve songs, they often included a wi'-gi-e (recitation) and even one or more we'-ga-xe, which were dramatized acts in which a participant used one or more of the ritual objects.

Song groups served dual purposes. One was to transmit knowledge. Each song group was self-contained and dealt with some aspect of sacred or ritual knowledge. A particular song group might define a responsibility of the Sacred Warrior (the leader of a war party) or of the eight commanders (the men who led the attack), or even of the individual warriors. It might concern some ritual act or sacred objects. A song group might address the general relationship between humans and Wa-kon-da. Thus every song group, through the use of songs, wi'-gi-e, and we'-ga-xe, contained substantive knowledge considered valuable and important.

Because every clan served as custodian for only part of the collective knowledge of the tribe, the ideas and information being conveyed in a particular song group were limited to the information in the keeping of that clan. Not infrequently a number of clans had song groups of the same name, such as Wolf or Deer. Each clan, however, had its own version of these songs, and although overlapping ideas and information might be presented, each clan addressed a different aspect of the topic. As a result, a song group of a particular clan presented only a fragment of the collective knowledge pertaining to that topic.

The Osage priests deliberately restricted knowledge. True knowledge of the meaning of a particular song group was limited only to the priests of the clan who owned it. To protect their knowledge, the priests made extensive use of metaphors in their songs and wi'-gi-e to hide their true meanings. In other cases they deliberately corrupted the words to make them unintelligible.[43] La Flesche recounted one such case concerning a song he was recording:

The opening lines of five stanzas were unintelligible . . . and [I] asked what they meant. With a slight frown . . . [the old priest] said "Oh, they mean nothing; they are only o'-ni-on (vocables)." . . . Being unsatisfied and knowing the native custom of hiding the true meaning of the words of sacred songs from an uninitiated person, [I] remarked: "The words to me sound like A ha a-tsin da ha the ka we (Aha! I have come, here to this place)." Thereupon the old man, with a hearty laugh, said: "That's just what they are!"[44]

With most songs and wi'-gi-e there was also a narrative story. Although priests from other clans could probably understand the main ideas contained in most songs and wi'-gi-e, they did not have total comprehension of what was being conveyed. Indeed, few if any priests fully understood the meanings of all of the songs and wi'-gi-e of their own clan, let alone those of other clans.

The more serious priests devoted their lives to studying and discussing the meaning and significance of their songs, wi'-gi-e, and we'-ga-xe. These things were not merely to be memorized and performed; they were intended to be studied. The songs, wi'-gi-e, we'-ga-xe, and ritual objects, with their multiple symbolism, were the depository of the knowledge of the Osages. At the same time, songs, wi'-gi-e, and we'-ga-xe were also prayers to Wa-kon-da.

Songs (wa-thon) were sung sometimes without accompanying musical instruments and sometimes with a rattle. Sometimes they consisted of words, sometimes only of vocables, and sometimes of both words and vocables. It is possible that many of the "vocables" were, as in the instance recounted by La Flesche, really disguised words. In many, if not most, cases a narrative story was associated with a song.

Wi'-gi-e, or recitations, were spoken passages in which were "set forth the relation in which the tribe stood to nature in all its various forms."[45] In terms of understanding Osage cosmology, the wi'-gi-e were far more informative and important than the songs. Wi'-gi-e were frequently quite long; they could include hundreds of lines of text. The longest recorded by La Flesche had 1,542 lines.[46]

A we'-ga-xe was a ritual action involving one or more of the ritual participants and one or more of the ritual items. These acts were dramatizations of particular events that the Osages felt words were inadequate to describe.[47] In the Songs of the Wa-xo'-be, there are a number of we'-ga-xe: the Approach to the House, the Opening of the Hawk Bundle, and the Shooting of the Arrows, to name only a few.

The performance of a we'-ga-xe was accompanied by songs and the recitation of a wi'-gi-e. As La Flesche stated, "all of these acts are given simultaneously and would be confusing and meaningless to a stranger . . . or to a member of the tribe not initiated into the rite."[48]

During the course of this initiation rite and others, ritual acts were performed that do not appear to have been we'-ga-xe but were none-theless integral parts of the ritual. One such ritual act was the Instructions to the Wife of the Initiate. For lack of a better term, I have called them "other events."

The initiation of a priest into the Songs of the Wa-xo'-be was divided into four stages. The first stage, becoming a candidate for the degree, involved a formal ceremony. After a man was prepared to be initiated, the ritual itself was performed in three stages: the preliminary rituals, the seven songs, and the six songs. For the sake of clarity I introduce and then present La Flesche's descriptions of each of the four stages separately. My discussions and occasional comments are enclosed in brackets; all the other material is La Flesche's.

## BECOMING A CANDIDATE[49]

[The decision to become a priest was a major one for a man and his family. Initiation into the clan priesthood was expensive, and it took several years to acquire the food and gifts that were needed. Food had to be collected and stored to feed the hundreds of visitors who would gather for the initiation. Expensive gifts of robes, blankets, and horses had to be accumulated to "pay" all the priests who would take part. Finally, the man had to devote much of his time to securing the necessary ritual items—that is, the skins of the seven sacred animals.[50]

The priests were selective about whom they accepted as candidates,[51] and the acceptance of a candidate for one of the degrees involved a short, formal ceremony. The most important ritual portion of this ceremony was a wi'-gi-e.—Ed.]

A man who makes up his mind to take the Songs of the Wa-xo'-be degree may send his wife or some friend, informally, for a Sho'-ka. A Sho'-ka must be chosen from a clan or subclan whose established office is to act as Sho'-ka (Ceremonial Messenger) for a clan or a group of clans in the ceremonies of the tribal rites. From the moment that the man chosen to act as Sho'-ka responds to the call and appears before the candidate for the degree, the relation between the two becomes formal and ceremonial. The candidate addresses the Sho'-ka, saying: "My nephew," or whatever the kinship term may be that he ordinarily uses in speaking to him, "I have sent for you so that you may call for me my elder brother," giving the name of a member of his own clan. The term "my elder brother" used by the candidate is not the ordinary kinship term but a ceremonial one. Having thus made his formal request, the candidate places in the hand of his Sho'-ka a filled pipe to carry as his badge of office and to show that the message he bears is of a ceremonial character.

The Sho'-ka having delivered his message, and the elder brother having arrived and taken the seat assigned him in the house, the candidate addresses him, saying: "My elder brother, I have called you because I want to ask you to act as Xo'-ka for me." The office of Xo'-ka is teacher or initiator.

The elder brother asks, in reply: "In what rite do you wish me to act as Xo'-ka for you, my younger brother?" The elder brother asks this question because if he had not taken the degree desired by the candidate he could not properly act as Xo'-ka for him.

The candidate replies: "My elder brother, I wish to have you act as my Xo'-ka in the Songs of the Wa-xo'-be."

Then the elder brother, without any doubt or hesitancy, replies: "It is well, my younger brother. I have myself sung the songs (taken the degree) of that rite and can, therefore, act as Xo'-ka for you."

The two men having thus come to a definite understanding, the elder brother proceeds at once to enter upon his duties as Xo'-ka. He commands the Sho'-ka to summon the heads of two of the principal war clans to appear at the house of the candidate, namely: the Elder Sky clan of the Sky division, and the Elder Water clan of the Earth division.[52] The Xo'-ka also commands the messenger to call an A'-ki-ho' Xo'-ka, an Assisting Xo'-ka. This assistant is chosen by the Xo'-ka himself from the clan of which both he and his candidate are members, knowing him to be a man well versed in this rite and competent to conduct the ceremony in all the details. The call of the heads of the two clans, the Elder Sky and the Elder Water, to witness the preliminary ceremony serves as notice to all the clan priests that a member of one of the clans of the Sky division has offered himself as a candidate for initiation into the mysteries of the Songs of the Wa-xo'-be degree of the war rites.

The two men who represent the Elder Sky and the Elder Water clans promptly arrive and are assigned seats appropriate to their dignity. Almost at the same time the Assisting Xo'-ka enters and is motioned to his place. After the ordinary greetings are exchanged between the men, the Xo'-ka, in a formal address, announces to the two representatives of the principal war clans the application of the candidate for initiation into the mysteries of the Songs of the Wa-xo'-be rite and at the same time expresses his willingness to act as his Xo'-ka during the ceremony. The two representatives give their approval and consent with expressions of pleasure at the coming initiation.

The Xo'-ka then asks the Assisting Xo'-ka to recite for the benefit of the candidate the Wa'-xpe-gthe A-don-be Wi'-gi-e, which may be freely translated as the Wi'-gi-e of the Guardians of the Suspended Penalties. The meaning of this wi'-gi-e may be explained as follows: when the candidate has chosen his Xo'-ka and through him summoned to his house the representatives of two of the principal war clans in order to obtain their consent to his initiation into the Songs of the Wa-xo'-be, the candidate had by these acts taken upon himself the vow that he will without fail be initiated into the rite and will perform all the acts necessary to be done in the initiatory ceremonies. The moment the two representatives give their consent to the conferring of the Songs of the Wa-xo'-be degree, the penalties attached to the vow become effective and hang suspended over the head of the candidate, to drop upon him as soon as he violates any of the obligations put upon him as a candidate. For instance: he may lay aside some articles of value with the thought, I will use these for fees in my initiation, or he may gather stores of food for entertaining the priests when they assemble to witness or to take an active part in his initiation. Should the candidate, in the stress of adverse circumstances, use for his personal comfort or that of his family any of these provisions, although his acts may be known only to himself, the penalties will fall upon him.

The Penalty Wi'-gi-e[53]

1 Verily, at that time and place, it has been said, in this house,
2 In the midst of the Winds that precede the approaching storm,
3 Move the Wa'-ca-ki-the[54] of the little ones.
4 My grandfather[55] (referring to a great butterfly, one of the Wa'-ca-ki-the)
5 Is, verily, a being from whom nothing is hidden,
6 He is the Great Butterfly (Dsin-tha' ton-ga),
7 Who moves amidst the winds that precede the storm,
8 My grandfather, it is said,
9 Ever moves amidst those advancing winds,
10 From him nothing can be hidden, as he moves onward amidst the winds,
11 Guarding the acts over which hang the penalties.
12 In the very depths of secret places these acts may be performed,
13 Yet he watches over them as he moves in the midst of the winds.
14 The guilty ones travel along life's pathway,
15 My grandfather
16 Overtakes them and makes them to become languid, to seek solitude and to sit in wretchedness,
17 Verily, he makes their skin to become sallow and of sickly hue;
18 He makes them to become restless and to lie here and there in distress.
19 My grandfather

20 Causes them to fail to reach the four divisions of the days (four stages of
   life),
21 My grandfather
22 Even causes them to lose consciousness and never to recover,
23 Verily, at that time and place, it has been said, in this house,
24 He even takes from the guilty their spirit (sanity) when bidden to do so.
25 The Great Butterfly stands as a Wa'-ca-ki-the of the little ones, it has been
   said, in this house.
26 And the Swallow (Ki-gthu'-ni-ka),
27 Amidst the winds that precede the storm,
28 Moves always, it is said,
29 Verily, nothing is hidden from him as he moves in the winds,
30 Guarding the acts over which hang the penalties.
31 My grandfather (the Swallow)
32 Overtakes the guilty persons,
33 And verily makes them to become languid,
34 He makes them to lose flesh which they never regain,
35 Verily, he makes their faces to become sallow and of sickly hue,
36 Makes them to lay their heads here and there in distress,
37 My grandfather
38 Takes from the guilty even their spirit (sanity) when asked to do so,
39 Verily, at that time and place, it has been said, in this house,
40 The swallow stands as a Wa'-ca-ki-the of the little ones.
41 The mottled eagle also (A'-hiu-ta-ta),
42 Moves amidst the winds that precede the storm,
43 Guarding the acts over which hang the penalties,
44 My grandfather (the Eagle)
45 Overtakes the guilty persons,
46 And verily makes them to become languid,
47 Makes their skin to become sallow and of sickly hue,
48 And to lay their heads here and there in restlessness, in distress,
49 My grandfather
50 Takes from the guilty even their spirit when asked to do so,
51 The mottled eagle stands as a Wa'-ca-ki-the of the little ones.
52 And there is a little pipe (Non-ni'-on-ba zhin-ga),
53 That moves amidst the advance winds of the storm,
54 Guarding the acts over which hang the penalties.
55 My grandfather
56 Overtakes the guilty and verily makes their skin to become sallow, and of
   sickly hue,
57 Makes them to become languid,
58 To lie here and there in restlessness, in distress,
59 My grandfather
60 Takes from the guilty even their spirit when asked to do so.

61 Verily, at that time and place, it has been said, in this house,
62 The nighthawk that lies outstretched (Tse-shin'-shin-e),
63 Moves amidst the winds that precede the storm,
64 Verily there is nothing hidden to my grandfather,
65 He overtakes the guilty persons,
66 And verily makes them to become languid,
67 Verily, at that time and place, it has been said, in this house,
68 He makes their skin to become sallow and of sickly hue,
69 To lie here and there in restlessness, in distress,
70 Verily at that time and place, it has been said, in this house,
71 My grandfather
72 Takes from the guilty even their spirit when asked to do so.
73 Amidst the winds that precede the storm,
74 The great dragonfly (Tse'-pi-tha ton-ga),
75 Moves always.
76 To my grandfather nothing is hidden as he moves forth in the winds,
77 Guarding the acts over which hang the penalties,
78 My grandfather overtakes the guilty,
79 And verily makes them to become languid,
80 Makes their skin to become sallow and of sickly hue,
81 He makes them to lie here and there in restlessness, in distress,
82 My grandfather
83 Takes from the guilty even their spirit when asked to do so.
84 What is the Wa'-ca-ki-the of the little ones, they said to one another,
85 My grandfather,
86 The swallow that lies outstretched (Ni-shku'-shku),
87 Amidst the winds that precede the storm,
88 Moves always,
89 Guarding the acts over which hang the penalties.
90 My grandfather
91 Overtakes the guilty persons,
92 And verily makes them to become languid,
93 Verily, he makes their flesh to wither,
94 He makes them to lie here and there in restlessness, in distress,
95 My grandfather
96 Takes from the guilty even their spirit when asked to do so.

The symbols mentioned in this wi'-gi-e belong to seven different clans. They are as follows:

1. The great butterfly belongs to the Isolated Earth clan. The name used in the wi'-gi-e, Dsin-tha' ton-ga, is an archaic name and not that in ordinary use. The common name is Dsi-on'-dsi-on.

2. The swallow belongs to the Bear and the Puma clans. The identity of the bird seems to be in doubt among the priests of today. Ki-gthu'-

ni-ka, the name used in the wi'-gi-e, is archaic and its meaning has become obscure. Charley Wah-hre-she, who recited the wi'-gi-e, believes that the buzzard is referred to in the archaic name, but Wa'-thu-xa-ge of the Gentle Sky clan is certain that the name refers to the swallow. In the free translation, however, the swallow is used.

3. The mottled eagle, the immature golden eagle of the dark plumage, belongs to the Eagle clan. The name, A'-hiu-ta-ta, used in the wi'-gi-e, is archaic but it is still known to what bird the name refers. The name in common use for this bird is Hon-ga gthe-zhe, the mottled eagle, from the mottled marks on its tail feathers.

4. The little pipe, Non-ni'-on-ba zhin-ga, belongs to the Elder Water clan of the Earth People. This pipe was used in the supplicatory ceremonies of the people, and it is probably for this reason that it was included in this wi'-gi-e. It may be safe to presume that this symbolic pipe was used in the rite calling for the punishment, by supernatural means, of persons treating with contempt the sacred rites.

5. The nighthawk belongs to the Elder Sky and the Buffalo [Face] clans. The name, Tse-shin'-shin-e, used in the wi'-gi-e, is archaic; that commonly used is Pshu'-shka.

6. The great dragonfly belongs to the Sun Carrier clan. The ordinary name for the insect, Tse'-pi-tha ton-ga, is used in the wi'-gi-e.

7. The bank-swallow belongs to the Men of Mystery and the Buffalo Bull clans. The common name of the bird, Ni-shku'-shku, is used in the wi'-gi-e.

After the recitation of the wi'-gi-e, the Xo'-ka and his assistant, the Assisting Xo'-ka, fold up their fees preparatory to going to their homes, but before leaving they inform their candidate that he is allowed, by custom, seven years in which to prepare for the initiation. Within this time he must lay aside various articles of value to use as fees to be given to the officers who are to take an active part in the initiatory ceremony. He must also store away food supplies to be used in entertaining the priests whom he will have to invite to the initiation. For ceremonial and symbolic use he must collect the skins of seven animals, namely: (1) the skin of a lynx; (2) the skin of a gray wolf; (3) the skin of a male puma; (4) the skin of a male black bear; (5) the skin of a male buffalo; (6) the skin of an elk; (7) the skin of a deer. Having given these instructions to their candidate as to his duties, the Xo'-ka and the Assisting Xo'-ka depart for their respective homes.

In the early days, when the arrow with its bow was the only weapon possessed by the Osage that was effective at a distance, it was difficult for a candidate, even with the generous assistance of his friends and relatives, to procure so great a supply of goods, provisions, and animal skins as were required for use in the initiation. Taking this difficulty into account, the priests allowed a candidate seven years in which to prepare himself to take the degree. In later days, when the Osage came into contact with the traders who supplied the people with flintlock muskets, powder, and balls, as well as other commodities, the task of the candidate was not as great, and with the help of his friends he could prepare himself for the initiation in a shorter time.

[After a man was accepted as a candidate for a priestly degree, he worked diligently to accumulate all the ritual items, gifts, and food necessary for his initiation. There was no ritual training for a candidate, however. Not until after he was actually initiated would he have the right to learn the ritual knowledge, the songs, wi'-gi-e, and we'-ga-xe associated with his degree. The initiation ceremony bestowed on the new priest only the authority and rights associated with the degree; it was not a test of his ritual knowledge. Indeed, many priests never learned the words of the wi'-gi-e or the songs of the degree they held. Only a few priests had in-depth knowledge of the rituals. Thus the selection of the Assisting Xo'-ka was extremely important: he had to be among the minority of priests who had commited these wi'-gi-e and songs to memory.—Ed.]

## THE PRELIMINARY CEREMONIES[56]

After a lapse of time, when the candidate has fully prepared himself for the degree, he calls his Sho'-ka, whom he sends to the Xo'-ka and his assistant to give them notice that he is ready to proceed with the initiatory ceremony. The two men go to the candidate's house to examine the amount of food supplies he has provided as well as the quality and the number of goods he has collected to be used as fees. When the Xo'-ka and his assistant have satisfied themselves that there is an adequate amount of provisions to be distributed to the priests during the ceremony, and that there is a sufficient amount of goods to be given to the heads of the clans who will take part, they set a day for the initiatory ceremony. The Sho'-ka is then sent to give formal notice to the priests to attend the initiation. This notice is called the U'-thu-ce U-tha-ge, Notice to Come and Participate. On every ceremonial occasion, the Sho'-ka thus sent goes from house to house to deliver his message, carrying in his hand a little pipe as the credential of his office. Only those of the priests who have taken this or the Ni'-ki-e degree of the tribal rites respond to the call.[57] This formal notice is equivalent to a command that cannot be ignored when given to members of a clan having a passive or an active part in the ceremony. A good representation of such clans is always desired because of the symbolic character of the group.

At the appointed time for the initiation the priests gather at the village of the candidate, where some of them camp and others are entertained at the homes of relatives or friends. Before the ceremonies begin, which occupy from three to four days, as well as at the intermissions, there is much feasting and visiting between the inhabitants of the candidate's village and the families who have come from a distance to attend the ceremonies.

[After all the participants had arrived, the preliminary ceremonies began. In them, all the ritual elements needed for the ceremony were brought together. The ritual itself required the recreation of the House of Mystery, the symbolic universe. Thus part of the preliminaries were concerned with bringing together the clan priests needed to create this symbolic universe. Symbolic items used in the ritual had to be consecrated for use. Finally, the main symbolic figure, the Xo'-ka, who would represent the sun and the symbolic man, had to be prepared for his role. The subject matter of the preliminary ceremonies was, therefore, the cosmos and its various elements.

The preliminary ceremonies consisted of six segments or parts spread over a three-day period: (1) the consecrating of the sacred animal skins, a ceremony called the *non'-ni' a-tha-sho-dse*, or "the Smoking"; (2) the making of the symbolic moccasins, called the *hon-be'-cu*, or "Moccasin Cutting"; (3) the selection of the man to act as the Wa-don'-be; (4) the rehearsal of the songs, known as the *hon wa-thon*, or "Night Singing"; (5) the painting and preparing of the Xo'-ka, a ceremony called *ki'-non*, or "Painting"; and (6) the formal procession to the House of the Mystery, called the *tsi ta'-pe wa-thon*, or "Song of Approach to the House."—Ed.]

The ceremony of sending the Sho'-ka to summon the priests whose duty it is to take part in the Non'-ni' A-tha-sho-dse ceremony, the blowing of smoke on the skins of the animals that symbolize courage and strength, occurs in the evening [preceding the first day]. To the ceremony are summoned only the priests belonging to the clans having the title Wa-non, Elders, all of which are war clans, and are the Elder Water belonging to the Earth People, the Elder Sky and the Mi-k'in' Wa-non [Sun Carrier] of the Sky People.[58]

*Day One*

*The Smoking (Non'-ni' A-tha-sho-dse):*[59] About sunrise the next morning the members summoned prepare themselves to go to the house of the candidate, the place of meeting, by putting upon themselves the signs of the earth and sky. For the sign of the earth they blacken the upper portion of the face with moistened black soil, and for the sign of the sky they spread the white down of the eagle upon the crown of the head. At the outer corner of one eye a figure is drawn resembling an ovate leaf, from the pointed end of which a short line is drawn running slantwise toward the ear [photo 5.1]. No satisfactory explanation could be obtained as to the signification of this figure, but it is said to belong to the Men of Mystery. From the inner corner of the eye a line is drawn toward the corner of the mouth. The meaning of this line is explained as representing the tears shed during the rite of vigil. These figures are made by removing from the skin, with the nail of the index finger, the moistened black soil. The men belonging to the Earth People put these figures on the right side of the face and those belonging to the Sky People on the left side. The men of both divisions paint upon the middle of the forehead a round red spot to represent the sun which travels over the earth and across the sky. Each member wears his buffalo robe with the hair outside, and that, with the symbolic painting and decoration, completes his sacerdotal attire.

When the priests have finished painting and dressing, they form a procession and solemnly march to the house of the candidate.[60]

While the house in which the ceremony is to take place may not have been built with reference to the cardinal points, it was, for ceremonial purposes, treated as though it had been [so] oriented. The end of the long house at the left of its entrance is regarded as the east and the opposite end as the west. The initiating clan enter the house first, the members taking their places at the east end of the lodge. The candidate, his Xo'-ka, the Assisting Xo'-ka, and the chosen singers occupy the middle space, and all sit facing the west. Then follow the other priests, those of the Earth People taking their prescribed places at the south side of the lodge, and those of the Sky People, the north side. Thus the house, together with the priests, seated in groups according to divisions, becomes symbolic of the visible universe, for the ceremony to be performed is largely a dramatization of the movements of the great life-giving power, the Sun, through the heavens and over the earth. The initiating clan personate the sun, the Sky People, the sky, with its celestial bodies, and the Earth People, the earth, with its water and all terrestrial life.

PHOTO 5.1. The face painting of the priests (reproduced from La Flesche 1925: Plate 12).

When the priests have taken their places in the order described above, and ordinary conversation among the members has ceased, the candidate rises in response to a signal given by the Assisting Xo'-ha, who now conducts the ceremonies, and receives from him a little pipe. This marks the beginning of the initiatory ceremonies.

The first act is in three parts, which are performed simultaneously. This act is called "Wa'-in Xa-ge," which, freely translated, means "Carrying (a pipe) and Wailing." The candidate carries in his right hand the pipe he received from the Assisting Xo'-ka, his left hand is outspread, and in this attitude he passes along the lines of priests sitting on either side of the lodge, places his hands upon the heads of two men at a time, and wails. The pipe carried by the candidate is a symbol of supplication to Wa-kon-da, and the wailing is an appeal to the priests to recite the sacred wi'-gi-e in full and not to hold any of it back. The second part is the reciting of the sacred wi'-gi-e by the priests. As the candidate passes along, carrying the emblem of supplication, and as he touches each couple, the priests who have memorized the wi'-gi-e at once begin its recitation, simultaneously but not in concert. This recital is an expression of the wish that the candidate shall succeed in all his enterprises as a warrior, and in all his other acts that pertain to the maintenance of life. The third part is performed by the women, who wail in sympathy with the candidate as an appeal to the priests that they will perform their part without reserve or prejudice. Widows of deceased members of the degree take their husbands' places at the ceremony and are honorary members.

When the candidate begins this act, "Carrying (the pipe) and Wailing," he observes the courtesy due from an initiating division (in this instance the Sky) to the opposite division. The candidate therefore approaches the two men sitting at the east end of the line of priests of the Earth People and places his hands upon their heads. The moment the candidate touches the heads of these two men, he and the women begin to wail and all the priests begin to recite the Smoking Wi'-gi-e. The candidate passes from couple to couple until he has reached the west end of the lodge. He then crosses over to the Sky side and continues wailing and touching the heads of the priests until he comes to the east end of the lodge. If the reciting of the wi'-gi-e goes on when he reaches the east, he stands waiting until the recitation ceases, when he and the women stop wailing.

There are two Smoking Wi'-gi-es; the first is called Wa-k'on'-ci Thu-ce Pe-thon-ba tse, "the Taking of Seven Animals." The second, Wa-k'on'-ci Thu-ce Sha'-pe tse, is "the Taking of Six Animals."

The Taking of Seven Animals Wi'-gi-e[61]

1 What shall the little ones make to be a symbol of courage as they travel the path of life? they said to one another.

2 The lynx that lies outstretched, they said,

3 Our grandfather, whose courage is great, we shall make to be a symbol of courage.

4 It was he who, at the beginning of the day,

5 Rushed forth in attack,

6 Upon the young male deer with curved horns,

7 And threw him to the earth where he lay in death.

8 My grandfather returned to the deer,

9 After he had made the attack.

10 Verily, at that time and place, it has been said, in this house.

11 He uttered a loud cry of triumph,

12 Then spake, saying: When the little ones go toward the setting sun,

13 To strike and overthrow their foes,

14 They shall always fall upon them in this very manner,

15 And their hands shall always be upon the fallen foe, as they travel the path of life,

16 And as the lynx stood there he made the first cut,[62] it has been said, in this house.

17 What shall the little ones make to be a symbol of courage? they said to one another,

18 The dark gray wolf that lies outstretched, they said;

19 Our grandfather, whose courage is great, we shall make to be a symbol of courage.

20 It was he who, at the beginning of the day,

21 Rushed forth in attack,

22 Upon the young male deer with gray horns,

23 Verily, it was within the bend of a river,

24 Our grandfather overtook the deer and made it to lie upon the earth in death,

25 Our grandfather uttered a loud cry of triumph,

26 Then spake saying: When the little ones go forth to strike their foes

27 They shall always strike them in this manner, as they travel the path of life,

28 When they make my hands to be their hands,

29 Then shall their hands always be upon the foe, as they travel the path of life.

30 And as the gray wolf stood there he made the second cut, it has been said, in this house.

31 What shall the little ones make to be a symbol of courage? they said to one another,

32 The male puma that lies outstretched, they said,

33 Our grandfather, who is of great courage,

34 We shall make to be a symbol of courage.

35 It was at the beginning of the day,
36 That our grandfather rushed forth in attack,
37 Upon the full-grown male deer with dark horns,
38 Verily it was within the bend of a river,
39 That our grandfather struck the deer to the earth and made it to lie in death,
40 Then our grandfather uttered a loud cry of triumph,
41 And spake, saying: When the little ones go forth to strike their foes,
42 They shall always strike them in this manner, as they travel the path of life,
43 Their hands shall always be upon the foe, as they travel the path of life.
44 And as the puma stood there he made the third cut, it has been said, in this house.
45 What shall the little ones make to be a symbol of courage? they said to one another,
46 The male black bear that lies outstretched, they said,
47 Our grandfather we shall make to be a symbol of courage.
48 It was at the beginning of the day,
49 That our grandfather rushed forth in attack,
50 Upon a hummock,
51 Which he tore apart with his hands,
52 Exposing the little bugs that dwelt therein.
53 He attacked them and crunched them between his teeth,
54 And out of the corner of his mouth, on the right side,
55 Blood began to trickle down.
56 Then, at that very time and place, it has been said, in this house,
57 He uttered a loud cry of triumph,
58 And spake, saying: When the little ones go forth to strike their foes,
59 They shall always strike them in this manner, as they travel the path of life
60 Their hands shall always be upon the foe, as they travel the path of life.
61 And as the male black bear stood there he made the fourth cut, it has been said, in this house.
62 What shall the little ones make to be a symbol of courage, as they travel the path of life? they said to one another.
63 The great animal (buffalo bull) who stands firmly upon the earth,
64 Our grandfather who is of great courage, we shall make to be a symbol of courage.
65 It was at the beginning of the day,
66 That our grandfather rushed forth in attack,
67 Upon a high bank,
68 And in his anger tore it down with his horns,
69 Then he uttered a loud cry of triumph,
70 And spake, saying: When the little ones go forth to strike their foes,
71 They shall always strike them in this manner, as they travel the path of life,
72 Their hands shall always be upon the foe, as they travel the path of life.

73 What shall the little ones make to be a symbol of courage? they said to one another.
74 The tall animal (the elk) who stands firmly upon the earth,
75 Our grandfather, we shall make to be a symbol of courage.
76 Verily, in the midst of an open prairie,
77 There stood a plant whose blossoms always look up to the sun (silphium laciniatum),
78 The stalks of this plant he angrily attacked with his horns and reduced them to a twisted knot,
79 Then he uttered a loud cry of triumph,
80 And spake, saying: When the little ones go forth to strike their foes.
81 They shall always strike them in this manner, as they travel the path of life,
82 Their hands shall always be upon the foe, as they travel the path of life.
83 What shall the little ones make to be a symbol of courage? they said to one another.
84 The little animal (the deer) that lies outstretched, they said,
85 Although not possessed with the gall that excites anger,[63]
86 We shall make to be a symbol of courage.
87 Four villages lay side by side,
88 Along the outskirts of these villages the deer ran swiftly and escaped his pursuers,
89 Although the deer runs along the edges of the village in his flight,
90 The arrows of his pursuers flying about him in forked lines,
91 He escapes all dangers.
92 When the little ones make of the deer a symbol of courage,
93 They shall enable themselves to escape all dangers, as they travel the path of life,
94 Thus it shall be with the little ones,
95 Their hands shall always be upon their foes, as they travel the path of life.

At the close of the recitation of the wi'-gi-e by the priest, and when the wailing has ceased, the candidate returns to his seat by the side of his Xo'-ka. The Assisting Xo'-ka then gives to the Sho'-ka the skin of the little lynx, the animal first mentioned in the wi'-gi-e, and also a little pipe which he has filled with tobacco. As the Sho'-ka takes the pipe, he wraps around the stem the head of the lynx skin, letting the body hang down loosely, and having thus arranged the two sacred articles he carries them to the man sitting at the east end of the line of priests of the Earth People. He spreads the lynx skin upon the ground before the man and then presents to him the little pipe and touches the tobacco within the bowl with a small firebrand. The priest draws at the stem of the pipe, and when the smoke passes freely he blows four whiffs upon the skin of the animal chosen to be a symbol of courage. In this way the Sho'-ka passes the pipe and the lynx skin from man to man until all the priests of the Earth People have blown tobacco smoke upon the sacred emblem. When the Sho'-ka reaches the west end of the lodge and all the members of the Earth People have blown smoke upon the bobcat skin, he crosses over to the Sky People and moves eastward, presenting each member of that division with the pipe and lynx skin until he reaches the east end of the lodge. All the priests of both divisions having performed the ceremony of smoking upon the little lynx, the other animal skins, the symbols of courage, are smoked in the same manner and in the order in which they are mentioned in the wi'-gi-e.

This ceremony belongs to the Earth division. It was performed when a war party composed of men belonging to both the Earth and the Sky peoples was preparing to go against the enemy. Such a war party was called Do-don'-hin-ton-ga, War Party in Great Numbers. The animals mentioned in the wi'-gi-e were those ceremonially appealed to by the warriors.

The meaning of the title of the second Smoking ceremony [which follows] is not strictly literal. In the title of the first Smoking ceremony [the one just described], all of the seven symbols are in reality "Wa-k'on'-ci," or animals. In the title of the second Smoking ceremony, two of the symbols are not animals, as the term "Wa-k'on-ci" would imply, one of them being "the little pipe" through which the supplications of the people are vicariously offered to Wa-kon-da and the other the buffalo hair out of which cords were made for binding the captives to be taken by a war party.

The Taking of the Six Animals[64]

1 Verily, at that time and place, it has been said, in this house,
2 They spake to one another, saying: What shall they make to be a symbol of courage, as they travel the path of life?
3 It was a little pipe,
4 They made to be a symbol of courage.
5 They made the little pipe to be a symbol of courage,
6 So that when they go toward the setting sun against their enemies,
7 They may overcome the foe with ease and make them to lie low in death, as they travel the path of life.
8 Verily, at that time and place, it has been said in this house,
9 They made this symbol of courage to stand forever, it has been said, in this house.
10 The shell of the mussel, they said to one another,
11 We shall make to be a symbol of courage.

12 When we make the shell of the mussel to be a symbol of courage,
13 And go toward the setting sun against our enemies,
14 We shall always go forth with courage, as we travel the path of life.
15 Verily, at that time and place, it has been said, in this house,
16 They made this symbol of courage to stand forever, it has been said, in this house.
17 This buffalo hair, they said to one another,
18 We shall make to be a symbol of courage.
19 When we make the buffalo hair to be a symbol of courage,
20 And go toward the setting sun against our enemies,
21 We shall always go forth with courage, as we travel the path of life.
22 Verily, at that time and place, it has been said, in this house,
23 They made this symbol of courage to stand forever, it has been said, in this house.
24 Verily, at that time and place, it has been said, in this house,
25 They said to one another: The bird that is without stain (golden eagle)
26 We shall make to be a symbol of courage.
27 Verily, at that time and place, it has been said, in this house,
28 The bird, at the beginning of day,
29 Suddenly rushed forth in attack.
30 Verily, in the midst of a lowland forest,
31 Upon the great turkey that sat therein,
32 Verily, at that time and place, it has been said, in this house,
33 He struck the turkey to the earth where it lay in death, as its feathers floated away in the wind.
34 Verily, at that time and place, it has been said, in this house,
35 Off in the distance the eagle was heard to say,
36 When they (the little ones) go in small bodies to strike the foe,
37 They shall strike them in this manner, as they travel the path of life.
38 Behold my hands,
39 When the little ones make these hands to be their hands,
40 And go toward the setting sun against their foes,
41 Their hands shall always be upon the foe, as they travel the path of life.
42 Verily, at that time and place, it has been said, in this house,
43 They made the eagle as a symbol of courage to stand forever, it has been said, in this house.
44 The great horned owl, it has been said, in this house,
45 At the beginning of the day,
46 Suddenly rushed forth in attack.
47 Verily, in the midst of a lowland forest,
48 Upon the male raccoon that sat therein,
49 Verily, at that time and place, it has been said, in this house,
50 And threw him to the earth, where he lay doubled up in death.
51 Quickly he (the owl) uttered a loud cry of triumph,

52 Then spake, saying: When they (the little ones) go forth in small bodies to strike the foe,

53 Verily, in this manner they shall always strike them.

54 Behold my hands,

55 When they make these hands to be their hands, as they travel the path of life,

56 And go toward the setting sun against their enemies,

57 Their hands shall always be upon the foe, as they travel the path of life.

58 Verily, at that time and place, it has been said, in this house,

59 They made (the horned owl) this symbol of courage to stand forever, it has been said, in this house.

60 The great gray owl, they said to one another,

61 We shall also make to be a symbol of courage.

62 The great gray owl they made to be a symbol of courage.

63 Verily, at that time and place, it has been said, in this house,

64 At the beginning of the day,

65 The gray owl suddenly rushed forth in attack,

66 Verily, among the groves that were strung along a little stream,

67 Upon the young male raccoon,

68 And threw him to the earth where he lay doubled up in death.

69 Then, far away in the distance, he was heard to say:

70 When the little ones go forth in small bodies to strike the foe,

71 Verily, in this manner they shall always strike them, as they travel the path of life.

72 Verily, at that time and place, it has been said, in this house,

73 He was heard to say: Behold my hands,

74 When they make these hands to be their hands,

75 And go toward the setting sun against their enemies,

76 Their hands shall always be upon the foe, as they travel the path of life.

77 Verily, at that time and place, it has been said, in this house,

78 They made (the gray owl) this symbol to stand forever, it has been said, in this house.

In the second Smoking ceremony the wailing of the candidate and the women is omitted and only the wi'-gi-e is recited by the priests. The symbolic articles, however, are passed around by the Sho'-ka and smoke is blown upon them by the priests in the same manner as in the first Smoking ceremony. The second Smoking ceremony was performed when a small war party composed of warriors of a few of the clans of each division were about to go against the enemy. A war party of this class was called Tsi'-ga-xa Do-don, the meaning of which term has become obscure. At the close of these two ceremonies food was distributed among the priests from the stores of the candidate. In the early days the food consisted of jerked buffalo and deer meat, and corn; in modern times the food is beef, flour, coffee, sugar, etc. After this distribution of provisions the priests adjourn until the next day.

## Day Two

*The Moccasin Cutting:*[65] At sunrise on the following day, the priests again assemble at the house of the candidate for the ceremony next in order, called Hon-be'-cu, the literal translation of which is, Hon-be, moccasins; cu, to cut. This title means to the Osage the cutting of the material from which to make the symbolic moccasins to be worn by the Xo'-ka and the Sho'-ka during the entire ceremony as a part of their sacerdotal attire.

When the priests had entered the house and taken their places in the clan order, the Assisting Xo'-ka directs the Sho'ka to take to the head man of the Buffalo Face clan a piece of buffalo skin and to spread it before him. The Sho'-ka performs this duty and also presents to the head man of the clan a blanket as a fee for the reciting of the Moccasin Wi'-gi-e. Having performed this act, the Sho'ka takes up a knife and holds it in readiness to perform his part of the ceremony. The head man then begins to recite the wi'-gi-e relating to the cutting of the material for the symbolic moccasins. When he comes to the fourth line of the fourth section the Sho'-ka cuts, in pantomime, the skin, beginning at the center and ending at the edge on the right side. In like manner he cuts the skin from the center to the edge nearest to himself. This ceremonial act has a triple meaning: (1) The act of cutting implies a wish that when the Osage warriors go against the enemy they shall always succeed in destroying the warrior of the enemy who is honored for his military prowess. (2) The cut toward the right indicates the east. (3) The cut toward the Sho'-ka indicates the south.

Without pause the recitation continues, and when the fourth line of the eighth section is reached the Sho'-ka cuts again, in pantomime, beginning at the center of the skin and ending at the edge at his left; then beginning again at the center he cuts to the edge farthest from himself. This act also has a triple meaning: (1) There is implied in the act of cutting that the Osage warriors who go against the enemy shall always succeed in slaying the woman of the enemy who has given birth to her first child. (2) The cut running from the center to the left indicates the west. (3) The cut running from the center to the edge farthest away from the Sho'-ka indicates the north.

When these ceremonial acts have been performed the Sho'-ka lays aside the knife and takes up an awl, which he holds in readiness for the acts that are to follow.

The recitation continues, and when the fourth line of the ninth section is reached the Sho'-ka gives an imaginary thrust with the awl into one corner of the skin. This thrust implies a determination to destroy the adolescent youth of the enemy.

The recitation goes on without pause, and when the fourth line of the tenth section is reached the Sho'-ka gives a thrust to the second corner of the skin. This second thrust is for the destruction of the adolescent maiden of the enemy.

The recitation moves on, and at the fourth line of the eleventh section the Sho'-ka gives a thrust to the third corner of the skin. This thrust is for the destruction of the warrior of the enemy distinguished for his military honors.

When the fourth line of the twelfth section is reached the Sho'-ka gives a thrust to the fourth corner of the skin. This thrust is for the destruction of the woman of the enemy who has given birth to her first child.

Moccasin Wi'-gi-e[66]

1 Verily, at that time and place, they said, it has been said, in this house,
2 The turtle that has a tail with seven serratures,
3 We shall make to be the symbol of our foot, O younger brothers.
4 When we make this turtle to be the symbol of our foot,
5 And go forth against our enemies who dwell toward the setting sun,
6 We shall enable ourselves to tread down the harmful grasses, as we travel the path of life.
7 What shall we make to be a symbol of our moccasin string? they said, it has been said, in this house.
8 The garter snake that lies outstretched
9 Shall be a symbol of our moccasin string, as we travel the path of life.
10 When we make this snake to be our moccasin string,
11 The harmful grasses that lie in our course, as we travel the path of life,
12 Shall not cut or break our moccasin string, O younger brothers, they said to one another.
13 What shall we make to be a symbol of our knife? they said, it has been said, in this house.
14 There is the young buffalo bull,
15 It is his right horn,
16 That shall be a symbol of our knife.
17 When we make the right horn of the young bull to be a symbol of our knife,
18 And go against our enemies who dwell toward the setting sun,
19 Our knife shall always be sharp and ready for use, as we travel the path of life, O younger brothers, it has been said, in this house.

20 Upon what shall we cut this skin? they said, it has been said, in this house.
21 Toward the setting of the sun,
22 There is a man of our enemies who is honored for his valor.
23 It is upon him that we shall cut this skin.
24 When we do our cutting upon that valorous man,
25 It shall be easy for us to do our cutting, as we travel the path of life, O younger brothers, they said to one another.
26 Verily, at that time and place, they said, it has been said, in this house,
27 The turtle that has a tail with six serratures,
28 We shall make to be a symbol of our foot, O younger brothers.
29 When we make that turtle to be our foot,
30 And go forth against our enemies who dwell toward the setting sun,
31 We shall enable ourselves to tread down the harmful grasses, as we travel the path of life.
32 What shall we make to be a symbol of our moccasin string? they said, it has been said, in this house.
33 The garter snake that lies outstretched,
34 Shall be a symbol of our moccasin string, as we travel the path of life.
35 When we make this snake to be our moccasin string,
36 The harmful grasses that lie in our course
37 Shall not cut or break our moccasin string, as we travel the path of life, O younger brothers, they said to one another.
38 What shall we make to be a symbol of our knife? they said, it has been said, in this house.
39 There is the young buffalo bull,
40 It is his right horn
41 That shall be a symbol of our knife.
42 When we make the right horn of the young bull to be a symbol of our knife,
43 And go against our enemies who dwell toward the setting sun,
44 Our knife shall always be sharp and ready for use, as we travel the path of life, O younger brothers, it has been said, in this house.
45 Verily, at that time and place, they said, it has been said, in this house,
46 Upon what shall we cut this skin? they said, it has been said, in this house.
47 Toward the setting of the sun
48 There is a woman of our enemies who has given birth to her first child.
49 It is upon her that we shall cut this skin.
50 When we do our cutting upon that woman,
51 It shall be easy for us to do our cutting, as we travel the path of life, O younger brothers, they said to one another.
52 Upon what shall we perforate this skin? they said, it has been said, in this house.
53 Toward the setting of the sun
54 There is an adolescent youth of our enemies.
55 It is upon that youth we shall perforate this skin.

56 When we perforate this skin upon that youth,
57 It shall be easy for us to do our perforating, as we travel the path of life, O
younger brothers, they said to one another.
58 Upon what shall we perforate this skin? they said, it has been said, in this
house.
59 It is the adolescent maiden
60 Upon whom we shall perforate this skin.
61 When we perforate this skin upon that maiden,
62 It shall be easy for us to do our perforating, as we travel the path of life, O
younger brothers, they said to one another.
63 Verily, at that time and place, they said, it has been said, in this house,
64 Upon what shall we perforate this skin? they said, it has been said, in this
house.
65 It is the man of our enemies who is honored for his valor
66 Upon whom we shall perforate this skin.
67 When we perforate this skin upon the valorous man,
68 It shall be easy for us to do our perforating, as we travel the path of life, O
younger brothers, they said to one another.
69 Upon what shall we perforate this skin? they said, it has been said, in this
house.
70 It is the woman of our enemies who has given birth to her first child
71 Upon whom we shall perforate this skin.
72 When we perforate this skin upon that woman,
73 It shall be easy for us to do our perforating, as we travel the path of life, O
younger brothers, they said to one another.

After the recital of the wi'-gi-e, the Sho'-ka, without any further ceremony, fashions the moccasins [fig. 5.1] and roughly sews together the edges of the skin. Three pairs of moccasins are made, two pairs for the Xo'-ka and one pair for the Sho'-ka. One of the pairs is to be worn by the Xo'-ka when he ceremonially approaches the place where the ceremony is to be given. This pair of moccasins symbolizes the journey of the dawn that precedes the approaching sun. The journey of the dawn comes to an end at the west entrance to the House of Mystery, where the dawn moccasins are slipped off. Here the Sho'-ka helps the Xo'-ka to put on the second pair of ceremonial moccasins. These represent the journey of the sun from the east across the sky to the west, giving life to the earth as it travels.[67] This pair he wears throughout the rest of the ceremony.

The dual form of the tribal organization, one part representing the sky and the other the earth, is not only expressive of the duality of nature as observed by the ancient priests, but it is also expressive of their faith that the Life-giving Power which abides within these two

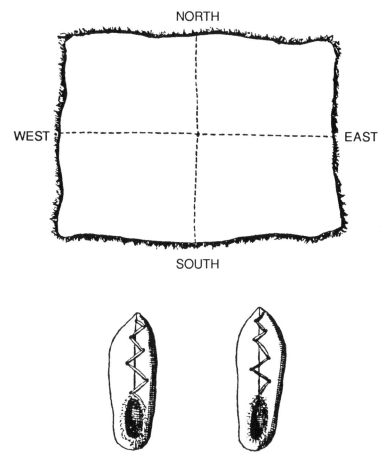

FIG. 5.1. Cutting of the symbolic moccasins (adapted from La Flesche 1925:62).

great cosmic bodies and gives form and life to all things therein will also give to the peoples of the two symbolic divisions the natural increase necessary for the continuity of the tribal life. While the priests continued to give much thought to the mysteries of life and to the dependence of the people upon Wa-kon-da for their existence, they also dwelt upon the efforts that must be made by the people themselves in order to fully attain the desired end, that is, the continuity of the tribal life. The belief became firmly fixed in the minds of the people that Wa-kon-da would give the desired natural increase, and also that the defense of the life thus granted must be made by the people themselves. In order to meet and successfully overcome the enemies that beset life's pathway there must be a complete unity of purpose and of action between the men of the two great tribal divisions, and all the people must share alike in the fortunes and misfortunes of the common defense.

Having thus determined upon a principle by which the people must govern themselves in order to guard and protect their tribal life by the strong arm of valor, the priests, to give vital force to that principle, added a symbolic figure to the complex life symbol for which the two tribal divisions stand. The symbol was the figure of a man perfect in all his physical structure, well prepared to take life's long journey, and confident in his ability to combat the perils that might arise to impede his progress.

It is this figure or principle that the Xo'-ka is to impersonate in the initiatory rite which is dramatic in form. Symbolically the two pairs of moccasins ceremonially prepared for him as a part of his sacerdotal attire represent the long and hazardous journey contemplated; the nights and days that mark the division of time; the strength, the courage, and the ability of the people as an organized body to crush the "harmful grasses" (figuratively, enemies), as they step forth upon life's perilous journey.

When the symbolic moccasins have been finished, another distribution of provision is made to the priests from the stores of the candidate.

*Choosing the Wa-don'-be:* At the close of the ceremonies relating to the making of the symbolic moccasins for the Xo'-ka and the Sho'-ka, the priests await with interest the choice to be made by the candidate of a man to act as Wa-don'-be. The literal translation of the title of this office is Wa, over; don'-be, to see or to guard. When used in connection with the tribal war rites, the word is understood to mean a protector of the tribal life.

If the candidate happens to be a young man who is not familiar with the details of the ceremony, he may be prompted by the Xo'-ka or by the Assisting Xo'-ka as to the proper man to nominate for the office of Wa-don'-be. The man to be nominated must be one who has won certain prescribed military honors [o-don']. He must have won thirteen military honors, seven to be counted for the Earth division and six for the Sky.

O-don' is the name of all classes of the prescribed war honors which can be counted by a warrior chosen for the office of Wa-don'-be at the initiatory ceremonies of the tribal war rites. The name may be freely translated as: a valorous act by which a warrior can win rank and become honored by the people.

If the candidate belongs to the Earth division he must nominate for the office of Wa-don'-be a warrior of the Sky division, but if of the Sky division he must name for the office a warrior of the Earth division.

When the candidate has chosen his Wa'-don-be, the priests adjourn to meet again at sundown for the Hon Wa-thon, or Night Singing.

At sunset, the priests who are members of the clan to which the candidate belongs gather, informally, at his house, where the Assisting Xo'-ka, assisted by the Xo'-ka, and together with certain chosen singers, rehearse the songs of the ceremony which actually begins on the following morning. The priests occupy the back part of the eastern end of the house while, in a row in front of them, sit the Assisting Xo'-ka, the Xo'-ka, the candidate, and the chosen singers. Members of other clans also attend, but more as a matter of courtesy to the initiating clan and for social pleasure than to form a formal assemblage. The Assisting Xo'-ka has at his side a bundle of consecrated tally sticks for keeping a correct count of the songs as he sings them. The Assisting Xo'-ka and his three assistant singers each has at his side a gourd rattle to be ceremonially taken up and used to accentuate the rhythm of the music of the Rattle-songs and those to be sung throughout the rest of the ceremony. This rehearsal lasts until about two or three o'clock in the morning. The members of the candidate's clan are obliged to sit through the entire rehearsal, but the members of the other clans are allowed to go to their homes when they become tired.

Up to this stage of the ceremony the candidate has no definite title, but when he takes his seat at the eastern end of the lodge together with his Xo'-ka, Assisting Xo'-ka, and the members of his clan for the Night-singing, he thenceforth is spoken of as Wa-thon A-ka, the Singer. He may not know any of the songs to be sung, may not even know how to sing, but he thus becomes the Singer, and bears that title throughout the ceremony. At the close of the ceremony, when the Wa-xo'-be of his clan is given over to him, he will then have the right to say: "I sang the songs of the Wa-xo'-be," and be entitled to act as Xo'-ka at the initiation of a candidate for the degree.

*Day Three*

*The Ki'-non (Painting):*[68] The ceremonies next in order are called Ki'-non, Painting, and relate to the symbolic painting of the Sho'-ka and the Xo'-ka as well as to the putting upon them of their sacerdotal attire, preparatory to the processional approach to the place prepared for the ceremony.

Before sunrise on the morning following the Night-Singing, the Assisting Xo'-ka, the Sho'-ka, the Singer, and the priests of their clan assemble for the Ki'-non ceremony at the house of the Singer. At this time each man puts upon his forehead moistened earth as a token that he is now a supplicant in the presence of the Life-giving Power. When the gathering has placed upon themselves this sacred sign, the Singer, following the instructions of the Assisting Xo'-ka, blackens with charcoal the face of the Sho'-ka, fastens to the base of the braided lock on the crown of his head a deertail headdress, puts upon his feet the symbolic moccasins ceremonially prepared for him, and ties to each of his arms, just above the elbow, a yard or two of calico. The moccasins are symbolic of life's long and perilous journey and the strips of calico represent the thongs to be used by the warrior in tying such captives as he may take on his journey. In early days skins of snakes were used as symbols for the captive thongs. The Sho'-ka wraps around his body a buffalo robe which is fastened at the waist with a girdle [photo 5.2].

Having thus painted his Sho'-ka, the Singer places in his hand a pipe filled with tobacco, to be taken by him as a supplicatory offering to the Xo'-ka, who is to impersonate throughout the ceremony not only the symbolic man, but also the sun. Four times the Sho'ka must proceed to the house of the Xo'-ka and quietly present to him the filled pipe, touching the tobacco with a live brand taken from the fireplace as the Xo'-ka smokes. At the fourth time the Singer, the Assisting Xo'-ka, and the priests of their clan follow the Sho'-ka to the house of the Xo'-ka, where the Sho'-ka carries the symbolic articles to be worn by the Xo'-ka as his sacerdotal attire: red paint, a downy feather taken from the undertail covert of the eagle, a gorget made from the shell of a freshwater mussel and attached to a woven neckband with fringes, a pair of woven wristlets with fringes, a woven belt, a puma skin, and one pair of the symbolic moccasins.[69]

When all four men have entered and taken their seats at the eastern end of the house, and the Xo'-ka has concluded his fourth ceremonial smoke, the Assisting Xo'-ka sings the following song. Each one of the four stanzas is followed by a section of a wi'-gi-e. Both the song and the wi'-gi-e refer to the story of the descent of the people from the sky to the earth, as given in the genesis wi'-gi-e of the Puma clan; to their dismay at finding the earth covered with water; and to their appeals to the water-spider, to the water-beetle, to the white leech, and to the

PHOTO 5.2. The painting and dress of the Sho'-ka (reproduced from La Flesche 1925:Plate 13).

black leech. In the free translation no attempt is made to give the words of the song the metrical form used in the original.

The Ki'-non Song and Wi'-gi-e[70]

1

The earth shall appear, it was said,
The earth shall appear, it was said,
Through the powers of the spider-like (water-spider),
My grandfather, it shall appear, it was said,
The earth shall appear, it was said.

1 Ha! it was to the spider-like
2 They spake, saying: The little ones have nothing of which to make their bodies, O my grandfather,
3 Verily, at that time and place, it has been said, in this house,
4 The spider-like replied: The little ones shall make of me their bodies,
5 Behold the parting of the waters as I push forth,
6 Verily, it is the movement of the forces to make a way for me as I go forth,
7 When the little ones make of me their bodies,
8 The forces shall make way for them also, as they go forth upon life's journey.

2

The earth shall appear, it was said,
The earth shall appear, it was said,
Through the powers of the black-bean-like (water-beetle),
My grandfather, it shall appear, it was said,
The earth shall appear, it was said.

9 Ha! it was to the one that is like a black bean
10 They spake, saying: The little ones have nothing of which to make their bodies, O my grandfather,
11 Verily, at that time and place, it has been said, in this house,
12 The black-bean-like replied: The little ones have nothing of which to make their bodies, you say.
13 The little ones shall make of me their bodies,
14 Behold the parting of the waters as I push forth,
15 Verily, it is the movement of the forces to make way for me as I go forth,
16 When the little ones make of me their bodies,
17 The forces shall make way for them also as they go forth upon life's journey.

3

The earth shall appear, it was said,
The earth shall appear, it was said,

> Through the powers of the whitleather-like (white leech),
> My grandfather, it shall appear, it was said,
> The earth shall appear, it was said,

18 Ha! it was to the one that is like whitleather
19 They spake, saying: The little ones have nothing of which to make their bodies, O my grandfather.
20 Verily, at that time and place, it has been said, in this house,
21 The whitleather-like replied: The little ones have nothing of which to make their bodies, you say.
22 The little ones shall make of me their bodies.
23 Behold the parting of the waters as I push forth,
24 Verily, it is the movement of the forces to make way for me as I go forth.
25 When the little ones make of me their bodies,
26 The forces shall make way for them also, as they go forth upon life's journey.

### 4

> The earth shall appear, it was said,
> The earth shall appear, it was said,
> Through the powers of the leech (black leech),
> My grandfather, it shall appear, it was said,
> The earth shall appear, it was said.

27 Ha! it was to the black leech
28 They spake, saying: The little ones have nothing of which to make their bodies, O my grandfather.
29 Verily, at that time and place, it has been said, in this house,
30 The black leech replied: The little ones have nothing of which to make their bodies, you say.
31 The little ones shall make of me their bodies.
32 Behold the parting of the waters as I push forth.
33 Verily, it is the movement of the forces to make way for me as I go forth.
34 When the little ones make of me their bodies,
35 The forces shall make way for them also, as they go forth upon life's journey.

At the close of the recital of the wi'-gi-e relating to the four water insects, the Singer, prompted by the Assisting Xo'-ka, rubs red paint upon the palms of his hands in readiness to put the symbolic color upon the face of the Xo'-ka. As the approaching sun reddens the eastern horizon, the Assisting Xo'-ka begins to recite the first section of the wi'-gi-e relating to the painting and the dressing of the Xo'-ka [the Wi'-gi-e of the Symbolic Painting, which follows], and the Singer lifts his outspread hands toward the sun, as though to receive from the Power of Day the sacred color and its life-giving power. At the end of the last (seventh) line the Assisting Xo'-ka pauses and the Singer passes his hands over the face and body of the Xo'-ka, who sits partly nude awaiting the painting, without touching him. This done, the Singer paints the face and body of his Xo'-ka with the sacred red paint [photo 5.3]. This ceremonial act is supplicatory. By it the Singer expresses his craving that through the sun his life may be made fruitful and that he may be blessed with a long line of descendants. The putting of the symbolic paint upon the face and body of the Xo'-ka is like putting it upon himself, for the Xo'-ka represents, among other things, the Singer. When all of the body of the Xo'-ka has been painted red, a dark line is drawn on his face running upward from one cheek to the forehead, then across to the opposite side and downward to the middle of the other cheek. This line represents the dark horizon line of the earth and is called ho'-e-ga, a snare, or an enclosure into which all life is drawn and held captive. From the line as it runs across the forehead, four black lines are drawn downward to the eyebrows. These four lines represent the four winds that symbolize the breath of life. Upon the right side of the Xo'-ka the Singer makes the picture of a man, which represents his soul or spirit. When a man who has taken the Wa-xo'-be degree of the tribal rites dies, his face and body are painted in this manner in preparation for burial.

The Assisting Xo'-ka proceeds to the next section of the wi'-gi-e while the Singer picks up from the pile of sacred articles a white, downy plume taken from under the wing of an eagle and holds it in his hand as the Assisting Xo'-ka recites. The downy feather represents one of the two shafts of light that are sometimes seen on either side of the sun as it rises above the eastern horizon. In this instance the shaft of light at the left of the sun is mentioned in the wi'-gi-e for the reason that the ceremony is being performed by a clan belonging to the Sky division. If the ceremony was given by a clan of the Earth division, the shaft of light on the right side of the sun would be mentioned. The shaft represented by the downy plume symbolizes the strong active life of a warrior. At the end of line 14 the Assisting Xo'-ka pauses while the Singer fastens to the base of the braided lock of the Xo'-ka that hangs from the crown of his head, the downy plume, which is so adjusted that it stands in its place upright and firm.

The Singer next picks up from the sacred articles a shell gorget which is fastened to the ends of a woven neckband and, as the Assisting Xo'-ka goes on with the third section of the wi'-gi-e, holds it in readiness. At the end of line 21 the Singer slips the neckband over the

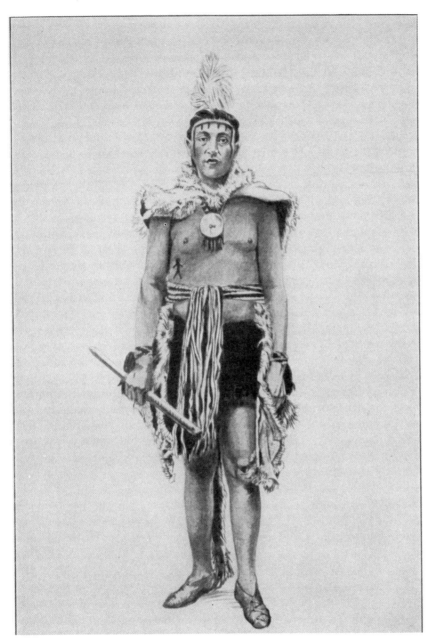

PHOTO 5.3. The painting and dress of the Xo'-ka (reproduced from La Flesche 1925:Plate 14).

head and around the neck of the Xo'-ka so that the gorget hangs at his chest. The gorget typifies the Power of Day, the sun. This act of the Singer is also supplicatory and expressive of a desire for a long and fruitful life, not only for himself but for all his descendants.

As the Assisting Xo'-ka begins to recite the fourth section of the wi'-gi-e, the Singer takes up two narrow woven bands and holds them in readiness. At the end of line 29 he quickly ties on the Xo'-ka's wrists the woven bands. In early times the woven bands were made of buffalo hair, but in modern days various colored yarn is used. Lines 24 and 25 of this section declare that the bonds to be put upon the wrists of the Xo'-ka are captive bonds, but lines 26 to 29 say that in truth it is not the bond of a captive that is tied to each wrist of the Xo'-ka, but a spirit. It would appear that these lines refer to the likening of the earth to a snare into which all life is drawn and held captive, not only in body but also in spirit.

The symbolic gorget having been put upon the chest of the Xo'-ka, the Assisting Xo'-ka continues to the fifth section and the Singer takes up a woven belt, in early days of buffalo hair but now of yarn, which he holds in readiness. In the wi'-gi-e the belt is spoken of as a captive's belt and as a spirit. At the close of the section the Singer wraps around the body of his Xo'-ka a puma skin robe and fastens it at the waist with the woven belt. The puma symbolizes the merciless, destructive fire and is a war emblem.[71] (For the symbolism of the puma skin robe, see lines 31–44 of the first Smoking wi'-gi-e.)

The Assisting Xo'-ka continues to the sixth section and the Singer picks up a pair of the symbolic moccasins ceremonially made for the Xo'-ka and holds them in readiness. In this section the Xo'-ka is referred to as a captive (line 38) and as a spirit (line 41) upon whose feet will be put the sacred moccasins.

Wi'-gi-e of the Symbolic Painting[72]

1 With what shall they (the little ones) adorn their bodies, as they tread the path of life? it has been said, in this house.

2 The crimson color of the Power of Day who sitteth in the heavens,

3 They shall make to be their sacred color, as they go forth upon life's journey.

4 Verily, the Power who reddens the heavens as he approaches,

5 They shall make to be their sacred color, as they go forth upon life's journey.

6 When they adorn their bodies with the crimson hue shed by that Power of Day,

7 Then shall the little ones make themselves to be free from all causes of death, as they go forth upon life's journey.

8 What shall the people use for a symbolic plume? they said to one another, it has been said, in this house.

9 Verily, the Power who always comes out at the beginning of day,
10 Has at his left side
11 A beam of light that stands upright like a plume.
12 That beam of light shall the people make to be their sacred plume.
13 When they make of that beam of light their sacred plume,
14 Then their sacred plume shall never droop for want of strength, as they go
   forth upon life's journey.
15 What shall they place as a pendant upon his (the Xo'-ka's) breast? they said
   to one another.
16 The shell of the mussel who sitteth upon the earth,
17 They shall place as a pendant upon his breast.
18 It is as the Power of Day who sitteth in the heavens,
19 Close to his breast they shall verily press this Power,
20 As a pendant upon his breast they shall place this Power,
21 Then shall the little ones become free from all causes of death, as they go
   forth upon life's journey.
22 Verily, at that time and place, it has been said, in this house,
23 They said to one another: What shall the people place upon his wrists?
24 It is a bond spoken of as the captive's bond,
25 That they shall place upon his wrists.
26 Verily, it is not a captive's bond
27 That is spoken of,
28 But it is a soul
29 That they shall place upon his wrists.
30 Verily, at that time and place, it has been said, in this house,
31 They said to one another: What is he upon whom a girdle is to be placed?
32 It is a captive, they said,
33 Upon whom a girdle is to be placed.
34 Verily, it is not a captive that is spoken of,
35 It is a spirit upon whom they will place a girdle, they said, it has been said,
   in this house.
36 Verily, at that time and place, it has been said, in this house,
37 They said to one another: What is he upon whose feet these moccasins are
   to be placed?
38 It is a captive
39 Upon whose feet these moccasins are to be placed.
40 Verily it is not a captive that is spoken of,
41 It is a spirit
42 Upon whose feet these moccasins are to be placed, they said, it has been
   said, in this house.

When the symbolic moccasins have been securely fastened to his feet
the Xo'-ka sings the first stanza of the Non-zbin' Wa-thon, the Rising
Song. At the close of this stanza the Sho'-ka takes the Xo'-ka by the

right arm and assists him to rise. When he has risen to his feet the Xo'-ka sings the second stanza. At its close the Assisting Xo'-ka, the Xo'-ka, the Singer, and the Sho'-ka walk out of the house, the Singer carrying in his arms the Wa-xo'-be to be used in the ceremony.

1

Ha! Sho'-ka, let us now arise,
Ha! Sho'-ka, let us now arise,
Let us now arise,
Ha! Sho'-ka, let us now arise,
Ha! Sho'-ka, let us now arise.

2

Ha! Sho'-ka, let us now go forth,
Ha! Sho'-ka, let us now go forth,
Let us now go forth,
Ha! Sho'-ka, let us now go forth,
Ha! Sho'-ka, let us now go forth.

*The Processional Approach to the House:*[73] When the Xo'-ka, the Singer, the Assisting Xo'-ka, and the Sho'-ka come out of the house of the Xo'-ka, the Sho'-ka leads the way toward the Sacred House [the symbolic House of Mystery] and the three men follow. After taking a few paces from the house, all four stop, the Xo'-ka himself (if he has memorized them) sings the Song of Processional Approach to the House and recites the first section of the wi'-gi-e, called Wa'-ci-thu-ce Wi'-gi-e or Footsteps Wi'-gi-e. At the close of the last line of the wi'-gi-e he takes from the bowl of a little pipe he carries a pinch of tobacco and drops it upon his right foot, which he is to put forward first as the procession moves. He also tosses a pinch over his right shoulder and one over his left shoulder. Then the procession moves forward. At the second stop he repeats the song, recites the second section of the wi'-gi-e, drops a pinch of tobacco on his left foot, which he first puts forward as the procession again moves. These ceremonial acts are repeated for the third and fourth stops. The fourth movement brings the men to the entrance of the Sacred House. Throughout this processional approach to the Sacred House the Singer carries in his arms his wa-xo'-be, and it is to this act of the Singer that the last line in each section of the wi'-gi-e refers.

It appears that the Footsteps Wi'-gi-e is an epitome of the story of the finding of the foe, given in lines 1,447 to 1,542 of the Ni'-ki Wi'-gi-e of the Puma clan (which will be given in the segment on the Rite of the Chiefs). The priests of this clan (Puma) leave the story unfinished because the right to recite it with all its details belongs to another clan. The Footsteps Wi'-gi-e, as given by the various clans, is substantially the same, but some refer to four bends of a river as the objects of approach while others refer to four valleys as well as four bends of a river. All, however, refer to the "Little House" as the real object of approach, the place where all must go to make their warlike movements authoritative.

1

> It is to a Sacred House that I am going,
> It is to a Sacred House that I am going,
> It is to a Sacred House that I am going,
> It is there that I am going.
> It is to the House of the Earth that I am going,
> To the House where they dwell I am going,
> To the House where they dwell I am going.

1 Toward what shall they direct their footsteps, they said to one another, it has been said, in this house.
2 Toward the setting of the sun,
3 There is a bend in a river,
4 Toward which they shall direct their footsteps,
5 Verily, it is not the bend of a river that is meant.
6 It is a Little House,
7 Toward which they shall always direct their footsteps.
8 When they direct their footsteps toward that Little House,
9 Then shall they take their footsteps with ease,
10 When they direct their footsteps toward that Little House
11 Then shall you all come there, carrying your little wa-xo'-be, it has been said, in this house.

2

> It is to a Sacred House that I am going, etc.

12 Toward what shall they direct their footsteps, they said to one another, it has been said, in this house.
13 Toward the setting of the sun,
14 There is a second bend of the river, toward which they shall direct their footsteps,
15 Verily, it is not two bends of a river that is meant,
16 There is a second Little House toward which they shall direct their footsteps.
17 When they direct their footsteps toward that Little House,
18 Then shall the little ones always take with ease their footsteps.
19 When they direct their footsteps toward that Little House,

20 Then shall you all come there, carrying your little wa-xo'-be, it has been said, in this house.

### 3
#### It is to a Sacred House that I am going, etc.

21 Toward what shall they direct their footsteps, they said to one another, it has been said, in this house.
22 Toward the setting of the sun,
23 There is a third bend of the river,
24 Toward which they shall direct their footsteps.
25 Verily, it is not three bends of a river that is meant,
26 There is a third Little House toward which they shall direct their footsteps.
27 When they direct their footsteps toward that Little House,
28 Then shall the little ones always take with ease their footsteps.
29 When they direct their footsteps toward that Little House,
30 Then shall you all come there, carrying your little wa-xo'-be, it has been said, in this house.

### 4
#### It is to the Sacred House that I am going, etc.

31 Toward what shall they direct their footsteps, they said to one another, it has been said, in this house.
32 Toward the setting of the sun,
33 There is a fourth bend of the river, toward which they shall direct their footsteps.
34 Verily, it is not four bends of a river that is meant,
35 There is a fourth Little House toward which they shall direct their footsteps.
36 When they direct their footsteps toward that Little House,
37 Then shall the little ones always take with ease their footsteps.
38 When they direct their footsteps toward that Little House,
39 Then shall you all come there, carrying your little wa-xo'-be, it has been said, in this house.

The division of the wi'-gi-e into four sections, each of which mentions a "little house" as the real object of the processional approach, has reference to the original organization of the four great tribal divisions established for the government of war movements. To each one of these great divisions was given an eagle symbol. While four "little houses" are severally mentioned in the wi'-gi-e, there is but one house that must be ceremonially approached when about to organize a war party or at an initiation of a member into the mysteries of the war rites, that of the Isolated Earth People.

The initial line in each section of the wi'-gi-e: "Toward what shall they direct their footsteps, they said to one another," refers to the discussions of the ancient priests when formulating the war rites.

The second line of each section: "Toward the setting sun," is a cryptic reference to the life journey of the people as an organized body, a journey which is likened to that of the sun (the great life symbol), taken daily and always westward.

The line: "Then shall the little ones always take with ease their footsteps" means that only by following the established rules can a war leader conscientiously proceed, without fear of giving offense to any of the clans composing the tribe or to any individual member of a clan. Whatever steps he may contemplate taking toward the attacking of another tribe, either as an individual enterprise or on behalf of all the people, he must first approach the "little house" and obtain therein the sanction of the people.

The last line in each section was always recited by the Xo'-ka in a low tone close to the ear of the initiate and to impress upon his mind that the warrior, in order to "take with ease his footsteps," must always make the tribe a party to his enterprise.

The purpose of the ancient priests in formulating the "Footsteps Wi'-gi-e" and ceremonies was to impress their people with the importance of proceeding in an orderly ceremonial manner when deliberating upon the question of going forth against the enemy, or upon the question of going on the tribal buffalo hunt. Only by observing an orderly procedure in deliberating on all tribal matters can the people take with tribal sanction, with safety, and with "ease" their "footsteps."

The fourth movement of the Tsi Ta'-pe [Song of Approach to the House] brings the men to the southwest end of the ground chosen for the ceremony, which is out of doors, in the open air, but is referred to in the Song of Approach as the "House of the Hon'-ga" [or the Sacred House or House of Mystery]. Arrived at this point, the solemn procession of the four men pauses. The Xo'-ka stands directly behind the second pair of the symbolic moccasins which had been placed in readiness for him and so arranged that the toes pointed eastward, for he is to wear them in place of the first pair at the next movement and throughout the principal part of the ceremony that follows. The Xo'-ka at once begins to recite a wi'-gi-e having two titles: Wa'-non-sdo-dse and Wa'-non-shki-ge Wi'-gi-e. Freely translated, the words of the first title signify the Act of Slipping Off (the first pair of moccasins); the second title, the Treading Upon Certain Objects (so that they shall be crushed into the earth). The objects to be trodden upon and crushed (figuratively) are certain classes of persons upon whom an enemy tribe depends for its potential power.

1 Upon what shall we slip off our moccasins? they said to one another, it has been said, in this house.
2 Toward the setting of the sun,
3 There is an adolescent youth,
4 Upon whom we shall always slip off our moccasins, they said to one another, it has been said, in this house.
5 When we slip off our moccasins upon the adolescent youth,
6 We shall make it possible to slip off with ease our moccasins, my younger brothers, they said to one another.
7 Upon what shall we slip off our moccasins? they said to one another, it has been said, in this house.
8 Toward the setting of the sun,
9 There is an adolescent maiden,
10 Upon whom we shall always slip off our moccasins, they said to one another, it has been said, in this house.
11 When we slip off our moccasins upon the adolescent maiden,
12 We shall make it possible to slip off with ease our moccasins, my younger brothers, they said to one another.
13 Upon what shall we slip off our moccasins? they said to one another, it has been said, in this house.
14 Toward the setting of the sun,
15 There is a man who is honored for his military prowess,
16 Upon whom we shall always slip off our moccasins, they said to one another, it has been said, in this house.
17 When we slip off our moccasins upon the man honored for his military prowess,
18 We shall make it possible to slip off with ease our moccasins, my younger brother, they said to one another.
19 Upon what shall we slip off our moccasins? they said to one another, it has been said, in this house.
20 Toward the setting of the sun,
21 There is a woman who has given birth to her first child,
22 Upon whom we shall always slip off our moccasins, they said to one another, it has been said, in this house.
23 When we slip off our moccasins upon the woman who has given birth to her first child,
24 We shall make it possible to slip off with ease our moccasins, my younger brothers, they said to one another.

At the close of the wi'-gi-e the Sho'-ka removes from the head of the Xo'-ka the white downy plume he had been wearing and replaces it with a red one which he takes from within the right foot of the second pair of symbolic moccasins. When the red plume has been fastened to the base of the braided lock on the crown of his head, the Xo'-ka, with a backward sliding movement of his right foot, slips off the moccasin, and in the same manner removes the moccasin from the left foot. He then slips on the second pair, beginning with the right foot, and the Sho'-ka fastens them at the ankles. The Sho'-ka then places the white plume in the right foot of the pair of moccasins that had been slipped off by the Xo'-ka and leaves it in that spot, where it remains throughout the rest of the ceremony.

When the white symbolic plume of the Xo'-ka has been exchanged for the red one, and the first pair of moccasins for the second pair, the Xo'-ka sings the first stanza of the Song of the Walking Upon the Animal Skins, which is more like a call than a song. The title of this song should not be taken literally, for the procession does not walk upon the skins, but only passes by the symbolic articles which are hung upon racks about the middle of the ground. The open space running from the east to the west on the ground arranged for the ceremony symbolizes the earth, and the animal skins hung upon racks along a part of this open space represent all living creatures of the earth. The sun, in passing over the earth, touches with its light all these creatures and gives them life. It is, therefore, the sun, which is represented by the Xo'-ka, who travels (figuratively) upon or over the symbolic animal skins.

The words of the song picture the Xo'-ka and his attendants as approaching and entering the village and finally the House of Mystery, by a succession of pauses, at each of which the Xo'-ka sings a stanza descriptive of some conspicuous object along the line of march to the eastern end of the House of Mystery.

This song, the music of which is of the nature of a call, has twelve stanzas. The same processional form is used, with some modifications, by a successful war leader as he triumphantly marches with his warriors into the village, and into the House of Mystery.

1

To the border of the village I have come.

2

To the footworn grounds of the village I have come.

3

To the frequented parts of the village I have come.

4

To the back side of the House of Mystery I have come.

5
To the door of the House of Mystery I have come.
6
To the whitened skins of the sacred animals I have come.
7
To the sacred animal skins, swaying in the winds, I have come.
8
To the inner side of the House of Mystery I have come.
9
To the middle of the east end of the House I have come.
10
To the sacred fireplace of the House I have come.
11
Beneath the smoke vent of the House I have come.
12
Into the light of the days I have come.

The expression used in the final stanza of this song, "Into the light of the days I have come," and expressions of like import used in other songs of these symbolic rites, appear to be employed to mark the completion of important ceremonial acts, for instance, the acts of the Xo'-ka. In this ritual, from the time of his symbolic painting, this stage of the ceremony is a dramatization of the coming of the Power of Day (the Sun). As the Power of Day emerges from the darkness of night to take his journey, he first heralds his coming by the pale dawn that stretches along the eastern horizon. Then, as he comes near, the pale light fades away and he casts upon the eastern edge of the earth a crimson color that takes the place of the white dawn. It is this crimson color, the color of day, that is put upon the face and body of the Xo'-ka. As the Xo'-ka and his attendants take their places at the eastern end of the House of Mystery, the act of the coming of the Power of Day is completed, as the sun is about to pursue his westward journey over the earth and across the sky. The final stanzas of the corn planting and harvesting songs may also be referred to as examples of the manner in which some ceremonial acts are closed, as well as the songs of the triumphal entry of a victorious war leader into the village and the House of Mystery, that close with these words: "Into the light of the days I have come home, I have come home."

The Singer, the Xo'-ka, and the Assisting Xo'-ka stand at the eastern end of the house, facing the west, as the Xo'-ka sings the ninth, tenth, eleventh, and twelfth stanzas of the song, "Walking Upon the Animal Skins." At the close of the last stanza the three men sit down upon blankets or robes that have been spread on the ground for their comfort. The Sho'-ka, who is still standing, takes the wa-xo'-be, and places it on the ground in front of the Xo'-ka, being careful to see that the sacred hawk, enshrined therein, lies with its head toward the Sky side of the house. He at the same time places in front of the Assisting Xo'-ka a gourd rattle. Having performed this duty, the Sho'-ka takes his seat at the left, toward the Earth side of the house.

## THE SEVEN SONGS[74]

[The preliminaries collectively have brought together and placed in their proper positions all the elements needed to symbolically recreate the cosmos in all its known dimensions. The main body of the initiation rite now commences, beginning with the portion known as the seven songs. The Buffalo Bull clan's version of the seven songs consisted of seventeen song groups including a total of fifty-one songs, three wi'-gi-e, four we'-ga-xe, and a rite called Instructions to the Wife of the Initiate.

The subject of the seven songs was the first stage of Osage tribal organization, particularly the organization of a tribal war party. A tribal war was as much a religious ritual as it was a military action. The *wa-sha'-be a-thin*, or war ceremony, began when the priests decided to declare a state of war, and it did not end until the warriors returned home from battle and claimed their war honors, or o-don'. Because rituals were performed continuously, the leader of the tribal war party had to be a priest. The first act in organizing a war party was the selection by the clan priests of one of their number to act as the *do-don-hon-ga*, or Sacred Warrior. This priest would be responsible for carrying out the rituals required as the party advanced toward the enemy, attacked, and returned home. The Sacred Warrior's role was strictly ceremonial; he did not take part in the battle. Eight other priests, four from the Sky People and four from the Earth People, were chosen to act as *xthe'-ts'a-ge*, or commanders. Two of these men, one representing the Sky and one representing the Earth, were appointed as chief commanders. These men actually planned the attack and led the warriors into battle.[75]

With the beginning of the seven songs, the cosmos is "brought to life" and put into motion. Although the Osages themselves did not divide the seven songs into parts, it can be useful to describe the ritual in three parts. (1) The first part brings the cosmos to life by opening the clan bundle and thus symbolically recreating the "birth" of the hawk. (2) The second and longest part of the ritual is concerned with the early organization of the tribe and the tribal war parties. In a series of songs, the Sacred Warrior is chosen and undergoes his vision quest, the eight commanders are selected, the warriors are prepared, and the party is sent on its way in search of the enemy. In the segment known as the Song of the Wa-don'-be, a complex segment with three concurrent sets of activities involving virtually everyone present, a "battle" is symbolically fought. This second part ends with the Crow Songs, which describe the dead on the field of battle. (3) In the third part—the Buffalo and Corn Songs—the whole tone changes to one of life and of Wa-kon-da's gifts of buffalo and corn for the sustenance of humans.

It is important to remember that this is one of twenty-four different sets of the seven songs. In this particular set, only that part of the knowledge entrusted to the Buffalo Bull clan is included. In what follows, I have presented the seventeen song groups under numbered subheadings to assist readers in following the order of the ceremony. —Ed.]

*1. The Song of the Opening of the Wa-xo'-be*[76]

When the four men are seated, the Sho'-ka takes from the candidate his Wa-xo'-be, places it on the ground before the Xo'-ka, the head of the bird within the shrine toward the Earth side of the house; next he puts before the Assistant Xo'-ka a gourd rattle and a bundle of tally sticks with which to keep count of the songs. These tally sticks are made, consecrated, and kept for ceremonial use; they are regarded as belonging to the same class of articles treasured for symbolic purposes.

The ceremonial acts are performed by the Xo'-ka while the Assisting Xo'-ka does the singing [of the Songs of the Opening of the Wa-xo'-be]. All of these movements are symbolic of the birth of a child [and/or the hawk].[77]

For a better understanding of the ceremonial acts that accompany each stanza of the song it may be well to give a brief description of the movements that attend the singing. Only two lines of each stanza will be translated.

1

He is about to come into the light of day,
Let him be touched with gentle hands.

As the Assisting Xo'-ka begins to sing the song, the Xo'-ka places his hands upon the shrine, one hand at each end, and in this attitude he waits. [The Xo'-ka first raises his right hand and lets it fall gently upon the wa-xo'-be. He then raises his left hand and lets it gently drop]. This alternate lifting of the hands by the Xo'-ka and letting them fall softly upon the shrine to awaken the Wa-xo'-be continues to the close of the stanza.[78]

2

He is about to come into the light of day,
He will turn himself from side to side.

The Xo'-ka turns the shrine endwise, so that the head of the hawk within the shrine is toward the Sky side. The second stanza is sung four times in order to complete the prescribed number of turnings, for the head of the hawk must be turned twice toward the Sky and twice toward the Earth moiety.

These ceremonial acts of the Xo'-ka emphasize the idea of the ancient priests who formulated the rites, that in all war movements there must be unity of purpose and of action by the people of the two great tribal divisions [Earth and Sky], and that all must share alike in the fortunes and misfortunes of the tribal enterprises.[79] On the other hand, there were men of the tribe less gifted mentally, to whom the symbolic movements that accompany the stanza meant simply that the dead bird within the shrine had actually been awakened and had of its own volition inclined its head with favor toward one division and then toward the other.[80]

At the close of these movements the Xo'-ka takes off the hanging strap of the shrine and lays it aside; then he opens, without ceremony, the buffalo-hair bag and lays that aside; next he opens the deerskin bag; and lastly the woven rush case, from the pocket of which he removes the hawk in its deerskin pouch. In the opening of the three bags, the mouth of each bag must be away from the Xo'-ka, and in taking one bag from the other the withdrawal must be made with a forward movement, for the reason that each movement has a cosmic significance and no cosmic body moves backward.

In response to a remark relating to the perfunctory manner in which the Xo'-ka removed the buffalo hair case and the deerskin case from the shrine, Charles Wah-hre-she said, "They are of no account." He did not intend the words to be accepted in their ordinary sense, but what he meant to convey was that the two symbolic articles had no special part to play in this particular ceremony.[81]

### 3

He is about to come into the light of day,
Let the cord of the mouth be untied.

The Xo'-ka puts the tips of his fingers on the knot of the narrow thong that closes and holds together the mouth of the pouch in which the hawk is kept. At the close of the stanza he unties the knot. This act is called thu-shke, untie.

### 4

He is about to come into the light of day,
Let the mouth unfold and be opened.

The Xo'-ka, at the close of this stanza, loosens the thong so that in opening the mouth of the pouch it may open freely and without a catch.

### 5

He is about to come into the light of day,
Let the mouth be opened wide.

At the close of this stanza the Xo'-ka opens wide the mouth of the pouch so that the hawk may freely pass out through it.

### 6

He is about to come into the light of day,
Let him pass through and be born.

This stanza speaks figuratively of the symbolic hawk as being born.

### 7

He is about to come into the light of day,
Let him be taken with gentle hands.

At the close of this stanza the Xo'-ka gently grasps the head of the bird and takes it from the pouch as a child is gently taken at its birth.

In the ceremonial acts of the Xo'-ka, when taking the hawk, still within its pouch, from the woven rush cases, and when removing the hawk from its deerskin pouch, particular care must be observed by him to make his movements forward, that is, the motion must be away from and not toward himself, for the reason that each of these movements of the Xo'-ka refers to birth into life.[82] [Because of the seating location of the Xo'-ka, this movement will be from east to west, the symbolic directional movement of all living things.] After the sacred hawk has thus been brought forth from its shrine, the Xo'-ka blesses himself with it. This he does by touching with it the crown of his head, his arms, body, and legs.[83]

At the close of the Song of Opening the Shrine, and the ceremonial acts with which the Wa-xo'-be, the sacred hawk, is brought into the light of day, the priests of the initiating clan, the Buffalo Bull, enter the House of Mystery in single file and take their seats at the eastern end, back of the candidate, the Xo'-ka, and the Assisting Xo'-ka. They are followed by the priests of the other clans. The priests of the clans of the Water enter first, followed by the Land clan priests and then the priests of the Sky clans. The last to enter were the priests of the Men of Mystery clan. If this was not an initiation for the Buffalo clan, they would enter after the Men of Mystery. The order in which the clans entered the House of Mystery was symbolic of the order of the march of the people in their early history. Inside the symbolic house, the priest of the Earth People took their seats on the south side, while those of the Sky People took their seats on the north [fig. 5.2].[84]

## 2. Standing at His Fireplace[85]

The title of the next song in order is Standing at His Fireplace. The song refers to the head of a throng of people journeying together who rises at break of day and stands at his fireplace as he gives his commands. The song refers particularly to the Sacred Warrior of a body of warriors. Two lines only of each stanza of this song are translated, as the other lines are repetitions.

1

Look you! 'tis day, kindle ye the fire,
The day has now come; kindle ye the fire.

2

Look you! arise and sit ye up,
Arise, arise, and sit ye up.

3

Look you! bestir yourselves, make ready,
Bestir yourselves, make ready.

4

Look you! move forward, begin the journey,
Move forward, begin the journey.

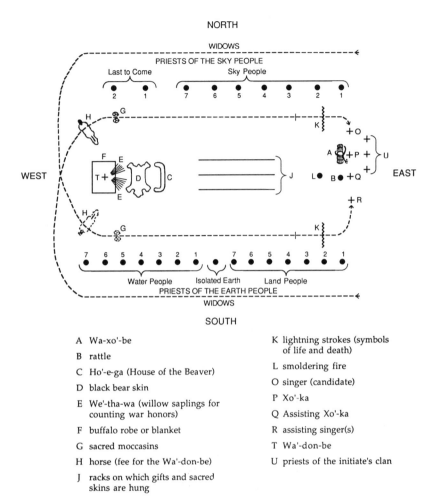

A  Wa-xo'-be

B  rattle

C  Ho'-e-ga (House of the Beaver)

D  black bear skin

E  We'-tha-wa (willow saplings for counting war honors)

F  buffalo robe or blanket

G  sacred moccasins

H  horse (fee for the Wa'-don-be)

J  racks on which gifts and sacred skins are hung

K  lightning strokes (symbols of life and death)

L  smoldering fire

O  singer (candidate)

P  Xo'-ka

Q  Assisting Xo'-ka

R  assisting singer(s)

T  Wa'-don-be

U  priests of the initiate's clan

FIG. 5.2. Organization of the House of Mystery (adapted from La Flesche 1925:84). In this diagram, the seating positions for all twenty-four clans are indicated. In the actual ritual, the priests from the initiate's clan would not be in their normal positions but would be seated behind the candidate and Xo'-ka.

### 3. Early Morning Songs[86]

The title of the song next in order is Early Morning Song. The song is like a hymn of adoration to the sun, an object that has ever been the wonder of the Osage people, and to which they gave a reverential place in their solemn rites, not in adoration of the sun itself, but as the visible manifestation of the presence therein of a higher power. They glorified its regularity of movement; the matchless color it displays as it rises mysteriously from behind the eastern horizon; its journey to the center of the heavens; and thence to the western horizon behind which it vanishes in mystery.

The theme of the Early Morning Song is the coming forth of the sun into the visible world from beyond the horizon which lies hidden in mystery. The coming of the sun is in this version likened to the coming forth of the human race from the invisible to the visible world. The song gives to the sun the form of the human body. The part that first appears is its head, then its arms; its body; its legs; and, lastly, its feet.

I spoke to Saucy Calf of this order given in the song as being the reverse of that given in other tribal ritual songs and asked him the meaning of the difference. He replied by a downward, sweeping gesture with his hands and said that the order given in the Early Morning Song and in other songs of the ritual refers to the birth of man. The order given in the rituals of other clans, which begins with the feet and ends with the mouth, refers to the growth of man, to his life's journey from infancy to old age.

The translation of the first three lines of each stanza will suffice to give the meaning of the song.

### Song 1

#### 1

He who is in the heavens is coming anew,
Coming anew into the visible world,
His head appears first as he approaches.

#### 2

He who is in the heavens is coming anew,
Coming anew into the visible world,
His arms appear as he approaches.

#### 3

He who is in the heavens is coming anew,
Coming anew into the visible world,
His body appears as he approaches.

#### 4

He who is in the heavens is coming anew,
Coming anew into the visible world,
His legs appear as he approaches.

5

He who is in the heavens is coming anew,
Coming anew into the visible world,
His feet appear as he approaches.

In Song 2 of the Early Morning Songs, the sun is personified and made to speak of his going forth into the visible from the invisible world in obedience to a command; of his coming forth with all the potential strength of his head, his arms, his body, legs, and feet. In these two songs and in other songs of like character the ancient priests aimed to express the idea that the sun and all other forms into which life flowed in obedience to the commanding will of an unseen power move together in their endless journey. This power is continuous in its action; therefore the sun and all attendant life come anew each day and continue to travel upon an endless path. This idea is also expressed by the priests in the dramatic action of the ceremony. The Xo'-ka, who sits beside his candidate at the eastern end of the house facing westward, takes the part of the sun in the great life drama; the candidate represents not only human life but all other forms of life that move apace with the sun on its endless journey.

Two lines only of each stanza are translated.

Song 2

1

It is said that I must go into the visible world,
My head shall be first to appear.

2

It is said that I must go into the visible world,
My arms shall be next to appear.

3

It is said that I must go into the visible world,
My body shall then appear.

4

It is said that I must go into the visible world,
My legs shall also appear.

5

It is said that I must go into the visible world,
My feet shall at last appear.

The third song of this group carries one back to the ancient priests, who sat around their hallowed fireplace contemplating the mystery of life. These men, in their mind's vision, beheld the onward movement of life as the onward movement of the sun that never fails to come anew each day from the unseen to the visible world, adorned in a color that awakens and pleases the sense of beauty. In their mind's vision they saw beauty and joy in human life and craved its continuity. Alongside all this they also saw the tragedies and the sorrows of life; that, at times, the best of their men must go and kill and be killed in order that the individual and the tribal life might continue. They likened such a movement to a plunge into the mysterious darkness of death. The conflict over, the living emerge from the darkness and return to the light of day.

In this song those men of the ancient days have attempted to portray such a return. They represent the people of the village as seeing in the distance the warriors returning, signaling their victory, over which they rejoice.

The first stanza tells of the emergence from the darkness and of the military honors won.

The second stanza speaks of the warriors returning, girdled with the trophies of the conflict.

The third stanza pictures the returning warriors as moving in two lines, each representing one of the two great symbolic tribal divisions.

The fourth stanza tells of the finding of the men of the enemy and of their defeat.

### Song 3

#### 1

Look you! they return to the visible,
They return to the visible,
Behold! they come with honors won in battle,
They come with honors won in battle,
Look you! they return to the visible.

#### 2

Look you! they return to the visible,
They return to the visible,
Behold! they come girdled with trophies,
They come girdled with trophies,
Look you! they return to the visible.

#### 3

Look you! they return to the visible,
They return to the visible,
Behold! they come as in a forked line,
They come as in a forked line,
Look you! they return to the visible.

4

Look you! they return to the visible,
They return to the visible,
Behold! they return, having found men,
They return, having found men,
Look you! they return to the visible.

### 4. Wolf Songs[87]

The group of songs following the Early Morning Songs is called Shon'-ge Wa-thon; Shon'-ge, wolf; Wa-thon, songs. The name Shon'-ge is also applied to the domesticated dog.

These songs refer to the eight men chosen as active commanders of the warriors when a large war party is ceremonially organized; four commanders for the warriors of the Sky People and four for those of the Earth People. These commanders are subordinate to the Sacred Warrior, whose office throughout the expedition is that of a mediator between Wa-kon-da and the people of the tribe by whom he is chosen for that duty. Only in the first stanza of Song 1 are these commanders referred to as men. In the other four stanzas they are spoken of as wolves.

The word Shon'-ge includes the gray wolf, the coyote, and the domestic dog, but the gray wolf is particularly referred to in these songs. The distinctive quality of the animal so aptly chosen to be the symbol of these officers is alertness which partakes of a divining nature, a quality that has for its aid an extraordinary sense of hearing and of smell.

The wolf is also esteemed by warriors for his power of endurance; he can travel long distances and resist hunger for many days. When a buffalo is taken sick or is wounded, the wolf will wait a long time without feeding for the animal to die in order to feast upon him.

The wolf is envied by the warrior for another quality, that is, his contentment to be alone and far away from his native habitat for long periods of time. A Sacred Warrior of a war party often had difficulty in keeping his men from deserting when suffering from attacks of homesickness.[88]

These commanders are spoken of as wolves because they are men of great fortitude; men who, like wolves, are ever alert, active, and tireless; men who can resist the pangs of hunger and the craving for sleep and who can also overcome nostalgia, that disheartening mental condition that sometimes seizes a man and unfits him for military duty.[89]

Song 1

1

On what day shall they begin their journey,
The four men who are to go forth.

2

On what day shall they begin their journey,
They who are to go like blue-gray wolves.

3

On what day shall they begin their journey,
They who are to go like black wolves.

4

On what day shall they begin their journey,
They who are to go like brown wolves.

5

On what day shall they begin their journey,
They who are to go like yellow wolves.

In Song 2, a commander is represented as speaking; speaking of the mystery amid which move the day, the man, the wolf, and which makes them all akin. The song implies an appeal to this mystery, the invisible power that controls the actions of all life in whatever form. The commander, conscious of his own limitations, craves the enduring qualities of the ever-moving day, and those of the wolf who, undaunted, travels far and wide over strange lands.

Four lines of the first stanza and one line from each of the other four will suffice to give the meaning of the song.

Song 2

1

Lo! I am ever traveling with the day,
With the day I am traveling as its kin,
I am ever traveling, ever traveling,
With the gray wolf I am traveling as its kin.

2

With the black wolf I am traveling as its kin.

3

With the roan wolf I am traveling as its kin.

4

With the yellow wolf I am traveling as its kin.

5

With the white wolf I am traveling as its kin.

*5. Isolated Song of the Hawk*[90]

The title of the next song sung by the Assisting Xo'-ka is Isolated Song of the Hawk. The title in Osage, Gthe-don' Wa-thon U-kon-dsi, means isolated or standing alone or apart from others.

There is no intimation as to what particular part of the tribal rites this song refers, but it may be said that the song belongs to two clans, namely, the Men of Mystery clan who made of the hawk their life symbol and took from it their sacred clan names,[91] and also to the Buffalo Bull clan. These two clans are jointly credited with the ownership of the hawk symbol, representing the courage of the warrior.[92]

The Osage warrior adores the hawk for the power he displays when "far above the earth he spreads his wings," in search of his prey; for his courage and the intrepidity with which he drops upon his victim and strikes it with unerring precision.

When about to attack the foe, the Sacred Warrior of a war party puts upon the back of each of his eight commanders a hawk,[93] then gives the signal for the attack. There can be no turning back, no turning aside, for the warrior must charge straight upon the foe.

When old Saucy Calf sang this song his face brightened with pleasure as though he saw at a glance all the movements of the hawk and the impetuous charge of the warriors upon the enemy.

1

Far above the earth I spread my wings,
Over these broad lands I fly,
A the, the, he the,
Over these broad lands I fly,
Far, far above the earth I spread my wings,
As over these broad lands I fly.

2

Far above the earth I spread my wings,
As over these grassy plains I fly,
A the, the, he the,
Over these grassy plains I fly,
Far, far above the earth I spread my wings,
As over the grassy plains I fly.

3

Far above the earth I spread my wings,
As over the wide valleys I fly,
A the, the, he the,
Over these wide valleys I fly,
Far, far above the earth I spread my wings,
As over these wide valleys I fly.

4

Far above the earth I spread my wings,
As over the great forests I fly,
A the, the, he the,

Over the great forests I fly,
Far, far above the earth I spread my wings,
As over the great forests I fly.

5

Far above the earth I spread my wings,
As over the lofty trees I fly,
A the, the, he the,
Over the lofty trees I fly,
Far, far above the earth I spread my wings,
As over the lofty trees I fly.

6

Far above the earth I spread my wings,
As over the high hills I fly,
A the, the, he the,
Over the high hills I fly,
Far, far above the earth I spread my wings,
As over the high hills I fly.

## 6. Songs of Taking the Rattle[94]

The song following the Isolated Song of the Hawk is called Song of Taking the Rattle, Pe'-xe Thu-ce Wa-thon.

This group composes one wi'-gi-e and five songs. Up to the rattle songs the Assisting Xo'-ka does not use the rattle to beat time to the music, but as he sings he strikes his thigh with the palm of his hand to accentuate the time. The assistant singers who sit at his left use bunches of the tally sticks which they strike against each other and make a clashing sound like that of gourd rattles.

During the singing of the songs, the Singer, following the instructions of the Assisting Xo'-ka, goes to the man of the Men of Mystery clan who holds the office of ceremonially painting the sacred hawk and conducts him to a place in front of the Xo'-ka. The Sho'-ka then sets before the man a brass kettle in which are placed the bird-hawk and a blanket. By this act the Men of Mystery priest understands that he is required to perform a ceremonial duty, that of reconsecrating the symbolic bird. The kettle is to hold the water to be used in moistening the blue clay when painting the bird. The man also understands that the valuable vessel and the blanket are offered to him as fees for his official services. When the Sho'-ka places the kettle before the man of mystery he says: "Have compassion upon us"; whereupon the official rises and returns to his seat, taking with him the kettle and its contents.[95]

The gourd rattle to be taken up and used from this time on is a sacred symbol of the Isolated Earth clan, whose people did not come from the sky but always belonged to the earth. These people used for their weapons the four winds that were destructive to life.[96]

The wi'-gi-e is a cryptic reference to the military organization of the Isolated Earth clan, an organization which it held before the reorganization took place. In those days the Isolated Earth had seven fireplaces (clans), and it may be that the tribe mentioned in the wi'-gi-e as having seven divisions refers to the ancient war organization of the Isolated Earth people.

A few words concerning the emblematic character of the ceremonial gourd rattle of the Isolated Earth people may be helpful toward a clearer understanding of what the authors of the tribal rites intended it to represent.

The ancient priests, when formulating the tribal rites, persistently held up before the people the fundamental principle that in all their activities as an organized body, a tribe, they must have unity of purpose and unity of action.

They gave iterative emphasis to this fundamental principle for the reason that during their long years of contemplation of the great cosmic bodies that move through the heavens in orderly precision they had discerned the strength and power of this principle. Moreover, they thought they discerned that all cosmic and other movements in the sky and upon the earth were governed and guided by an all-controlling, though unseen, Power.

At the time when the priests formulated the tribal rites, rites observed even down to the present day, these ancient men had no written literature to shed a light from the past upon their days of thoughtful search, nor could they fix in writing the thoughts that played in their minds as they sat around the sacred fire in silent contemplation of the cosmic wonders that on every side surrounded them. Nevertheless the men of the days gone by used means, although crude in character, by which to transmit to their posterity something of what they had learned from nature's open book.

Thus these old men formulated for their people rites composed of wi'-gi-es, spoken passages in which was set forth the relation in which the tribe stood to nature in all its various forms. These wi'-gi-es were frequently accompanied by dramatic action and broken by songs that illustrated the meaning or intent of the spoken words. The underlying principle that had led to the formulating of these rites was embodied in a symbol.

This symbol was the figure of a man, perfect in physical form, possessed of mental powers and the ability to express thought. This symbolic man stood as the unification of the two great tribal divisions, the Sky, representative of the sky with its cosmic bodies, and the Earth, the earth into which life descends to take on bodily forms.

When the tribe was at peace with all the world, the face of the symbolic man was always turned toward the east whence arises the sun, the great life symbol. As he thus stands, his left side is toward the north, the place of the Sky great division, representing the sky, and his right side toward the south, where is the Earth great division, representing the earth with its teeming life on land and in water. When the tribe goes forth to war against its enemies to protect the life of the people, their cultivated fields, or their hunting grounds, then the symbolic man, who represents the tribe as a unit in purpose in its action, turns and stands facing the west, the direction of the darkness of death. His left side is then turned to the south and his right side toward the north.

This turning of the symbolic man of the tribe is mentioned in all the rites, controls the movements of the two great divisions of the tribe, and emphasizes the unity of purpose and action of the tribe in peace and in war.

The gourd rattle, the symbolism of which is the theme of the wi'-gi-e belonging to this group of songs, was the official insignia of the Isolated Earth people, which was at the head of the military affairs of the tribe in the early part of its ceremonial life. The Isolated Earth people was a tribal division [orginally] having seven fireplaces (clans), as have at the present time the Sky great division and the Land and Water subdivisions of the great Earth division of the tribe. It appears that at the reorganization, the number of clans of the Isolated Earth people was reduced to one clan, to which was given a new office, but the property right to the insignia of the gourd rattle, with its songs, was undisturbed and still remains with the Isolated Earth clan and is counted as one of its life symbols.

The gourd rattle symbolizes a head; this symbol has two aspects. In one it represents the head of a puma, a symbol of the relentless fire of which the charcoal is a sign when a warrior puts it upon his face in preparing to attack the enemy. In the other aspect it represents the head of a man, figuratively, the seventh clan [fireplace] of the Isolated Earth, the head of the division.

When, at an initiation, the Rattle Wi'-gi-e is recited by a member of the Earth great tribal division, the rattlers within the rattle were referred to as being the teeth of the right jaws and the handle of the rattle as the right forearm of the symbolic animal or man. If the Assisting Xo'-ka reciting the wi'-gi-e is a member of the Sky great tribal division, he would designate the rattlers as the teeth from the left jaws and the handle of the rattle as the left forearm of the symbolic animal or man. (See sections 1 and 2 of the wi'-gi-e.) Thus the fundamental principle of the unity of the tribe in purpose and in action is emphasized in the rattle, the ancient life symbol of the Isolated Earth people.

This fundamental principle of unity of purpose and of action was expressed, as has been shown, in various ways in the tribal rites, but it was set forth clearly by a symbolic pipe in the custody of the Elder Water, a war clan of the Water subdivision of the Earth Peoples.

The bowl of this pipe is of black pipestone; under the bowl is carved the face of a man. On the thong which holds the bowl and stem together are threaded seven native beads made of shell, to represent the Earth People, and on the same thong are strung six native copper tubes to represent the Sky People. This unique symbolic pipe, both by its workmanship and symbolic decoration, shows that it was made before articles of European manufacture were in use by the Osage, but the organization of the tribe as it is known today was even then in active existence.

The first act performed by the warriors when preparing to go to war is to seek divine aid by certain ceremonial acts, the first of which is to call upon the head of the Elder Water clan to lay before the council the sacred pipe in his custody. Upon the performance of this duty the council proceeds to select a man who is to act as mediator between the people and Wa-kon-da. When this man accepts the office of Sacred Warrior, the sacred pipe is solemnly filled and then placed in the hands of the mediator whose duty it is to offer it to Wa-kon-da.[97] Within the sacred pipe was placed, figuratively, the prayers of all the people of the two great tribal divisions. To perform this sacred duty, undisturbed by human activities, the Sacred Warrior goes far away from the village to the hills, where he remains thinking only of the prayers of the people to Wa-kon-da, to whom he cries continually, carrying in his hand the prayer-pipe. For the period of seven days he must fast and cry, resting only at night.[98]

Thus by the use of the symbolic pipe the ancient priests brought together in the pipe the people of the two great tribal divisions with their cry for aid, and Wa-kon-da, to whom they offered their prayers vicariously.

Rattle Wi'-gi-e[99]

1

1 What shall the little ones make to be their rattle, as they travel the path of
   life? it has been said, in this house.
2 There dwell together a people who are divided into seven villages (clans),
3 It is the seventh one of these villages, the odd one in number,
4 Whose head
5 They shall make to be their rattle,
6 Then shall they travel the path of life, free from all causes of death, it has
   been said, in this house.
7 When they use the rattle against those seven villages,
8 They shall easily overcome them, as they travel the path of life.

2

9 What shall the little ones make to be the handle of their rattle?
10 There dwell together a people who are divided into seven villages,
11 It is the seventh one of these villages
12 Whose left forearm
13 They shall make to be the handle of their rattle.
14 When they make the forearm of the seventh village to be the handle of their
   rattle,
15 They shall travel the path of life, free from all causes of death.
16 When they use the rattle against those seven villages,
17 They shall easily overcome them, as they travel the path of life.

3

18 What shall the little ones make to be the rattlers of their rattle?
19 In the direction of the setting sun
20 There dwell together a people who are divided into seven villages (clans),
21 It is the seventh one of these villages
22 Whose teeth of the left jaws
23 They shall make to be the rattlers of their rattle.
24 When they use the rattle against those seven villages,
25 They shall easily overcome them, as they travel the path of life.

4

26 Verily at that time and place, they said,
27 Behold the opening at the top of the rattle,
28 Which they did not make without a purpose.
29 They made the opening in order that their petitions may readily pass to Wa-
   kon-da.
30 Behold the opening at the lower part,
31 Which they did not make without a purpose.
32 They made the opening in order that their petitions may readily pass to Wa-
   kon-da.

5

33 Behold the dust that stirs within the rattle from each stroke,
34 Which they did not make without a purpose.
35 There are peoples toward the setting sun
36 Who have possessions in great numbers,
37 They have made that dust to represent all those spoils.

6

38 They gave the first stroke of the rattle,
39 When the hollows of every part of the earth
40 Trembled with the shock of the blow.

7

41 They gave the second stroke,
42 And all the little creatures of the earth
43 Became deafened with the shock of the sound.

8

44 They gave the third stroke,
45 And all the little creatures of the earth
46 Fell and lay scattered over the length and breadth of the land.

9

47 They gave the fourth stroke,
48 And all the little creatures of the earth
49 Became motionless throughout all the land.

The first song of the group of Rattle Songs refers to the hawk. Birds of this species were the life symbol of the Men of Mystery clan, so that to the members of this clan all hawks were sacred. The first two stanzas of this song refer to the black hawk and the red hawk. These are not real birds, but they are symbols. The black hawk represents the night. It is spoken of first because it is the greater of the two, for out of the darkness of the night proceed the mysteries of life. The red hawk typifies the glowing color of the luminous day. These two, the force of night and the force of day, are forever coming and going, and it is to this endless recurrent movement that the song refers. The third and fourth stanzas mention the gray and the little hawk. These are also cosmic symbols.

The translation of two lines of each stanza will suffice to give the meaning.

Song 1

1

At this place he shall appear, he shall appear,
The black bird, the hawk shall appear.

2

At this place he shall appear, he shall appear,
The red hawk, the hawk shall appear.

3

At this place he shall appear, he shall appear,
The gray hawk, the hawk shall appear.

4

At this place he shall appear, he shall appear,
The little hawk, the hawk shall appear.

It was explained that the theme of the second and third songs of this group is the birth of mankind.

In this general creative movement man is seen emerging from the invisible to the visible world. The actual appearance of the fathers of the Osage people is definitely spoken of in these two songs. Although their emerging into view in this world is not definitely stated, it is implied in the words that picture the appearance.

There is no expression in either of the songs of emotion or of marvel; only the bare fact is given of the appearance of the fathers as they came to view. A translation of two lines of the first stanza and one line from each of the other four stanzas will give the import of the song.

Song 2

1

My fathers appeared, they appeared,
Their heads first appeared, first appeared.

2

Their arms first appeared, first appeared.

3

Their bodies first appeared, first appeared.

4

Their legs first appeared, first appeared.

5

Their feet first appeared, first appeared.

Song 3

1

When my fathers appeared, how did they appear?
Their heads first appeared, their heads first appeared.

2

When my fathers appeared their arms first appeared.

3

When my fathers appeared their bodies first appeared.

4

When my fathers appeared their legs first appeared.

5

When my fathers appeared their feet first appeared.

In composing the fourth and fifth songs of this group, the ancient priests seem to have been suddenly struck with the marvelousness of the coming of their ancestors, their emergence from the unseen to the visible world.

The people sing of their fathers with fervor, particularly in the fifth song. When their ancestors emerged from the unseen world they appeared with a perfect physical structure, with the additional capabilities of thinking and of bringing to pass, capabilities not possible to the animals who also drew their life from Wa-kon-da. Hence the fathers of the Osage are spoken of as Wa-kon-da-gi, men of mystery. [They should not be confused with the clan of the same name.]

The Assisting Xo'-ka sings the fifth song with vim, and the Xo'-ka joyfully dances to the rhythm of the music.

The translation of two lines of the first stanza of the fourth song and one of each of the other four stanzas is here given.

Song 4

1

When the Wa-kon-da-gi appeared, how did they appear?
Their beads were the first to appear, the first to appear.

2

Their arms were the first to appear, the first to appear.

3

Their bodies were the first to appear, the first to appear.

4

Their legs were the first to appear, the first to appear.

5

Their feet were the first to appear, the first to appear.

Three lines only of the first stanza of the fifth song of this group and one of each of the other four stanzas are given.

Song 5

1

When the men of mystery appeared,
What part of their bodies was the first to appear?
Look you, their heads were the first to appear.

2

Look you, their arms were the first to appear.

3

Look you, their bodies were the first to appear.

4

Look you, their legs were the first to appear.

5

Look you, their feet were the first to appear.

## 7. Songs of the Rite of Vigil[100]

The title of the next group of five songs is Songs of the Rite of Vigil: Non'-zhin-zhon, Rite of Vigil; Wa-thon, Songs.

The Rite of Vigil, it is said, was instituted by the people of the Crawfish clan of the Land subdivision of the Earth Peoples. Sometimes the people of this clan speak of themselves as Mon-in'-ka-zhin-ga, Little-earth, a name that refers to the various colored soils of the earth the crawfish (according to the myth) revealed to the people in order that they might use them as a sign of the presence of Wa-kon-da in the earth as well as in the sky, when they offer their supplications.[101]

These songs refer to the vigils of a man who is chosen for the office of leader of a war party [The Sacred Warrior]. His office is one of great hardship, because he must act as intermediary between the people and Wa-kon-da and offer to that power the prayers of the people for aid in an enterprise that is serious and uncertain in its future consequences. The chosen leader is required, for the time, to abandon all thoughts of human affairs, even to disregard his physical comforts or discomforts, to keep his mind fixed only upon the supplications of the people and upon the divine power to whom he offers them. He must keep awake while he offers the prayers so as not to lose any sign of approval that might be revealed to him in answer to the prayers. To insure wakefulness, the supplicant must stand or he must move about, or if forced by exhaustion to rest he must sit in an upright position, although he may lean against a rock or against the trunk of a tree. He must, however, remain awake whether he stands or sits and keep his mind fixed upon the divine power to whom he must cry continually for a period of four days, or seven if his strength holds out for that length of time. Thus it will be understood that the title of this group of songs is figurative and means that when the chosen war leader takes this rite he is to be, as it were, asleep to all human affairs but stand awake as he offers the appeals of his people to Wa-kon-da.

In his seven days' vigil, this chosen leader represents all of the people, and at the end of the four or seven days his duty as representative of all the people has been performed. When he returns to his home he then begins the rites pertaining to the organization of the war party, and the leader's responsibility as intermediary shifts from the people to the warriors who are to risk their lives for the tribe. Throughout the expedition the leader must maintain his vigil and his appeals to the divine power for aid to the warriors. During the march he must walk apart and at night must camp alone with no one for companion, for he must be alone when in the presence of Wa-kon-da. When he lies down for required sleep he must always lie on his side, never on his back, in order that the vigil might remain unbroken, in spirit at least, until the expedition comes to an end. This is what Non'-zhin-zhon, the native title of the Rite of Vigil, means. By some authors on Indian customs the term "fast" is applied to this rite; while the term is correctly used, it nevertheless is very partial, as it covers only one phase of this complex rite.[102]

The first song of this group has a subtitle, Wa-thon, Song; Pi-zhi, meaning in ordinary usage "bad," but as used in the subtitle the word is a trope for mysterious.[103]

The priests, who represent the entire tribe, select a man to act as Sacred Warrior. This man, in his turn, chooses from his clan a Xo'-ka, a master of ceremonies, who must be versed in all the details of the war ritual.[104] The song points to the first act of this "master of ceremonies," who instructs the Sacred Warrior that he must withdraw and exclude himself from every human association in order that he may perform the Rite of Vigil. This means that he is to go far away from home and be in solitude when he offers to Wa-kon-da the supplications of the people in behalf of their proposed hazardous undertaking. The supplicatory prayers of the people are contained, figuratively, in the pipe which is to be continually carried by the Sacred Warrior. For seven days and nights this Sacred Warrior must be watchful and wakeful and must abstain from food while amid his physical and mental anguish he continues to appeal to Wa-kon-da on behalf of the people.[105]

If on any of the days mentioned in the song some sign should be given that his prayers are heard, the Sacred Warrior becomes at liberty to return to the House of Mystery wherein he had been instructed to take the Rite of Vigil.

A translation of two lines from each stanza will be sufficient to give the meaning of the song.

### Song 1

**1**

Go thou, and pass through the period of anguish,
To return, mayhap, on the first night.

**2**

Go thou, and pass through the period of anguish,
To return, mayhap, on the second night.

**3**

Go thou, and pass through the period of anguish,
To return, mayhap, on the third night.

**4**

Go thou, and pass through the period of anguish,
To return, mayhap, on the fourth night.

**5**

Go thou, and pass through the period of anguish,
To return, mayhap, on the fifth night.

**6**

Go thou, and pass through the period of anguish,
To return, mayhap, on the sixth night.

**7**

Go thou, and pass through the period of anguish,
To return, mayhap, when the number of days is completed.

In the second song, the man delegated to offer the prayers of the people is represented as speaking. He speaks of the sanctity of the bits of the soil of the earth he puts upon his forehead and head as a sign that he recognizes the earth as one of the abiding places of Wa-kon-da.

The word ki'-non which is used in the song means a ceremonial adornment with a sacred sign.

A translation of two lines of the first stanza and one line of each of the other stanzas will suffice to give the meaning of the song.

### Song 2

**1**

I adorn myself, adorn myself with the sacred sign,
Upon my face I put the blue sod, the sacred sign.

2

Upon the hair of my head I put the sacred sign.

3

A waving line I put upon my face, a sacred sign.

4

Upon my smoothed hair I put the sacred sign.

5

A straight line I put upon my face, a sacred sign.

6

Upon my hair, whitened with down, I put the sacred sign.

In the third song, that portion of the priests who estabished the sacred tribal rites of the Osage are represented as addressing the general membership of the order, who are told that it is obligatory upon all priests when preparing themselves about sunrise to enter the House of Mystery to adorn their face and head with the sacred signs and also to fast throughout the ceremonies that follow. This part of the ceremony is called Non'-zhin-zhon, the Rite of Vigil.

The first stanza refers to the blue soil of the earth which is put upon the forehead and upon the top of the head; the second and fourth, to the act of putting the clay upon the hair of the head; the third and fifth stanzas, first, a waving line which typifies those northern and southern parts of the earth which the sun in its westward course does not pass directly over but which are touched with the life-giving power of the sun as it passes; second, a straight line which typifies the straight path of the sun over the earth from east to west; the sixth, to the eagle down which a priest puts upon his head when he prepares to enter the House of Mystery. A translation of the first two lines of the first stanza and one line from each of the other stanzas will suffice to give the meaning of the song.

Song 3

1

You are one of us and use our sacred signs,
You must put upon yourselves the sacred blue soil.

2

You must put upon your hair the sacred sign.

3

You must put upon your face the waving line.

4

You must put upon your smoothed hair the sacred sign.

5

You must put upon your face the straight line.

6

You must put upon your head the white down, a sacred sign.

The fourth song of the Rite of Vigil group differs from the third only in the music and in a few of the words. The song represents the head of the order[106] as addressing the younger or subordinate members, telling them of the signs with which they had adorned themselves in order to indicate them as being a part of the priestly order. A translation of two lines of each stanza will suffice to give the meaning of the song.

Song 4

1

The sign on your face marks you as one of us,
The blue soil on your face marks you as one of us.

2

The sign on your head marks you as one of us,
The blue soil on your hair marks you as one of us.

3

The sign on your face marks you as one of us,
The waving line on your face marks you as one of us.

4

The sign on your head marks you as one of us,
The soil on your smoothed hair marks you as one of us.

5

The sign on your face marks you as one of us,
The straight line on your face marks you as one of us.

6

The sign on your head marks you as one of us,
The white down on your hair marks you as one of us.

The fifth song represents a member of the priesthood as expressing his contentment that he has put upon himself the sacred emblems of the order and invites the members to look upon him as having fulfilled the requirements of adornment. A translation of two lines from each stanza will suffice to give the meaning of the song.

Song 5

1

Look you, I am adorned with the sacred emblems,
Adorned with the blue soil of the earth.

2

Look you, I am adorned with the sacred emblems,
On my hair is the sacred soil of the earth.

3

Look you, I am adorned with the sacred emblems,
Adorned with the waving line, the sacred emblem.

4

Look you, I am adorned with the sacred emblems,
On my smoothed hair is the sacred soil of the earth.

5

Look you, I am adorned with the sacred emblems,
Adorned with the straight line, the sacred emblem.

6

Look you, I am adorned with the sacred emblems,
On my hair is the white down, the sacred emblem.

### 8. Making of the Bow[107]

The next group of three songs bears the title Min'-dse Ga-xe Wa-thon, Songs of Making of the Bow: Min'-dse, bow; Ga-xe, make; Wa-thon, songs. The theme of the first song of this group is the conclusion of the rites and ceremonies by which a war party is ceremonially organized, when the Sacred Warrior is ready to march against the enemies of the tribe. The duty imposed upon this officer is to pray continually for his men and for the success of the undertaking. To enable the Sacred Warrior to perform his duties, eight subordinate officers are chosen to perform the actual duties of commanders. These officers are chosen from the warriors of the two great tribal divisions, four from the Sky People and four from the Earth People.

The words of the song imply that the Sacred Warrior is speaking of the completion of the rites instituted by the priests; of the ceremonial pipe which he carries; of the ceremonial war club, which typifies all the war clubs of the warriors; of the ceremonial knife, which typifies all the knives to be used by the warriors; of the scalp that is tied to the wa-xo'-be; of the bows of his men; of the arrows of the warriors; of the standards carried by the subordinate commanders; and of the sacred eagle down used in the ceremonies. All of these articles are regarded as the property of the Sacred Warrior, as are also all the honors attending the success of the expedition, the trophies, the captives, and spoils taken by his warriors. A translation of two lines of each stanza will suffice to give the meaning of the song.

Song 1

1

Lo, the rites are ended, I march against the foe,
Bearing the mystic pipe, I march.

2

Lo, the rites are ended, I march against the foe,
Bearing the mystic club, I march.

3

Lo, the rites are ended, I march against the foe,
Bearing the mystic knife, I march.

4

Lo, the rites are ended, I march against the foe,
Bearing the mystic scalp, I march.

5

Lo, the rites are ended, I march against the foe,
Bearing the bows, I march.

6

Lo, the rites are ended, I march against the foe,
Bearing the arrows, I march.

7

Lo, the rites are ended, I march against the foe,
Bearing the standards, I march.

8

Lo, the rites are ended, I march against the foe,
Bearing the symbol of spoils, I march.

The theme of the second song is the selection of the Sacred Warrior by the priests, to whom that officer speaks. He refers to his selection as bearer of the mystic pipe in which are placed (figuratively) the prayers of the people; to the ceremonial articles used in the rites and also to the weapons of his warriors. A translation of one line from each stanza will suffice to give the meaning of the song.

Song 2

1

At dawn you made me bearer of the mystic pipe.

2

At dawn you made me bearer of the mystic club.

3

At dawn you made me bearer of the mystic knife.

4

At dawn you made me bearer of the mystic scalp.

5

At dawn you made me bearer of the bows.

6

At dawn you made me bearer of the arrows.

7

At dawn you made me bearer of the standards.

8

At dawn you made me bearer of the symbol of spoils.

In the third song the Sacred Warrior warns the foe of his coming to destroy them, the people having determined in solemn council to move against the enemy. The priests are represented in this song as bringing their mystic pipe and other ceremonial articles to the assembly.

A translation of two lines from each stanza will suffice to give the meaning of the song.

Song 3

1

Look ye, I come to slay you, to make you die,
The holy men have assembled, bringing their mystic pipe.

2

Look ye, I come to slay you, to make you die,
The holy men have assembled, bringing their mystic club.

3

Look ye, I come to slay you, to make you die,
The holy men have assembled, bringing their mystic knife.

4

Look ye, I come to slay you, to make you die,
The holy men have assembled, bringing their mystic scalp.

5

Look ye, I come to slay you, to make you die,
The holy men have assembled, bringing the bows of the warriors.

6

Look ye, I come to slay you, to make you die,
The holy men have assembled, bringing the warriors' arrows.

7

Look ye, I come to slay you, to make you die,
The holy men have assembled, bringing the standards.

### 9. Spirit Songs[108]

The next group of songs in order is called Wa-non'-xe Wa-thon: Wa-non'-xe, Spirit; Wa-thon, Songs. The belief in a future spiritual state of existence is strong among the Osage people. These songs teach the initiate that even as he lives and moves about in the midst of earthly life he also lives in the midst of the realm of death; that there is continuity of life not only in this world but in the spirit world as well.

These songs refer to the spirits of his ancestors, of the men who have fallen in battle, who belonged to his own tribe, and also to the spirits of the men of the foe, for all travel upon the same well-trodden path to the spirit land.[109] The words of the first song of this group imply that the initiate speaks of his visits to the land of spirits. A translation of two lines from each stanza will suffice to give the meaning of the song.

Song 1

1

Often in my travels I come to the land of spirits,
As day approaches I travel and come to the land of spirits.

2

Often in my travels I come to the land of spirits,
As the sun drops, I travel and come to the land of spirits.

3

Often in my travels I come to the land of spirits,
In my dreams I travel and come to the land of spirits.

4

Often in my travels I come to the land of spirits,
As a spirit I travel and come to the land of spirits.

The second spirit song has but one stanza. The theme of the song is the spirit path which every living creature must finally take on entering the unseen world. The singer speaks of his footprints as being already upon that mystic path, even as he lives.

### Song 2

Lo, my footprints are even now upon the mystic path,
The spirit path that ever lies before us,
Verily my footprints are on that path.
My footprints are even now upon that mystic path.

In the third song of this group there is no mention of a spirit or of the spirit land, but the theme of the song is the sorrow that fills the heart of the singer as he approaches the House of Mystery where are assembled the holy men; they of the Sacred Eagle; they of the Red Eagle; they of the Shining Eagle; and they of the Little Eagle, who are about to perform the solemn rites.

A translation of two lines from each stanza will suffice to give the meaning of the song.

### Song 3

1

Sorrow fills my heart as I go to the holy men,
To those of the Sacred Eagle.

2

Sorrow fills my heart as I go to the holy men,
To those of the Red Eagle.

3

Sorrow fills my heart as I go to the holy men,
To those of the Shining Eagle.

4

Sorrow fills my heart as I go to the holy men,
To those of the Little Eagle.

### 10. Songs of the Midday Sun[110]

The group of songs following the spirit songs is called Mi Tho-ton-don Wa-tho: Mi, sun; Tho-ton-don, vertical; Wa-thon, songs; songs of the midday sun.

The theme of the first song of this group is the rite performed by the Sacred Warrior of a war party whereby he seeks for a sign in the midday sun that will give him hope for success in his hazardous undertaking. This rite is performed on approaching the home of the enemy when there is most need for courage.

A translation of two lines from each stanza will suffice to give the import of the song.

Song 1

1

I go to learn if I shall go on
To learn of the sun if I shall go on.

2

I go to learn if I shall go on
To make the foe to lie reddened on the earth.

3

I go to learn if I shall go on
To make the foe to lie blackened on the earth.

4

I go to learn if I shall go on
To make the earth brown with the bodies of the foe.

5

I go to learn if I shall go on
To make the foe to lie scattered on the earth.

6

I go to learn if I shall go on
To make their bones to lie whitened on the earth.

7

I go to learn if I shall go on
To make their locks to sway in the wind.

The second song of this group implies that the Sacred Warrior has received the desired sign that he is to proceed upon his journey to punish the troublesome foe. Encouraged by a hopeful sign from the midday sun, he continues his journey and assumes the title Wa-kon-da-gi, man of mystery.

A translation of two lines from each stanza will suffice to give the import of the song.

Song 2

1

Verily, by the midday sun, I, as a man of mystery, go
To fall, unawares, upon the foe.

2

Verily, by the midday sun, I, as a man of mystery, go
To make the foe to lie reddened on the earth.

3

Verily, by the midday sun, I, as a man of mystery, go
To make the foe to lie blackened on the earth.

4

Verily, by the midday sun, I, as a man of mystery, go
To make the earth brown with the bodies of the foe.

5

Verily, by the midday sun, I, as a man of mystery, go
To make the foe to lie scattered on the earth.

6

Verily, by the midday sun, I, as a man of mystery, go
To make the bones of the foe to lie whitened on the earth.

7

Verily, by the midday sun, I, as a man of mystery, go
To make the locks of the foe to wave in the winds.

The theme of the third song of this group is the continuance of the
march of the Sacred Warrior, with his warriors, toward the enemy with
all confidence that he will overcome.

A translation is given of two lines from each stanza of this song.

Song 3

1

Onward I march toward the foe,
To fall upon them unawares.

2

Onward I march toward the foe,
To make them to lie reddened on the earth.

3

Onward I march toward the foe,
To make them to lie blackened on the earth.

4

Onward I march toward the foe,
To make the earth brown with the bodies of the foe.

5

Onward I march toward the foe,
To make them to lie scattered on the earth.

6

Onward I march toward the foe,
To make their bones to lie whitened on the earth.

7

Onward I march toward the foe,
To make their locks to wave in the winds.

### 11. *Little Songs of the Sun*[111]

The next group of three songs is called Mi Wa-thon Zhin-ga: Mi, sun; Wa-thon, songs; Zhin-ga, little; little songs of the sun. There is also a subtitle to this group, Mi A-po-ga, Wa-tho: Mi, sun; A-po-ga, downward; postmeridian songs. These titles are complex as to their significance. They probably refer to the birth of the hawk, the symbolic child of the power of night and the power of day, of the godlike greatness of the sun at dawn, of its dominance at midday, and its unabated greatness as it travels downward to the west. [These songs were given earlier in the discussion of the organization of the tribe.] They are now repeated in their proper place in the ritual of the [Songs of the] Wa-xo'-be as given by Saucy Calf. This old man took pride in the accuracy of his work when he conducted the ceremonies of the tribal rites, and as he gave me the Wa-xo'-be ritual he felt troubled, lest it be not recorded in the way he had given it. He was willing to give the ritual because he knew that it was going to be lost as the people came more under the influences of civilization. The old man was much amused when he gave the songs of the birth of the hawk and told me the mythical story of that event. The priests of his clan [Buffalo Bull] had something to do with the birth of the blackbird, and he knew the purposes of its institution in the tribal rites, that there was nothing in it of a supernatural character, yet the very people who made the symbolic article became afraid of it, thinking that it had become possessed with power to do harm. Two lines only of the first song are translated; the other two songs are given in full.

### Song 1

1

I go to the call of those who are assembled,
To the call of those who are gathered around the hawk.

2

I go to the call of those who are assembled,
To the call of those who are gathered around the blackbird.

3

I go to the call of those who are assembled,
To the call of those who are gathered around the One of the Night.

### 4

I go to the call of those who are assembled,
To the call of those who are gathered around the One of the Day.

## Song 2

### 1

He is born! He is born!
Behold, the hawk, he is born,
They have said. They have said,
He is born!

### 2

He is born! He is born!
Behold, the blackbird, he is born,
They have said. They have said,
He is born!

### 3

He is born! He is born!
Behold, he is born of the One of the Night,
They have said. They have said,
He is born!

### 4

He is born! He is born!
Behold, he is born of the One of the Day,
They have said. They have said,
He is born!

## Song 3

### 1

Lo, it has come to pass,
Behold, the hawk that lies outstretched,
Is now born they proclaim. Is now born they proclaim.
Welcome! be it said. Lo, it has come to pass.

### 2

Lo, it has come to pass,
Behold, it is of the One who is of the Day,
He is born they proclaim. He is born they proclaim.
Welcome! be it said. Lo, it has come to pass.

### 3

Lo, it has come to pass,
Behold, the blackbird that lies outstretched,
Is now born they proclaim. Is now born they proclaim.
Welcome! be it said. Lo, it has come to pass.

4

Lo, it has come to pass,
Behold, it is of the One who is of the Night,
He is born they proclaim. He is born they proclaim.
Welcome! be it said. Lo, it has come to pass.

## 12. Fish-Turtle Song[112]

The title of the song next in order is Ho-Ke' Wa-thon: Ho-Ke', fish-turtle; Wa-thon, song. The name Ho-Ke' is archaic and its true meaning has become obscured by careless transmission. I asked Saucy Calf its significance and he replied, "It is Ho, fish; and Ke', turtle, of course." He gave a hearty laugh as he explained that the meaning had become lost and the priests formed the habit of defining the name as Ho-Ke', fish-turtle.

It would appear, however, from the theme of the song that it is a part of the group of wolf songs which follow it. The theme of each song in the group is mon-zhon', land. A translation of one line of the Fish-Turtle Song, which has but one stanza, will suffice to give its meaning.

Lo, there lies the land whither I am going.

## 13. Wolves Wandering the Land Songs[113]

The group of songs next taken up by the Assisting Xo'-ka is called Shon'-ge Mon-zhon' Op'-she Wa-thon: Shon'-ge, wolves; Mon-zhon', lands; Op'-she, march upon; Wa-thon, songs; songs of the wolves who march upon the land. The theme of these two wolf songs is the authority conferred upon the eight commanders of a war party, four chosen from the Earth great tribal division and four from the Sky great tribal division. These two songs refer only to the four commanders chosen from the Sky division, the Sky being in this ritual the initiating division. The eight commanders form a council to designate each day the lands over which the warriors are to march. There is another group of wolf songs in which are mentioned these eight officers. Of Song 1, the first stanza is translated in full and two lines of each of the other stanzas.

Song 1

1

'Tis mine to say on what lands the warriors shall march,
'Tis mine to say on what lands the warriors shall march,
'Tis mine, as one of four men, to say on what lands
The warriors shall march,
'Tis mine to say on what lands the warriors shall march.

### 2

'Tis mine, I the gray wolf, to say on what lands
The warriors shall march.

### 3

'Tis mine, I the black wolf, to say on what lands
The warriors shall march.

### 4

'Tis mine, I the brown wolf, to say on what lands
The warriors shall march.

### 5

'Tis mine, I the yellow wolf, to say on what lands
The warriors shall march.

### 6

'Tis mine, I the white wolf, to say on what lands
The warriors shall march.

The theme of Song 2 of this group is the same as that of Song 1. In Song 2 no mention is made of the lands over which the warriors are to march. In this song each of the four commanders (the wolves) is represented as singing of his general authority as a commander.

A translation of two lines of each stanza will suffice to give the meaning of the song.

### Song 2

### 1

Upon me has fallen the authority to speak,
Upon me, the gray wolf.

### 2

Upon me has fallen the authority to speak,
Upon me, the black wolf.

### 3

Upon me has fallen the authority to speak,
Upon me, the brown wolf.

### 4

Upon me has fallen the authority to speak,
Upon me, the yellow wolf.

### 5

Upon me has fallen the authority to speak,
Upon me, the white wolf.

## 14. The Weeping Song[114]

[This song group and the following one, the Seizing of the Wa-don'-be, are closely related, with the second following after only a short pause. Preparations are made for both of them just preceding the singing of the Weeping Song. The Xo'-ka announces that they have now come to this part of the ceremony.—Ed.]

At the close of this announcement the Xo'-ka rises and informs the priests that he has performed all the acts required of him to make complete the ceremony of initiation; that he has presented to the warrior who is to act as Wa-don'-be and recount his o-don' [war honors] a horse, together with other valuable goods, which have been by him accepted. Thereupon the priests signify their approval by saying, "Ho!"

The Sho'-ka then prompts the Singer as to the part he is to perform during the singing of the songs. Following the Sho'-ka's instructions, the Singer crosses over to the south side [the Earth side, since he is of the Sky People and his Wa-don'-be has to be the opposite] of the House of Mystery to his Wa-don'-be, where he "seizes" the warrior by the edge of his blanket and conducts him to a place ceremonially prepared for him at the west end of the house. When the Wa-don'-be is seated, the Singer fastens to his scalp lock a scarlet deer's tail headdress badge which only a warrior who has won military honors is privileged to wear, and he also places upon the back of the Wa-don'-be a rawhide shield painted with symbolic designs and ornamented with eagle feathers.[115]

The Sho'-ka brought to the Assisting Xo'-ka a bunch of willow saplings which he divided into two parts, one containing seven and the other six. The Assisting Xo'-ka crossed the lower ends of the bunches of saplings and handed them to the Sho'-ka without saying a word. The Sho'-ka put these in the hands of the Singer, observing the same manner that they had been put into his hands. He then directed the Singer to take them to the Wa-don'-be and place the saplings on the ground before him, keeping the two bunches of saplings as they had been handed to him. Having performed this duty, the Singer then returned to his place at the right of the Xo'-ka.[116]

[The preliminaries completed, they then begin the Song of Weeping. In this song group, four ritual actions take place concurrently: (1) the Assisting Xo'-ka and his assistant singers sing the Weeping Song; (2) the Singer carries the pipe and hawk, while wailing and touching the heads of the priests—the same ritual act, called the *wa'-in xa-ge*, that we saw earlier in the Smoking of the Animals; (3) the women wail; and (4) the priests recite the Dream Wi'-gi-e.—Ed.]

Charley Wah-hre-she explained that the wailing of the candidate was an appeal for long life and an endless line of descendants; the reciting of the Dream Wi'-gi-e was in the nature of a supplication to Wa-kon-da that the cry of the candidate might be heard and his prayer granted; the wailing of the women was in remembrance of their husbands or sons who had gone to the spirit land and whose places they filled in the organization of the priests.

While it is true, as explained by Charley Wah-hre-she, that this entire ceremony is in the nature of a supplication, it is also clear that it is a dramatization of the rite of the seven days' vigil which a man is required to take who is chosen to offer the appeal of the people for divine aid in overcoming their enemies, as also the continuance of the rite throughout the entire war expedition.

The pipe referred to in the first stanza of the Wa'-in Xa-ge Song contains (figuratively) the petitions of all the people and is in the possession of their priestly representative throughout the seven-day period of the rite and throughout the entire war expedition. The other stanzas mention certain ceremonial articles used in the war rites.

A translation of two lines from each stanza of the first song is here given.

1

I cry to Wa-kon-da for aid as I go forth,
Bearing the mystic pipe I go.

2

I cry to Wa-kon-da for aid as I go forth,
Bearing the mystic club I go.

3

I cry to Wa-kon-da for aid as I go forth,
Bearing the mystic knife I go.

4

I cry to Wa-kon-da for aid as I go forth,
Bearing the mystic trophy I go.

5

I cry to Wa-kon-da for aid as I go forth,
Bearing my bow I go.

6

I cry to Wa-kon-da for aid as I go forth,
Bearing my arrows I go.

### 7
I cry to Wa-kon-da for aid as I go forth,
Bearing the mystic standards I go.

### 8
I cry to Wa-kon-da for aid as I go forth,
Bearing the symbol of trophies I go.

When the Singer had touched the heads of all the priests sitting on both sides of the house, he stood still but continued to wail, as did the women, until the last word of the Dream Wi'-gi-e had been spoken.

### Dream Wi'-gi'-e[117]

1 Verily, at that time and place, it has been said, in this house,
2 The youngest of the brothers,
3 Arose and stood in silent contemplation.
4 Verily, it was at the time when the earth sat glorified amid her blossoms and ripening fruit,
5 That the young brother stood in silent contemplation.
6 It was in the evening of the day,
7 When he stood at one end of the house,
8 With his head inclined to the left,[118]
9 He fell prone to the earth, where he lay outstretched.
10 Night passed. The Sun struck the heavens with a pale light,
11 Then the young brother arose, took that which was made sacred (the soil of the earth),
12 Put it upon his brow and stood motionless.
13 The Sun ascended to a point midway between the eastern horizon and the zenith;
14 The Sun moved on to the middle of heaven;
15 The Sun descended to a point midway between the zenith and the western horizon;
16 Then, in the evening of the day,
17 While yet the sacred soil remained upon the young brother's brow,
18 He shed tears while he slowly moved
19 To the borders of the village where,
20 With head inclined to the left,
21 He fell prone to the earth and lay outstretched,
22 And Wa-kon-da made the eyes of the youth to close in sleep.
23 Night passed. The Sun struck the heavens with a pale light,
24 The young brother arose, took that which was made sacred,
25 Put it upon his brow and stood upright.
26 He wandered from place to place as the Sun ascended to a point between the eastern horizon and the zenith;

27 He wandered from place to place as the Sun descended to the middle of heaven;

28 Still he wandered from place to place as the Sun descended to a point midway between the zenith and the western horizon.

29 Then, in the evening of the day,

30 He came to a great spring where he paused and spake, saying:

31 Even in this spot, within this spring itself, may be an abiding place of Wa-kon-da.

32 He removed from his brow the sign of vigil, the consecrated soil of the earth.

33 Then, with head inclined to the left,

34 He fell prone to the earth, where he lay outstretched,

35 And Wa-kon-da made the eyes of the youth to close in sleep.

36 Night passed. The Sun struck the heavens with a pale light,

37 The young brother arose and took that which was made sacred,

38 Put it upon his brow and stood upright.

39 He wandered from place to place as the Sun ascended to a point midway between the eastern horizon and the zenith;

40 He wandered from place to place as the Sun ascended to the middle of heaven;

41 Still he wandered from place to place as the Sun ascended to a point midway between the zenith and the western horizon;

42 Then, in the evening of the day,

43 He came to a great elm tree where he paused and spake, saying:

44 Even in this spot, within this tree itself, may be an abiding place of Wa-kon-da.

45 He removed from his brow the sign of vigil, the sacred soil of the earth.

46 Then, with head inclined to the left,

47 He fell prone to the earth where he lay outstretched,

48 And Wa-kon-da made the eyes of the youth to close in sleep.

49 Verily, at that time and place, it has been said, in this house,

50 At the beginning of the day,

51 The young brother arose and took that which was made sacred,

52 Put it upon his brow and stood upright.

53 He wandered from place to place as the Sun ascended to a point midway between the eastern horizon and the zenith;

54 He wandered from place to place as the Sun ascended to the middle of heaven;

55 Still he wandered from place to place as the Sun decended to a point midway between the zenith and the western horizon;

56 Then, in the evening of the day,

57 He came to a low hill that resembled the breast of a turkey.

58 Close to the hill the young brother stood and spake, saying:

59 Even in this spot, within this hill itself, may be an abiding place of Wa-kon-da.

60 Upon this very hill I shall recline and sleep,
61 Lo, I am weary in body and mind,
62 I feel ready to depart for the spirit land.
63 My elder brothers
64 May never find my body in this lonely spot.
65 After a pause he said: Toward the places where men
66 Are wont to pass to and fro I must arise and go;
67 He arose and wearily strode forth.
68 In time he came to a little brook,
69 Whose banks were covered here and there with groves of trees.
70 Close to the brook he paused to rest.
71 Near by stood a willow, a tree that never dies.
72 To that tree he slowly moved and sat down,
73 Then, clinging to the trunk of the tree, he tried to rise for a further effort.
74 He spake as to a responsive being, saying to the willow:
75 Ha! my grandfather,
76 It seems impossible for me to go on, O grandfather.
77 The tree replied, saying: O little one!
78 The little ones shall always cling to me for support, as they travel the path of life.
79 Behold the base of my trunk which sends forth its supporting roots.
80 I have made them to be the sign of old age, O little one.
81 When the little ones make of me their symbol of old age,
82 They shall not fail to live to see old age, as they travel the path of life.
83 Behold my bark that is roughened with age,
84 That also,
85 I have made to be the sign of old age.
86 When the little ones make of me their symbol of old age,
87 They shall not fail to live to see their faces roughened with age, as they travel the path of life.
88 These lower outspreading limbs,
89 I have made to be my arms, as I stand here.
90 When the little ones make of my lower limbs the symbols of their arms,
91 They shall not fail to live to see their arms strengthened with age, as they travel the path of life.
92 These curved limbs, bent with their weight,
93 I have made to be the sign of old age.
94 When the little ones make of me their symbol of old age,
95 They shall not fail to live to see old age, as they travel the path of life.
96 The white blossoms upon my topmost branches,
97 I have made to be the sign of old age.
98 Aged men
99 Are spoken of as having scant, yellowish hair.

100 The little ones shall not fail to live to see their hair grown scant and yellowish with age, as they travel the path of life.
101 The young brother wearily stode homeward, and in time
102 Came to the borders of the village,
103 Where he paused to rest.
104 Then, as in a passing vision, he saw men,
105 In deadly strife, their war clubs rising and falling in blows and parries.
106 The vision passed; the young brother thought: Lo, I suffer in body and mind,
107 Is it true, as has been said, that Wa-kon-da holds in favor young men of my age?
108 Even in this spot,
109 Within this spot itself may be an abiding place of Wa-kon-da.
110 Then with head inclined to the left,
111 He fell prone upon the earth, where he lay outstretched.
112 Suddenly a man
113 He heard approaching, treading softly upon the earth as he came.
114 The young brother lifted his head to see,
115 But, verily, there came to him as he lay waiting no sign of a man.
116 After a moment's pause, a man
117 He again heard approaching, the grass rustling at his every step.
118 The young brother lifted his head to see,
119 But, verily, there came to him no sign of a person as he lay waiting.
120 After a moment's pause,
121 The right foot of the young brother was touched
122 By the man with his foot,
123 And the stranger spake, saying:
124 It is said that a man is wandering over the earth, suffering in body and mind.
125 Is it you who is thus spoken of, my younger brother, the stranger asked.
126 Yes, my grandfather, it is I,
127 I who sit here, the young brother replied.
128 The stranger spake, saying: Ha! my younger brother,
129 Then it is you whose mind is steadfastly fixed upon the whole earth, with a longing desire.
130 Look upon me!
131 The young man replied: O my grandfather,
132 I look upon you
133 And see every part of your body covered with red (the red dawn).
134 The stranger spake: Your mind is steadfastly fixed upon the power whose every part is stained with red.
135 Look upon me again!
136 The young man replied: Little pipes (pipes used in ceremonies),
137 Seven in number, I see you holding in your hands, as you stand,

138 The odd one in number
139 Profusely adorned with the scalps of men, O my grandfather.
140 The stranger spake: Even upon the sacred pipes your mind is steadfastly
      fixed, my younger brother.
141 Look upon me again!
142 The young man replied: I look upon you, O my grandfather,
143 A little (hawk) bundle,
144 Most pleasing to look upon,
145 You hold under your arm, as you stand there, O my grandfather.
146 The stranger spake: Ha! my younger brother,
147 Even upon the sacred shrines your mind is steadfastly fixed, my younger
      brother.
148 Look upon me again.
149 The young man replied: I look upon you, O my grandfather,
150 Animal skins (the seven symbolic skins used in ritual)
151 Lie spread beneath your feet,
152 Upon them you stand as they yield softly to the weight of your feet.
153 The stranger spake: Ha! younger brother,
154 Even upon the sacred animal skins your mind is steadfastly fixed.
155 Look upon me again!
156 The young man replied: As an aged man,
157 Your face roughened with the wrinkles of age, I see you, O my grandfather.
158 The stranger spake: Even upon the appearance of an aged man your mind
      is steadfastly fixed, my younger brother.
159 Look upon me again!
160 The young man replied: As an aged man (in sacerdotal attire),
161 With fluttering down of the eagle
162 Adorning his head, I see you, O my grandfather;
163 As an aged man,
164 With the stem of a pipe between his lips, I see you, O my grandfather.
165 Again, I see you as amidst the four great divisions of the days,
166 Standing there as though in your personal abode, O my grandfather.
167 The stranger spake: Ha! my young brother,
168 Even upon the four great divisions of the days your mind is steadfastly
      fixed, my younger brother.
169 The young man replied: Verily, amidst the days that are beautiful and
      peaceful,
170 I see you standing as though in your personal abode, O my grandfather.
171 The stranger spake: Even upon the days that are beautiful and peaceful,
      your mind is steadfastly fixed, my young brother.

No explanation could be obtained as to whether the story of the
dream was from the actual experience of a man who had taken the
Rite of Vigil when chosen for the office of Sacred Warrior, or whether it

is an allegorical myth designed to aid the man taking the rite to limit the range of his thoughts only to objects of a sacred character. It is clear from the wi'-gi-e, however, that the man chosen to perform the rite is required, when in his vigils, to fix his thoughts only upon the objects that are sacred to the people and used by them as symbols when appealing for divine aid. It also follows that any vision that may come to him from the suggestion of these objects may be taken by him as a sign that his appeal has been heard and accepted by Wa-kon-da.

The sacred objects specially mentioned in the wi'-gi-e are as follows: Wa-kon-da and his abiding places, the waters, trees, and hills; the observance of certain sacred ceremonies, as when each morning a bit of the soil, a sacred symbol, must be put on the forehead, and while the sign is upon the supplicant's face he must utter his cry of prayer. At night this symbol may be removed, and when he takes his rest he must lie with his face to the earth, never on his back. If he belongs to the Earth People he must lie with his head to the right side, if to the Sky People his head must be toward the left. The "willow that never dies" is a symbol of old age or of the long continued life craved for the people as a tribe; the battles in which men have risked their lives for the continued existence of the tribe; the earth in which Wa-kon-da abides; the red dawn, a sacred symbol of life; the little pipe that bears the messages of the people to Wa-kon-da; the bundle containing the sacred hawk, symbol of the courage of the warrior; the seven sacred animal skins; the face of the old man roughened and wrinkled by time; the aged man who in the councils sits clothed in ceremonial attire, his head covered with eagle down, a sacerdotal insignia; the four seasons of life through which all persons must strive to pass; finally the calm and peaceful days to the tribe will at last arrive.[119]

When all had become quiet the candidate resumed his seat at the right of the Xo'-ka.

### 15. Song of the Seizing of the Wa-don'-be[120]

[This song group has three concurrent parts: (1) the singing of the songs by the Assisting Xo'-ka and his singers, (2) the simultaneous recital of three different versions of the wi'-gi-e by the priests, and (3) the Wa-don'-be's counting of his war honors.—Ed.]

After a brief pause, the Assisting Xo'-ka again took up his rattle and began to sing, which is a call to the Wa-don'-be to retrace his steps, meaning, that he must now count his o-don' in the order that he had won them. As the Wa-don'-be arose he picked up one of the bunches of saplings,[121] the one containing six, and began to count. At the same moment all the priests present began to recite three different wi'-gi-es. The priests of the Land subdivision of the Earth great tribal division recited the Wi'-gi-e of the Thirteen Footprints of the Black Bear.[122] The priests of the Water subdivision of the Earth great division recited the Wi'-gi-e of the Male Beaver and the Thirteen Willow Saplings.[123] The priests of the Sky great division recited the Wi'-gi-e of the Thirteen Sun-rays.[124] [Although classified as Sky People,] the priests of the Buffalo Bull and the Men of Mystery clans recited the Wi'-gi-e of the Male Beaver and the Thirteen Willow Saplings as here given by Saucy Calf.

As the singing of the first and second songs of this group continued without pause, and the reciting of the three wi'-gi-e took place at the same time, the Wa-don'-be, in a steady, deliberate, and even voice recounted his o-don', seven for the Earth great division and six for the Sky great division. The Wa-don'-be dropped a sapling on the earth at his feet as he finished giving the history of the o-don' it represented.

Wi'-gi-e of the Beaver and the Thirteen Willow Saplings[125]

1

1 Verily at that time and place, it has been said, in this house,
2 The male beaver
3 At the left side of one end of his house,
4 Lay with moistened soil upon his face.
5 He spake, saying: The soil upon my face
6 I have not put there without a purpose.
7 When the little ones go toward the setting sun against their enemies,
8 It shall serve them as a sign of their appeal for divine aid to overcome with ease their enemies.
9 From the left side of his house
10 The male beaver
11 Pushed forth, rippling the surface of the water,
12 And he spake, saying: Behold the ripples upon the water,
13 Which I have made to be the sign of old age.
14 May even one of the little ones
15 Live to see his skin furrowed as the ripples on the water.
16 The splashing of the water as I push forth
17 Is not without a purpose,
18 The voices of the little ones, lifted in appeal, shall be heard by Wa-kon-da, as are the splashes I make on the water.

2

19 Verily at that time and place, it has been said, in this house,
20 The male beaver came to a bend of the river,

21 Where stood a yellow willow tree,
22 Which he quickly cut down,
23 Then spake, saying: This act of cutting down the tree
24 Is not performed without a purpose.
25 The people who dwell toward the setting sun
26 I have made this fallen tree to represent.
27 May even one of the little ones
28 Enable himself to cut down with ease his enemies, as he travels the path of life.

3

29 After a pause
30 He started to drag the tree.
31 Against the current of the river
32 He dragged the tree.
33 Splashing with his tail the surface of the water as he pushed forth,
34 He spake, saying: These splashes of the water
35 Are as my voice that is heard by Wa-kon-da.
36 So shall it be with the little ones,
37 Their voices, lifted in appeal, shall always be heard by Wa-kon-da.
38 After a pause
39 He put at the left side of the entrance of his house
40 The lower part of the trunk of the willow tree.

4

41 After a pause,
42 At the right side of one end of his house,
43 The male beaver
44 Lay with moistened soil upon his face.
45 He spake, saying: The soil upon my face
46 I have not put there without a purpose.
47 When the little ones go toward the setting sun against their enemies
48 It shall serve them as a sign of their supplication for divine aid to overcome with ease their enemies.
49 Verily at that time and place, it has been said, in this house,
50 From the left side of his house,
51 The beaver pushed forth, rippling the surface of the water,
52 Then spake, saying: Behold the ripples upon the water,
53 Which I have made to be the sign of old age.
54 May even one of the little ones
55 Live to see his skin furrowed with age as the ripples on the water.

5

56 The beaver came to another bend of the river,
57 Where stood a yellow willow tree,
58 Which he quickly cut down,

59 Then spake, saying: This act also
60 I have performed not without a purpose.
61 There dwell toward the setting sun many people,
62 It is for the counting of these people I cut down this tree.
63 When the little ones go toward the setting sun against their enemies,
64 And they appeal for divine aid, they shall always overcome their enemies
    with ease.
65 After a pause
66 He started to drag the willow tree.
67 Against the current of the river
68 He dragged the willow tree.
69 Splashing the surface of the water with his tail as he pushed forth,
70 He spake, saying: The splashes that I make as I push forth,
71 Are as my voice that is heard by Wa-kon-da.
72 So shall it be with the little ones,
73 Their voices, lifted in appeal, shall always be heard by Wa-kon-da.

6

74 Verily at that time and place, it has been said, in this house,
75 The male beaver,
76 From the left side of his house,
77 Pushed forth, rippling the surface of the water.
78 He reached another bend of the river,
79 Where stood a yellow willow tree,
80 Which he quickly cut down,
81 Then spake, saying: This act also
82 I have performed not without a purpose.
83 There dwell many people toward the setting sun,
84 It is for the counting of those people that I have cut this.
85 When the little ones go to cut down their enemies
86 They shall always cut them down with ease, as they travel the path of life.

7

87 After a pause
88 He went on and reached the seventh bend of the river,
89 Then spake, saying: This bend of the river, also,
90 I have made to represent the honors of the warrior.
91 The little ones shall use this river's bend for counting their honors.
92 When they use it to count their military honors,
93 They shall count with ease their honors, as they travel the path of life.

The first song [of the Seizing of the Wa-don'-be] has two stanzas.[126] The words are addressed to the Wa-don'-be, the man of valor chosen by the candidate to recount the deeds he performed when he fought in defense of the tribe. By the first stanza the honored warrior is commanded to go to the place prepared for him, there to travel again (retrospectively) the path of honor he had made in his warlike career. In the second stanza the Wa-don'-be is commanded to go to the seat of honor and there count, one after the other, the thirteen military honors he has won, in accordance with the tribal rites. A free translation of one sentence of each of the two stanzas of the song is given.

Song 1

1

Go thou and travel again the path thou hast made.

2

Go thou and count in sequence the honors thou hast won.

The second song has thirteen stanzas. These are divided into two groups, one containing six and the other seven stanzas. The group of six stanzas is for the Sky great division and that of seven stanzas for the Earth great division. When the ceremony is given by a clan of the Earth great division, the group of seven stanzas is sung first, and when the ceremony is given by a clan of the Sky division, the group of six stanzas is sung first. Saucy Calf, who gave this ritual, belonged to a clan of the Sky, so he sang first the group with six stanzas.

In order to avoid repetition, the seven stanzas only are here given, the words of all the stanzas except the seventh being the same. The numbers given throughout the seven stanzas may be read as ordinal numbers, thus: first, second, third, etc. They refer to the willow saplings to be used by the Wa-don'-be in recounting his o-don' (war honors) at the singing of the song. The words of the song are addressed to the Wa-don'-be and as though offering to him the saplings one by one.

The words of two lines of each stanza of this song are freely translated. In the last or seventh stanza the ordinal number is not used for the reason that the Osage word for the ordinal form of the number seven contains four syllables, so that the word does not fit the music; therefore the word "e'-non" is substituted, a word which means the last one to complete the prescribed number.

Song 2

1

Thou art a man, O Wa-don'-be, O Wa-don'-be,
Take thou the first of these, the first of these.

2

Thou art a man, O Wa-don'-be, O Wa-don'-be,
Take thou the second of these, the second of these.

3

Thou art a man, O Wa-don'-be, O Wa-don'-be,
Take thou the third of these, the third of these.

4

Thou art a man, O Wa-don'-be, O Wa-don'-be,
Take thou the fourth of these, the fourth of these.

5

Thou art a man, O Wa-don'-be, O Wa-don'-be,
Take thou the fifth of these, the fifth of these.

6

Thou art a man, O Wa-don'-be, O Wa-don'-be,
Take thou the sixth of these, the sixth of these.

7

Thou art a man, O Wa-don'-be, O Wa-don'-be,
Take thou the final one of these, the final one.

[When the singing and reciting begin, the Wa-don'-be stands up and starts his count.] "I rise to count my o-don'. It is at your request, O Water People, Land People, and Men of Mystery, that I rise to recount my o-don'. You well know that the o-don' that have been awarded me are not altogether clear of doubt (a conventional plea of modesty), but it is your wish that I recount them on this occasion, and I cannot but give consent to your request."[127]

*The Seven O-don':* (1) "This (willow sapling) represents the o-don' known as 'Striking the Enemy within the Camp Limits.' A Pawnee warrior was slain within the camp limits on Salt Creek. Do-don'-i-non-hin [a personal name] was first to strike the warrior, and being next to him in the attack I gave the enemy the second stroke, which entitles me to a like o-don'. O thou Wa-xo'-be that lies before me, I place this upon thee.

(2) "This (willow sapling) represents the o-don' called Wa'-thu-xpe [not translated]. I won it in a fight by a great war party, composed of both the great divisions of the tribe. The sacred charcoal was still upon my body and face when I performed this act and there exists no doubt of my title to count this o-don'. O thou Wa-xo'-be that lies before me, I place this upon thee.

(3) "This (willow sapling) represents the o-don' known as 'Triumph of a Sacred Warrior of a Great War Party.' Ni'-ka-ga-xthi [a personal name] came to me in his bereavement and, weeping, asked me to go forth to slay an enemy because of his loss. I went forth and came back

in triumph. O thou Wa-xo'-be that lies before me, I place this upon thee.

(4) "This (willow sapling) represents the o-don' called 'Victory.' I won the o-don' when as the officer carrying one of the standards of a war party, I struck an enemy. O thou Wa-xo'-be that lies before me, I place this upon thee.

(5) "This (willow sapling) represents the o-don' called 'Striking of an Enemy in an Attack by a Great War Party.' I won this o-don' when, under the leadership of Little Mi-ka [a personal name], a war party attacked and slew a number of the enemy. O thou Wa-xo'-be that lies before me, I place this upon thee.

(6) "This (willow sapling) represents the o-don' called 'the Killing of an Enemy in the Open Country.'[128] I won this o-don' by striking a single enemy attacked at break of day by a war party of which I was a member. O thou Wa-xo'-be that lies before me, I place this upon thee.

(7) "This (willow sapling) represents the o-don' called 'Taking a Head in an Attack by a War Party Composed of Warriors of Only One of the Great Divisions.'[129] I won this o-don' in an attack made by a war party led by Wa-kon'-da-u-ki-e [a personal name]. O thou Wa-xo'-be that lies before me, I place this upon thee."

*The Six O-don':* (1) "This (willow sapling) represents the o-don' called 'Award to a Member of a Clan War Party.' I won this o-don' in an attack made upon the enemy by a war party led by Ku'-zhi-wa-tse. O thou Wa-xo'-be that lies before me, I place this upon thee.

(2) "This (willow sapling) represents the o-don' called 'Award to a Leader of a Clan War Party.' I won this o-don' as leader of a war party carrying a single Wa-xo'-be. O thou Wa-xo'-be that lies before me, I place this upon thee.

(3) "This (willow sapling) represents the o-don' called 'Striking of an Enemy in an Attack of a Clan War Party.' I won this o-don' in an attack made by a war party led by Gthe-mon'-zhin-ga. O thou Wa-xo'-be that lies before me, I place this upon thee.

(4) "This (willow sapling) represents the o-don' called 'the Hitting of an Enemy in an Attack in the Open Country.'[130] I won this o-don' in an attack made by a war party led by Tse-do'-a-mo-in. O thou Wa-xo'-be that lies before me, I place this upon thee.

(5) "This (willow sapling) represents the o-don' called 'Award to the Sacred Warrior of a War Party of Only One of the Great Divisions.' I won this o-don' as the successful Sacred Warrior of a war party. O thou Wa-xo'-be that lies before me, I place this upon thee.

(6) "This (willow sapling) represents the o-don' called 'Talking the Head of an Enemy in an Attack of a Clan War Party.' I won this o-don' in an attack made by a war party carrying but one Wa-xo'-be. O thou Wa-xo'-be that lies before me, I place this upon thee."

At the close of the singing, the Assisting Xo'-ka puts down his rattle, the Wa-don'-be returns to his seat among the members of his own clan, and the priests seek relaxation from their mental strain in social conversation.[131]

## 16. Crow Songs[132]

At the close of the Wa-thu'-ce songs, the Assisting Xo'-ka gives the following notice: "O priests, I have come to the Crow songs. At this time the holy men drink water." Thereupon the women bring in water and the "holy men," in accordance with ancient custom, proceed to refresh themselves and to wash from their faces the sign of the Rite of Vigil which they had put on their faces before the dawn.

The Sho'-ka and his assistants also bestir themselves and apportion to the families of the holy men the provisions supplied by the candidate and his relatives, first serving the Wa-don'-be a large portion. The activity in the serving of cold water and food to the holy men at the singing of the Crow Songs, of which there are two, is a dramatization of the scenes that take place upon a battle field when the conflict is over, and the combatants, both the living and the slain, have departed.

The crow is a bird that figures prominently in rites not only of the Osage but also those of other Siouan tribes. The men of ancient days who formulated the tribal rites observed that nature had endowed this bird with faculties that served him well. His strong sense of sight enabled him to follow the movements of a war party, and when foe met foe and the hills were strewn with the slain the bird feasted upon the remains of the fallen warriors. Should it happen that he was not present to witness the deadly strife, the winds carried to him the message that a feast awaited him beyond the hills—a message received through his keen sense of smell. The wi'-gi-e of the Seizing the Wa-don'-be, the ceremonial movements, and the Crow Songs all dramatize the rallying of the people to go and chastise their foes. The warriors who march to the country of their enemies leave the hill strewn with the dead, upon which the black birds of mystery feast. Thus the warriors return triumphant to their village, where the o-don' won by them are ceremonially confirmed.[133]

The theme of the first Crow song is the person (the crow) who first approaches the abandoned field of conflict where lie the bodies of the slain. In the song the crow is represented as speaking while he approaches to feast upon the fallen warrior, from the back, from the left side, from the breast, and, lastly, from the right side.

In this song two men only are mentioned as having gone. Saucy Calf could not explain what was meant by this, but thought it meant one of the slain from each side, as the bodies of the slain on both sides are left upon the field of combat. A free translation is given of three lines from each stanza.

Song 1

1

Lo, two men have gone to the spirit land,
A he the, two men have gone to the spirit land,
I go to feast upon their backs with zest.

2

Lo, two men have gone to the spirit land,
A he the, two men have gone to the spirit land,
I go to feast upon their left sides with zest.

3

Lo, two men have gone to the spirit land,
A he the, two men have gone to the spirit land,
I go to feast upon their breasts with zest.

4

Lo, two men have gone to the spirit land,
A he the, two men have gone to the spirit land,
I go to feast upon their right sides with zest.

The second Crow song, which Saucy Calf next takes up, is descriptive of the actions of the crow when feasting upon the bodies of the slain warriors. The first stanza refers to the cries of the birds as they spring into the air and tear each other in fight over the bodies of the fallen; the second stanza refers to the ravenous manner in which they feed. The third refers again to the fighting and to the way in which the birds tumble through the air in their struggles. The fourth to the peaceful manner in which the crows depart from the battle field, flying abreast by twos, having satisfied their hunger.

A translation of one line from each stanza will suffice to make clear the meaning.

Song 2

1

The crows fight and scream where lie the two.

2

The crows eat with zest where lie the two.

3

The crows wrestle in the air above the two.

4

The crows, in pairs, leave the place where lie the two.

At the close of the Crow songs, all the priests, excepting those belonging to the clan that is conducting the initiation, go out for a recess, during which they give themselves up to social pleasures and enjoy the food furnished by the Singer. After a rest of about two hours, the priests return to the [symbolic] lodge and take their places without formality.[134]

## 17. Buffalo Songs

Two themes are united in the group of songs next in order. The first theme is of an animal life form, the buffalo, and the second is of a vegetal life form, the corn. These two forms of life are held by the Osage as specially sacred, for they are recognized as special gifts from Wa-kon-da, the power that is the source of all forms of life. This composite group of songs bears the title Tse Wa'-on, Buffalo Songs. The myth which tells of the buffalo and the corn implies that the buffalo was first to become the principal food supply of the people and later the corn took an important and a permanent place in the secular and religious life of the tribe.

The corn must be ceremonially planted by woman; therefore when the buffalo and the corn songs are to be sung, the Singer's wife and her uninitiated woman relatives are invited to be present in order to receive instructions in the rites which must be observed when planting the corn.

When Saucy Calf is about to sing the buffalo and corn songs he gives the following notice to the members of the order: "Priests! I have come to the Buffalo Songs. On arriving at these songs it is customary to have the Ki'-non present, O priests!"

The Sho'-ka, who has gone to gather the women, reenters, followed by the wife of the candidate and her friends, who take seats in front of and facing the Xo'-ka, the Assisting Xo'-ka, and the Singer to be instructed.[135]

[This ritual has two parts. The first part consists of the Instructions to the Wife of the Singer. Only after the instructions are finished does the singing of the Buffalo Songs begin.—Ed.]

When the women have taken their places, the Assisting Xo'-ka begins his instructions. He begins by addressing the wife of the Singer by the term of relationship that he is accustomed to use when speaking to her.

"My granddaughter, this Wa-xo'-be is now yours, to take care of until there comes a time when it will be passed on to someone else. There may come a time when a warrior will wish to use this particular Wa-xo'-be in a war expedition. If ever that happens the warrior will come to your house in an appeal to you, not only for its use but also for your good wishes for success during the time that he is gone on the expedition. When you hear that a warrior is about to come to you, then you shall prepare yourself to receive him ceremonially. Should you happen to have a robe of black bearskin you will be fortunate, for the black bear is a symbol of strength and courage. This robe you will spread upon the ground at your accustomed place in the house ready for you to sit upon while you wait for the coming of the warrior. Dress yourself in any garment that you think will be most becoming to you, but do not fail to remember to paint the parting of your hair red. The red line symbolizes the path of the force of day and also represents the path of life. When you have put upon your head this symbol then you will take your seat upon the bearskin robe and put this Wa-xo'-be in your lap. Upon the departure of the warrior from the house with the Wa-xo'-be you will remove the symbol from your head and say while doing so: 'My grandfather bade me to say, when I do this act, "I remove this symbol from my head and wipe my hands upon the bodies of the enemy."'

"In time you will hear that the warrior has started on his journey. Then you are to remember him. On the following morning, as the sun begins to rise, paint the parting of your hair red, put a narrow blue line upright on your right cheek, one horizontally on your forehead, and one on your left cheek like that on the right. This is the symbolic painting by which you send to the warrior sympathy and courage, and your wish for his success. You must remove these symbols from your head and face before the sun reaches the zenith and say, while you do so: 'My grandfather bade me to say, when I do this, "I remove these symbols from my head and face and wipe my hands upon the body of the chief of the enemy."' On the next day, as the sun rises, you will again paint yourself in the same manner, but add a red line to each of the blue ones on your face. Before the sun reaches the zenith you must remove the symbols, and as you do so repeat the words I have just given you. On the third morning you will repeat this ceremony, this time adding a blue line to the red and blue lines, and later remove them as you did the others. On the fourth morning you must perform the same ceremony, adding to the three lines on your face a red line, and later remove them in the same manner as before.

"Before the sun rises on the fifth morning you must arise and go out of your house and take from the earth a bit of soil and put it on your head. This is the Rite of Vigil and the Sending of Courage. You must give all your thoughts to the warrior who has gone against the enemy carrying your Wa-xo'-be. In this way you will give him aid. When the shadow of evening comes, making indistinguishable the faces of men, then remove from your head the soil of the earth. In doing so remember to repeat these words: 'My grandfather bade me to say, when doing this, "I remove from my head the soil of the earth and wipe my hands upon the body of the chief of our enemies, that he may come to his death at the hands of our warriors."' You will repeat this rite for a period of four days, when your duty to your Wa-xo'-be and to the warrior will be fulfilled."[136]

The Assisting Xo'-ka next proceeds to instruct the woman as to her duties as a mother. "You have a child. Other children are yet to be born to you. There is in you the same desire that there is in all good mothers to bring your children successfully to maturity. In this you need the aid of a power that is greater than that of the human being. There is a rite by which an appeal can be made to this power. It is this: Let the father of your child secure the skin of an old male buffalo. You will dress and soften the skin with your own hands. When you have made it soft and pliable, take some red paint and with it draw a straight, narrow line from the head, through the length of the body of the skin, to the tip of the tail. This straight line represents the path of the power of day that liveth forever. You will paint all four legs of the robe red, to represent the dawn, the coming of the force of day and of life [fig. 5.3]. Let each child to whom you have given birth sleep in the consecrated robe and you will have aid in bringing to maturity your children."

The Assisting Xo'-ka continues his instructions to the woman as to the ceremonial planting of the corn. "The planting of the field is also a responsibility that has been bestowed upon you and has to do with the feeding of your children. In this duty also you need aid such as no human effort can give you. There is a way by which you can appeal for aid in performing this duty and reach the power that controls all things. When the time for planting has come, aim to rise with the sun so that your task will begin at the same time the sun begins to take its course. The parting of your hair must be painted red for this work. The red line will represent the path of the force of day and will make the

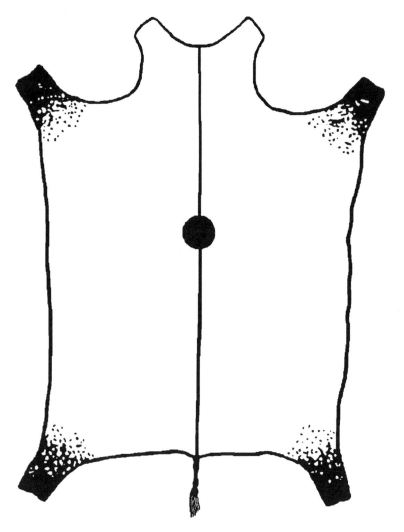

FIG. 5.3. Painting of the robe according to the Instructions to the Wife of the Initiate.

paths of all the animals converge toward you, for upon them you and your children must depend for food. When you reach your field you must, first of all, prepare seven hills which you shall regard as the 'Mysterious Hills'. Open the first hill with your planting stick and put into it one grain of corn, after which you will cover up the opening and tamp it with your foot; in the second hill you will put two grains in the same manner; three in the third hill; four in the forth; five in the fifth; six in the sixth; and seven in the seventh. This ceremony is a supplication for three things: first, the growing of corn to maturity; second, the success of the hunter; third, the success of the warrior who protects the home and the field. When you have finished planting the seven sacred hills you may proceed to plant the rest of your field without further ceremony."[137]

The woman is next instructed how to gather ceremonially the roots of the water lily for food for her little ones. "The water lily with which you feed your children is also a sacred food and should be gathered with proper ceremony. It is a symbol of life. When you set a day to go and gather this food, aim to rise with the sun and paint the parting of your hair red. The red line represents the path of the force of day and the paths of all living things which converge toward you and give to you and your children both food and clothing. When you come to the lake where you are to gather the water lily, cut a willow pole. The willow is a tree that never dies and is a symbol of life. When you have cut the pole remember to say: 'My grandfather bade me to say: "This is to be my staff."' Upon entering the water to begin your work, take from the bottom of the lake a bit of the mud and touch your head and body with it. This act is your prayer to the earth. Then proceed to dig. When you have secured the first root, rub your arms and body with it, that you may receive the blessing of life, and then throw it back into the water and remember to say: 'My grandfather bade me to do this act.' This is all of my instructions, my granddaughter."

If the singer has no children, the instructions relating to the rites of the buffalo robe and to the gathering of the water lily roots may be omitted. At the conclusion of these instructions the wife of the Singer and her companions take off their gala dresses, having put them on over other garments before entering, and leave them as they go out. The various articles of clothing worn by the wife of the Singer are intended as a part of the fee given to the Assisting Xo'-ka. A horse is the usual fee to which the clothing is added.

[After the instructions are completed and the wife and her female relatives have gone, the singing of the Buffalo Songs begins.] The songs of this group belong to the clan called the Buffalo Bull, and are distributed among the rites of the various clans. Some of the rites are said to include as many as thirteen or more of these songs, while others have only from six to twelve. Many of the songs of this group are corn-planting songs. These are classed as buffalo songs because the buffalo is said to have given corn to the people. The Buffalo Bull clan can use all or only a part of these songs in their ceremonies, while each of the other clans can use only those songs that have been given to them to include in their rites.[138]

The first song of this composite group relates to the coming of the buffalo from the mysterious invisible world to the material and visible world. The first two stanzas imply the creation of the male and female with their full procreative powers; the third stanza speaks of the birth of the young buffalo; the fourth stanza refers to the completion of this creative act, the appearance of the father, mother, and the little one in the material world, in the light of day. A free translation of all the five lines of the first stanza and two lines from each of the three other stanzas will suffice to give the meaning of the song.

Song 1

1

My grandfathers are rising,
A ho! my grandfathers are rising,
A ho! my grandfathers are rising,
I shall go to them, go to them, when they have risen,
When the males have risen.

2

I shall go to them, go to them, when they have risen,
When the females have risen.

3

I shall go to them, go to them, when they have risen,
When the young one has risen.

4

I shall go to them, go to them, when they have risen,
And come into the light of day.

The first and second songs of this group differ in both character and expression. The first song indicates a thoughtful, contemplative mood, having for its object the performance of an act that will greatly affect the welfare of the people; the music of the song expresses dignity, solemnity, and a reverence for the power that gives thought to a vast and far-reaching movement. The words of the second song, the rhythm, and quick time of the music indicate a happy spirit that rejoices at the actual coming of the buffalo into the material world, together with the promise of continuance through natural increase for the lasting benefit of the tribe. A free translation of the first stanza in full and two lines of each of the other stanzas of the second song is given.

Song 2

1

My grandfathers rise, they rise,
They rise; look ye! they rise,
Look ye! Look ye!
The males rise, the males rise,
Look ye! they rise. Look ye! Look ye!

2

The females rise, the females rise,
Look ye! they rise. Look ye! Look ye!

3

The little one rises, the little one rises,
Look ye! the little one rises. Look ye! Look ye!

4

In the light of day they stand, they stand,
Look ye! they stand. Look ye! Look ye!

The third song of this group differs from the second only in the music. The words and rhythm have the same tone of happiness at the coming of the buffalo into the visible world. Saucy Calf gave only the first and fourth stanzas of this song, leaving the words of the second and the third to be implied.

It is the practice of the singers of the ritual songs to give only the first and last stanzas of the songs that have the same theme and which dwell upon the same subject. This practice is called "Pa-ci a ki'-tha ha thu-ce," taking only the first and the last. The first and fourth stanzas are translated in full.

Song 3

1

My grandfather, my grandfather rises,
Look you! he rises; look you! he rises,
Look you! he rises; the male rises,
The male rises; look you! he rises.

4

My grandfather, my grandfather rises,
Look you! he rises; look you! he rises,
Look you! he rises; he stands in the light of day,
He stands in the light of day. Look you! he stands.

It was explained by Saucy Calf that the fourth song of this group speaks of the readiness of the buffalo to come to the material world, into the light of day, and that all things necessary to be accomplished for their coming are completed.

A free translation is given of the first stanza and one line from each of the other stanzas.

Song 4

1

My grandfather comes and stands,
It is done, soon shall I go! It is done,
It is done, soon shall I go,
It is done! I, the male, stand.

2

It is done! I, the female, stand.

3

It is done! I, the little one, stand.

4

It is done! In the midst of day we stand.

The fifth song dwells upon the continued approach of the buffalo to the world that is sensible to the sight as well as to the touch.

The music and the words of the song denote happiness and faith that the buffalo will come into the world, not once, but for all time. The final stanza sings of that day. A word, on'-ba, is here used in two senses, namely, the light of day into which all things come and live, and the attainment or the accomplishment of a desired end. The bringing of the buffalo from the world of mystery into the material world was for a definite purpose, and when that purpose was accomplished the object stood in the light of day, as a thing completed.

All of the lines of the first stanza are translated and one line from each of the other three stanzas.

Song 5

1

Along the borders of the earth ye move,
Amidst the visible forms the male will come,

The male will come,
Amidst the visible forms the male will come.

2

Amidst the visible forms the female will come.

3

Amidst the visible forms the little one will come.

4

Amidst the visible forms, in the light of day they will come.

The next two songs, the sixth and seventh, bear the subtitle Wa-dsu'-ta Gi-bon Wa-thon, Songs of Calling the Animals.

In many of the Siouan tribes there are rites by which the people call the buffalo to come to their aid in the struggle to maintain life. From the words of the ritual songs of this character, a stranger who is not familiar with the Indian ceremonial mode of thought and expression would fall into the belief that the supplications for aid were addressed to the animal itself, but a closer, thoughtful study would lead him to the understanding that the call for aid was made through the animal to the Mysterious Power that gave it life and form.

The ancient priests who composed these songs mention the buffalo in the sequential order of their creation as dictated to them by wa-thi'-gthon, or a carefully studied reasoning, namely, the male first, the female next, and lastly the little one. While by the final stanza they call the three in their triple relationship to come into the light of day, the call is, in reality, a song of adoration of the power that made the light of day for the benefit of all living creatures.

Song 6

1

O ye with new-grown hair, new-grown hair, come,
My grandfathers, come ye, come ye,
Come ye hither, come;
Come ye with the males, come ye;
My grandfathers, come ye hither, come ye;
Come ye hither, come.

2

Come ye with the females, come ye.

3

Come ye with the little one, come ye.

4

Come ye with the day, come ye.

In the seventh song the ancient priests continue to call to the buffalo, the valued gift coming from Wa-kon-da, the Giver of Life. Those men of the ancient days gave to this song words that are undisguised and can be understood by any person having a knowledge of the language. The music has a mysterious tone which, to them, was one of reverence and of adoration.

Song 7

1

Come ye hither, Come ye hither;
Come ye! Come ye!
Where I may see thee, ye of the males,
Come ye hither! Come ye hither!
Come ye! Come ye!

2

Where I may see thee, ye of the females.

3

Where I may see thee, ye of the little ones.

4

Where I may see thee, here in the light of day!

In songs 1 to 7 of this group, the ancient priests have attempted to give expression, in music and words, to their belief in the coming of the buffalo from the unseen to the visible, material world, not of its own accord but out of and guided by a divine creative mind.

This belief concerning the source of the life, not only of the buffalo but of life in all its forms, fixed itself firmly upon the minds of the Osage men of the ancient days after they had spent years of studious thought upon the activities of nature, upon the great cosmic bodies and particularly upon those of the earth and the sun. The buffalo was an animal of widespread usefulness. It gave to the Indians of the plains food, clothing, and shelter. It was given prominence in the myths, rituals, sacred songs, tribal ceremonials, and the clan organizations. In the tribal hunting of the buffalo the herd was approached with solemn rites, always with recognition of the Great Creative Power that brought this sacred animal to man.

The theme of the eighth song is the actual arrival of the buffalo to the visible world, into the light of day. The song is in the form of a little drama. The first stanza dwells upon the shooting of the buffalo by man; the second, upon the death of the animal; in the third, the man is joined by another who is asked to assist and to hold steady the hind leg as the first man performs the task of cutting up the flesh; in the fourth, he is asked to hold steady the head; in the fifth, he is asked to hold the foreleg. A translation of one line only from each stanza will suffice to give the meaning.

Song 8

1

My grandfather I have shot, I have shot.

2

My grandfather I have killed, I have killed.

3

Hold for me his leg, hold for me his leg.

4

Hold for me his head, hold for me his head.

5

Hold for me his arm, hold for me his arm.

The ninth song of this group is the first of the Songs of the Corn. It is thought that the priests represent the people as speaking in this song, each for himself or herself, the men who guard the village and the women who work in the fields.

The words and the music of the song express joy at the awakening of the earth from its long winter sleep; the smoke arising from the fields where the women are preparing the soil for planting; the sight of the long rows of little hills within which are to be put the precious seeds from which the people hope for a rich harvest; the sight of the young stalks as they spread their blades in the winds and take their place amid other living forms; the sight of the bright light of day that touches every form of life and urges each onward toward maturity.

Amid all this awakening, this activity of life, the old priests perceived a first token of the presence of the Divine Creative Power, a presence that is indicated by some visible mark, like footprints upon the earth's surface.

Only the lines of the first stanza are translated and the last two lines from each of the other three stanzas.

Song 9

1

Amid the earth, renewed in verdure,
Amid rising smoke, my grandfather's footprints
I see, as from place to place I wander,

The rising smoke I see as I wander.
Amid all forms visible, the rising smoke
I see, as I move from place to place.

2

Amid all forms visible, the little hills in rows
I see, as I move from place to place.

3

Amid all forms visible, the spreading blades
I see, as I move from place to place.

4

Amid all forms visible, the light of day
I see, as I move from place to place.

The tenth song of this group is expressive of a feeling of reverence for woman, a feeling akin to that of adoration, for it is she upon whom nature has imposed the sacred duty of motherhood.

In this song the priests have represented the woman as speaking of her task of planting, cultivating, and harvesting the corn for food for her children. This plant must bear the fruit which the children must eat that they may live, and the woman has learned that the plant will require as much care from her as the little ones in order to bring it to maturity and fruition.

Stanzas 1 to 5 are descriptive of the work of preparing the soil to receive the seeds to be planted. Stanzas 6 to 8 refer to the sacred act of the woman and to the seeds she must plant in the seven consecrated hills. Stanzas 9 to 17 tell of the successive stages of the growth and fruition of the plant. Stanzas 18 to 20 speak of the harvesting that brings joy in the woman's house and to the day that marks the fulfillment of her duty. A translation of one line from each stanza will give the meaning of the song.

### Song 10

1

Footprints I make! Smoke arises from their midst (burning of the old stalks).

2

Footprints I make! The soil lies mellowed.

3

Footprints I make! The little hills stand in rows.

4

Footprints I make! Lo, the little hills have turned gray.

5

Footprints I make! Lo, the hills are in the light of day.

6

Footprints I make! Lo, I come to the sacred act.

7

Footprints I make! Give me one (grain), two, three, four.

8

Footprints I make! Give me five, six, the final number.

9

Footprints I make! Lo, the tender stalk breaks the soil.

10

Footprints I make! Lo, the stalk stands amidst the day.

11

Footprints I make! Lo, the blades spread in the winds.

12

Footprints I make! Lo, the stalks stand firm and upright.

13

Footprints I make! Lo, the blades away in the winds.

14

Footprints I make! Lo, the stalk stands jointed.

15

Footprints I make! Lo, the plant has blossomed.

16

Footprints I make! Lo, the blades sigh in the wind.

17

Footprints I make! Lo, the ears branch from the stalk.

18

Footprints I make! Lo, I pluck the ears.

19

Footprints I make! Lo, there is joy in my house.

20

Footprints I make! Lo, the day of fulfillment.

In the eleventh song the priests represent the woman as being in a thoughtful mood upon the arrival of the season when the seeds she had planted amidst her footprints should have grown to maturity and fruition. As she plans to visit the field, her thoughts run back to the time when she finished making the little hills in which to plant the seeds of the corn. She follows again, in memory, the plant in its various stages of growth, from the time it pushed upward through the soil and spread its leaves in the sun to the time when the stalk strengthened and stood with broad leaves swaying in the four winds; to the time when it stood in full maturity, crowned with yellow blossoms. She pictures in her mind the ripening ears reaching out like arms from the stalks, and she fancies herself standing in the clear day of reality, the day of the fulfillment of her motherly duty. All the lines of the first stanza are translated and one line from each of the other stanzas.

Song 11

1

I shall go to see, I shall go to see,
The footprints I have made, I shall go to see,
I shall go to see, I shall go to see,
The hills standing in rows, I shall go to see,
I shall go to see, I shall go to see.

2

The stalks with outspreading leaves, I shall go to see.

3

The stalks standing upright, I shall go to see.

4

The leaves swaying in the wind, I shall go to see.

5

The yellow blossoms, I shall go to see.

6

The overhanging ears, I shall go to see.

7

The final day of my task, I shall see.

In the twelfth song, the woman, the tiller of the soil, is represented as hastening to the field with light footsteps. As she enters the field she stands with exultant pride amidst the rustling leaves of the fruit-laden stalks crowned with yellow blossoms. She gathers some of the fruit for the evening meal. When she finds red, blue, or speckled ears she keeps them separate for the little ones and anticipates the joy of hearing their cries of delight when they see the corn. With a heavy load, but a light heart, she hastens homeward, enters her house, and meets the demonstrations of joy in the "Welcome home." To the mother it is a day of contentment. One line is translated from each stanza of this song. The music is the same as that which accompanies the tenth song.

### Song 12

#### 1

Footprints I make! I go to the field with eager haste.

#### 2

Footprints I make! Amid rustling leaves I stand.

#### 3

Footprints I make! Amid yellow blossoms I stand.

#### 4

Footprints I make! I stand with exultant pride.

#### 5

Footprints I make! I hasten homeward with a burden of gladness.

#### 6

Footprints I make! There's joy and gladness in my home.

#### 7

Footprints I make! I stand amidst a day of contentment!

At the close of this song, when Saucy Calf presides as master of ceremonies, he speaks to the priests in a voice that all can hear: "Ha! priests, this closes the Buffalo Songs. I have now come to the "Six Songs." Henceforth, many of the songs will be accompanied with ceremonial forms and acts. Therefore, you will give us all your attention."

The Buffalo Songs, just given, close the first part of the ritual known to the priests as the "Seven Songs."

## THE SIX SONGS [139]

[With only a brief announcement, the six songs part of the ceremony begins immediately after completion of the seven songs.][140]

Wa-thon Sha-pe Tse, the Six Songs, is the title of that part of the tribal war rite that belongs to the Sky People. The origin of this second part of the tribal war rite is accredited jointly to the Men of Mystery clan and the Buffalo Bull clan.

The mythical story of the origin of this part of the tribal war rite, briefly told, is as follows:

The first war organization of the tribe was composed of four tribal divisions, bearing the names: the Black Bear,[141] the Water, the Sky, and the Isolated Earth. The war emblems of these four divisions were four golden eagles, varying in plumage according to the different stages of the bird's maturity. For purposes of initiation into the mysteries of this organization, the priests formulated a ritual which they called "Wa-thon Pe-thon-ba Tse," The Seven Songs. The rites by which this organization was governed permitted but one kind of ceremonially organized war party, which bore the [name] Do-don'-hin ton-ga, Great War Party. Consequently, one division could not act independently of the other three and muster warriors to go on the warpath, since all of the four divisions must act as one body in order to make a war movement authoritative. This arrangement served, in a way, the military activities of the people, but because of its intricate ceremonials that took several days to perform during the assembling of the warriors it lacked mobility and so did not admit of prompt action in an emergency.

After a long period of varied experiences, the priests at last determined not to upset the old organization but to supply its defect by formulating a supplementary rite which permitted: (1) the assembling of a war party composed of the warriors from the clans of one of the two great tribal divisions; (2) a war party made up of two or more of the clans of one of the two great divisions; (3) a war party organized by one clan that belonged to only one of either of the two great divisions. These three classes of war parties could be organized, under the new arrangement, independently of the four divisions and regardless of ceremonies. These classes of war party were called Tsi'-ga-xa Do-don, which probably means war party organized outside of the House of Mystery.

In formulating this supplementary rite, the priests, in order to give their action a mystic effect, resorted to a mythical story in which the Men of Mystery and the Buffalo Bull clans figured prominently as the givers of a hawk as a war emblem to each of the Seven Fireplaces (clans) of the Land People; to each of the Seven Fireplaces (clans) of the Water People; and to each of the Seven Fireplaces (clans) of the Sky People. These hawks were called Wa-xo'-be Zhin-ga, Little Bundles, and symbolized the courage of the warrior. There seems to be no tradition as to whether the four eagles above mentioned were enshrined or not, but if they were, they appear to have been supplanted by the sacred hawks that were enshrined (figuratively) in the space between the arch of the sky and the earth beneath, [both of] which are symbolically represented by the woven rush case within which lies the hawk.

The hawk symbols were used in two ways: (1) when a war party is about to attack the enemy, the commander of a group is ceremonially given the hawk belonging to his clan to carry so that his men may charge upon the enemy as swiftly and as courageously as the hawk that falls upon its prey; (2) at an initiation by a clan of one of its members into the mysteries of the tribal war rites, the hawk occupies a sacred place and becomes the central figure in the initiatory ceremonies. To the Men of Mystery clan was given the office of reconsecrating the symbolic hawk at an initiation, an office that ranks high in honor. To the Buffalo Bull clan, the companion clan of the Men of Mystery, was given the office of awarding to the warriors the prescribed military honors won by them, honors which are termed o-don', acts for which one is honored. To this supplementary rite the priest gave the title Wa-thon Sha-pe Tse, The Six Songs, and dedicated it to the clans of the Sky People.[142]

[The Buffalo Bull clan's version of the six songs, as used in their Songs of the Wa-xo'-be initiation rite, was divided into fifteen song groups. In these groups there were thirty-nine songs (some of which Saucy Calf could not remember), three wi'-gi-e (the Charcoal Wi'-gi-e, the Penalties Wi'-gi-e, and the War Standard Wi'-gi-e, which Saucy Calf could not relate because it belonged to the Deer clan), and three dramatic acts ("Striking the Earth," "Striking the Scalp," and "Shooting the Sacred Bow").

The Buffalo Bull clan version starts with a set of Buffalo Songs, a continuation of the Buffalo Songs that were the last song group in the seven songs. These songs are concerned with life, not war. The theme of the songs changes abruptly with the second song group, the Deer Songs, which are about the courage of the warriors. From the second song group on, the thematic structure parallels that found in the seven songs. In a highly fragmented way, these song groups tell of the warriors preparing for war, going to find the enemy, defeating them, and returning victorious. As in the seven songs, the full story is not presented, but rather discontinuous pieces of relevant knowledge. The only information presented was that which "belonged" to the Buffalo Bull clan.

Even though the picture is fragmentary, there is a clear difference between these songs and the seven songs. In the seven songs, the Sacred Warrior and the eight commanders were the focus of attention; here the primary emphasis is on the individual warrior. Of particular concern in the Buffalo Bull clan version is the responsibility of the warrior. When a man joins a war party, he in effect takes a vow to follow through to victory. The joining of a war party imposes on the warrior the same obligations that a man incurs when he becomes a candidate for the priesthood. This obligation becomes clear in song group 10, the Great Rain Songs, which includes a Penalties Wi'-gi-e.

Although the warriors are the main focus of the six songs, some of the song groups are concerned with the Sacred Warrior and the eight commanders, as well as with rituals used by tribal war parties. Why these songs are included here and not with the seven songs is unclear.—Ed.]

### 1. Buffalo Songs[143]

The Six Songs, as given by Saucy Calf, begins with four buffalo songs, bearing the common title Tse-do'-a Ni'-ka I-non-zhin Wa-thon: Tse-do'-a, Buffalo; Ni'-ka, Men; I-non-zhin, Stand-by; Wa-thon; freely translated, Songs of the Buffalo, the Stand-by of Men.

The two groups of buffalo songs, the one which closes the Seven Songs, and the other which opens the Six Songs, are regarded as one group and as supplicatory in character. They relate to the buffalo, a food animal, and to the corn, a food plant. Both of these forms of life are held sacred because they are believed to be direct gifts to the people from the Mysterious Power, whence comes life in all its multifarious forms, the ability to move, to reproduce its kind, in order that each one may bear its particular part in the great drama of life.

The priests who arranged the songs and the wi'gi-es to be used in the tribal rites as expressions of the desire for divine aid did not employ terms that could be taken as direct appeals to the Mysterious Power, but cryptic forms were used, the real meaning of which could be understood only by the initiated. For instance, the ancient men did not say in these songs and wi'-gi-es: "O Wa-kon-da, give us continually the buffalo in order that we may live," nor did they ask, "Wa-kon-da, give us ever the harvests of corn that we may continue to have food." These supplications are implied by the language used in the songs and wi'-gi-es as well as by the general acceptance of the tribal rites as expressive of appeals for divine aid.

The buffalo and corn songs in their entirety belong to the Buffalo Bull clan, who gave permission to each of the other clans to use a designated number in their versions of the tribal rites.[144]

At the singing of these songs, the Xo'-ka, the Assisting Xo'-ka, and the Singer rise and stand throughout the singing. The theme of these songs tells of the coming of the buffalo from the unseen to the visible world in order to give support to the lives of men.

The third and fourth lines of each stanza of the song are translated.

Song 1

1

Lo, my grandfathers rise and stand,
They of the shaggy mane, rise and stand.

2

Lo, my grandfathers rise and stand,
They of the curved horns, rise and stand.

3

Lo, my grandfathers rise and stand,
They of the humped shoulders, rise and stand.

4

Lo, my grandfathers rise and stand,
They whose tails curl backward in anger, rise and stand.

5

Lo, my grandfathers rise and stand,
They, the four-legged ones, rise and stand.

6

Lo, my grandfathers rise and stand,
They who paw the earth in anger, rise and stand.

In the second song of this group the buffalo are represented as advancing from the unseen to the visible world. The third and fourth lines of each stanza are translated.

Song 2

1

Lo, my grandfathers are advancing,
They of the shaggy mane, are advancing.

2

Lo, my grandfathers are advancing,
They of the curved horns, are advancing.

3

Lo, my grandfathers are advancing,
They of the humped shoulders, are advancing.

4

Lo, my grandfathers are advancing,
They whose tails curl in anger, are advancing.

5

Lo, my grandfathers are advancing,
They, the four-legged ones, are advancing.

6

Lo, my grandfathers are advancing,
They who paw the earth in anger, are advancing.

The third song represents the buffalo as rising with cheerful quickness, to move to the visible world. Two lines from each stanza are translated.

Song 3

1

Look you, my grandfathers rise,
They of the shaggy manes, rise quickly.

2

Look you, my grandfathers rise,
They of the curved horns, rise quickly.

3

Look you, my grandfathers rise
They of the humped shoulders, rise quickly.

4

Look you, my grandfathers rise,
They whose tails curl in anger, rise quickly.

5

Look you, my grandfathers rise,
They, the four-legged ones, rise quickly.

6

Look you, my grandfathers rise,
They who paw the earth in anger, rise quickly.

In the fourth song the rising of the buffalo is again referred to. They are represented as approaching from every corner of the earth, the west, east, south, and north. The song is an expression of joy at the coming of the animals so useful to the life of men.[145]

Song 4

1

Look you, my grandfathers rise to come,
They rise and come from the land of the west.

2

Look you, my grandfathers rise to come,
They rise and come from the land of the east.

3

Look you, my grandfathers rise and come,
They rise and come from the land of the south.

4

Look you, my grandfathers rise and come,
They rise and come from the land of the north.

## 2. The Deer Songs[146]

The song next in order is the Ta Wa-thon, Deer Song. Saucy Calf sang but one deer song, although in the list of songs permanently fixed by the priests he gives the number as four. Hin-ci'-mon-in, also a Buffalo Bull priest, gives three in his list.[147] The name of the deer appears in the song only in the title.

This song refers to the choice of the deer as one of the seven animals chosen for use in the tribal war rites as symbols of courage. The deer, having no gall, is not a courageous animal, yet it so happens some-times that when hotly pursued by the hunter he will run into the village amidst the houses and excape harm as though by some super-natural influence. It was because of its fleetness that the old priests gave the deer a prominent place in the war rite. Two lines of the first stanza and one of each of the other stanzas are translated.

1

O where shall I run? where shall I run?
O ho, amidst these houses I shall run.

2

O ho, I run along the rear of the houses.

3

O ho, amid the light of day I run in safety.

## 3. Black Bear Songs[148]

The next group of songs is called Wa-ca'-be Wa-thon, Black Bear Songs. These songs refer to the close of the great war ceremony that takes place in the House of Mysteries, after which the warriors march toward the country of the enemy. While the office of setting up the House of Myste-ries was specifically conferred upon the Black Bear clan, it was under-stood that the Puma, a kindred clan, was included in the appointment.

The black bear and the puma are both symbols of the fire that knows no mercy when once it takes a destructive course. The sign of this ruthless quality is charcoal made from the redbud tree, which was consecrated for the purpose. The warriors, when about to attack the enemy, blacken their faces with the sacred charcoal, and he who ne-glects to put upon his face this sign is ignored when honors are con-ferred upon the men who had performed the prescribed acts of valor.

In each stanza of the two songs here given, an archaic term is used which could not be translated or analyzed by any of the men who gave the tribal rituals. Saucy Calf expressed the belief that the archaic term "wa'-ca-ki-the" refers to a person or a group of persons appointed to perform certain mystic acts by which success may be brought about in a tribal enterprise. The term is also frequently used in the penalty wi'-gi-es, wherein certain birds, animals, and insects are appealed to, to punish, by supernatural means, any person who may violate his initiatory obligations.

Two lines from each stanza of this song are translated.

Song 1

1

You have closed the mystic rites, O Wa'-ca-ki-the,
You have closed the rites, O Great Black Bear.

2

You have closed the mystic rites, O Wa'-ca-ki-the,
You have closed the rites, O Great Puma.

The second song of this group refers again to the closing of the final mystic rites performed by the priests within the House of Mysteries set up by the Black Bear and the Puma clans. The closing of the rites is a signal to the warriors that they are to hold themselves in readiness to march against the enemy. The warriors with their weapons are figuratively assembled in the House of Mysteries.

A translation of three lines from each stanza will suffice to give the meaning of the song.

Song 2

1

Thou hast closed the mystic rites, O Wa'-ca-ki-the,
Wheresoever thou goest, there I shall go.
Thou hast closed the mystic rites, O Great Black Bear.

2

Thou hast closed the mystic rites, O Wa'-ca-ki-the,
Wheresoever thou goest, there shall I go.
Thou hast closed the mystic rites, O Great Puma.

*4. Songs of the Rush for Charcoal*[149]

The next group of songs is called Non-xthe' I-kin-dse Wa-thon, Songs of the Rush for Charcoal. It is an epitome of the Fire Ritual that belongs to the great war ceremony which is performed when the two tribal divisions organize a war party to go against a common enemy. In preparing for the ceremonies that pertain to this ritual, two great fires [one for the Earth People and one for the Sky People] are built in the morning while it is yet dark.

When the two sacred fires are kindled and are burning, the warriors gather around their (respective) fires, stripped of nearly all clothing [except for the loin cloth and moccasins], and wait for the fray. The officer belonging to the Earth People side stands by the fire holding in his hand one of the [war] standards, while the officer on the Sky People side stands before his fire also holding in his hand one of the standards. Both officers begin at the same time to recite the fire wi'-gi-e, each using his own version.

[The young warriors then begin grabbing burning limbs from the fire.] From the burning brand snatched out of the symbolic fire, the warrior scrapes off the charcoal and puts it into a small deerskin pouch which he carries upon some part of his clothing as he marches against the enemy. When the foe is discovered and an attack is to be made, the warrior paints his face with this charcoal, an act by which he expresses his determination to show no mercy to the enemy and to expect none toward himself.[150]

Saucy Calf gave only four songs belonging to this rite, including the charcoal wi'-gi-e, although in his formal list of the ritual songs he gave the number as 10.

The black bear, the male puma, and the golden eagle are mentioned in the charcoal wi'-gi-e as the animals who gave to the "little ones" the sacred symbolic color (black) to use in their war rites. While these animals and the color of the charcoal are brought into prominence in the ritual, they are solely as the color emblem of a mysterious force—fire. This force, fire, has a dual character; it is a destructive power, and it is a beneficial power. When the warrior blackens his face with the symbolic charcoal as he is about to attack the enemy, the color (black) symbolizes the destructive character of fire. To that characteristic of fire the appeal is made. The act of putting the black on the face is equivalent to the warrior taking a vow to show no mercy to his enemy.

The Charcoal Wi'-gi-e[151]

1 What shall the little ones use as charcoal? they said to one another, it has been said, in this house.

2 Then arose the male black bear with a stubby tail, and spake,

3 Saying: I am a person who is fit to be used as charcoal for blackening the face.

4 When the little ones make of me their charcoal,
5 Black indeed shall be the charcoal they use in their life's journey.
6 The color of the tip of my nose, which is black,
7 Is fit for the little ones to use for blackening their faces.
8 When they use this to blacken their faces,
9 Black indeed shall be the charcoal they use in their life's journey.
10 When they go against the enemy who dwell toward the setting sun
11 And use the color as a symbol of their supplications for divine aid,
12 Their prayers shall always be readily granted, in their life's journey.
13 Then shall they always succeed in making the foe to fall.
14 The color of the edges of my mouth, which is black,
15 Is also for use as a symbolic color.
16 When the little ones make use of this as a sacred color,
17 Black indeed shall be the charcoal they use to blacken their faces.
18 When they go toward the setting sun, against their enemies,
19 And use this color as a symbol of their supplications for divine aid,
20 Their prayer shall always be readily granted.
21 Then shall they always succeed in making the foe to fall.
22 The color of the tips of my ears
23 Is also fit for the use as a sacred color.
24 When the little ones use it as a sacred color,
25 Black indeed shall be the charcoal they use to blacken their faces.
26 When they go toward the setting sun, against their enemies,
27 They shall use the color as a sign of the supplication for aid.
28 Then shall they never fail to make fall the foe, as they travel the path of life.
29 The color of the hair along the ridge of my back, which is black,
30 Is also fit for use as a symbolic color.
31 When the little ones use it as a sacred color,
32 Black indeed shall be the charcoal they use to blacken their faces.
33 When they go toward the setting sun, against their enemies,
34 They shall use the color as a sign of their supplication for aid.
35 Then shall they never fail to make fall the foe.
36 The color of the tip of my tail, which is black,
37 Is also fit for use as a symbolic color.
38 When the little ones use it as a sacred color,
39 Black indeed shall be the charcoal they use to blacken their faces.
40 When the little ones use it as a sacred color,
41 As they go toward the setting sun, against their enemies,
42 They shall use it as a sign of their supplication for divine aid.
43 Then shall they never fail to make fall the foe,
44 The color of my toes, which is black,
45 Is also fit for use as a symbolic color.
46 When the little ones use it as a sacred color,
47 Black indeed shall be the charcoal they use to blacken their faces.

48 When they go toward the setting sun, against their enemies,
49 They shall use the color as a sign of their supplication for aid.
50 Then shall they never fail to make fall the foe.
51 What shall they use as charcoal? they said to one another, it has been said, in this house.
52 Then the male puma spake,
53 Saying: I also am a person fit to be used as charcoal for blackening the face.
54 When the little ones make of me their charcoal,
55 Black indeed shall be the charcoal they use in their life's journey.
56 The color of the tip of my nose, which is black,
57 Is fit for the little ones to use for blackening their faces.
58 When they use this for blackening their faces,
59 Black indeed shall be the charcoal they use to blacken their faces.
60 The color of the edge of my mouth, which is black,
61 The little ones shall use as a symbolic color.
62 When the little ones use this as a sacred color,
63 Black indeed shall be the charcoal they use to blacken their faces.
64 What shall they use as charcoal? they said to one another, it has been said, in this house.
65 Then spake the eagle, the faultless in plumage,
66 Saying: I am a person who is fit for use as charcoal.
67 The color of my beak, which is black,
68 They shall also use as a sacred color.
69 I am a person who is ever under the watchful care of Wa-kon-da.
70 May some of the little ones also
71 Come under the watchful care of Wa-kon-da.
72 When they make of me their sacred charcoal,
73 As they go toward the setting sun, against their enemies,
74 They shall never fail to make the foe to lie low.
75 The color of the feathers on the crown of my head, which is black,
76 Shall be as charcoal to the little ones a symbolic color.
77 When the little ones make of me their charcoal,
78 Black indeed shall be the charcoal they use to blacken their faces.
79 When they go toward the setting sun, against their enemies,
80 They shall use it as a sign of their supplication for aid.
81 Then shall they easily make fall their foe, in their life's journey.
82 The black tip of my tail
83 Shall also be as charcoal to them.
84 When they make of it their charcoal, a symbolic color,
85 Black indeed shall be the charcoal they use to blacken their faces.
86 When they go toward the setting sun against their enemies
87 They shall use this color as a sign of their supplication for aid.
88 Then shall they easily make the foe to fall, in their life's journey.
89 The color of my feet, which is black,

90 Shall also be to them as charcoal, a symbolic color.
91 When the little ones make of it a sacred color,
92 Black indeed shall be the charcoal they use to blacken their faces.
93 When they go toward the setting sun, against their enemies,
94 They shall use it as a sign of their supplication for aid.
95 Then shall it be easy for them to make the foe to lie low, as they travel the path of life.

The three songs of this group relate to the hereditary office of the men of certain clans to assemble the various symbolic articles to be used in the fire ceremony and the reciting of the rituals pertaining thereto.

These articles are feathers from the immature golden eagle to be used in the making of the dark [war] standards; feathers of the mature eagle to be used in making the white [war] standards. Eight standards are made, four for the commanders chosen from the Sky People and four for the commanders chosen from the Earth People; the eight standards: the deerskins which are to be attached to the lower part of each of the standards; the sacred wood (redbud) to be burned to make the symbolic charcoal to be used by the warriors on the successful day hoped for. A translation of two lines from the first stanza and one line from each of the other stanzas of the song is given.

Song 1

1

Let the men gather here to sing, I say!
I say! I say! I say!

2

They who have the sacred bird, I say!

3

They who have the mystic standards, I say!

4

They who have the golden eagle, I say!

5

They who have the deerskins, I say!

6

They who have the mystic fires, I say!

7

They who have the mystic charcoal, I say!

8

They who have the day of success, I say!

After a short pause, the Assisting Xo'-ka sings the second song, when the Xo'-ka rises and dances to the music.

Lines 1 and 2 of the first stanza and 1, 2, and 3 of the other stanzas are translated.

### Song 2

#### 1

The men here gathered shall sing, they alone,
They alone, e he the he the,

#### 2

The men here gathered shall sing, they alone,
They alone, e he the he the,
They who have the sacred bird shall sing.

#### 3

The men here gathered shall sing, they alone,
They alone, e he the he the,
They who have the standards shall sing.

#### 4

The men here gathered shall sing, they alone,
They alone, e he the he the,
They who have the white eagle shall sing.

#### 5

The men here gathered shall sing, they alone,
They alone, e he the he the,
They who have the deerskins shall sing.

#### 6

The men here gathered shall sing, they alone,
They alone, e he the he the,
They who have the mystic fire shall sing.

#### 7

The men here gathered shall sing, they alone,
They alone, e he the he the,
They who have the mystic charcoal shall sing.

#### 8

The men here gathered shall sing, they alone,
They alone, e he the he the,
They who have the day of success shall sing.

As the second song is coming to a close, the Sho'-ka places in the hands of the Xo'-ka a [war] standard made for this ceremony. The

Assisting Xo'-ka goes to the third song without pause while the Xo'-ka continues to dance, holding aloft the standard. The chorus sings louder, the rattles are beaten faster, and the Assisting Xo'-ka calls to the Xo'-ka: "Dance, young man! You may never have another chance to dance before these people!"

At the end of the last stanza in this ceremony the Xo'-ka, with a dramatic motion, tosses the standard toward the Deer clan of the Water people as he cries out: "Oh! Deer's lung of the Water, what doest thou! look upon this, an emblem of thy making!" Whereupon the member of that clan who had made the standard picks it up, takes it to his seat and then recites the wi'-gi-e relating to the emblem [not recorded].[152]

Song 3

1

They alone, they alone, hi hi-i,
The men here gathered shall stand alone.

2

They alone, they alone, hi hi-i,
They who have the sacred bird shall stand alone.

3

They alone, they alone, hi hi-i
They who have the standards shall stand alone.

4

They alone, they alone, hi hi-i
They who have the white eagle shall stand alone.

5

They alone, they alone, hi hi-i
They who have the deerskins shall stand alone.

6

They alone, they alone, hi hi-i
They who have the mystic fires shall stand alone.

7

They alone, they alone, hi hi-i
They who have the mystic charcoal shall stand alone.

8

They alone, they alone, hi hi-i
They who have the day of success shall stand alone.

## 5. Songs of the Waters[153]

The next group of songs is the Ni'dsi Wa-thon, Songs of the Waters. When a war party comes to a stream that looks dangerous, these songs are sung as supplication to Wa-kon-da for permission to cross safely and without harm. Certain water animals are also appealed to for strength and courage, for Wa-kon-da had given to them a power not given to man, that of successfully overcoming the dangers of angry waters. These animals are: (1) the wingless, or finless one. No definite information could be obtained as to what fish is meant, but Saucy Calf believed it to be the eel; (2) the sacred beaver. This animal is at home in both land and water and is a powerful swimmer; (3) the great otter, whose home is in the water and on the land and is known to be one of the strongest swimmers; and (4) the great turtle, who is another swimmer who is never afraid of dangerous water.

Three land animals are also appealed to because they are known to be great and courageous swimmers. When crossing a river too deep to be waded, the warriors make little boats [so-called bull-boats] of the skins of these animals, into which they put their sacred hawk bundles and clothing and tow them as they swim across. These animals are: (1) The great black bear, who is mysterious in its habits; (2) the great puma, possessed of great courage; (3) the sacred gray wolf, an animal always tireless and alert.

Three lines of each stanza of this song are translated.

### Song 1

#### 1

Wa-kon-da, thou holy one, permit us to cross this water,
Permit us to cross, permit us to cross,
Thou wingless one, thou who art our grandfather.

#### 2

Wa-kon-da, thou holy one, permit us to cross this water,
Permit us to cross, permit us to cross,
Thou Sacred Beaver, thou who art our grandfather.

#### 3

Wa-kon-da, thou holy one, permit us to cross this water,
Permit us to cross, permit us to cross,
Thou Great Otter, thou who art our grandfather.

#### 4

Wa-kon-da, thou holy one, permit us to cross this water,

Permit us to cross, permit us to cross.
Thou Great Black One, thou who art our grandfather.

### 5

Wa-kon-da, thou holy one, permit us to cross this water,
Permit us to cross, permit us to cross,
Thou Great Puma, thou who art our grandfather.

### 6

Wa-kon-da, thou holy one, permit us to cross this water,
Permit us to cross, permit us to cross,
Thou Great Wolf, thou who art our grandfather.

### 7

Wa-kon-da, thou holy one, permit us to cross this water,
Permit us to cross, permit us to cross,
Thou Great Turtle, thou who art our grandfather.

In the second song the warriors address the animals mentioned in the first song, calling upon them for aid in crossing the angry waters. Four lines of the first stanza and two lines of the other stanzas of this song are translated.

### Song 2

### 1

O grandfather, here I stand at the water's edge,
Thou Finless One,
Lo, at the water's edge I stand,
Look you, look you.

### 2

Thou Sacred Beaver,
Lo, at the water's edge I stand.

### 3

Thou Great Otter,
Lo, at the water's edge I stand.

### 4

Thou Great Black One,
Lo, at the water's edge I stand.

### 5

Thou Great Puma,
Lo, at the water's edge I stand.

### 6

Thou Sacred Wolf,
Lo, at the water's edge I stand.

7

Thou Great Turtle,
Lo, at the water's edge I stand.

The third of the water songs speaks in definite terms of the dwelling place that is in a great lake of the land and water animals appealed to for aid.

The idea that land animals as well as water animals dwell in great bodies of water is common among some of the Siouan tribes.

### Song 3

1

Here he shall appear, he shall appear,
Out of the great lake the Finless One shall come.

2

Here he shall appear, he shall appear,
Out of the lake the Sacred Bear shall come.

3

Here he shall appear, he shall appear,
Out of the lake the Great Otter shall come.

4

Here he shall appear, he shall appear,
Out of the lake the Great Black One shall come.

5

Here he shall appear, he shall appear,
Out of the lake the Great Puma shall come.

6

Here he shall appear, he shall appear,
Out of the great lake the Sacred Wolf shall come.

7

Here he shall appear, he shall appear,
Out of the lake the Great Turtle shall come.

### 6. Songs of the Stars[154]

The group following the Songs of the Waters is the Wa'-tse Wa-thon, Songs of the Stars. The two songs here given belong to the Buffalo Bull clan, and both songs refer to the morning star. A translation of one line of the [only?] stanza will be sufficient to give the meaning.

### Song 1

Lo, the star again appears, yonder he stands.

The second song has only one stanza. A translation of one line will suffice to give the meaning of the song.

Song 2

Lo, the star! Yonder he stands with throbbing brilliancy.

### 7. The Great Evening Songs[155]

The next group of songs is the Pa'-ce-don Wa-thon Ton-ga, the Great Evening Songs.

The words of the Great Evening Songs are clear but are obscure as to what part of the tribal rite they refer. Saucy Calf passed them without any remarks. Both songs perhaps refer to the Night People or to some rite of the people of the Night clan, the sixth of the Sky clans, and to the people of all the clans who have put symbolic marks upon their foreheads and bodies. The night is regarded by the Osage as one of the greatest of the mystic cosmic powers. Only lines 1 and 5 of the stanzas of this song are translated.

Song 1

1

To the people of the night I am going,
To the people whose foreheads bear a mystic mark.

2

To the people of the night I am going,
To the people on whose bodies there are mystic marks.

Lines 1 and 4 of the stanzas of the second song are translated.

Song 2

1

There are peoples of the night, you have said.
Peoples whose foreheads bear a mystic mark.

2

There are peoples of the night, you have said,
Peoples on whose bodies there are mystic marks.

### 8. The Little Evening Songs[156]

The next group of songs is the Pa'-ce-don Wa-thon Zhin-ga, Little Evening Songs, or Wa-po'-ga Wa-thon, Songs of the Gray Owl. In each of the three songs of the Little Evening Songs, the Sacred Warrior of a war party is represented as speaking. This officer, who acts as mediator between his warriors and the Mysterious Power that governs all things, travels apart from his men throughout the day, and at night he stands alone, far away from the camp, to listen, in the gloom of evening, for the word of approval that might come through the medium of the gray owl, the horned owl, the gray wolf, or the peculiar sounds made by a snake. [It may be that the Morning Star Song and the Great Evening Song also refer to this nightly vigil of the Sacred Warrior.]

It is implied by the words of the first song of this group that the Sacred Warrior listens for the voices of the owls or the wolf or for the sounds made by the snake during his nightly vigil and accepts as a favorable answer to his supplications the first one of these he hears.

The first two lines of each stanza of this song are translated.

### Song 1

#### 1

Hark! I hear a voice in the evening gloom,
Lo! it is the gray owl who speaks in the dark of evening.

#### 2

Hark! I hear a voice in the evening gloom,
Lo! it is the horned owl who speaks in the dark of evening.

#### 3

Hark! I hear a voice in the evening gloom,
Lo! it is the gray wolf who speaks in the dark of evening.

#### 4

Hark! I hear a sound in the evening gloom,
Lo! it is the snake who moves in the dark of evening.

### Song 2

#### 1

Lo! from the dark of the evening I am bidden to go,
It is the gray owl who speaks, bidding me go.

#### 2

Lo! from the dark of the evening I am bidden to go,
It is the horned owl who speaks, bidding me go.

#### 3

Lo! from the dark of the evening I am bidden to go,
It is the gray wolf who speaks, bidding me go.

#### 4

Lo! from the dark of the evening I am bidden to go,
It is the snake who, from the gloom of night, signals me to go.

Three lines of the first stanza of the third song and two lines of each of the other stanzas are translated.

Song 3

1

Lo! a man speaks, telling me of my success,
'Tis the gray owl who speaks to me,
Amid night's gloom he gives to me the word.

2

'Tis the horned owl who speaks to me,
Amid night's gloom he gives to me the word.

3

'Tis the gray wolf who speaks to me,
Amid night's gloom he gives to me the word.

4

'Tis the snake who gives to me the signal,
Amid night's gloom he gives to me the sign.

## 9. The Snake Songs[157]

The next group of songs is called We'-ts'a Wa-thon, Snake Songs; literally, We'-ts'-a, he-who-kills; Wa-thon, songs. These songs refer to snakes that have a death-dealing power. The rattlesnake is referred to particularly. The name We'-ts'a is applied to the harmless as well as to the poisonous snakes. Two peculiarities of the poisonous snake are mentioned in these songs: its skill in secreting itself in the grass and the quickness with which it reveals itself and strikes. The first song refers to the rattlesnake, the second song to the other venomous snakes. The first and third lines of each stanza of the first song are translated.

Song 1

1

Look you! how quickly it reveals itself, reveals itself,
A rattle reveals itself.

2

Look you! how quickly they reveal themselves, reveal themselves
Four rattles quickly reveal themselves.

In the second song the venomous snake is represented as speaking of itself. The first and fourth lines of each stanza are translated.

Song 2

1

Lo, it is I, the mysterious one,
I am he who is invisible to all.

2

Lo! it is I, the mysterious one,
I, who makes them to lie low in death.

## 10. The Great Rain Songs[158]

Ni-zhiu' Wa-thon Ton-ga, the Great Rain Songs, is the title of the next group. As here given, this group is composed of two songs and a wi'-gi-e, which is first recited. The wi'-gi-e dwells upon the punishment meted out by supernatural means to a candidate who violates his initiatory vow. The swallow, the great dragonfly, and the great butterfly are mentioned as the mystic avengers. These three creatures of the air are appointed to guard the vows of a candidate and to impose the penalties when a candidate violates his vows and treats the "little ones" with contempt. These guardians of the penalties are ever at the back of the candidate, or hover around his head from the time he makes his vow, but the moment he violates his vow they let fall upon him the awarded penalty. A little pipe is used when calling upon these guardians to impose the penalty that follows the violation of the obligations.

All of these avengers are associated with the rain and thunder and travel amidst the winds that rush in advance of the approaching storms. They are spoken of as possessing a power of discernment from which no harmful act can be concealed.

Wi'-gi-e of the Penalties[159]

1 It has been said, in this house,
2 That an avenger of the little ones,
3 Amid the winds of the west,
4 My grandfather, the avenger, travels.
5 Even amidst the winds that rush before the storms,
6 He travels and moves
7 With a power of discernment from which no evil act can be concealed.
8 It is he who is chosen to guard with watchful care the penalties.
9 It is the swallow,
10 My grandfather, who travels amidst the winds,
11 Verily with a power from which no evil act can be concealed.
12 He stands ever at the back of the man who takes the vow,
13 Or ever hovers about his head.
14 Even as the man violates his vow and goes upon his life journey, unmindful of his broken vow,
15 The skin of his face shall become sallow and of sickly hue;
16 Blood shall gush from his nostrils with twirling motion,
17 Even as the man goes upon his journey, unmindful of his broken vow,

18 His spirit shall be suddenly taken from him, when demanded.
19 The avenger of the little ones
20 Shall forever stand.
21 Amidst the winds of the rising sun,
22 Amidst the rushing winds that lead the storms,
23 The great dragonfly,
24 My grandfather, moves and travels
25 With a power from which no evil act can be concealed.
26 He it is who is chosen to guard with watchful care the penalties.
27 As the man who violates his vow goes upon his life journey,
28 The dragonfly ever follows at his back,
29 Or ever hovers around his head,
30 Making the skin of his face to become sallow upon the breaking of his vow,
31 Making the blood to gush from his nostrils, when it is demanded.
32 Thus will he punish the man who breaks his vow, even to the taking of his spirit.
33 The avenger of the little ones
34 Shall forever stand.
35 Amidst the winds of the north,
36 The great butterfly,
37 My grandfather, moves and travels
38 With a power from which no evil act can be concealed.
39 He it is who was chosen to guard with watchful care the penalties.
40 He is ever at the back of the man who makes the vow,
41 He ever hovers around his head.
42 Upon the violation of the vow he makes the face of the candidate to become sallow,
43 Makes the blood to gush from his nostrils with a twirling motion,
44 He even takes from the man his spirit, when it is demanded.
45 The avenger of the little ones
46 Shall forever stand.
47 Amidst the winds of the south,
48 Amidst the rushing winds that lead the storms,
49 The little mystic pipe,
50 My grandfather, moves and travels
51 With a power from which no evil act can be concealed.
52 He is ever at the back of the man who makes the vow,
53 Ever hovers around his head.
54 Upon the breaking of the vow he makes the face of the man to become sallow,
55 Makes the blood to gush from his nostrils, in a twirling motion,
56 Even takes from the man his spirit, when it is demanded.

The first song is descriptive of the approaching thunderclouds, of their varying colors and awe-inspiring movements. The power that moves the clouds with fear-inspiring, angry violence is addressed as "grandfather." Two lines of each stanza of the first song are translated.

### Song 1

#### 1

Lo, my grandfather is coming,
Darkening the heavens with black clouds.

#### 2

Lo, my grandfather is coming,
Amid gray clouds that overspread the sky.

#### 3

Lo, my grandfather is coming,
Amid yellow clouds that overspread the sky.

#### 4

Lo, my grandfather is coming,
Amid angry clouds rolling through the sky.

The second song is descriptive of the movements of the approaching clouds with flashes of lightning, ever controlled by the Mysterious Power. Two lines from each stanza are translated.

### Song 2

#### 1

Lo, my grandfather is coming,
Moving hither and thither with the winds.

#### 2

Lo, my grandfather is coming,
Lighting up the heavens with fire.

#### 3

Lo, my grandfather is coming,
With jagged bolts of lightning.

#### 4

Lo, my grandfather is coming,
With the gray clouds moving onward.

#### 5

Lo, my grandfather is coming,
Swiftly, swiftly through the heavens.

## 11. The Little Rain Songs[160]

The group following the Great Rain Songs is the Ni-zhiu' Wa-thon Zhin-ga, the Little Rain Songs. [In this song group and the one that follows, a sacred war club is used in the dramatic acts.] To each wa-xo'-be belonging to certain clans is attached a symbolic club, typical of the one originally made by the people of the Elder Sky clan, to symbolize the indestructible life, or the never-ending life craved by the people for their tribal existence and which is the theme of these elaborate supplicatory rites.[161] If the wa-xo'-be used at an initiation happens to be one that has attached to it a symbolic club, the Xo'-ka will use the mystic club when performing the dramatic acts that accompany the songs. But should the wa-xo'-be have no club, the Sho'-ka will provide a stick of some kind that will be used as a substitute.[162]

The first song has a composite significance: first, the seizure of the sky by the earth. This act is indicated by a symbolic mark, a dent made on the ground with a ceremonial club. Second, the path of the sun from the eastern horizon to the midheavens, thence to the western horizon. These paths are indicated by two straight lines made on the ground with the club. Third, the spreading of the sun's life-giving touches to the earth, upon the right and the left side of the path. These touches of the life-giving power of the sun are shown by undulating lines made upon the earth with the club. The five stanzas of this song are accompanied by dramatic acts performed by the candidate and his Xo'-ka. When the Assisting Xo'-ka comes to the song, the Sho'-ka takes up a club which he puts in the hands of the candidate, then leads him to a certain spot on the Sky side of the House of Mystery and instructs him as to what he is to do when the singer comes to the third line of the first stanza. The Sho'-ka gives a signal to the Assisting Xo'-ka, who then begins to sing.

At the third line the candidate strikes the earth with the end of the club, imitating as he does so the roar of the thunder; then he puts the club down on the dent made in the ground and returns to his seat.

The Xo'-ka then picks up the club and the singer goes on to the second stanza. At the third line the Xo'-ka strikes the dent made by the candidate, imitating the sound of thunder, and quickly makes a straight line westward.

Without pause the singer goes on to the third stanza, and at the third line he again strikes the central spot and with a quick motion makes a waving line northward.

The singer proceeds to the fourth stanza; at the third line the Xo'-ka strikes the central spot and quickly makes a straight line eastward.

The singing continues, and at the third line of the fifth stanza the Xo'-ka strikes the central spot and with a violent motion makes a waving line southward.

The singing ceases and the Xo'-ka goes to his seat having, in this dramatic fashion, brought together the sky and the earth, the two great cosmic forces whence proceeds life in all material forms.

The first and third lines of each stanza of this song are translated.

### Song 1

#### 1

I go to see my grandfather who is to be seized,
He who is to be seized by the earth I go to see.

#### 2

I go to see my grandfather who is to be seized,
He will mark the earth with a straight line.

#### 3

I go to see my grandfather who is to be seized,
He will mark the earth with a waving line.

#### 4

I go to see my grandfather who is to be seized,
He will mark the earth with a straight line.

#### 5

I go to see my grandfather who is to be seized,
He will mark the earth with a waving line.

At the close of the first rain song the Sho'-ka brings the branch of a cottonwood tree, which he plants in the central mark of the symbolic figure roughly made by the Xo'-ka and which represents the unity of the sky and the earth.

When this was done, the Xo'-ka took his place beside the tree and the Assisting Xo'-ka took up the second song, which relates to the cottonwood tree, used here as a symbol of the continuity of the life jointly given by the sky and the earth.

At the third line of the first stanza the Xo'-ka touches caressingly the buds of the cottonwood tree, which symbolize the continuity of life; those on the west side, the north side, the east side, and on the south side of the tree.

At the third line of the second stanza he breaks off a bud from the west side of the tree, one from the north side, one from the east side, and one from the south side, tossing each bud over his shoulder. The buds represent the distribution of life over the earth.

At the third line of the third stanza he breaks the tree into pieces, downward from the top to the root. The broken pieces of the tree represent the natural end of life.

At the third line of the fourth stanza he gathers up the broken pieces of the tree into one bunch and throws it backward over his head toward the setting of the sun, a setting toward which all life forms travel.

All of the acts accompanying the first and the second rain songs are a dramatization of the activities of the sky and the earth, which affect all forms of life.

A translation of the first and third lines of each stanza of the song will suffice to give the meaning.

Song 2

1

In four stages my grandfather shall walk around the tree,
Touching, touching the buds of the sacred tree.

2

In four stages my grandfather shall walk around the tree,
Breaking off here and there the buds of the sacred tree.

3

In four stages my grandfather shall walk around the tree,
Breaking in pieces the body of the sacred tree.

4

In four stages my grandfather shall walk around the tree,
Throwing westward the broken pieces of the sacred tree.

### 12. Songs of Making One Strike the Other[163]

The group of songs following the Little Rain Songs is called Ki-ka'-xe I-ki-tsin, freely translated, Making One Strike the Other. In the first song the warrior is represented as speaking at a time when the men are about to go forth to attack a troublesome foe. In the first and third stanzas the warrior speaks of the red hawk, which he holds up as being closest to him, particularly in times of peril; in the second and fourth stanzas he speaks of the black hawk also as being close to him when he is threatened with danger.

Not only do these birds symbolize the courage of the warrior but they are also emblematic of the unerring precision of the night and day in their movements, a quality necessary for the fighting man, and the weapons he must use to overcome his enemy. When going upon the warpath, each commander carries with him one of these symbolic hawks, and must have it upon him as he charges with his men upon the foe. A translation of the first two lines of the first and second stanzas will suffice to give the meaning of the songs.

### Song 1

1

I am ever close to the red hawk, the bird of courage,
Lo, I go against the foe, having close to me the bird.

2

I am ever close to the black hawk, the bird of courage,
Lo, I go against the foe, having close to me the bird.

The second song, which has but one stanza, speaks of the warriors returning in triumph, having overcome the foe, and bringing home the birds, emblematic of courage and precision of action. A translation of the first and third lines of the stanza will be sufficient to give the meaning of the song.

### Song 2

Lo, the warriors are coming home,
Bringing home their sacred hawks.

[Before singing the third song] the Sho'-ka removes the scalp that is fastened to the hanging strap of the Wa-xo'-be and wraps the scalp around the middle of the war club, which he places in the left hand of the Xo'-ka. The Sho'-ka then takes up the Wa-xo'-be and puts it into the right hand of the Xo'-ka. When that official [the Xo'-ka] has been thus equipped for ceremonial acts that accompany the song, the Assisting Xo'-ka takes up his rattle and begins to sing and the Xo'-ka rises to dance. [The song speaks of the red hawk and the black bird as coming home in triumph and standing side by side before the waiting throng.] The Xo'-ka dances in one place until the Assisting Xo'-ka comes to the third line in each stanza, when the Xo'-ka takes two steps forward, holds the war club aloft, and strikes the scalp wound around the club with the Wa-xo'-be, uttering as he does so the magic cry:

He  hi hi    hi hi    e  e

Then he steps back to his place where he continues to dance. This symbolic act forms a little drama of the warriors going forth to strike and overcome the enemy,[164] an act which implies that the courageous warrior, armed with a club, is able to overcome the enemies of the tribe.

One line from each of the first and second stanzas is translated.

Song 3

1

Lo, the red hawk is home, and stands beside the black bird.

2

Lo, the black bird is home, and stands beside the red hawk.

### 13. Songs of Releasing the Arrows[165]

The title of the group of songs next in order is Mon-gthu-stse-dse Wa-thon, Songs of Releasing the Arrows. These songs, with their mystic symbols and dramatic action, are supplicatory in character; they are expressions of a craving for divine aid toward the perpetuity of the tribal existence and the continuity of the life of the individual by an unbroken lineage.

[The preceding song group tells that man is able to overcome his enemies physically, but this alone is insufficient for continuity.] It was necessary that the life put into his being should be given perpetuity by a never-ending line of descendants. This could not be attained except by divine favor, a favor to be sought by supplication in a ceremonial form, to consist in the sending forth of two mystic arrows, one to overtake the Day and the Night, in both of which forever moves the power to be appealed to for the favor desired.[166]

The little bow and the two arrows used in the act accompanying the songs are made in accordance with a ritual formulated by the ancient priests and presented for an initiation ceremony by the clan called Sole Owners of the Bow [or Bow clan], who hold the office of making these ceremonial articles. The breast of the bow is painted red as a symbol of the recurrent day, and the back is painted black, a symbol of the night that ever follows the day. One of the arrows is painted red and the other black, so that both together symbolize day and night.

When the Songs of the Arrows are about to be sung, the people whose houses happen to be in the line over which the arrows are to be set in flight move out, even the horses that happen to stand in the way are driven aside, for there are many persons who believe that any man or beast over which the magic arrows make their flight will die within the year.

While the people are scurrying out of the way, the Sho'-ka picks up the sacred hawk [wa-xo'-be] and places it upon the back of the Xo'-ka, where it hangs suspended from a cord that goes around his neck. The Sho'-ka then puts in the hands of the Xo'-ka the symbolic bow and the two arrows. The Assisting Xo'-ka takes up his rattle and begins to sing. The Xo'-ka quickly rises and dances to the rhythm of the music. When the fourth line of the first stanza is reached, the Xo'-ka takes two or three steps forward, fits the red arrow to the cord of the bow, [aims it toward the setting sun to pursue forever the day and the night that mark the duration of all life], and as he pulls the cord utters the magic cry:

He   hi hi      hi hi      e   e

But he does not release the arrow. [He only symbolically shoots the arrows.] Before turning around to come back to his place, the Xo'-ka takes pains to remove from the bow the arrow, in order to avoid bringing its point into line with priests sitting on both sides of the lodge. At the fourth line of the second stanza, the Xo'-ka repeats the magic cry and simulates the act of releasing the black arrow. At the fourth line of the third stanza, the same magic cry and the same act of simulation is repeated, but the red arrow is now drawn. When the Assisting Xo'-ka sings the fourth line of the fourth stanza, the Xo'-ka again gives the magic cry as he goes through the act of drawing and releasing the black arrow.[167]

This symbolic and dramatic invocation is addressed to the Mysterious Power in all its abiding places, but directly to the day and the night wherein it makes its everlasting abode.

By these symbolic acts the initiate is not only assured that he will be protected by the Red Hawk, the Black Bird, and the Sacred Warrior, as all of these represent the warriors of the tribe, but that he will have a line of descendants that will continue through all time.[168]

Saucy Calf gave only one song of this group, although on his counting stick five songs were given to the group. The first and the fourth lines of each stanza are translated.

Song ?

1

Behold! the red hawk releases the arrow,
Lo, he releases the arrow of the day.

2

Behold! the blackbird releases the arrow,
Lo, he releases the arrow of the night.

3

Behold! the red hawk releases the arrow,
Lo, he releases the arrow of the day.

4

Behold! the blackbird releases the arrow,
Lo, he releases the arrow of the night.

### 14. Victory Song[169]

The next song bears the title Wa-tsi'-a-dsi Wa-thon, which may be freely translated as Victory Song. The song is in praise of the hawk. This bird symbolizes the courage and the unity of purpose of the warriors in action, regardless of the number of men who achieve victory. A war party may be small or composed of men drawn from the tribe as a whole, but the hawk represents the spirit that actuates the warrior, irrespective of the number engaged, and the song glorifies this fundamental quality of the tribal warriors.

The hawk is here personified as a fighting man. The song speaks of the parts that are vital to his physical structure, beginning with the head and ending with the feet. In songs of this character belonging to other clans, the enumeration begins with the feet and closes with the mouth. Saucy Calf, in explaining the difference of the order, said, "This song refers to the birth of man, and the songs of the other clans refer to both the physical and mental growth of man." [Although Saucy Calf did not mention it, it is assumed that the Xo'-ka continues to dance with the hawk on his back and the bow and arrows in his hand during this song. It is unclear why La Flesche did not include a text of this song or of the Song of Closing the Ceremony, which follows.—Ed.]

### 15. Song of Closing the Ceremony[170]

The last song of this ritual is called U'-thu-ce I-non-zhin Wa-thon, which, freely translated, means song by which the participants of the ceremony rise to go home. When the Xo'-ka has taken his seat [at the close of the Victory Song?], the Assisting Xo'-ka begins to sing the Song of the Rising to Depart. The priests promptly rise, those of the Earth People passing in single file between the fireplace and the Xo'-ka, the Singer, and the Assisting Xo'-ka and going out on the Sky side. Those of the Sky People march in the same manner and go out on the Earth side. Each head of the various clans on both sides of the two great tribal divisions greets the Singer with the words, "Many animals shall appear for you," meaning, abundant shall be your food and many shall be your descendants. Some whose relationship to the Singer permits of it make a jesting remark, to which the Singer responds seriously, without the slightest sign of a smile, with the greeting, "Ho!"[171]

This song again refers to the hawk, the symbol of the warrior, but the use of archaic and corrupted words make it practically impossible to give a literal translation.

When the initiatory ceremony is over, the wa-xo'-be that had been used remains in the initiate's possession until such time as an initiation is applied for by some [other] member of the clan.

At the beginning of the work, Saucy Calf explained that for a long time he had not attended any of the initiations or had occasion to recite the rituals; consequently his memory of the songs in their established sequential order had become faulty. He made the further remark that if he had lost any of the songs it would be those that are of no particular importance, or would be songs that are merely repetitions. He did not give all the songs marked on his counting stick, but he gave enough to indicate what each group of songs signified.

## EDITOR'S SUMMARY

The Songs of the Wa-xo'-be were concerned with the conduct of war. The Osages saw the world as filled with human enemies who could destroy them, and so defensive war was a part of human life. In this never-ending struggle for survival, it was not sufficient merely to defeat one's enemies; one had to try to destroy them absolutely. Only through their enemies' destruction could the Osages hope to find peace, which was the objective of war. Perhaps not surprisingly, the subject matter of this ritual is at times grisly. War was not depicted as some glorious game but as deadly and bloody acts of violence. If our knowledge of the Osages were limited to just this one ceremony, we might assume that they were among the most vicious and bloodthirsty people in North America. Such an assumption would also cause us to misinterpret the true significance of what was being communicated.

The Osages were not an aggressive, bloodthirsty, and hostile people. Indeed, they were almost the opposite in their daily social behavior. Reverend William Vaill, one of the early missionaries to the Osage, wrote in 1826:

They [the Osages] are naturally amiable and friendly, and always shake hands with a smile on their countenances. Though they love hunting and delight in war, they have never been known to torture prisoners. If they decide on war, they will to war, and kill, and take all they can; but it is soon over, and prisoners are well treated. If anyone has lost a child the prisoner is made to supply its place. A Pawnee boy or girl sometimes receives, if possible, more affection and attention than an own child. . . . Strangers are always pleased with the hospitality of these people. They will divide the last meal, and never suffer one to go hungry from their village, or remain there in want, if they have to give. . . . They are not quarrelsome among themselves, but they are remarkable for mildness. . . . The Osages are remarkable for always being at war, without being a war-like people.[172]

In the Songs of the Wa-xo'-be, four interrelated themes or subjects are addressed simultaneously: authority/unity, purpose, the organization of war parties, and the required behavior of the warriors. The dominant theme, expressed implicitly throughout the ritual, is that of authority and unity. The Osages believed that the people had to act together in all of life's endeavors in order to succeed. To accomplish this, they created an organizational structure in which authority was dispersed and which thus necessitated collective action. Almost every aspect of the ritual was controlled by one or another of the clans, phratries, or moieties. Only the priests of a specific clan, phratry, or moiety had the authority to perform or authorize the performance of particular parts of the ritual. This ritual and other major rituals were, by necessity, group efforts that required the participation and support of every clan, phratry, and moiety. The rituals served as a social paradigm communicating the idea that the individual, like the clan, was not independent but merely part of the larger unit and therefore dependent upon others.

The idea of purpose was a second theme implicit in the ritual. Just as all living things had a purpose, all human actions had to have purpose. There was no glory in the mere act of killing or destroying an enemy. War and killing had to have purpose, by which the Osages meant that war had to serve the unified objectives of the people. Spontaneous acts of aggression by individuals were dangerous. Individual aggressiveness, even against one's enemies, had to be controlled and directed. Thus o-don' (war honors) were bestowed upon men only for their actions as members of organized war parties—that is, war parties organized under the authority of a clan priest (clan/moiety war parties) or the collective authority of priests acting in unison (tribal war parties).

The core of the rituals, the seven songs and the six songs, was concerned with the organization of war parties. The seven songs tell of the organization and conduct of a tribal party, a war party involving the members of all twenty-four clans acting in concert. In fifty-one songs, three wi'-gi-e, and four we'-ga-xe grouped into seventeen song groups, the universe was symbolically recreated, the Sacred Warrior who was to lead the party was chosen and made ready, the eight commanders were selected, the warriors were prepared, the party moved against the enemy, a battle was fought, and the battlefield after the fighting ended was described. The whole story was not told, and only those parts of the ritual belonging to the Buffalo Bull clan were mentioned. Theoretically, the seven songs of all twenty-four clans would have to be brought together to reveal the full organizational structure and conduct of a tribal war party. The actual meaning of the song groups is further obscured by the rich use of symbols and metaphors. Even though it is a fragmentary account, the basic plot can be seen if one is aware of the general story.

The six songs were concerned with war parties at the clan and/or moiety level. This ritual knowledge was presented in fifteen song groups that consisted of thirty-nine songs, three wi'-gi-e, and three we-ga-xe. The information, however, was presented in such a fragmentary manner that even knowing the subject of the six songs is little help in understanding the Buffalo Bull clan version of them. In these songs, the focus is on the warriors' individual conduct in war parties that lacked Sacred Warriors and commanders. In a highly fragmented manner, these songs tell of the warriors preparing for battle, their search for and defeat of the enemy, and, finally, their victorious return. As in the case of the seven songs, it would be necessary to bring together the information presented in all twenty-four clan versions to gain a complete picture of the organization and conduct of these war parties.

The fourth subject addressed in this ritual was the conduct of individual warriors. When a man assumed the role of a warrior, he could not act or behave like a normal man. In war, young men had to overcome their normal fears and feelings of humanity and instead act with merciless courage. The hawk was a symbol of the Osage warrior. The most courageous of all birds, a hawk would unhesitatingly attack a much larger bird in defense of its nest. Warriors were expected to do likewise in defense of their people, particularly women and children. The fire also symbolized the Osage warrior. Like the pitiless prairie fire that consumes everything in its path, so should warriors attack their enemies, killing all. The ritual made it clear that when a man put the black ash of a warrior on his face, he was transformed into a fearless and merciless destroyer of his people's enemies.

The seven songs and the six songs speak of the first and second stages of tribal organization as described in the story of the organization of the tribe. In both these stages the primary reason for tribal organization was to control warfare. The third and last stage of tribal organization, the creation of the two chiefs to manage the day-to-day internal problems of the tribe, is the subject of the rite of the chiefs.

## CHAPTER 6

*Rite of the Chiefs*

$\text{T}$HE Rite of the Chiefs, associated with the great bundle (wa-xo'-be ton-ga), was the initiation rite of a man into one of the three tribal priesthoods. Whereas the clan bundles were associated with the visible world—the world of the living and thus primarily warfare—the great bundle was associated with the invisible world, the realm of Wa-kon-da and thus of fertility and long life. As a result, the theme of the material presented in the rite of the chiefs is very different from that in the Songs of the Wa-xo'-be. Instead of the destructive forces of the universe, this ritual addresses the major life-giving and life-renewing forces of Wa-kon-da. Although it was the more important ritual, the Rite of the Chiefs was much shorter than the Songs of the Wa-xo'-be.

Compared to clan bundles (wa-xo'-be zhin-ga) and clan priests (non-hon'-zhin-ga), there were very few great bundles and great bundle priests (ton'-won a-don-be). La Flesche was able to determine of the existence of only five great bundles.[1] These bundles were basically identical to each other in construction and were associated with the same ritual knowledge and authority.

The great bundle priests had authority over at least two, and undoubtedly more, important tribal rituals: the new year rite and the tattooing rite. The tattooing instruments were part of the bundle itself, and the great bundle priest personally performed the tattooing. Unlike clan bundles, these bundles were rarely transferred. Only when a great bundle priest became too old or infirm to perform the tattooing would a bundle be transferred and a new priest initiated. In contrast to the clan priests, the great bundle priest effectively retired after the bundle was transferred. It is not clear whether the old priest actually surrendered his authority to the initiate with the transfer or whether he simply withdrew from an active role in the rituals. In another contrast to the transferring of a clan bundle, a great bundle priest chose the man who received the bundle. The initiate was an involuntary candidate.

The ritual elements of the Rite of the Chiefs differed from those used in the Songs of the Wa-xo'-be. Participants in the rite of the chiefs were: (1) the candidate, (2) the Xo'-ka, (3) the Assisting Xo'-ka, (4) the *u-dse'-the a-don-be,* or Keeper of the Fireplace, (5) the clan priests, and (6) the wife of the initiate.

*The candidate.* The candidate was asked to join this priesthood. No title was given to him; the term "Singer" was not applied, and his actual role in the ritual was minor.

*The Xo'-ka.* The role of the Xo'-ka was performed by the retiring great bundle priest. Great bundle priests, unlike clan priests, were always men who possessed great ritual knowledge. Only the great bundle priest himself had the knowledge of and authority to perform certain ritual acts. Thus, in the Rite of the Chiefs, many of the important wi'-gi-e were recited by the Xo'-ka himself and not by the Assisting Xo'-ka. Symbolically, the Xo'-ka represented the sun and the "symbolic man." The sun symbolism, however, is slightly different from that in the clan initiations. In this rite, the Xo'-ka wears a bearskin robe, the symbolic significance of which is not clear. In his hair he wears tufts of swan feathers that symbolize "the days of cloudless skies, the days of perpetual peace."[2]

*The Assisting Xo'-ka.* In comparison to his role in the clan bundle initiation rites, the role of the Assisting Xo'-ka in the Rite of the Chiefs was limited. Because there were so few great bundle priests, this role was probably filled by a clan priest who had neither the knowledge nor the authority to recite or perform many of the required ritual acts.

*The Keeper of the Fireplace.* This position was filled by the last man initiated as a great bundle priest. Seated near the door, he represented "all of the people." He sang one song and made a statement during the ritual.[3]

*Clan priests.* Priests representing all twenty-four clans were required for this ritual, not only to create the symbolic House of Mystery but also to recite their clan wi'-gi-e. The head priest of the Crawfish clan played an additional role in the ritual.[4]

*The wife of the initiate.* The same ritual that was performed in the Songs of the Wa-xo'-be for the wife of the initiate—"Instructions to the Wife of the Initiate"—was performed in the Rite of the Chiefs as well.

*Ritual items.* Only three ritual items were used in this rite: the wa-xo'-be ton-ga (great bundle), the counting sticks, and the sacred bow and arrows. The great bundle was described in chapter 3. Although the great bundle being transferred was physically present during the rite of the chiefs, it was neither opened nor used in the ritual acts. The counting sticks consisted of two bundles, one of seventy sticks and the other of sixty. They were held by the Keeper of the Fireplace during the ritual and given to the wife of the initiate afterwards.[5] Their symbolic importance was not recorded. The sacred bow and two arrows used in this ritual have the same symbolic importance and use as those in the Songs of the Wa-xo'-be.

*Ritual segments.* The Rite of the Chiefs was structured very differently from the clan initiation rites. It had only one song group, "The Approach to the House," which was a standard part of the preliminary rituals. The main body of the rite consisted of the reciting of wi'-gi-e and the performance of we'-ga-xe (dramatic acts).

Charley Wah-hre-she gave La Flesche only a very brief description of the ritual events preceding the main part of the Rite of the Chiefs. It is doubtful that any formal ceremony was involved in a man's becoming a candidate for this rite. The priest asked the initiate to take the bundle. Whereas candidates for the clan priesthood had seven years to acquire the required items, the transferring of a great bundle appears to have been more immediate. A man who was a great bundle priest waited until he was too old to perform the associated ritual functions before naming a successor. Under these circumstances, it was imperative to hold the initiation as soon as possible. The initiate and his family seem to have gathered the required items as quickly as possible. After the initiate had collected the necessary food and gifts, the initiation was held.

The preliminary rituals for the Rite of the Chiefs differed in several ways from those described for the Songs of the Wa-xo'-be. There was no Smoking rite, since there were no animal skins to be consecrated. Although it is not definite, there possibly was no Moccasin Cutting rite. The underlying theme of the Moccasin Cutting was warfare and destruction, a theme absent in the Rite of the Chiefs. There was no selection of a Wa-don'-be, and no Night Singing. It is possible that the preliminary rituals consisted of nothing more than the ki'-non[6] and the Approach to the House.[7] If this interpretation is correct, then the Rite of the Chiefs was only a one-day ceremony. Charley Wah-hre-she gave brief descriptions of the ki'-non and the Approach to the House rituals used in the Rite of the Chiefs. Because these are basically the same as those used in the Songs of the Wa-xo'-be and described in chapter 5—except that the references to killing and destruction were replaced by appeals for life—I have not included them in this chapter.

The Rite of the Chiefs itself, after any preliminary rituals, was divided into five segments or parts. (1) The ritual begins with the Wi'-gi-e of the Chief's Vigil, in which the vision of the Gentle Ponca chief is told. (2) Next follows the "Sending," in which symbolic items are sent to the priests of all the clans. (3) After the Sending, each clan priest recites the wi'-gi-e of his clan. This act seems to symbolize the clans' collective recognition of and subordination to the greater power. (4) Next, the "Instructions to the Wife of the Initiate" are given and the clan priests leave. (5) The performance of the shooting of the sacred arrows ends the ritual.

What follows is La Flesche's description of the Rite of the Chiefs and his translations of its texts. My occasional comments and explanations appear in brackets.

## THE CHIEF'S VIGIL

When the priesthood has come to order, the Xo'-ka recites the Wi'-gi-e of the Chief's Vigil. This wi'-gi-e is in three parts, each one relating to a mystical revelation during the vigil. The first part bears the subtitle He-Who-Becomes-Aged-While-Yet-Traveling (a Pelican); the second part is called The-Very-Aged-Eagle; the third part is the Metal Wi'-gi-e. The third wi'-gi-e indicates a foreign influence, the substitution of steel needles or awls as scarifiers in place of the wing bones of the pelican and eagle.

### Wi'-gi-e of the Chief's Vigil

#### Part I. Vision of the Aged Pelican

1 Verily, at that time and place, it has been said, in this house,
2 The Water people, a people who possess seven fireplaces, were gathered together.
3 One of the Water people (of the Ponca clan)
4 Fell into deep meditation (upon his future course).
5 Verily, at the end of the lodge he sat,
6 Where he fell prostrate and lay with head bowed low.
7 Verily, at that time and place, it has been said, in this house,
8 He took that which was made sacred by the people (the soil of the earth)
9 And put it upon his face (the forehead).
10 Then, in the early dawn,
11 He cried without ceasing as he moved
12 And walked away forthwith (toward the unfrequented parts of the land).
13 Verily, he arrived at the borders of the village, where he sat to rest,
14 While the sun reached mid-heaven.
15 As the darkness of the evening came upon him,
16 Verily, in the midst of an open prairie, where trees grow not,
17 He inclined his head toward his right side,

18 Sat to rest upon the earth, with his body bent low,
19 And Wa-kon-da made him close his eyes in sleep.
20 Night passed while he yet sat.
21 He woke and saw the signs of the approach of the force of Day.
22 Then he took that which was made sacred by the people
23 And put it upon his face.
24 At break of day
25 He cried without ceasing as he wandered away.
26 Then, as he paused and stood to rest,
27 The force of Day reached mid-heaven.
28 The darkness of evening came upon the man,
29 Yet he ceased not his cry as he wandered.
30 In the midst of the open prairie, where trees grow not,
31 As he sat upon the earth to rest he thought: This spot, also, may be Wa-kon-da's abode.
32 Then he inclined his head toward his right side,
33 Bent his body low,
34 And Wa-kon-da made him close his eyes in sleep.
35 Verily, at that time and place, it has been said, in this house,
36 He awoke and thought: The light of the force of Day is spreading over me.
37 Then he took that which was made sacred by the people,
38 Put it upon his face,
39 And in the early dawn
40 He cried without ceasing as he moved,
41 Even as he went forthwith to wander.
42 As he sat down upon the earth to rest the force of Day reached mid-heaven.
43 The darkness of evening came upon the man,
44 Yet he ceased not his cry as he wandered.
45 In the midst of the open prairie, where trees grow not,
46 As he sat down upon the ground he thought: This spot may, also, be Wa-kon-da's abode.
47 Then he inclined his head toward his right side,
48 Bent his body low to rest,
49 And Wa-kon-da made him close his eyes in sleep.
50 He awoke while yet he sat and thought:
51 Even now the light of the force of Day is spreading over me.
52 He raised his head and arose,
53 Took that which was made sacred by the people,
54 Put it upon his face.
55 Then, in the early dawn,
56 He cried without ceasing as he wandered.
57 He sat down upon the earth to rest.
58 The force of Day reached mid-heaven.
59 The darkness of evening came upon the man,

60 Verily, in the midst of the open prairie, where trees grow not,
61 And he thought: In this spot, also,
62 Wa-kon-da must make his abode, and he sat upon the earth to rest.
63 Verily, at that time and place, it has been said, in this house,
64 He inclined his head toward his right side,
65 Bent his body low for rest,
66 And Wa-kon-da made him close his eyes in sleep.
67 Verily, at that time and place, it has been said, in this house,
68 He arose as day approached, took that which was made sacred by the people,
69 Put it upon his face.
70 Then, in the early dawn,
71 He cried without ceasing as he wandered.
72 Verily, at that time and place, it has been said, in this house,
73 While he yet cried and wandered,
74 The force of Day reached mid-heaven.
75 In the evening of the sixth day (of his vigil)
76 He approached the head of a stream.
77 Close to its banks he stood and thought:
78 Here, in this spot, also, Wa-kon-da must make his abode.
79 Here, in this very spot, I shall rest and sleep.
80 Verily, at that time and place, it has been said, in this house,
81 Wa-kon-da made him close his eyes in sleep.
82 He awoke, saw that night had passed, and he thought: The light of the force of Day is spreading over me.
83 Verily, at that time and place, it has been said, in this house,
84 He raised his head and arose,
85 Took that which was made sacred by the people,
86 Put it upon his face.
87 Then, in the early dawn,
88 He cried without ceasing as he wandered.
89 He came to the head of a stream
90 And stood close to it.
91 Verily, at that time and place, it has been said, in this house,
92 There sat the Pelican, He-who-becomes-aged-while-yet-traveling.
93 The man stood near to him and spake, saying:
94 O grandfather,
95 The little ones have nothing of which to make their bodies!
96 In quick response, the Pelican said: O little one,
97 You have said the little ones have nothing of which to make their bodies.
98 The little ones shall make of me their bodies.
99 When the little ones make of me their bodies,
100 They shall always live to see old age.
101 Behold, the skin of my feet,

102 Which I have made to be the means to reach old age.

103 They (the little ones), also, shall always live to see old age by its means.

104 Behold, the muscles of my jaws,

105 Which I have made to be the means by which to reach old age.

106 When the little ones, also, make of them the means by which to reach old age,

107 They shall always live to see old age.

108 Behold, the inner muscles of my thighs,

109 Which I have made to be the means by which to reach old age.

110 When the little ones make of them the means by which to reach old age,

111 They shall always live to see, in the muscles of their thighs, the signs of old age.

112 Behold, the muscles of my breast, gathered in folds by age,

113 Which I have made to be the means by which to reach old age.

114 When the little ones, also, make of them the means by which to reach old age,

115 They shall always live to see old age.

116 Behold, the flaccid muscles of my arms,

117 Which I have made to be the means to reach old age.

118 When the little ones, also, make of them the means to reach old age,

119 They shall always live to see, in the muscles of their arms, the signs of old age.

120 Verily, at that time and place, it has been said, in this house,

121 He said: Behold, my wings.

122 They, also,

123 Are not without meaning.

124 I offer them for use as awls.

125 When the little ones make use of them as awls,

126 They shall always have awls that are sharp, indeed.

127 When they make use of them as awls,

128 The little ones shall always live to see old age.

129 Even though they pass away to the realm of spirits,

130 They shall, by the use of the awls (as scarifiers), bring themselves back to consciousness.

131 Behold, the stooping of my shoulders,

132 That I have made to be the means by which to reach old age.

133 When they, also, make it the means by which to reach old age,

134 They shall always live to see old age.

135 Behold, the muscles of my throat,

136 Which I have made to be the means to reach old age.

137 When they make of them the means by which to reach old age,

138 They shall always live to see, in the flaccid muscles of their throats, the signs of old age.

139 Behold, the locks on the crown of my head that have grown scant with age.

140 When they make of them the means by which to reach old age,
141 They shall always live to see, in their thinned locks, the signs of old age.

## Part II. The Aged Eagle

1 Verily, at that time and place, it has been said, in this house,
2 He (the Chief), with the close of the words (of the pelican), arose to his feet
3 And thought as he stood: I will now go to my home,
4 It being the seventh day (of his vigil).
5 He approached a small stream as he moved homeward.
6 As he drew near to it
7 He came face to face with the Very Aged Eagle.
8 He stood close to him and spake, saying:
9 O my grandfather,
10 The little ones have nothing of which to make their bodies.
11 Verily, at that time and place, it has been said, in this house,
12 The Aged Eagle made reply: The little ones shall make of me their bodies.
13 When the little ones make of me their bodies,
14 They shall always live to see old age.
15 Behold, the skin of my feet,
16 That I have made to be the means to reach old age.
17 When the little ones, also, make of it the means to reach old age,
18 They shall always live to see old age.
19 Behold, the wrinkles upon my ankles,
20 Which I have made to be the means to reach old age.
21 When they, also, make of them the means to reach old age,
22 They shall always live to see, upon their ankles, the signs of old age.
23 Behold, the inner muscles of my thighs,
24 Which I have made to be the means to reach old age.
25 When they make of them the means to reach old age,
26 They shall always live to see, in the inner muscles of their thighs, the signs of old age.
27 Behold, the muscles of my breast, gathered in folds,
28 Which I have made to be the means to reach old age.
29 When they, also, make of them the means to reach old age,
30 They shall always live to see, in the folds of the muscles of their breasts, the signs of old age.
31 Behold, the flaccid muscles of my arms,
32 Which I have made to be the means to reach old age.
33 When they, also, make of them the means to reach old age,
34 They shall always live to see old age.
35 Verily, at that time and place, it has been said, in this house,
36 He said: Behold, my wings!
37 The little ones shall make awls (of the bones) of my wings.
38 When they take to making awls of my wings,

39 They shall have awls that will be sharp, indeed.

40 Even if any of the little ones pass into the realm of spirits,

41 They shall, by the use of the awls (as scarifiers), bring themselves back to consciousness.

42 When they use the awls to bring the little ones back to life,

43 They shall always live to see old age.

44 Behold, the stooping of my shoulders,

45 That I have made to be the means to reach old age.

46 When they, also, make of it the means to reach old age,

47 They shall always live to see old age.

48 Behold, the muscles of my throat,

49 Which I have made to be the means to reach old age.

50 When the little ones make of them the means to reach old age,

51 They shall always live to see, in the flaccid muscles of their throats, the signs of old age.

52 Behold, the locks on the crown of my head that are thinned with age.

53 These locks, also,

54 I have made to be the means to reach old age.

55 When they, also, make of them the means to reach old age,

56 They shall always live to see, in their scant locks, the signs of old age.

Part III. Mon'-ce (Metal)

1 Verily, at that time and place, it has been said, in this house,

2 On the seventh day (of his vigil)

3 He (the Chief) came to the borders of the village

4 And he paused and stood.

5 There, upon the ground, lay a piece of metal.

6 Close to it he stood and spake, saying:

7 O grandfather,

8 The little ones have nothing of which to make their bodies, O grandfather.

9 The metal spake, in quick response: O little one,

10 You say the little ones have nothing of which to make their bodies.

11 They shall make of me their bodies.

12 I am difficult to overcome by death.

13 When the little ones make of me their bodies,

14 They shall be as I, difficult to overcome by death.

15 Verily, at that time and place, it has been said, in this house,

16 He also said: The little ones shall make awls of me.

17 When the little ones take to making bone awls of me,

18 They shall have awls that will be sharp, indeed.

19 When the little ones make of me their bodies,

20 When they take to making awls of me,

21 And should any of them pass, even to the realm of spirits,

22 They shall, by the use of the awls (as scarifiers), bring themselves back to consciousness.
23 When, by this means, they bring themselves back to life,
24 They shall always live to see old age.
25 When the little ones make of me their bodies,
26 They shall always be free from all causes of death.
27 When the little ones make of me their bodies,
28 They shall know that there is no power whose skin is as hard as mine.
29 I am the only power whose skin is hard.
30 When the little ones make of me their bodies,
31 Their skins shall become as hard as mine.
32 The four great divisions of the days (stages of life)
33 They shall always successfully reach.
34 The day that is free from anger and violence,
35 I, as a person, can bring to your presence.
36 The little ones shall, as a people, dwell in the days that have no anger as they travel the path of life.

## THE CEREMONY OF SENDING[8]

At the close of the recitation of the Wi'-gi-e of the Chief's Vigil, the Xo'-ka takes up the ceremonial act next in order, called Wa-the'-the (the Sending), i. e., the sending to the various clans of the two great tribal divisions the life symbols belonging to each. The candidate, in his preparations for initiation, is required to collect such of the life symbols of the various clans as are of a tangible character. At the beginning of the Wa-the'-the ceremony, these symbolic articles are brought by the Sho'-ka and placed in a pile before the Xo'-ka. While these symbolic articles are not actually sent to each clan, yet they must be present. The symbols that are of an intangible nature and therefore not collectible, such as the earth, sun, moon, stars, sky, night, and day, are borne in mind by the Xo'-ka and are counted by him as being actually present.

Before the Wa-the'-the ceremony begins, the heads of the clans having symbols that are collectible ask of the Sho'-ka if the symbolic articles are actually present. When all the clans are satisfied that such is the case, the Xo'-ka begins the ceremony. He sends to each of the clans the fees collected and offered by the candidate for his initiation. Ceremonial etiquette requires the Xo'-ka[9] to begin the "sending" with the clan sitting nearest to him but belonging to the division opposite to his own, then to the clan nearest to him belonging to his own division, after which the distribution proceeds in sending alternately to the clans of the two great divisions. When all the fees have been thus distributed, the members of each clan recite simultaneously the wi'-gi-e which tells of the meaning of some of its own life symbols.[10]

## RECITAL OF THE WI'-GI-E OF THE CLANS

This simultaneous recitation by all the clans is not in unison. The members of one clan pay no attention to the recitation of those of another clan. Each person is busy with his own part of the ceremony. The result is a confused sound of words, and the sight is expressive of individual devotion to the task in hand.

[Charley Wah-hre-she did not know, or did not remember, all of the clan wi'-gi-e, and there is one discrepancy between his list of clan wi'-gi-e and the clan listing given in chapter 3. He gives a wi'-gi-e (or notes the lack of one) for all seven Water People clans, the Isolated Earth clan, and six of the seven Land People clans. However, although he gives nine wi'-gi-e for the nine Sky clans, he gives one for the Buffalo-Face clan and another for the Buffalo Back clan.[11] Other data indicate that these were a single clan and that Buffalo Back was merely an alternative name. If this was true, then he gave a wi'-gi-e for only eight of the Sky People clans.—Ed.]

Wi'-gi-e of the Water People Clans

The Elder Water People
1 Verily, at that time and place, it has been said, in this house,
2 The Water People, a people who possess seven fireplaces,
3 Spake to the Elder Water (clan),
4 Saying: O grandfather,
5 The little ones have nothing fit for their use as symbols.
6 Verily, at that time and place, it has been said, in this house,
7 The Elder Water replied, saying:
8 Behold the turtle that has a tail with seven serrations (snapping turtle).
9 That turtle
10 The little ones shall always use as a symbol.
11 Behold the seven serrations on the tail of the turtle.
12 Those also
13 I have made to be symbols.
14 The o-don', spoken of as the seven o-don' (war honors),
15 I have made them to symbolize.
16 Six of the serrations on the tail of the turtle
17 I have also
18 Made to symbolize
19 The o-don', spoken of as the six o-don'.
20 The o-don' of every description I have made them to symbolize.

21 Verily at that time and place, it has been said, in this house,

22 He continued: Behold the figures on the back of the turtle.

23 I have not made them without a purpose.

24 The little ones shall use them as a means to reach old age as they travel the path of life.

25 When they use these figures as a means to reach old age,

26 They shall always live to see old age.

27 When the little ones make of me their bodies,

28 Their skins shall become impenetrable.

29 Behold the figures on my breast (the turtle).

30 Those figures also

31 I have made to be a symbol.

32 A symbol of the power of the upper regions (the arch of the sky),

33 The gray line that lies across my breast,

34 A force of the upper regions (the galaxy),

35 I, as a person, have verily made to symbolize.

36 When the little ones make of me their bodies,

37 They shall enable themselves to live to see old age.

38 When the little ones of the Earth people and those of the Sky people

39 Make of me their bodies,

40 They shall enable themselves to live to see old age.

41 The four great divisions of the days (stages of life)

42 They shall always successfully reach and enter, as they travel the path of life.

### The Cattail People

The Cattail clan is brought to this ceremony to take its place as a mute representative of an aquatic plant, its clan symbol, namely, the cattail. The presence of this clan is necessary to complete the tableau representing the water part of the earth, for the reason that the plants which draw their nourishment from within the water are regarded as a part of that element. Although the priests of this clan remain silent throughout the ceremony, a fee is sent to its head, and the members share in the distribution of the supplies furnished by the candidate. This silent representation by a clan of its clan symbol explains the statement that each clan is a we'-ga-xe (we', that with which; ga-xe, to make)—i. e., that part which is used to make a whole; in this instance the universe is the whole. This clan takes a more active part in some of the other tribal rites.

### The White Water People

1 Verily, at that time and place, it has been said, in this house,

2 The Water, a people who possess seven fireplaces,

3 Spake to the White Water (clan),

4 Saying: O grandfather,

5 The little ones have nothing that is fit for their use as symbols.

6 Verily, at that time and place, it has been said, in this house,

7 The Water replied, saying: You say the little ones have nothing that is fit for their use as symbols.

8 I am one who is fit for use as a symbol.

9 Behold the shellfish that sitteth in the water.

10 Verily, I am the person who has made of the shellfish his body.

11 When the little ones make of me their bodies,

12 They shall always live to see old age.

13 Behold the wrinkles upon my skin (shell),

14 Which I have made to be the means of reaching old age.

15 When the little ones make of me their bodies,

16 They shall always live to see the signs of old age upon their skins.

17 The seven bends of the river (river of life)

18 I always pass successfully,

19 And in my travels the forces themselves

20 Have not the power to see the trail I make.

21 When the little ones make of me their bodies,

22 No one, not even the forces, shall be able to see the trails they make.

23 Behold the power of day that sitteth in the heavens.

24 Verily, I am a person who has made of that power his body.

25 Behold, the power of day that sitteth in the heavens.

26 The little ones also shall make of that power their bodies.

27 Then the four great divisions of the days (stages of life)

28 They shall always reach and enter, as they travel the path of life,

29 And they shall always live to see old age as they travel the path of life.

The Gentle Ponca People[12]

1 Verily, at that time and place, it has been said, in this house,

2 The Water, a people who possess seven fireplaces.

3 Spake to one of the Water (clans),

4 The Wa'-tse-tsi (They who came from the stars),

5 Saying: O grandfather,

6 We have nothing that is fit for use as a symbol.

7 Verily, at that time and place, it has been said, in this house,

8 He replied, saying: You say you have nothing that is fit for use as a symbol.

9 I am a person who is fit for use as a symbol.

10 Behold, the female red cedar.

11 Verily, I am a person who has made of that tree my body.

12 When the little ones make of me their bodies,

13 They shall always live to see old age.

14 Behold, the male red cedar.

15 The little ones shall always use the male red cedar as a symbol.

16 Behold the male red cedar.

17 When the little ones use that tree for a symbol,

18 They shall always live to see old age.

19 Verily, at that time and place, it has been said, in this house,
20 He said to them: Behold these waters,
21 That we shall make to be companions to the red cedar.
22 When the little ones make use of these waters,
23 The means by which to reach old age,
24 They shall always live to see old age.
25 Behold the grass that never dies (the sedge).
26 When the little ones make of it the means to reach old age,
27 They shall always live to see old age.
28 I, myself, have made it to be the means to reach old age.
29 Behold the bend of my shoulders (refers to the drooping of the sedge),
30 That I have made to be the means to reach old age.
31 Behold, the white blossoms on the top of my stalk,
32 Which I have made to be the means to reach old age.
33 The little ones shall reach old age
34 And see their scanty locks turn yellowish with age as have these blossoms.

The Deer People

 1 Verily, at that time and place, it has been said, in this house,
 2 The Water, a people who possess seven fireplaces,
 3 Spake to a Water (clan)
 4 Called the Lungs of the Deer,
 5 Saying: O grandfather,
 6 We have nothing that is fit to use as a symbol.
 7 The Deer hastened to say: O little ones,
 8 You say you have nothing that is fit to use as a symbol.
 9 I am a person who is fit for use as a symbol.
10 There is a little animal (the deer),
11 Of which I have always made my body.
12 The little ones shall use that animal as a symbol.
13 When they use that little animal as a symbol,
14 They shall have a symbol that will satisfy their desires.
15 Verily, at that time and place, it has been said, in this house,
16 He said to them: Behold the color of my hoofs, that is black in color.
17 I have made that color to be as my charcoal.
18 When the little ones also make that color as their charcoal,
19 They shall have charcoal that will easily sink into their skin.
20 Behold the tip of my nose, that is black in color.
21 I have made that color to be as my charcoal.
22 When the little ones make that color as their charcoal
23 They shall have charcoal that will easily sink into their skin.
24 Behold the color of the tips of my ears, that are black.
25 I have made that color to be as my charcoal.
26 When the little ones make of that color their bodies,

27 They shall have charcoal that will easily sink into their skin.
28 All these shall stand as symbols for the little ones.
29 Behold the young male deer whose horns are still of a dark gray hue.
30 That animal shall always be a symbol to the little ones.
31 They shall have power, even as I have, to evade all dangers.
32 When my enemies hurl at me their shafts that fly around me in forked lines,
33 As they pursue and surround me and my companions,
34 Yet with the power (of fleetness) I possess I can escape these dangers.
35 When the little ones make of me their bodies,
36 They also shall have power to overcome the dangers that lie in their life's pathway.
37 The four successive days (stages of life)
38 I successfully reach and cause myself to enter.
39 When the little ones make of me their bodies,
40 The four successive days (stages of life),
41 They also shall successfully reach and enter.
42 When they make of me the means to reach old age,
43 They shall always live to see old age.
44 Verily, at that time and place, it has been said, in this house,
45 He said: Why should they make of this little animal a symbol?
46 It is for the little ones to use for making the animals to appear.
47 When they use it for making the animals appear,
48 The animals shall not fail to appear.
49 Under the branches of the white oak,
50 Where the earth is trodden soft by many hoofs,
51 I have made a playground for the little animals (the deer).
52 When the little ones use this playground to make the animals appear,
53 The animals shall not fail to appear.
54 Verily, at that time and place, it has been said, in this house,
55 He continued: Under the branches of the red oak,
56 Where the earth is trodden soft by many hoofs,
57 I have made a playground for the little animals.
58 When the little ones use this playground to make the animals appear,
59 There, under the branches of the red oak, the animals shall not fail to appear.
60 Under the branches of the long-acorn tree,
61 Where the earth is trodden soft by many hoofs,
62 I have made a playground for the little animals.
63 When the little ones use this playground to make the animals appear,
64 There, under the branches of the long-acorn tree, the animals shall not fail to appear.
65 Under the branches of the gray-acorn tree,
66 Where the earth is trodden soft by many hoofs,
67 I have made a playground for the little animals.

68 When the little ones use the playground to make the animals appear,
69 There, under the branches of the gray-acorn tree, the animals shall not fail
   to appear.
70 Under the branches of the twisted oak,
71 Where the earth is trodden soft by many hoofs,
72 I have made a playground for the little animals.
73 There, under the branches of the twisted oak, the animals shall not fail to
   appear.
74 Under the branches of the dark-acorn tree,
75 Where the earth is trodden soft by many hoofs,
76 I have made a playground for the little animals.
77 When the dark-acorn tree is
78 Approached by the little ones when hunting,
79 There the animals shall not fail to appear.
80 Under the branches of the low stunted oaks,
81 Where the earth is trodden soft by many hoofs,
82 I have made a playground for the little animals.
83 When the low stunted oaks
84 Are approached by the little ones,
85 There the animals shall not fail to appear.
86 These (the playgrounds)
87 I have not made without a purpose.
88 I have made them to be ho'-e-ga (places in which the little animals are
   ensnared).
89 When the little ones also make ho'-e-ga of the playgrounds,
90 The animals shall not fail to appear.
91 Verily, at that time and place, it has been said, in this house,
92 He said to them: Behold, this bunch of grass,
93 Which is also not without a purpose.
94 When the little ones approach the grasses of the earth,
95 The animals shall not fail to appear.
96 Even before the beginning of the day
97 The animals shall not fail to appear,
98 And in the evening of the day
99 The animals shall not fail to appear.
100 When the little ones make of me their bodies,
101 Those of the Earth,
102 And those of the Sky,
103 The animals shall not fail to appear.

### The Bow People

1 Verily, at that time and place, it has been said, in this house,
2 The Water, a people who possess seven fireplaces,
3 Spake to the Bow (clan),

4 Saying: O Water,
5 We have nothing that is fit for use as a symbol.
6 Verily, at that time and place, it has been said, in this house,
7 The Bow people replied: You say you have nothing that is fit for use as a symbol.
8 I am a person who is fitted for use as a symbol.
9 Verily, in the midst of the rushing waters (in the midst of the shallow rapids)
10 Abides my being.
11 Verily, I am a person who has made of the waters his body.
12 Behold the right side of the river.
13 Of it I have made the right side of my body.
14 When the little ones make of me their bodies
15 And use the right side of the river
16 To make their bodies,
17 The right side of their bodies shall be free from all causes of death.
18 Behold the left side of the river.
19 Of it I have made the left side of my body.
20 When the little ones also make of that the left side of their bodies,
21 That side of their bodies shall always be free from all causes of death.
22 Behold the channel of the river.
23 Of it I have made the hollow of my body.
24 When the little ones make of me their bodies,
25 The hollow of their bodies shall always be free from all causes of death.
26 There is also an animal of which I have made my body.
27 It is the redfish
28 Of which I have made my body,
29 That I might be free from all causes of death.
30 When the little ones make of the redfish their bodies,
31 They shall always live to see old age.
32 Behold the blackfish.
33 Of it I have made my body.
34 When the little ones make of it their bodies,
35 They shall always live to see old age.
36 Verily at that time and place, it has been said, in this house,
37 He said to the people: Behold the otter.
38 Of it also I have made my body.
39 When the little ones make of the otter their bodies,
40 They shall always live to see old age.
41 When the people of the Sky
42 And of the Earth
43 Make of the otter their bodies,
44 They shall always be free from all causes of death.
45 Behold the male beaver.
46 Of it also I, as a person, have, verily, made my body.

47 When the little ones make of the beaver their bodies,
48 They shall always live to see old age.
49 Seven willow saplings
50 The beaver brought to the right side of his house,
51 Dragging them with his teeth to his house, laying them down in a pile.
52 Then he spake, saying: These saplings
53 I have made to represent certain things,
54 The things spoken of as o-don' (war honors).
55 Verily, I, as a person, have made them to represent the o-don'.
56 Against the current of the river the beaver went forth,
57 Rippling the surface of the water as he made his way,
58 Saying as he did so: Behold the parting of the waters in forked lines as I push forth,
59 The ripples of the waters I have made the means to reach old age.
60 When the little ones make of me their bodies
61 The powers shall always make way for them as do these waters for me.
62 He struck the surface of the water with his tail, making a cracking noise, as he pushed forth,
63 And he said: These strokes
64 I make not without a purpose.
65 Toward the setting of the sun are our enemies.
66 In striking the waters I strike our enemies.
67 The beaver went again against the current and came to the second bend of the river,
68 Where stood a sapling of the never-dying willow.
69 He cut down the sapling and dragged it to his house,
70 Then he spake, saying: When the little ones use this for counting,
71 They shall always count their o-don' with accuracy.
72 Verily, at that time and place, it has been said, in this house,
73 The beaver went again against the current and came to a third bend of the river,
74 Where stood a sapling of the never-dying willow.
75 He cut down the sapling and dragged it to his house,
76 Then he spake, saying: When the little ones use this for counting,
77 They shall always count their o-don' with accuracy.
78 The beaver went again against the current and came to the fourth bend of the river,
79 Where stood a sapling of the never-dying willow.
80 He cut down the sapling and dragged it to his house,
81 Then he spake, saying: When the little ones use this for counting,
82 They shall always count their o-don' with accuracy.
83 The beaver went again against the current and came to the fifth bend of the river,
84 Where stood a sapling of the never-dying willow.

85 He cut down the sapling and dragged it to his house,
86 Then he spake, saying: When the little ones use this for counting,
87 They shall always count their o-don' with accuracy.
88 The beaver went again against the current and came to the sixth bend of the river,
89 Where stood a sapling of the never-dying willow.
90 He cut down the sapling and dragged it to his house,
91 Then he spake, saying: When the little ones use this for counting,
92 They shall always count their o-don' with accuracy.
93 The beaver went again against the current and came to the seventh bend of the river,
94 Where stood a sapling of the never-dying willow.
95 He cut down the sapling and dragged it to his house,
98 Then he spake, saying: This also the little ones shall use.
97 When the little ones use this for counting,
98 They shall always count their o-don' with accuracy.

In bringing this wi'-gi-e to a close, Charley Wah-hre-she remarked that he omitted the section relating to the six willow saplings for counting o-don', it being the practice of the priests to omit it when giving this ritual. It seems that where a practice of this kind is established, it is not necessary to ask the customary permission to make such omission. The candidate or his relatives may, however, insist upon the reciting of the wi'-gi-es without any omissions, although the lines may be merely tiresome repetitions. Wah-hre-she remarked, further, that to recite the section relating to the six willow saplings would be a repetition of the first six lines, word for word, of the section relating to the seven willow saplings.

### The Ga-Tsiu' People[13]
According to Wah-hre-she, this clan has no clan symbol of its own: nevertheless it is given a place in this ceremony as a we'-ga-xe and counted as the seventh clan of the Water People because of its office of Sho'-ka. It is the Sho'-ka of both the Deer people and the Fish [Bow] people clans. Wah-hre-she hesitated to give the meaning of the name Ga-tsiu', but suggested that possibly it means "Turtle with a serrated tail." (See line 8, wi'-gi-e of the Elder Water.)

### The Isolated Earth People
1 Verily, at that time and place, it has been said, in this house,
2 They (the people) spake to the Isolated Earth,
3 Saying: O grandfather,
4 We have nothing that is fit to use as a symbol.
5 The Isolated Earth replied: O little ones,
6 You say you have nothing fit to us as a symbol.
7 I am one who is fitted for use as a symbol.

8 Verily, at that time and place, it has been said, in this house,

9 He set up a house,

10 And then he said: I have not set up this house without a purpose.

11 I have set it up so that within it the necks of living creatures shall be broken.

12 I have not set up this house without a purpose.

13 I have made it to represent and to be a symbol of the spider.

14 Verily, this house, like a snare, draws to itself

15 All living creatures, whosoever they may be.

16 Into it they shall throw themselves and become ensnared.

17 When the little ones use its power to make the animals appear,

18 Even before the break of day

19 The animals shall not fail to appear;

20 And in the evening of the day

21 The animals shall not fail to appear.

22 The oldest of all animals (the buffalo bull)

23 That lies upon the earth,

24 The little ones shall use its power to make the animals appear.

25 With the life blood of that animal,

26 Even before the break of day

27 They shall always renew their own life blood.

28 And in the evening of the day

29 The little ones shall renew their life blood with that of this animal.

30 Verily, at that time and place, it has been said, in this house,

31 He spake again, saying: These are the things that shall stand as symbols for the little ones:

32 The short snake (the spreading adder)

33 Shall always be a symbol to the little ones.

34 Then above the bunches of tall grass

35 The short snake lifted his head and spake, saying:

36 Even though the little ones pass into the realm of spirits,

37 They shall, by the use of my fangs, bring themselves back to life and consciousness.

38 When the little ones make of me their bodies,

39 The four successive days,

40 They shall always successfully reach and enter.

41 The Isolated Earth continued, saying: The little ones shall use for a symbol

42 The long snake dotted with yellow spots (the bull snake).

43 The little ones shall always use this snake for a symbol.

44 Then above the bunches of tall grass

45 The long snake with yellow spots lifted his head.

46 This snake also

47 The little ones shall always use as a symbol.

48 Then spake the snake, saying: Even though the little ones pass into the realm of spirits,

49 They shall by the use of my strength recover consciousness.
50 The four successive days
51 They shall always successfully reach and enter.
52 The Isolated Earth continued, saying: The little ones shall use for a symbol
53 The black snake.
54 The little ones shall always use it as a symbol.
55 Then above the bunches of tall grass
56 The black snake lifted his head.
57 This snake also spake, saying:
58 Even though the little ones pass into the realm of spirits,
59 They shall by my aid bring themselves back to consciousness.
60 The four successive days
61 They shall always successfully reach and enter.
62 The Isolated Earth continued, saying: The little ones shall use as a symbol
63 The great snake (the rattlesnake).
64 From amidst the bunches of tall grass
65 The snake caused itself to be heard by making a buzzing sound.
66 That snake also spake, saying:
67 Even though the little ones pass into the realm of spirits,
68 They shall, by clinging to me and using my strength, recover consciousness.
69 The great snake,
70 Making a sound like the blowing of the wind,
71 Close to the feet (of the sick),
72 He repeatedly sounded his rattle as he stood.
73 Close to the head (of the sick)
74 He repeatedly sounded his rattle.
75 Toward the east winds
76 He repeatedly sounded his rattle.
77 Toward the west winds
78 He repeatedly sounded his rattle.
79 Toward the winds from the cedars (the north)
80 He repeatedly sounded his rattle,
81 Then spake, saying: Even though the little ones pass into the realm of spirits,
82 They shall always with my aid bring themselves back to consciousness.
83 When the little ones make of me their bodies,
84 The four great divisions of the days
85 They shall reach successfully,
86 And then into the days of peace and beauty
87 They shall always make their entrance.

### Wi'-gi-e of the Land People Clans

#### The Eagle People

1 Verily, at that time and place, it has been said, in this house,
2 The Land peoples, a people who possess seven fireplaces,

3 Spake to the Hon'-ga A-hiu-ton [eagle],
4 Saying: O grandfather,
5 The little ones have nothing that is fit to use as a symbol.
6 Verily, at that time and place, it has been said, in this house,
7 The Winged Earth [eagle] replied, saying: You say the little ones have nothing that is fit to use as a symbol.
8 I am one who is fitted for use as a symbol.
9 Of the bird that is without stain (evil disposition, the golden eagle)
10 I, as a person, have, verily, made my body.
11 I am continually watched over by all the powers as one worthy of their notice.
12 When the little ones make of me their bodies,
13 They too shall be watched over by all the powers as worthy of their notice.
14 I am fitted for the use of the little ones as a means to reach old age.
15 Behold the skin of my feet.
16 I have made it to be the means to reach old age.
17 When the little ones make of it the means to reach old age,
18 They shall always live to see old age.
19 Behold the skin of my feet where they are dark in color.
20 I have made these dark parts of my feet to be as my charcoal.
21 When the little ones make them to be as their charcoal,
22 They shall have charcoal that will easily sink into their skin.
23 Behold, the tip of my beak is black in color.
24 My black beak I have made to be as my charcoal.
25 When the little ones make of me their bodies,
26 They shall have charcoal that will easily sink into their skins.
27 Behold the parts of my body that are black.
28 I have made the parts of my body that are black to be as my charcoal.
29 When the little ones make of me their bodies,
30 They shall have charcoal that will easily sink into their bodies.
31 Behold the tip of my tail, that is dark in color.
32 I have made the black tip of my tail to be as my charcoal.
33 When the little ones make of me their bodies,
34 They shall have charcoal that will easily sink into their skin.

### The Bear People
1 Verily, at that time and place, it has been said, in this house,
2 The Land people, a people who possess seven fireplaces,
3 Spake to the Black Bear (clan),
4 Saying: O grandfather,
5 The little ones have nothing of which to make their bodies.
6 The Black Bear made quick response: O little ones,
7 You say the little ones have nothing of which to make their bodies.
8 Let the little ones make of me their bodies.

9 Let them also make of me their charcoal.

10 Behold the skin of my feet, that is dark in color.

11 I have made my feet to be as my charcoal.

12 Behold the tip of my nose, that is dark in color.

13 I have made the tip of my nose to be as my charcoal.

14 When the little ones make the tip of my nose to be as their charcoal,

15 They shall always have charcoal that will easily sink into their skin as they travel the path of life.

16 Behold my body that in all its parts is black in color.

17 I have made my body to be as my charcoal.

18 When the little ones also make my body to be as their charcoal,

19 They shall always have charcoal that will easily sink into their skin as they travel the path of life.

20 Verily, at that time and place, it has been said, in this house,

21 The people spake again to the Black Bear, saying: O grandfather,

22 The little ones have nothing of which to make their bodies.

23 The Black Bear replied: The little ones shall make of me their bodies.

24 Of the male puma that lies upon the earth,

25 I, as a person, have, verily, made my body.

26 Of the power of day that sitteth in the heavens,

27 I, as a person, have, verily, made my body.

28 Verily, at that time and place, it has been said, in this house,

29 He continued (speaking as the puma): Behold the soles of my feet, that are black in color.

30 I have made the skin of the soles of my feet to be as my charcoal.

31 When the little ones also make of the skin of the soles of my feet to be as their charcoal,

32 They shall always have charcoal that will easily sink into their skin as they travel the path of life.

33 Behold the tip of my nose, that is black in color.

34 I have made the tip of my nose to be as my charcoal.

35 When the little ones make of me their bodies,

36 They shall always have charcoal that will easily sink into their skin.

37 Behold the tips of my ears that are black in color.

38 I have made the tips of my ears to be as my charcoal.

39 When the little ones make of me their bodies,

40 They shall always have charcoal that will easily sink into their skin.

41 Behold the tip of my tail that is black in color.

42 I have made the tip of my tail to be as my charcoal.

43 When the little ones make of me their bodies,

44 They shall always have charcoal that will easily sink into their skin as they travel the path of life.

45 Verily, at that time and place, it has been said, in this house,

46 The people spake to the great white swan (a subclan of the Black Bear),

47 Saying: O grandfather,

48 The little ones have nothing of which to make their bodies.

49 Verily, at that time and place, it has been said, in this house,

50 The great white swan replied: Behold the skin of my feet that is dark in color.

51 I have made the dark skin of my feet to be as my charcoal.

52 When the little ones make the dark skin of my feet to be as their charcoal,

53 They shall always have charcoal that will easily sink into their skin as they travel the path of life.

54 Behold the tip of my beak that is dark in color.

55 I have made the dark tip of my beak to be as my charcoal.

56 When the little ones make of me their bodies,

57 They shall always have charcoal that will easily sink into their skin as they travel the path of life.

58 Thus shall it be with the little ones when they make of me their bodies.

59 Even within half of a day

60 I reach, when making my flight, the farther side of the great lake,

61 Where I sit upon its waves swinging up and down.

62 When the little ones make of me their bodies,

63 Their arms, like my wings, I shall cause to become strong as they travel the path of life.

64 When all animals are gathered together for a test of endurance,

65 They become breathless sooner than I on my life's journey.

66 When the little ones make of me their bodies,

67 Verily, none of the living creatures shall surpass them

68 In power of strength and endurance as they travel the path of life.

## The Puma People

1 Verily, at that time and place, it has been said, in this house,

2 The Land people, a people who possess seven fireplaces,

3 Spake to the one who had made of the Puma his body,

4 Saying: O grandfather,

5 We have nothing that is fit to use as a symbol.

6 The Puma quickly replied: O little ones,

7 You say you have nothing that is fit to use as a symbol.

8 I am one who is fitted for use as a symbol.

9 Behold the male puma, that lieth upon the earth.

10 Verily, I am a person who has made of the male puma his body,

11 The knowledge of my courage has spread over the land.

12 Behold the force of day, that sitteth in the heavens.

13 Verily, I am a person who sitteth close to the force of day.

14 When the little ones make of me their bodies,

15 They shall always be free from all causes of death as they travel the path of life.

16 Behold the great red boulder, that sitteth upon the earth.

17 Verily, I am a person who draws to himself the power of the great boulder.

18 Behold the great red boulder, that sitteth upon the earth.

19 Even the great powers themselves

20 Stumble over me as I sit immovable as the great red boulder.

21 When the little ones make of me their bodies,

22 Even the great powers shall stumble over them and fall.

23 Even the great powers themselves

24 As they move over the earth pass around me as I sit immovable as the great red boulder.

25 When the little ones make of me their bodies,

26 Even the great powers themselves shall pass around them in forked lines as they travel the path of life.

27 Even the great powers themselves

28 Fear to stare me in the face with insolence.

29 When the little ones make of me their bodies,

30 Even the powers themselves

31 Shall fear to stare them in the face, as they travel the path of life.

32 Verily, at that time and place, it has been said, in this house,

33 He said to them: Behold the Black Bear, that is without a blemish, that lieth upon the earth.

34 Verily, I am a person who has made of the Black Bear his body.

35 Behold the force of night, that sitteth in the heavens.

36 Verily, I am a person who maketh the Black Bear to draw from the force of night its power.

37 Behold the great black boulder, that sitteth upon the earth.

38 Verily, I am a person who sitteth close to the great black boulder.

39 Behold the great black boulder, that sitteth upon the earth.

40 When the little ones make of the great black boulder their bodies,

41 Even the great powers themselves

42 Shall stumble over them and fall.

43 Even the powers themselves

44 As they move over the earth pass around me in forked lines as I sit immovable as the great black boulder.

45 When the little ones make of me their bodies,

46 Even the powers themselves

47 Shall pass around them in forked lines as they travel the path of life.

48 Verily, at that time and place, it has been said, in this house,

49 He said to them: Behold the great white swan.

50 Verily, I am a person who has made of the great white swan his body.

51 Behold, the force of night (the Wa'-tse Do-ga, The Male Star, the morning star).

52 Verily, I am a person who has made of the force of night his body.

53 Behold, the great white boulder, that sitteth upon the earth.

54 Verily, I am a person who has made of the great white boulder his body.

55 When the little ones make of me their bodies,
56 Even the powers themselves
57 Shall stumble over them and fall.
58 Even the powers themselves
59 As they move over the earth pass around me as I sit immovable as the great white boulder.
60 When the little ones make of me their bodies,
61 Even the powers themselves
62 Shall pass around them as they pass around the great white boulder.
63 Verily, at that time and place, it has been said, in this house,
64 He said to them: Behold the male elk, that lieth upon the earth.
65 Behold, the yellow boulder, that sitteth upon the earth.
66 Verily, I am a person who maketh the male elk to draw from the yellow boulder its power.
67 Behold Wa'-tse Mi-ga (the Female Star, the evening star).
68 Verily, I am a person who maketh the yellow boulder to draw from the evening star its power.
69 When the little ones make of me their bodies,
70 Even the powers themselves
71 Shall stumble over them and fall.
72 Even the powers themselves
73 As they move over the earth pass around me as I sit immovable as the great yellow boulder.
74 When the little ones make of me their bodies,
75 Even the powers themselves
76 Shall pass around them as they pass around the great yellow boulder.
77 Even the powers themselves
78 Fear to set teeth upon me in anger.
79 When the little ones make of me their bodies,
80 The powers themselves shall fear to set teeth upon them in anger.
81 Verily, at that time and place, it has been said, in this house,
82 He said to them: Even the powers themselves
83 Fear to stare me in the face with insolence.
84 When the little ones make of me their bodies,
85 Even the powers themselves
86 Shall fear to stare them in the face with insolence.
87 I am difficult to overcome by death.
88 When the little ones make of me their bodies,
89 They also shall always be difficult to overcome by death.
90 The four successive days
91 They shall cause themselves to reach and to enter.
92 The people of the Water
93 And those of the Sky
94 Shall make of me their bodies.

95 When they make of me their bodies,
96 They shall cause themselves to be difficult to overcome by death.
97 The powers themselves shall fear to set teeth upon them in anger.
98 They shall always live to see old age.
99 The four successive days
100 They shall always reach and enter.
101 Verily, at that time and place, it has been said, in this house,
102 The Land people, a people who possess seven fireplaces,
103 Spake to the one who had made of the Puma his body,
104 Saying: O grandfather,
105 We have nothing that is fit to use as a symbol.
106 Verily, at that time and place, it has been said, in this house,
107 The Puma replied: You say you have nothing that is fit to use as a symbol.
108 I shall go forth and make search.
109 Verily, at that time and place, it has been said, in this house,
110 He strode away forthwith to make search,
111 And he came to the margin of a lake,
112 Where, within its bed of mud, sat the cin (the bulbous root of Sagittaria latifolia).
113 He dug it up and sent it rolling on the bank, where he stood.
114 Then in haste he carried it home to the people,
115 And standing before them said: How will this serve as a symbol, O elder brothers?
116 With eager haste the people munched the bulbous root,
117 Then said: It cannot be used as food.
118 Verily, it is not what we desire, O younger brother.
119 Although that be true, nevertheless
120 We shall put it to use in other ways, O younger brother, as we travel the path of life.
121 Again he strode away forthwith
122 And came to the middle of a lake,
123 Where, within its bed of mud, lay the tse'-wa-the (the root of the Nelumbo lutea).
124 With a quick movement of his foot he lifted the root from its bed of soft earth.
125 Then in haste he brought it home to the people,
126 To whom he said: How will this serve as a symbol, O elder brothers?
127 With eager haste the people munched the root,
128 And, like milk, its juice squirted out as they pressed the root between their teeth,
129 And they spake, saying: It is fit for the little ones to use as food.
130 It is fit for them to use as a symbol, O younger brother.
131 The little ones shall use this for food in their life's journey.
132 The people of the Water

133 And those of the Sky
134 Shall always use this root for food.
135 Verily, at that time and place, it has been said, in this house,
136 The people said to one another: Verily, we shall make the young bull
137 And this plant to be companions, O younger brothers.
138 The little ones shall use the two together as food.
139 When the little ones eat of these foods, as they travel the path of life,
140 Their limbs shall always stretch in growth.
141 Again the Puma went forth and came to the farther margin of the lake,
142 Where, within the soft earth of its borders, sat the Do (the root of the
    Glycine apios).
143 He dug it up and sent it rolling upon the earth.
144 Then in haste he brought it home to the people,
145 Who said to him: This is what you have been continually searching for, O
    younger brother.
146 They munched it, and, like milk, its juice squirted within their mouths,
147 And they said: The little ones shall use this root as food in their life's
    journey.
148 When the little ones use this root as food,
149 Their limbs shall always stretch in growth.
150 Verily, at that time and place, it has been said, in this house,
151 The people said to one another: The deer with dark horns
152 We shall make this plant to draw, O younger brothers.
153 When we make this plant to draw to us the dark-horned deer,
154 The people of the Water
155 And those of the Sky
156 Shall always use these two foods together in their life's journey.
157 When they use these two foods together,
158 Their limbs shall always stretch in growth.
159 When they use these two foods to make their limbs to grow,
160 They shall always live to see old age.
161 Again the Puma went forth to the farther bank of the lake.
162 Verily, to a lowland forest,
163 Where, in the mellow earth, sat the Hon-bthin'-cu (a wild bean, Falcata
    comosa).
164 He dug it up and sent it rolling upon the earth.
165 This root also, the people said,
166 The little ones shall use as food in their life's journey.
167 When the little ones use this root as food in their life's journey,
168 They shall always live to see old age.
169 Verily, at that time and place, it has been said, in this house,
170 The people said: The turkey
171 Shall be drawn toward us by this plant, O younger brothers.
172 When the little ones use the two together for food,

173 They shall always live to see old age.
174 When the people of the Water
175 And those of the Sky
176 Use the bean and the turkey as food,
177 They shall always live to see old age.
178 The four great divisions of the days
179 They shall always reach and cause themselves to enter.

### The Elk People

1 Verily, at that time and place, it has been said, in this house,
2 The Land people, a people who possess seven fireplaces,
3 Spake to the clan who made of the Puma his body,
4 Saying, O younger brother,
5 We have nothing that is fit to use as a symbol.
6 Whereupon the Puma with hastened steps went forth
7 And came suddenly upon the male elk,
8 Who stood upon the earth.
9 The Puma returned in haste to his elder brothers,
10 Who said to him: O younger brother!
11 The Puma replied, saying: O elder brothers, I went forth and came upon a man who stands yonder.
12 The people spake to one another, saying: O younger brothers,
13 Whoever the man may be who stands yonder,
14 We will send him to the abode of spirits.
15 With heads bent thitherward they hastened to the man,
16 The oldest of the brothers moistening in his mouth his index finger in readiness to slay the stranger.
17 With quickened footsteps they set forth
18 Toward the male elk.
19 They came upon him and stood with heads inclined toward him.
20 The male elk hastened to say: O elder brothers,
21 I am a Hon'-ga (a sacred person), he stood saying.
22 I am the Great Elk, O elder brothers.
23 I am a person who is never absent from any important act.
24 I am a person who can be of use to you as a symbol.
25 Great Elk
26 Is a name that I have taken to myself, O elder brothers.
27 Verily, at that time and place, it has been said, in this house,
28 He repeated: I am a person who can be of use to you as a symbol.
29 When the little ones use me as an instrument for making the animals to appear,
30 The animals shall always appear for them.
31 Verily, at that time and place, it has been said, in this house,
32 The Great Elk started to perform some mysterious acts.

33 In the midst of each of the four winds
34 He threw himself upon the earth.
35 In the midst of the east wind
36 He threw himself upon the earth,
37 And as he stood, the sky of the day became calm and peaceful.
38 In the midst of the north wind
39 He threw himself upon the earth,
40 And the sky, as though touched with gentle hands, became permeated with gentleness and peace, as he stood.
41 In the midst of the west winds
42 He threw himself upon the earth,
43 And from the powers above (the overarching heaven)
44 As he stood he swept away all traces of anger.
45 In the midst of the south wind
46 He threw himself upon the earth,
47 And as he stood, from every part of the earth
48 He verily cleansed the land of all anger.
49 Verily, at that time and place, it has been said, in this house,
50 He spake to the people, saying: I am a person who is suitable to be used by you as a symbol.
51 Then again he threw himself upon the earth.
52 As he arose to his feet he left the surface of the earth covered with the hairs of his body,
53 And he spake again, saying: These hairs
54 I have scattered upon the earth so that the animals may appear in their midst.
55 They are the grasses of the earth.
56 I have made them for you for making the animals to appear, in order that you might live.
57 The little ones shall always see the animals appear in the midst of the grasses of the earth.
58 Verily; at that time and place, it has been said, in this house,
59 The Great Elk threw himself once more upon the earth,
60 And as he arose to his feet he stood with his buttocks toward the people,
61 And he spake, saying: Behold the ball-like muscles of my buttocks.
62 They are the round hills of the earth.
63 I have made them to represent all the round hills of the earth.
64 Amidst the round hills of the earth the little ones shall always see the animals appear.
65 Behold the right side of my body.
66 It is the level lands of the earth.
67 I have made it to represent all the level lands of the earth.
68 Behold the ridge of my back.
69 It is the ridges of the earth.

70 I have made it to represent all the ridges of the earth.
71 When the little ones approach the ridges of the earth,
72 They shall always see the animals appear in their midst.
73 Behold the curve of my neck.
74 It is the gaps in the ridges of the earth.
75 I have made it to represent all the gaps in the ridges of the earth.
76 When the little ones approach these gaps of the ridges,
77 They shall always see the animals appear in the gaps.
78 Behold also the tip of my nose.
79 It is the peaks of the earth.
80 I have made it to represent all the peaks of the earth.
81 When the little ones approach the peaks,
82 They shall always see the animals appear in the midst of the peaks.
83 Behold the bases of my horns.
84 They are the loose rocks of the earth.
85 When the little ones approach the loose rocks, they shall always see the animals appear in their midst.
86 Behold the branches of my horns.
87 They are the branches of the rivers.
88 The little ones shall always see the animals appear along the branches of the rivers.
89 Behold the smaller tines of my horns.
90 They are the creeks of the earth.
91 The little ones shall always see the animals appear along the creeks of the earth.
92 Behold the large tines of my horns.
93 They are the large streams that are dotted here and there with forests.
94 I make them to represent all the large streams of the earth.
95 When the little ones approach one of these streams in their life's journey,
96 They shall always see the animals appear along the banks.
97 Behold the largest parts of my horns.
98 They are the rivers.
99 I have made them to be the places where the animals shall appear.
100 When the little ones approach one of these rivers,
101 They shall always see the animals along the banks.
102 When the little ones go forth to hunt,
103 Even before the break of day,
104 They shall always see the animals appear,
105 And in the evening of the day
106 They shall always see the animals appear.
107 The people of the Water
108 And those of the Sky
109 Shall always make use of me as a symbol as they travel the path of life.

## The Crawfish People

1 Verily, at that time and place, it has been said, in this house,
2 The Land people, a people who possess seven fireplaces,
3 Spake to the clan who had made of the Puma his body,
4 Saying: O younger brother,
5 We have nothing that is fit to use as a symbol.
6 Verily, upon the utterance of these words by the people,
7 The Puma went forth to an open prairie, where trees grow not,
8 Where he came face to face with a man who stood upright
9 In the midst of the prairie with uplifted hand.
10 The Puma turned and hastened toward home.
11 The people spake to one another, saying: Our younger brother is returning.
12 His manner indicates that he bears great tidings.
13 Soon he stood before the people, saying: A man stands yonder, O elder brothers.
14 What sayest thou? O younger brother, they said to him.
15 And he repeated: A man stands yonder, O elder brothers,
16 With a cloven hand uplifted.
17 Then the peoples spake to one another, saying: O younger brothers,
18 Whatever man he may be who stands yonder
19 We shall send him to the abode of spirits, O younger brothers.
20 Then with heads bent toward the man
21 The people strode forth in haste,
22 And soon came face to face with the man who stood in the prairies.
23 Stood with a cloven hand uplifted.
24 Ho! younger brother, they said to him,
25 What man art thou that stands before us?
26 The man replied: I am a Hon'-ga (a sacred person).
27 I am the Crawfish.
28 I am the Little Earth, O elder brothers.
28 The man continued quickly: O elder brothers,
30 I am a person who is ever present at any important movement.
31 I am a person who, in truth, is a symbol.
32 A person who holds himself ready to be used as a symbol, O elder brothers.
33 Verily, at that time and place, it has been said, in this house,
34 Within a hillock of soft mud
35 He disappeared as though sucked into his home
36 And quickly reappeared with a bit of dark soil,
37 Which he held aloft as he stood offering it to the people, and he spake to them, saying:
38 This bit of dark earth, O elder brothers,
39 You shall use as a symbol when offering your supplications.
40 Then, even before the sun rises to the height of your houses,

41 You shall never fail to have your prayers granted in your life's journey, O elder brothers.

42 I have bestowed upon you a gift that will make you gratefully happy, O elder brothers.

43 Then, gently and slowly,

44 The man again descended into the earth

45 And reappeared with a bit of blue clay,

46 Which he stood offering to the people as he spake to them, saying:

47 This bit of blue clay, O elder brothers,

48 You shall always use as a symbol, O elder brothers.

49 When you use it as a symbol while offering your supplications,

50 You shall never fail to have your prayers granted, O elder brothers.

51 Verily, at that time and place, it has been said, in this house,

52 He continued: You shall always use the blue clay as a symbol, O elder brothers.

53 For a third time

54 The man descended into the earth

55 And reappeared with a bit of red clay,

56 Which he stood offering to the people as he spake to them, saying:

57 This bit of red clay also

58 You shall always use as a symbol, O elder brothers.

59 By its aid you shall with ease excite compassion and your prayers shall be granted, O elder brothers.

60 Verily, at that time and place, it has been said, in this house,

61 The man for the fourth time

62 Descended into the earth

63 And brought forth a bit of yellow clay,

64 Which he stood offering to the people as he spake to them, saying:

65 This bit of yellow clay also

66 You shall always use as a symbol.

67 When you use it as a symbol while offering your supplications,

68 Then, even before the sun rises to the height of your houses,

69 You shall never fail to have your prayers granted on your life's journey, O elder brothers.

70 Verily, at that time and place, it has been said, in this house,

71 He spake again, saying: Behold my cloven hand.

72 My cloven hand also

73 You shall always use as a symbol, O elder brothers.

74 There are poles that are spoken of as forked poles.

75 My cloven hand shall be represented by the forked poles that you may use for any purpose, O elder brothers.

76 When toward the setting sun you go against your enemies,

77 With a craving for success to vanquish them,

78 By the aid of this symbol you shall not fail to win success, O elder brothers.

The Wind People

1 Verily, at that time and place, it has been said, in this house,
2 The people spake to one another, saying: O younger brothers,
3 We have nothing that is fit to use as a symbol.
4 Then he who had made the Puma to be his body
5 Hastened forth to make search.
6 In the midst of an open prairie, where trees grow not,
7 There stood the Youngest Land (The youngest, or the last of the Land subdivision in the tribal order),
8 With whom he stood face to face.
9 The Youngest Land spake quickly, saying: O elder brother.
10 The Puma asked: What man art thou?
11 Youngest Land replied: I am Hon'-ga Gthe-zhe (the sacred spotted eagle).
12 I am a Hon'-ga (a sacred person), O elder brother,
13 A person who is fitted for use as a symbol.
14 The people shall always use me as a symbol as they travel the path of life.
15 When they so use me,
16 The people of the Water
17 And those of the Sky
18 Shall always use me as a symbol.
19 When they so use me,
20 Even before the sun rises to the height of their houses,
21 They shall easily win compassion and their prayers shall be granted as they travel the path of life.
22 I, who stand here, have given you that which will make you gratefully happy.

Wi'-gi-e of the Sky People Clans

The Elder Sky People

1 Verily, at that time and place, it has been said, in this house,
2 The Sky people, a people who possess seven fireplaces,
3 Spake to the Elder Sky,
4 Saying: O grandfather,
5 We have nothing that is fit for use as a symbol.
6 The Elder Sky replied:
7 You say you have nothing that is fit to use as a symbol.
8 I am a person who is fit to use as a symbol,
9 For of the force of day who sitteth in the heavens,
10 I, as a person, have verily made my body.
11 When the little ones make of me their bodies,
12 Even of the force of day who sitteth in the heavens,
13 The little ones as a people shall make their bodies.

14 When the little ones make of the power of day their bodies,

15 They shall be free from all causes of death.

16 When they make of the power of day the means of reaching old age,

17 They shall always live to see old age as they travel the path of life.

18 Verily, at that time and place, it has been said, in this house,

19 Of these powers the little ones shall make their bodies,

20 Of the force of night who sitteth in the heavens,

21 I, as a person, have verily made my body.

22 When the little ones make of me their bodies,

23 Even I, who am difficult to be overcome by death,

24 When the little ones make of me their bodies,

25 They shall cause themselves to be difficult to overcome by death as they travel the path of life.

26 Of the male star, who sitteth in the heavens (the morning star),

27 That power also,

28 The little ones shall make their bodies.

29 When the little ones make of the morning star their bodies,

30 They shall enable themselves to live to see old age as they travel the path of life.

31 The female star, who sitteth in the heavens (the evening star),

32 Of that power also

33 The little ones shall make their bodies.

34 Then they shall cause themselves to be difficult to overcome by death.

35 When they make of her the means of reaching old age,

36 They shall enable themselves to live to see old age as they travel the path of life.

37 Verily, at that time and place, it has been said, in this house,

38 There is a force who never fails to appear at the beginning of day.

39 Upon the left side of this power

40 There stand six rays (stripes, as though made by strokes):

41 These six rays

42 I have made to be symbols,

43 Symbols of the acts spoken of as o-don' (valorous or warlike acts).

44 When they make of these rays the symbols of their o-don'

45 They shall enable themselves to count with accuracy their o-don' as they travel the path of life.

46 Upon the right side of this power

47 There stand seven rays (rays of like appearance to the six rays).

48 Those seven rays also

49 I have made to be symbols,

50 Symbols of the acts spoken of as o-don' I have made them to be.

51 Verily, I have made them all to stand as the o-don' of the people.

52 When the little ones use these rays for counting their o-don',

53 They shall enable themselves to account with accuracy the deeds by which they won their o-don' as they travel the path of life.

54 Verily, at that time and place, it has been said, in this house,
55 It was said: Of what else shall the little ones make their bodies?
56 Verily, at that time and place, it has been said, in this house,
57 The Elder Sky replied:
58 There is a bird that has a long bill (the pileated woodpecker).
59 Of that bird also
60 I, as a person, have verily made my body.
61 The force of day, who sitteth in the heavens,
62 I have made the bird to symbolize.
63 The force of night, who sitteth in the heavens,
64 I have made the bird to symbolize.
65 The male star, who sitteth in the heavens,
66 I have made that bird to symbolize.
67 When the little ones make of me their bodies,
68 They shall always find a plentiful supply of the earth's riches.
69 When they go toward the setting sun against their enemies,
70 Taking with them the bird as a symbol through which to offer their supplications,
71 They shall never fail to succeed as they travel the path of life.
72 The female star, who sitteth in the heavens,
73 I have caused that bird to symbolize.
74 When the little ones go toward the setting sun against their enemies,
75 Taking with them the bird as a symbol through which to offer their supplications,
76 They shall never fail to succeed as they travel the path of life,
77 They shall always find a plentiful supply of the earth's riches.
78 When the little ones make of me their bodies,
79 They shall enable themselves to live to see old age as they travel the path of life;
80 The four great divisions of the days
81 They shall enable themselves to reach and enter.
82 When the people of the Water
83 And those of the Land
84 Make of me their symbol throughout their life's journey,
85 They shall never fail to succeed as they travel the path of life.

## The Buffalo-Face People

The presence of the Tse-do'-ga In-dse (Buffalo-face clan) is necessary in this ceremony in order to complete the tableau of the sky, the great bodies that move therein, and the animal life in the earth to which they are related. This clan occupies the second place in the ceremonial order of the clans composing the Sky moiety, but, as in the case of the Cattail clan, its members remain silent throughout the ceremony. The head of the clan, however, is given a fee for his services, and the members share in the distribution of the provisions provided by the candidate.

The Sun Carrier People

1 Verily, at that time and place, it has been said, in this house,
2 The Sky people, a people who possess seven fireplaces,
3 Spake to the Elder Sun Carrier,
4 Saying: O grandfather,
5 We have nothing that is suitable to use as a symbol.
6 The Elder Sun Carrier quickly replied:
7 You say you have nothing that is suitable to use as a symbol.
8 I am a person of whom you may well make your bodies,
9 For of the force of day who sitteth in the heaven,
10 I, as a person, have verily made my body.
11 When the little ones make of me their bodies,
12 Of the force of day who sitteth in the heavens,
13 They, as a people, shall verily make their bodies, as they travel the path of life.
14 When they make of the power of day their bodies,
15 They shall be free from all causes of death;
16 When they also make of him the means of reaching old age,
17 They shall enable themselves to live to see old age, as they travel the path of life.
18 Verily, at that time and place, it has been said, in this house,
19 He said to them: Of the force of night who sitteth in the heavens (moon),
20 I, as a person, have verily made my body.
21 When the little ones make of me their bodies,
22 Of the force of night who sitteth in the heavens,
23 They, as a people, shall make their bodies, as they travel the path of life.
24 I am difficult to be overcome by death.
25 When of the force of night
26 The little ones also make their bodies,
27 They shall cause themselves to be difficult to overcome by death;
28 When they make of the power of night the means of reaching old age,
29 They shall enable themselves to live to see old age, as they travel the path of life.
30 Of the male star (the morning star),
31 Who sitteth in the heavens,
32 I, as a person, have verily made my body;
33 When the little ones also make of him their bodies,
34 When they make of the morning star
35 Their bodies as they travel the path of life,
36 They shall cause themselves to be difficult to overcome by death.
37 When they make of him the means of reaching old age,
38 They shall enable themselves to live to see old age, as they travel the path of life.
39 Of the female star (the evening star)
40 I, as a person, have verily made my body.

41 When the little ones also make of her their bodies
42 They shall cause themselves to be difficult to overcome by death;
43 When they make of her the means of reaching old age,
44 They shall enable themselves to live to see old age as they travel the path of life.
45 Verily, at that time and place, it has been said, in this house,
46 He said to them: Of these powers the little ones shall make their bodies.
47 The force who never fails to appear at the beginning of day (the sun),
48 Has upon his left side (see lines 37 to 53 of the Elder Sky Wi'-gi-e)
49 Six rays (stripes) that stand upright.
50 These six rays
51 I have made to be symbols (of warlike acts).
52 When the little ones use these six rays for counting their o-don'
53 They shall count with accuracy their o-don' as they travel the path of life.
54 The force who never fails to appear at the beginning of day
55 Has upon his right side
56 Seven rays that stand upright.
57 These seven rays (stripes)
58 I have made to be symbols.
59 When the little ones use these seven rays for counting their o-don',
60 They shall count with accuracy their o-don' as they travel the path of life.

### The Night People

1 Verily, at that time and place, it has been said, in this house,
2 The Sky people, a people who possess seven fireplaces,
3 Spake to the People of the Night,
4 Saying: O grandfather,
5 We have nothing that is suitable to use as a symbol.
6 He hastened to reply, saying: O little ones,
7 I am a person who is suitable for use as a symbol.
8 Of the Black Bear, who is without a blemish,
9 I, as a person, have verily made my body.
10 When the little ones also make of him their bodies
11 They shall always be free from all causes of death,
12 And they shall enable themselves to live to see old age as they travel the path of life.
13 Behold the skin of my feet wherein it is dark in color.
14 The dark soles of my feet I have made to be as my charcoal;
15 When the little ones also make it to be as their charcoal
16 They shall have charcoal that will easily sink into their skin as they travel the path of life.
17 Behold, the tip of my nose is dark in color.
18 The dark tip of my nose I have made to be as my charcoal;
19 When the little ones also make it to be as their charcoal
20 They shall have charcoal that will easily sink into their skin.

21 Behold my body, that is black in color.
22 My body that is black in color I have made to be as my charcoal,
23 When the little ones also make it to be as their charcoal
24 They shall have charcoal that will easily sink into their skin.
25 When the little ones make of me the means of reaching old age
26 They shall always live to see old age;
27 And the four great divisions of days
28 They shall not fail to reach and to enter as they travel the path of life.

### The Gentle Sky People and Its Subclans[14]

1 Verily, at that time and place, it has been said, in this house,
2 The Sky people, a people who possess seven fireplaces,
3 Spake to the Gentle Sky people,
4 Who had made of the Red Eagle their body (red is here used as a trope),
5 Saying: O grandfather,
6 The little ones have nothing of which to make their bodies.
7 The Gentle Sky quickly replied: O little ones,
8 You say the little ones have nothing of which to make their bodies.
9 I am a person of whom the little ones may well make their bodies.
10 When they make of the Red Eagle
11 Their bodies in their life's journey,
12 They shall enable themselves to live to see old age as they travel the path of life.
13 The folds of the skin of my feet
14 I have made to be the means of reaching old age.
15 When the little ones also make of them the means of reaching old age,
16 They shall enable themselves to live to see old age as they travel the path of life.
17 The wrinkles of the muscles of my ankles also
18 I have made to be the means of reaching old age.
19 When the little ones also make of them the means of reaching old age,
20 They shall enable themselves to live to see in the muscles of their ankles the signs of old age.
21 The loose muscles of my legs
22 I have made to be the means of reaching old age.
23 When the little ones also make of them the means of reaching old age,
24 They shall enable themselves to live to see in the loose muscles of their legs the signs of old age.
25 The loose inner muscles of my thighs
26 I have made to be the means of reaching old age.
27 When the little ones also make of them the means of reaching old age,
28 They shall enable themselves to see old age as they travel the path of life.
29 The skin of my breast, gathered into folds,
30 I have made to be the means of reaching old age.
31 When the little ones also make of them the means of reaching old age,

32 They shall enable themselves to live to see in the skin of their breasts the signs of old age.
33 The loose muscles of my arms
34 I have also made to be the means of reaching old age.
35 When the little ones also make of them the means of reaching old age,
36 They shall enable themselves to live to see the muscles of their arms loosen with old age.
37 Behold my shoulders, that are bent with age,
38 Which I have also
39 Made to be the means of reaching old age.
40 When the little ones make of them the means of reaching old age,
41 They shall enable themselves to live to see in their shoulders the signs of old age.
42 The loose muscles of my throat
43 I have also
44 Made to be the means of reaching old age.
45 When the little ones make of them the means of reaching old age,
46 They shall enable themselves to live to see in the loosened muscles of their throats the signs of old age.
47 The hair on the crown of my head, grown thin with age,
48 I have also
49 Made to be the means of reaching old age.
50 When the little ones also make of my thin hair the means of reaching old age,
51 They shall enable themselves to live to see in the thinned hair of the crown of their heads the signs of old age.
52 The white hair on my head
53 I have also
54 Made to be the means of reaching old age.
55 When the little ones also make of my white hair the means of reaching old age,
56 They shall enable themselves to live to see that the hair on their heads has grown yellowish with age.
57 Of the power of day
58 I, as a person, as a people, have verily made my body.
59 Verily, there is a force who never fails to appear at the beginning of day,
60 The power who lies as though dipped in red (the dawn).
61 Of that power also
62 I, as a person, as a people, have verily made my body.
63 By the side of the force who never fails to appear at the beginning of day (the sun),
64 Even at his left side,
65 Stands a plumelike shaft of light.
66 I, as a person, as a people, have made my body of this plume.

67 When the little ones make their plumes like this shaft of light,
68 They shall always live to see old age.
69 When the little ones approach old age,
70 Having made their plumes like to the shaft of light,
71 Their symbolic plumes shall never droop as they travel the path of life.
72 By the side of the force who never fails to appear at the beginning of day (the sun),
73 Even at his right side,
74 There stands a plumelike shaft of light.
75 Of that shaft of light I have made my symbolic plume.
76 When the little ones make of that shaft of light their symbolic plumes,
77 They shall always live to see old age.
78 When the little ones approach old age,
79 Having made of that shaft of light their symbolic plumes,
80 Their symbolic plumes shall never droop as they travel the path of life.
81 I, as a person, verily make my abode in the days that are calm and peaceful.
82 When the little ones make of me their bodies,
83 They shall enable themselves to dwell as a people in the days that are calm and peaceful as they travel the path of life.
84 Verily, from all the powers
85 I, who stand here, have removed all signs of anger.
86 When the little ones make of me their bodies,
87 They shall enable themselves to remove from the forces
88 All signs of anger as they travel the path of life.
89 From the power who lies below (the earth)
90 I have removed all anger and violence.
91 From the power of daylight, who stands in the midst of the heavens,
92 I have removed all anger and violence.
93 From the power who lies above (the overarching sky)
94 I have removed all anger and violence.
95 Verily, from all the powers,
96 When the little ones make of me their bodies,
97 They shall enable themselves to remove all anger and violence as they travel the path of life.
98 When the people of the Water,
99 Together with those of the Land,
100 Make of me their bodies,
101 Verily, from over all the land,
102 They shall enable themselves to remove all anger and violence as they travel the path of life.
103 Verily, at that time and place, it has been said, in this house,
104 The Sky people, a people who possess seven fireplaces,
105 Spake to one of the Sky clan,
106 Verily, a person (clan) who stands having no anger or violence,

107 Saying: O my grandfather,
108 The little ones have nothing of which to make their bodies.
109 "No Anger" (the subclan of that name) replied, saying:
110 You say the little ones have nothing of which to make their bodies.
111 I am a person (a people) of whom the little ones may well make their
     bodies.
112 I am a person whose being abides in the moist, vibrating air of the earth.
113 When the little ones make of me their bodies,
114 They shall enable themselves to become a people of the moist, vibrating air
     of the earth as they travel the path of life.
115 Verily, in the days that are calm and peaceful,
116 I, as a person, make my abode.
117 When the little ones make of me their bodies,
118 They, as a people, shall abide in the days that are calm and peaceful as they
     travel the path of life.
119 The Peaceful Day
120 Is a personal name that I have taken.
121 When the little ones make of me their bodies,
122 They, as a people, shall abide in the days that are calm and peaceful, as
     they travel the path of life.
123 Of a little pipe (the Peace Pipe) I have made my body.
124 When the little ones also
125 Make of it their bodies,
126 They shall live without anger or violence as they travel the path of life.
127 When they use the pipe in seeking earthly riches,
128 They shall enable themselves to find riches in abundance.
129 It (the Pipe) shall also be the means by which they may obtain food.
130 When they use it as a means to obtain food,
131 They shall enable themselves to live to see old age as they travel the path of
     life.
132 Verily, at that time and place, it has been said, in this house,
133 He (No Anger) said to them: Of a little yellow flower
134 I, as a person, have, verily, made my body.
135 The little Ba-shta'-e-gon (Ratibida columnaris)
136 I, as a person, have, verily, made my body.
137 When the little ones make of it their bodies,
138 They shall cause themselves to live together without anger or violence,
139 And they shall live to see old age as they travel the path of life.
140 Verily, at that time and place, it has been said, in this house,
141 He further said to them: And when the little ones eat of this plant
142 They shall enable themselves to live to see old age as they travel the path of
     life.
143 Of the red corn
144 I, as a person, have, verily, made my body.

145 The little ones shall at all times make of the red corn their food.
146 When they make of it their food,
147 They shall enable themselves to live to see old age as they travel the path of life.
148 The blue corn
149 They shall also
150 Make to be their food at all times.
151 When they make the blue corn to be their food,
152 They shall enable themselves to live to see old age as they travel the path of life.
153 Verily, at that time and place, it has been said, in this house,
154 The speckled corn
155 They shall also
156 Make to be their food at all times.
157 When the little ones use the speckled corn for food,
158 They shall enable themselves to live to see old age as they travel the path of life.
159 When the little ones make the speckled corn to be their food,
160 They shall live to see their limbs stretch in growth as they travel the path of life.
161 Verily, at that time and place, it has been said, in this house,
162 He said to them: The yellow corn
163 They shall also
164 Use for food at all times.
165 When they use the yellow corn for food,
166 They shall enable themselves to live to see old age.
167 When the little ones use the yellow corn for food,
168 They shall live to see their limbs stretch in growth as they travel the path of life.
169 The people of the Water
170 And those of the Land
171 Shall use the corn for food at all times.
172 When they use it for food,
173 They shall enable themselves to live to see old age as they travel the path of life.
174 The four great divisions of the days,
175 They shall always cause themselves to reach and to enter,
176 Even to the days that are calm and peaceful
177 They shall bring themselves as they travel the path of life.

The Last Sky People
1 Verily, at that time and place, it has been said, in this house,
2 The Sky people, a people who possess seven fireplaces,
3 Spake to the Last Sky,
4 Saying: O grandfather,

5 We have nothing that is suitable to use as a symbol.
6 The Last Sky hastened to reply, saying: O little ones,
7 You say you have nothing that is suitable to use as a symbol.
8 I am a person who may well be used as a symbol.
9 Of the Red Black Bear (red is here used as a trope),
10 I, as a person, have verily made my body.
11 When the little ones seek refuge in me as they travel the path of life,
12 They shall always live to see old age.
13 When they make of me the means of reaching old age,
14 They shall enable themselves to live to see old age as they travel the path of life.
15 The skin of my feet that is dark in color
16 I have made to be as my charcoal.
17 When the little ones make it to be as their charcoal,
18 They shall have charcoal that will easily sink into their skin as they travel the path of life.
19 The tip of my nose, that is dark in color,
20 I have made to be as my charcoal.
21 When the little ones make it to be as their charcoal,
22 They shall have charcoal that will easily sink into their skin as they travel the path of life.
23 My body, that is black in color,
24 I have made to be as my charcoal.
25 When the little ones make it to be as their charcoal,
26 They shall have charcoal that will easily sink into their skin.
27 They shall also find in it the means of reaching old age.
28 When the little ones make of me their bodies,
29 They shall enable themselves to live to see old age as they travel the path of life.
30 The skin of my feet, that is gathered in folds,
31 I have made to be the means of reaching old age.
32 When the little ones also make it to be the means of reaching old age,
33 They shall enable themselves to live to see old age as they travel the path of life.
34 The muscles of my ankles, that are wrinkled,
35 I have made to be the means of reaching old age.
36 When the little ones also make them to be the means of reaching old age,
37 They shall always live to see in the muscles of their ankles the signs of old age.
38 The inner muscles of my thighs, that are gathered in folds,
39 I have made to be the means of reaching old age.
40 When the little ones make them to be the means of reaching old age,
41 They shall enable themselves to live to see old age.
42 The muscles of my breast, that are gathered in folds,

43 I have made to be the means of reaching old age.
44 When the little ones make of them the means of reaching old age,
45 They shall enable themselves to live to see old age as they travel the path of life.
46 The muscles of my arms, that are gathered in folds,
47 Shall be to them the means by which they shall see old age as they travel the path of life.
48 My shoulders also that are bent with age
49 I have made to be the means of reaching old age.
50 When the little ones make them to be the means of reaching old age,
51 They shall always live to see in their shoulders the sign of old age.
52 The muscles of my throat, that are loosened with age,
53 I have made to be the means of reaching old age.
54 When the little ones also make of them the means of reaching old age,
55 They shall always live to see in the loosened muscles of their throats the sign of old age.
56 The thin hair on the crown of my head also
57 I have made to be the means of reaching old age.
58 The little ones in their old age
59 Shall always see the hair on the crowns of their heads thinned with age.
60 The thin, yellowish hair of my head
61 I have also
62 Made to be the means of reaching old age.
63 When the little ones make of me their bodies,
64 They shall always live to see the hair of their heads thinned and yellowish with age.
65 The four great divisions of the days
66 They shall always enable themselves to reach and to enter.
67 When the people of the Water
68 And those of the Land
69 Make of me their bodies,
70 They shall enable themselves to live to see old age as they travel the path of life.

### The Buffalo Back People[15]

1 Verily, at that time and place, it has been said, in this house,
2 The Sky people, a people who possess seven fireplaces,
3 Spake to one of their number, the Buffalo Back,
4 Saying: O grandfather,
5 We have nothing that is suitable to use as a symbol.
6 The Buffalo Back quickly replied, saying: O little ones,
7 You say you have nothing that is suitable to use as a symbol.
8 I am a person who is suitable to use as a symbol.
9 The people of the Water
10 And those of the Land

11 Shall always use me as a symbol.

12 On their account I shall always be burning my fingers (referring to his duties as Sho'-ka, kindling fires, etc.).

13 When they cause me to burn my fingers by calling me to their service,

14 They shall enable themselves to live to see old age as they travel the path of life.

15 When they make of me the means of reaching old age,

16 The four great divisions of days

17 They shall enable themselves to reach and to enter as they travel the path of life.

### Men of Mystery People

1 Verily, at that time and place, it has been said, in this house,

2 The Sky people, a people who possess seven fireplaces,

3 Spake to one of their number, the Men of Mystery,

4 Saying: O grandfather,

5 We have nothing that is suitable to use as a symbol.

6 The Men of Mystery quickly replied, saying: O little ones,

7 You say you have nothing that is suitable to use as a symbol.

8 I am a person who is suitable to use as a symbol.

9 Of the red metal

10 I, as a person, have verily made my body.

11 When the little ones make of it their bodies,

12 They shall enable themselves to live to see old age as they travel the path of life.

13 When they make of it the means of reaching old age,

14 They shall be free from all causes of death as they travel the path of life.

15 Verily, at that time and place, it has been said, in this house,

16 He spake again, saying: Of the black metal

17 I, as a person, have, verily, made my body.

18 When the little ones make of it their bodies,

19 They shall enable themselves to live to see old age as they travel the path of life.

20 When of the black metal

21 They make their bodies in their life's journey,

22 Their skin, like that metal, shall be difficult to penetrate.

23 Verily, at that time and place, it has been said, in this house,

24 He spake again, saying: Of the loose, rough metal

25 I, as a person, have, verily, made my body.

26 When the little ones make of it their bodies,

27 When of the loose rough metal

28 They make their bodies,

29 They shall cause themselves to be difficult to overcome by death.

30 When they make of it the means of reaching old age,

31 They shall live to see old age, as they travel the path of life.

32 Verily, at that time and place, it has been said, in this house,
33 He spake again, saying: Of the yellow metal,
34 I, as a person, have verily made my body.
35 When the little ones make of it their bodies,
36 They shall be free from all causes of death.
37 They shall enable themselves to be difficult to overcome by death.
38 When they make of it the means of reaching old age,
39 They shall live to see old age, as they travel the path of life.
40 Verily, at that time and place, it has been said, in this house,
41 To the four great divisions of the days
42 They shall cause themselves to reach and to enter as they travel the path of life.
43 These shall stand for the bodies of the little ones.
44 Of the hard hailstone,
45 Also,
46 I, as a person, have verily made my body.
47 Of the hard corn (the flint corn),
48 Together with the hailstone, I have made myself to be a person.
49 When the little ones make of these their bodies,
50 They shall enable themselves to live to see old age as they travel the path of life.
51 When the little ones use the hard corn for food,
52 They shall enable themselves to live to see old age as they travel the path of life.

### Buffalo Bull People

1 Verily, at that time and place, it has been said, in this house,
2 The Sky people, a people who possess seven fireplaces,
3 Spake to the Buffalo Bull
4 Saying: O grandfather,
5 We have nothing that is suitable to use as a symbol.
6 Come down to us, O grandfather! they said to him (the Tho'-xe are a sky people).
7 Verily, at that time and place, it has been said, in this house,
8 The Gentle Sky (here personified), who sat with the Sky people of the seven fireplaces,
9 Had with him his red plume (symbol of the dawn and of peace),
10 Which he quickly took from its coverings
11 And shot into the mouth of the angry bull; it lodged by the left side of his tongue,
12 Where it lay lengthwise by the side of the tongue.
13 Thereupon the Bull lowered his tail, which he had lifted in anger, and stood subdued by the magic of peace.
14 Then the Bull spake, saying: O Sky people,
15 You say you have nothing that is suitable to use as a symbol.

16 I, who stand here, am a person who is suitable to use as a symbol.

17 Verily, at that time and place, it has been said, in this house,

18 The Bull, preparatory to an extraordinary effort, expanded with a quick motion the hairs of his tail

19 And tossed into the air a cloud of dust that obscured the scenes,

20 And he spake, saying: I am a person who is never absent from the activities of life, O Sky people.

21 Verily, at that time and place, it has been said, in this house,

22 The Bull threw himself with a quick motion upon the earth,

23 And the bulbous root of the little great medicine (the poppy mallow)

24 Rolled forth from his body upon the earth.

25 Whereupon he said: This root

26 Shall always be a medicine to the people.

27 When the little ones use it for medicine,

28 They shall enable themselves to live to see old age as they travel the path of life.

29 Verily, at that time and place, it has been said, in this house,

30 The Bull again threw himself, with a quick motion, upon the earth,

31 And the root of the Ha'-ba-kon-ce-da, "Ripens with the corn" (Laciniaria pycnostachya),

32 Rolled forth from his body upon the earth.

33 And the people said: Shall this root also

34 Be used by the people as medicine, O grandfather?

35 Then hastily they put pieces of it into their mouths to test its taste,

36 And said: It is bitter within the mouth, O grandfather!

37 It is astringent, O grandfather!

38 From this sacred plant we shall take a personal name, O grandfather, that it may ever be remembered.

39 The name "Astringent"

40 Shall have a place among our sacred names, O grandfather.

41 Verily, at that time and place, it has been said, in this house,

42 He (the Buffalo) led them to the Mon-kon-ton-ga, Great Medicine (Cucurbita foetidissima),

43 Before which they stood, and they said:

44 Shall this plant be a medicine to the people, O grandfather?

45 And the Bull spake, saying: When the little ones use this plant as medicine,

46 They shall enable themselves to live to see old age as they travel the path of life.

47 Verily, at that time and place, it has been said, in this house,

48 In the presence of the Mon-kon' Ni-ka-shi-ga, Man Medicine plant (Cucurbita perennis),

49 They came and stood,

50 And the people said: Shall this plant be a medicine to the little ones, O grandfather?

51 The Bull replied: When the little ones use this plant as medicine,
52 They shall enable themselves to live to see old age as they travel the path of life.
53 When the people of the Water
54 And those of the Land
55 Use this plant also for medicine,
56 They shall enable themselves to live to see old age as they travel the path of life.
57 Verily, at that time and place, it has been said, in this house,
58 The people said: Of what shall the little ones make their bodies?
59 And, in response, the Bull caused the red corn
60 To roll forth upon the earth.
61 In like manner he sent forth the red squash
62 To accompany the red corn.
63 Then the red-haired animal also
64 He made to accompany them.
65 All these he sent rolling forth upon the earth, out of sight (refers to the creation),
66 And he said: When the little ones use all of these as medicine,
67 They shall enable themselves to live to see old age as they travel the path of life.
68 Verily, at that time and place, it has been said, in this house,
69 The people said: What else shall the people use as medicine?
70 Then the Bull spake, saying: The blue corn
71 Shall also
72 Be used by the little ones as medicine.
73 And the people said to one another: The black squash
74 We shall make to accompany it, O younger brothers.
75 The dark-haired animal,
76 We shall make to accompany it, O grandfather.
77 The Bull spake, saying: When the little ones use these as medicine,
78 They shall enable themselves to live to see old age as they travel the path of life.
79 Verily, at that time and place, it has been said, in this house,
80 The Bull caused a speckled corn
81 To roll forth upon the earth,
82 Saying, as he did so: The speckled corn also
83 The little ones shall use as medicine.
84 When they use this corn as medicine,
85 They shall cause their limbs to stretch in growth as they travel the path of life.
86 And the people said: The speckled squash
87 We shall make to accompany it, O grandfather.
88 The speckled animal

89 We shall make to accompany it.
90 The Bull spake, saying: When the little ones use all of these as medicine,
91 They shall enable themselves to live to see old age as they travel the path of life.
92 Verily, at that time and place, it has been said, in this house,
93 The Bull spake, saying: These shall stand as medicine for the little ones.
94 The yellow corn,
95 The little ones shall use as medicine.
96 When the little ones use the yellow corn as medicine,
97 They shall enable themselves to live to see old age as they travel the path of life.
98 The people spake, saying: The yellow squash,
99 We shall make to accompany it, O grandfather,
100 The animal with yellow hair,
101 We shall make it to be the means of bringing, O grandfather.
102 And the Bull spake, saying: When the little ones use all of these as medicine,
103 They shall enable themselves to live to see old age.
104 When the people of the Water,
105 And those of the Land
106 Use all of these as medicine,
107 They shall enable themselves to live to see old age as they travel the path of life.
108 All of these they shall use to make their limbs to stretch in growth.
109 The four great divisions of the days,
110 Verily the four great divisions,
111 They shall enable themselves to reach and to enter,
112 To the days that are calm and peaceful,
113 They shall enable themselves to come and to enter as they travel the path of life.
114 Verily, at that time and place, it has been said, in this house,
115 The people said: What shall the little ones use as medicine?
116 The Bull replied: The aged animal (the buffalo bull),
117 The little ones shall use as medicine (the fat of the buffalo is used in various ways for medicine, and also for ceremonial purposes).
118 When the little ones use the aged animal as medicine,
119 They shall enable themselves to live to see old age as they travel the path of life.
120 Verily, at that time and place, it has been said, in this house,
121 The Bull spake, saying: Behold the thick ball-like muscles of my hindquarters.
122 When the little ones use this part of my body as medicine,
123 They shall enable themselves to live to see old age as they travel the path of life.

124 Behold, the left side of my body,
125 Which I have made for use as medicine.
126 When the little ones use this part of my body as medicine,
127 They shall enable themselves to live to see old age as they travel the path of life.
128 Behold, the muscles of my spine (one side),
129 Which I have made for use as medicine.
130 When the little ones use this part of my body as medicine,
131 They shall enable themselves to live to see old age as they travel the path of life.
132 Verily, at that time and place, it has been said, in this house,
133 The Bull spake, saying: Behold, the muscles of my spine (the other side),
134 The fat of which I, who stand here, have made for use as a healing ointment, and oil for ceremonial purposes.
135 The people of the Water
136 And those of the Land
137 Shall use the fat of this part of my body as ointment.
138 When they use the fat of this part of my body as a healing ointment, and oil for ceremonial purposes,
139 They shall enable themselves to live to see old age as they travel the path of life.
140 Verily, at that time and place, it has been said, in this house,
141 He said to the people: Behold, the right side of my body,
142 Which I, who stand here, have made for use as medicine.
143 When the little ones use this part of my body as medicine,
144 They shall enable themselves to live to see old age as they travel the path of life.
145 Behold, the muscles of my breast,
146 Which I have made for use as medicine.
147 When the little ones use this part of my body as medicine,
148 They shall enable themselves to live to see old age as they travel the path of life.
149 Behold also my heart sack,
150 Which I have made for use as medicine (used as a receptacle for the medicinal fat).
151 When the little ones use this part of my body as medicine,
152 They shall enable themselves to live to see old age as they travel the path of life.
153 The muscles of my limbs,
154 Those of the various parts of my body,
155 Verily, the muscles of every part of my body,
156 The little ones shall use as medicine.
157 When they use my body in all its parts as medicine,

158 Verily they shall enable themselves to live to see old age as they travel the
    path of life.
159 When the people of the Water
160 And those of the Land
161 Use my body in all its parts as medicine,
162 They shall enable themselves to live to see old age as they travel the path of
    life.

## SONG OF THE KEEPER OF THE FIREPLACE

At the beginning of this ceremony, the man who was the last to be initiated into the mysteries of the Rite of the Chiefs is chosen to act as U-dse'-the A-don-be, Keeper of the Fireplace. As the priests enter the lodge to take their places, this officer takes his appointed seat near the door, where he does not represent any clan but, rather, all of the people. When the Assisting Xo'-ka performs the ceremony of Wa-the'-the, the Sending (of the Symbolic Articles), he sends with a fee a bundle of counting sticks to the Keeper of the Fireplace. The Sho'-ka, who carries the bundle of sticks, divides it into two parts, one containing 70 and the other 60 sticks. He holds in his right hand the bunch containing 70 sticks and in his left the bunch having 60. He crosses his forearms at the wrists and in this manner carries the counting sticks to the Keeper of the Fireplace, who receives and holds the sticks in the same ceremonial manner. When the priests begin to recite the wi'-gi-e, this officer sings a song, beating from time to time the two bundles of sticks against each other. (Charley Wah-hre-she declined to give the song but offered no reason for declining.)

When the reciting of the wi'-gi-e had come to a close, the Keeper of the Fireplace speaks, saying: "I am about to return these counting sticks to the Xo'-ka, but before doing so I wish to give to all the priests present a word of warning before they rise to depart. These counting sticks are now to be put in the care of the wife of the initiate, and as long as these sticks are in her keeping she shall be exempt from the seizure of any of her property for ceremonial use—namely, her wood; her tent frames; stores of meat, fresh or dried; stores of corn; dried squash; or any other food supplies. If an officer, notwithstanding her claims to exemption, persists in seizing her property, then she shall present to him this bundle of counting sticks and challenge him to count the seven and six o-don' (war honors) he may have won in battle in defending the homes of his people. Should the officer accept the challenge and count the prescribed number of o-don', she shall then yield to him the property he demands, but let the officer beware of speaking falsely in counting his o-don'.

Having given his word of warning, the Keeper of the Fireplace beckons to the Sho'-ka to come and take the counting sticks, which he hands to him in the same ceremonial manner as they were received.

The Keeper of the Fireplace, in addition to the fee that accompanied the counting sticks, later receives two shares of the provisions furnished by the candidate.

## INSTRUCTIONS TO THE WIFE OF THE INITIATE

[At this point the ceremony known as Instructions to the Wife of the Initiate takes place. It is basically the same as that used in the Songs of the Wa-xo'-be, except that the first part related to war is omitted; see its earlier description in chapter 5.][16]

When the Assistant Xo'-ka has finished his instructions, the woman goes out of the lodge. The leader of the Crawfish clan then speaks, saying, "O priests, you may now remove from your faces the symbolic paintings." The women bring water, and all the men, excepting those of the Elder Sky, the Isolated Earth, and the clan of the initiate, wash their faces, while the men appointed to distribute the provisions furnished by the initiate perform their duties. Then, as the women carry away the portions given to the families, all the priests, excepting those of the Isolated Earth, the Elder Sky, and the initiating clan, go out of the lodge, those of the Sky People passing out by the south door and those of the Earth People by the north. Each priest as he passes the initiate addresses him by the name of his clan and greets him with the words, "O Hon'-ga (a sacred person), living creatures shall come to you," meaning that children will be born to him and to his wife and that they shall have plenty of animal food on which to live.

## THE ARROW CEREMONY

When the priests have left the lodge, the Sho'-ka approaches the Assisting Xo'-ka and places in his hands a small bow, the front of which is painted red to symbolize the day and the back black to symbolize the night. The bow is accompanied by two arrows, each of which has a dual significance—namely, the arrow painted red symbolizes day and the posterity of the initiate; the one painted black symbolizes night and also the posterity of the initiate.

These symbolic weapons are, in turn, put by the Assisting Xo'-ka into the hands of the Xo'-ka. The initiate rises, and with him the Xo'-ka, who is to fit the arrows to the bow and to speed them one after the other on an eternal course, even as the days and the nights move on in endless succession.

The Xo'-ka addresses the members of the two clans who remained to lend themselves for use as symbols, one as the sky and the other as the earth, in this ceremony relating to the life force, and says, "I call upon you, O Sky and Earth, to assist me" (in the speeding of this life). He then adjusts the red arrow to the string of the bow, and as he does so he speaks to the Elder Sky, saying, "O Sky, I am about to set in flight this arrow toward you, and it shall not be without success. Toward the setting of the sun there are seven villages; it is the seventh one at which I aim this arrow." At this the priests of the Elder Sky begin to recite their wi'-gi-e relating to life. The Xo'-ka points the arrow over the heads of the priests and goes through the motion of releasing it. At the same time he cries, "A-tha-tha tha tha-tha . . . !" a cry uttered by a person when suddenly stricken with pain, and follows the cry with the words, "Tsi'-zhu o-xo-be xtsi e-dsi a-ka, we-ton-in da!" "It is apparent the Tsi'-zhu (the Sky) sits yonder in mystery!" It was explained that the cry is a mimicking of the cries of the persons tattooed, but most likely this statement is to mislead the uninitiated, and the act undoubtedly has a deeper significance, one touching closely upon the coming of life into bodily form. The Xo'-ka then takes the black arrow, adjusts it to the string of the bow, turns to the priests of the Isolated Earth and addresses them in the same words he used to the Elder Sky. These also reply by reciting their wi'-gi-e, while the Xo'-ka goes through the motion of releasing the arrow over their heads and utters the cry of pain. Each of these acts is repeated, and the last brings the ceremony to a close.

## EDITOR'S SUMMARY

The Rite of the Chiefs tells the story of the last stage in the development of traditional Osage tribal organization: the creation of the two offices of chief. In the initiation rite for great bundle priests, however, only half of the story is told—that part concerned with the vigil of the Gentle Ponca chief and Wa-kon-da's revelations to him. The other half of the story, the vigil of the Gentle Sky chief, was told in the initiation rite of the great medicine bundle priests, a rite that is now lost.

The Rite of the Chiefs differed from the Songs of the Wa-xo'-be and from all clan bundle initiations in both substantive content and ritual structure. The two chiefs were men of peace, not war. Their concern and responsibility was for the health, life, and general well-being of the Osage people. The two bundles, the great bundle and the great medicine bundle, were not for things of this world, the world of the living, but the means by which the Osage people addressed the invisible world and asked for Wa-kon-da's blessing. In the main part of the rite, there were no references to blood or killing or destruction. The focus was only on life-giving forces and upon health and old age.

Compared to the initiation rites for the clan priests, this was a very short ritual, lasting only a single day and consisting, after a few preliminary rituals, of only five main segments or parts: (1) the Wi'-gi-e of the Chief's Vigil, (2) the "Sending" of the fees or gifts, (3) the simultaneous reciting of all of the clan wi'-gi-e and the singing by the Keeper of the Fireplace, (4) the Instructions to the Wife of the initiate, and (5) the shooting of the sacred arrows.

The important parts of this rite were found in its wi'-gi-e. Those of the chief's vigil were broken into three parts, all relating to old age. In each part, awls of pelican bone, eagle bone, or metal were referred to. These awls were used in the tattooing rite, which was an appeal to Wa-kon-da for long life. The presence of a metal awl is interesting. La Flesche believed the metal awl indicated a European influence and was thus added sometime during the historic period.[17] There is another possible explanation, however. Metal awls may originally have been made of copper, which was widely used during the Mississippian period.

The Wi'-gi-e of the Chief's Vigil was followed by simultaneous recitations of the clan wi'-gi-e. These wi'-gi-e were important because in them the major life-giving forces, symbolically represented by each clan, were defined. The act of simultaneous recitation of the clan wi-gi-e served to demonstrate the Osages' collective recognition of and subordination to a higher power. Thus the rite was not concerned solely with health and long life but also served to reaffirm the unity of the people (symbolized by the clans) in acknowledging the gifts and will of Wa-kon-da.

## CHAPTER 7

*Conclusion*

FRANCIS La Flesche preserved the best record we will ever have of the religion of an eastern, horticultural Native American tribe. Even more importantly, he concentrated on recording the secret initiation rites of the priesthoods, including the two described in this book. Unlike public rituals, accounts of which constitute the vast bulk of the literature on North American Indian religions, initiation rites were not merely descriptive; they were also explanatory. There was a major difference in the substantive content of public and initiation rituals.

La Flesche died before he could finish his studies of the Osage religion. He never wrote an overview and never fully analyzed or integrated most of the data he collected. In chapters 3 and 4, I offered introductions to Osage religion and rituals derived from La Flesche's work. In this final chapter I want to discuss some general characteristics of Osage religion not yet touched upon and then address the difficulty of comparing La Flesche's Osage data with data from other studies of American Indian religion.

## OSAGE RELIGIOUS BELIEFS AND PRACTICES

Osage religious beliefs were not based on divine revelation. At times Wa-kon-da did reveal certain things to particular individuals—for example, the power of the man medicine plant was revealed to the Sky chief. But such revelations were the exception. Most religious beliefs were derived from empirical observations of natural phenomena and from reasoning. These beliefs and their associated religious institutions and rituals were the conscious creations of the priests. Because they were consciously created by humans, religious beliefs, institutions, and rituals were subject to periodic revision by humans in response to changes they perceived in the world of the living. The allegorical story of the tribe makes it clear that the priests had on several occasions reorganized their socioreligious institutions.

The Osage religion was not concerned with death and the afterlife. The Osages had only vague concepts of what happened to a person's spirit after death. They held no concept of individual rewards or punishments for the conduct of one's life. The purpose and focus of their religion was the survival and perpetuation of the Osage people. Of primary concern was the maintenance of their population. Longevity and children were the blessings of Wa-kon-da, and Osage daily life was structured as a ritual to present a never-ending appeal for Wa-kon-da's blessing. The most direct and immediate physical threat to the Osages' well-being and survival came from other peoples. The Osages saw the world as filled with enemy peoples who could at any time strike and destroy them without warning. As a result, warfare and unity of action were recurrent themes in their religious life. Hunting, farming, healing, and weather control were of concern, but, not being seen as imminent threats to collective survival, they played a subordinate role in Osage ritual life.

La Flesche's writing and notes also made clear two points concerning Osage religious beliefs that most studies of American Indian religions have ignored: the Osages were not unanimous in their interpretations of religious rituals, and not all supernatural phenomena were integrated into their formal religion.

The leaders of the Osage priesthoods formed the intellectual elite of the tribe—what in Western society would be called the theologians, philosophers, and scholars. To these men the various rituals were both supplicatory and pedagogical. Sacred objects (wa-xo'-be) such as the bundles and pipes were merely symbols of the sacred and consisted of nothing more than hide, feathers, stone, and so forth. Religious narratives, songs, and recitations were filled with abstract symbols, metaphors, and multiple levels of meaning. These men spent their lives studying and interpreting the rituals and observing the world in an unending quest to expand their knowledge. This knowledge, in turn, would assist them as leaders of the Osage people.

To greater or lesser degrees, less intellectually oriented priests, as well as the common people, viewed rituals quite differently. To many of these people, rituals possessed mystical potency. Embodied within the wa-xo'-be were supernatural forces that were potentially dangerous and could be used for good or evil. The religious narratives, songs, and recitations were not to be interpreted but simply accepted literally. Interpretation of the meaning and significance of particular rituals and religious practices thus differed greatly from individual to individual. La

Flesche's accounts of the Osage religion, including those presented in this book, represent the interpretations of the intellectual elite. Not all supernatural phenomena recognized by the Osages were integrated into their formal religion. They held other beliefs that might best be called "folk beliefs"—including belief in prophets, were-animals, witchcraft, "little people," and ghosts. Although La Flesche recorded information about these other beliefs, he made no attempt to discuss them in relationship to formal religious beliefs and rituals. My calling them folk beliefs is not to imply that these were merely stories or fantasies.[1] The vast majority of Osages, including the priests, truly believed in the existence of these supernatural phenomena.

There were among the Osages women and men who had the ability to foretell the future. In dreams or visions—the distinction is not always clear—these prophets would see or sense something that was going to occur. Most commonly they warned of impending enemy attacks. Such prophecies were readily validated when a hidden enemy raiding party was discovered. The last and most famous of these prophets was Wah-tian-kah, whose Delphic-like predictions were interpreted as having foretold the Osages' eventual oil wealth, the coming of peyote, and even the automobile and airplane.[2] The supernatural origin of these prophecies was not clearly explained. Most appear to have come to individuals in a dream or dreamlike state, whereas others came as visions during a rite of vigil. Some prophets were women, and no prophets were known to have been priests.

Some people were thought to have the power to change themselves into animals. One man reportedly was able to transform himself into a snake; in other cases, men could change into deer.[3] Although no known cases were recorded in which people could change themselves into wolves or birds or other life forms, the potential for doing so existed. No explanation was recorded as to why some people had this ability. The particular life form into which a person could transform himself or herself was not related to the life symbols of the person's clan. Nor did the ability to change physical form indicate any evil intent on the part of the individual, and such people were not considered witches.[4]

There were Osage witches, however—individuals who used supernatural powers to harm others. It is not known whether the Osages recognized one or several categories of witches. There were individuals who prepared various "love medicines."[5] There were some malevolent people who could and did harm or even kill others.[6] At least some witches were called "Snakes" or "bean shooters," the latter because they killed others by magically shooting them with mescal beans. John Wilson, the peyote leader, was attacked by one of the Snakes in about 1900 when he was running a meeting at Black Dog's camp. Some Osages say that the last known Osage witch was a woman who died in Gray Horse in 1919.[7]

The Osages also believed in little people, or *mi'-a-gthu-shka*.[8] Little people were said to look just like other humans but to be only the size of children. They had their own villages, trails, and other places they frequented. There was a supernatural quality about the little people. Some Osages thought that they could be seen only when they wanted to be seen or were taken unawares. Because the little people were considered potentially dangerous, most Osages avoided contact with them.[9]

The Osages also believed in ghosts. They distinguished fictional tales from stories based on fact, and La Flesche recorded a number of Osage ghost stories that were told as true stories. In them, ghosts did not return from the dead; rather, ghosts of individuals remained among the living for some time after death.[10]

The degree to which the Osages believed in prophets, were-animals, witches, little people, and ghosts probably varied from person to person. Yet there is no doubt that the vast majority of Osages believed in some or all of these supernatural forces.

Thus the Osage religion did not consist of a single, unified, integrated set of beliefs and practices relative to the supernatural. There was, indeed, a formal, institutionalized religion, but there were significant individual differences in how particular aspects of that formal religion were interpreted. These "institutional" beliefs and practices coexisted with a wide range of folk beliefs and practices.

That the Osage religion encompassed a wide range of supernatural beliefs and interpretations should not come as a surprise. One has only to look at the Western Judeo-Christian religious tradition to see numerous parallels. Among Christians, there are people who believe in a literal interpretation of the scriptures, and others who believe the scriptures are metaphorical and symbolic and thus have to be studied if their real meanings are to be determined. Also found among European Christian populations are folk beliefs in supernatural powers that are not part of Christian teaching: werewolves, witches, visionaries, leprechauns, vampires, and ghosts.

It is important to realize, however, that folk beliefs have been more troublesome to European Christians than to the Osages. European religious leaders have traditionally reacted to these beliefs either by denying their validity or by calling them the work of the devil. Osage religious leaders did not view folk beliefs in the same threatening manner. The term *Wa-kon-da* referred to a mystery. To the Osages, the supernatural world was infinitely complex, and human beings could never hope fully to comprehend the cosmos. Their formal, institutionalized religious teachings explained only certain things that they understood. There were still other supernatural phenomena for which they had no explanation. To the Osage priests, these inexplicable supernatural phenomena could exist without threatening their authority and at times could even prove beneficial to the people.

## THE OSAGE RELIGION IN COMPARISON

Comparative studies of religion are the most difficult of all comparative studies of human culture. Religion is a highly complex subject because the religion of a people does not consist of a single, integrated set of beliefs and practices; it always encompasses a wide range of beliefs and individual interpretations. Comparative studies by their very nature must draw on the published accounts of many different researchers. Both quantitatively and qualitatively, the information recorded for the different tribes of North America varies greatly, depending in large part on the abilities and interests of individual researchers, as well as the knowledge, interests, and personal beliefs of the Native Americans who gave the information. Although a vast descriptive literature has been published on Native American religions, serious problems in comparability exist within it, and comparative studies of American Indian religions are still in their infancy. The studies that do exist are usually limited to comparisons of particular mythological themes or ritual forms, and they use illustrative examples drawn from only a few tribal religions.[11] Few scholars have attempted to analyze and define systematically the different religious traditions that existed in North America.

The scholar who has most recently attempted to define the major religious traditions of the American Indians is Ake Hultkrantz.[12] Hultkrantz defined four characteristics that all North American religions shared: a similar worldview, the idea of cosmic harmony, an emphasis on direct contact with supernatural powers through visions, and a common view of the cycle of life and death. Later he qualified this generalization by saying that the emphasis on direct contact with supernatural powers was not present among the tribes of the southwestern United States.[13] According to Hultkrantz, these shared characteristics were the result of a common origin and were brought with the people from Asia. The earliest form of North American Indian religion he called the Hunting Pattern. With the domestication of corn, beans, squash, and other plants in Mesoamerica, the second religious tradition—the Horticultural Pattern—later developed and spread north into the eastern and southwestern United States. He defined these two patterns on the basis of seven contrasting elements (Table 7.1)[14] To illustrate the two traditions, Hultkrantz used the Wind River Shoshone for the Hunting Pattern and the Zuni for the Horticultural Pattern.

With one exception, Osage religious beliefs and practices correspond to the four shared characteristics defined by Hultkrantz. In their worldview, their concept of cosmic harmony, and their cycle of life and death, the Osages were basically compatible with Hultkrantz's categories. Hultkrantz also noted that emphasis on direct experience with the supernatural was found throughout North America with the exception of the Southwest, implying that it was present among the eastern horticulturalists. In this respect he was mistaken. Although the Osages viewed such contact differently from the southwestern tribes, Osage religious practices did not emphasize personal supernatural contact.

An even more serious problem arises in attempting to apply Hultkrantz's Horticultural Pattern to the Osages. Although the Osages recognized the presence of male and female forces in the cosmos, they did not have named gods or goddesses with physical forms. As a result, their rituals did not include masked dancers representing supernatural beings. Nor did Osage religious beliefs include any named culture heroes. In Osage secular histories, individuals were frequently mentioned by their personal names, but in religious narratives, people who performed important actions were never mentioned by name but only by clan, phratry, or moiety affiliation. The Osages did not perform rain ceremonies, although they did have some minor rituals that would stop or divert storms. Although the Osages had rituals that would be classified as fertility rituals, these ceremonies were concerned with children and descendants and were parts of the generalized appeals for Wa-kon-da's blessings.

For the most part, Osage ritual life focused more overtly on social relations within the tribe and with other tribes. In the "living world," the realm for which humans bore primary responsibility, unity, war, and peace were of the highest concern. Although the Osages made repeated use of certain sites for rituals, they did not have the same concept of shrine or sacred place as that found among the Puebloan peoples.[15] In Osage religious narratives, no specific places are mentioned, and in the rituals themselves, only direction of movement (usually east to west) was significant, not specific places.

TABLE 7.1
**Elements of the Two Religious Patterns Defined by Hultkrantz**

| Hunting Pattern | Horticultural Pattern |
| --- | --- |
| Animal ceremonialism | Rain and fertility ceremonies |
| Quest for spiritual power | Priestly ritual |
| Male supreme being | Goddesses and gods |
| Annual ceremony of cosmic rejuvenation | Yearly round of fertility rites |
| Few stationary cult places | Permanent shrines and temples |
| Shamanism | Medicine society ritualism |
| Life after death beyond the horizon or in the sky | Life after death in the underworld or among the clouds |

If Osage religious practices and those of the horticultural tribes of the Southwest—the Puebloan peoples—are compared, some similarities can be noted. All had formally trained priests who had authority over particular crises and calendrical rituals. Beyond these very basic features, however, the differences far outweigh the similarities.

Over the past twenty years, North Americanists have drastically reevaluated their perspective on pre-Columbian North America. More than any other group, historical demographers have been responsible for this changing perspective. In 1910, James Mooney estimated the Indians of North America to have numbered slightly more than one million in 1492. This number was based on the population estimates given by explorers and others for various tribes at the time of earliest contact with Europeans.[16] It was not until the late 1960s and early 1970s that scholars began to question this estimate seriously, arguing that Old World diseases such as malaria, cholera, and smallpox had spread far in advance of European contact and produced devastating effects on the native population of North America.[17] Today, the most conservative estimates place the figure at over two million,[18] while some place it as high as seventeen million.[19] Not only has its estimated number increased dramatically, but the geographical distribution of this pre-Columbian population has also changed. The horticultural tribes of the eastern United States were by far the most severely affected by Old World diseases prior to contact. Most scholars now feel that these eastern horticulturalists constituted well over half of the total native population north of Mexico.[20]

The eastern horticulturalists were not only the most numerous peoples in North America, they were also the most highly developed in terms of social and political complexity. The core area, the Mississippi Valley and the Gulf Coastal Plain, was occupied by what archaeologists have called the Mississippian peoples. From archaeological research and early ethnohistoric accounts, the basic features of Mississippian culture can be reconstructed for the period sometime prior to 1492. Politically, the core area was characterized by chiefdoms or even incipient states that were ruled by hereditary chiefs or kings, some of whom were considered to be gods on earth. There were large temple mound complexes, such as Spiro, Cahokia, Moundville, and Etowah, which were associated with formal priesthoods and the ritual use of sacred fires, medicine bundles, stickball contests, and pipes. Trade networks for exchanging shell, copper, and other valued items extended from the Great Lakes to the Gulf of Mexico and from the Atlantic to the Great Plains and beyond.[21] Most of these horticulturalists were scattered village peoples, but major population centers were associated with some of the temple complexes. The one associated with Cahokia had an estimated population of twenty-five thousand or more.[22]

Although the Mississippians occupied only a portion of the eastern United States, their cultural influence permeated the entire region, giving the area its cultural distinctiveness.[23] Whether the Osages were originally part of the core Mississippian population or merely one of the many tributary groups who were culturally influenced, if not dominated, by the Mississippians is arguable.[24] But the overwhelming similarities in the social, political, and religious institutions of the Osages, the other Dhegiha Siouan peoples, and the adjacent Chewere Siouan and Central Algonkian peoples were not a chance occurrence. These institutions had to have a common historic origin,[25] and the only feasible explanation is that they were the products of the shared cultural influence of the Mississippian peoples.[26]

The problem facing students of North American Indian religions is the same one that confronts all scholars concerned with pre-Columbian North America. Little is known about the early cultural traditions of the eastern horticulturalists, and what data exist are usually fragmentary. Disease, warfare, displacement, and European contact destroyed most of these peoples while drastically changing the cultures of most survivors long before the first scholar attempted to record the culture of a North American tribe.[27] With few exceptions, the modern descendants of these peoples offer scant clues to their past cultural traditions. The eastern horticulturists constitute a major gap in our knowledge of early North American peoples.

For over a century scholars have attempted to define and interpret North American Indian cultural traditions, primarily using information obtained from the study of foraging peoples and the southwestern horticultural tribes. Francis La Flesche has given us a description of the religion of a horticultural people that differs significantly from what is known of the religions of the horticultural peoples of the Southwest. The question remains, where does one place the Osages? How representative are Osage religious beliefs and practices of the eastern horticulturalist tradition? This question may never be satisfactorily answered.[28] It is clear, however, that the Osages represent a religious tradition significantly different from those recorded for other North American Indian tribes, and they cannot be ignored.

## A UNIQUE LEGACY

This book is intended to serve only as an introduction to Francis La Flesche's Osage studies. I have presented a brief outline of the Osage religion and edited versions of just two of their initiation rituals. In my general discussion of Osage religion, I have tried to present La Flesche's ideas—but La Flesche did not always speak directly to the topics discussed. To fill in the gaps in his presentations, I had to analyze his data and draw conclusions from my analysis. My purpose in presenting detailed descriptions of two of the rituals was to demonstrate the basic structure and content of Osage rituals. Within La Flesche's published works are descriptions of eleven other rituals, each of which differs from the others to some degree in structure and content. The rituals were meant not merely to be seen or heard (or read), but rather to be experienced and contemplated. Rich in complex symbolism and meaning, these rituals offer something new and exciting to be discovered with every reading. There is a wealth of information yet to be gleaned from La Flesche's studies.

Saucy Calf, Black Dog, Charley Wah-hre-she, Shunkahmolah, Bacon Rind, and the other Osage priests have, through La Flesche, left the world a unique and invaluable legacy. They have given us a window into the past of a pre-Columbian America now gone. They have shown us a logical, rational, and pragmatic people struggling to understand and survive in a world of infinite complexity. They have provided us with a glimpse inside the minds of the ancient Osages and thus into the minds of their Mississippian forebears. They have presented us with a picture, however faint, of the intellectual and cultural traditions of at least some of the horticultural peoples who once inhabited the eastern United States. They have shown us how much has been lost and how little we truly understand the Native American past.

# Notes

PREFACE

1. See Levy-Bruhl (1923; 1926).
2. See Hallpike (1976).
3. This appears on an untitled and unsigned piece of scrap paper in La Flesche's files. It appears to have been part of an article that he discarded unfinished. See Fletcher and La Flesche Papers.

CHAPTER 1

1. Alexander (1933:329).
2. Kroeber (1939:75).
3. For example, he wrote that he was planning to publish volumes on the tattooing rite (La Flesche 1921:73) and on the *wa-do'-ka we-ko,* or scalp ritual (La Flesche 1925:309). He never finished his research on these volumes, and his notes on the two rituals are incomplete. See Fletcher and La Flesche Papers.

CHAPTER 2

1. See Berkhofer (1978:171).
2. For biographies and bibliographies of Native American writers during the nineteenth and early twentieth centuries, see Littlefield and Parins (1981; 1985).
3. La Flesche (1900:xv).
4. Francis La Flesche to George Vaux, Jr., October 14, 1916. Letter in Fletcher and La Flesche Papers.
5. La Flesche (1905:4–5).
6. Eastman (1911:xi).
7. Eastman (1911:xii).
8. Liberty (1978:46).
9. See Alexander (1933); Liberty (1976:106).
10. A number of biographies have been written about members of the La Flesche family. See Green (1969) and Barnes (1984) for studies of the La Flesche family. See Wilson (1974) and Crary (1973) for biographies of Susette La Flesche. See Alexander (1933) and Liberty (1976; 1978) for biographies of Francis La Flesche. The most complete account of the life of Francis La Flesche is found in Mark's (1988) biography of Alice Fletcher.
11. This trial was widely publicized. The Standing Bear case was used by Indian rights groups as an example of government abuse of the Indians. Immediately after the trial, Henry Tibbles (1879) published a popular account.

Helen Hunt Jackson (1881) used the Ponca case as one of her examples of mistreatment of Indians in *A Century of Dishonor*.

12. In the early twentieth century, some Omahas tried to have the La Flesche family purged from the tribal roll.

13. The break between La Flesche and Tibbles appears to have come in 1882 over the Omaha allotment bill. Francis La Flesche and Alice Fletcher supported the bill, while Susette and Henry Tibbles opposed it (see Mark 1988:123–124).

14. See Mark (1988) for an in-depth look at the relationship between Fletcher and La Flesche.

15. See La Flesche (1885).

16. This study was 650 pages in length.

17. This law school later became part of George Washington University.

18. Ridington (1992:1).

19. Mark (1988:351).

20. Mark (1988:352).

21. See Bailey (1973:110–111).

22. Howard (1965:107).

23. Mathews (1961:742–743); Mooney (1896:894–903). Mathews confuses the Arapaho, Sitting Bull, with the more famous northern Sitting Bull.

24. Bailey field notes.

25. Bailey field notes.

26. Bailey field notes; and see Sebbelov (1911) for a photograph and description of this dance.

27. La Flesche (1921:274).

28. Bailey field notes.

29. Bailey field notes.

30. See Fletcher and La Flesche (1911:57–66).

31. La Flesche (1921:52); Bailey field notes.

32. Black Dog died on November 17, 1910; see Tinker (1957:11).

33. La Flesche (1930:529).

34. See Tinker (1957:16)

35. Bailey field notes.

36. It is not surprising that La Flesche seriously underestimated the complexity of Osage ritual life. He probably assumed that it was similar to that of the Omahas, but the Osages were far more complex (see Fletcher and La Flesche 1911).

37. As early as the 1880s, special agent Eugene White (1965:203) had declared the Osages the "wealthiest people in the world" on the basis of the value of their reservation and money held in trust by the federal government. The development of their tribally owned oil resources during the first decades of the twentieth century greatly enhanced their incomes.

38. La Flesche (1921:plate 16, p. 73).

39. La Flesche (1928:30).

40. Bailey field notes.

41. La Flesche (1921:73).

42. Tinker (1957:2).

43. Bailey field notes.

44. Tinker (1957:3).

45. La Flesche (1925:179).

46. Bailey field notes.
47. Tinker (1957:20).
48. Bailey field notes.
49. La Flesche (1921:220).
50. Bailey field notes.
51. Wilson (1985:116).
52. Tinker (1957:20).
53. Bailey field notes.
54. La Flesche (1918:84).
55. La Flesche's 1923 fieldwork was very different from that of previous years. Instead of recording rituals, he seems to have spent most of his time talking with Fred and Julia Lookout about the economic uses of plants (see La Flesche 1924).

## CHAPTER 3

1. See Bailey (1973).
2. See McGee (1897:191); La Flesche (1915:459–62); Dorsey (1884:211–13).
3. See Chapman and Chapman (1964); Chapman (1974; 1980).
4. For historical information on the Central Algonkian tribes, see Tanner (1987); for the Kaws, see Unrau (1971); for the Ioways, see Blaine (1979); for the Otoes and Missouris, see Chapman (1965); and for the Quapaws, see Baird (1980).
5. For historical information on the Osages during this period, see Bailey (1973); Din and Nasatir (1983); and Rollings (1992).
6. Bailey (1973:110).
7. The cosmos was equated with Wa-kon-da. Osage peyotists later stated this concept as "God is truth! Religion is one's belief as to what this truth is" (McCarthy 1923:9). Thus the quest for knowledge was the search for a greater understanding of God.
8. La Flesche (1928:29).
9. La Flesche (1925:139); and see La Flesche (1930:563).
10. See also La Flesche (1928:29–30).
11. La Flesche (1928:29–30); and see also La Flesche (1925:38; 1930:577).
12. La Flesche (1932:193).
13. La Flesche (1932:194); and see also La Flesche (1921:302).
14. See La Flesche (1925:42).
15. See La Flesche (1928:29–30).
16. La Flesche (1921:277); and see also La Flesche (1930:670).
17. See La Flesche (1925:96, 101, 301–302; 1930:670).
18. La Flesche (1930:683). This space was also called *i-u'-thu-ga,* or "cavity of the mouth" (see La Flesche 1930:531n).
19. The Osage image of the universe is seen in their village arrangement (La Flesche 1921:50–51), in the organization of the House of Mystery (La Flesche 1925:84), and in the rush mat that held the sacred hawk (La Flesche 1930:682–83). See also La Flesche (1930:628).
20. This will be illustrated later in the "Instructions to the Wife of the Initiate" portion of the Songs of the Wa-xo'-be.
21. See La Flesche (1921:70).
22. See La Flesche (1925:327; 1930:574).

23. See La Flesche (1930:647).

24. See La Flesche (1925:327; 1930:574).

25. See La Flesche (1925:316; 1930:654; 1939:221).

26. See La Flesche (1921:70–71; 1925:251–52; 1930:555).

27. This term should not be confused with *ni'-ka wa-kon-da-gi,* the Men of Mystery, the name of one of the twenty-four clans.

28. La Flesche (1930:584).

29. La Flesche (1925:364). Osage peyotists expressed this by saying "We . . . have been given hearts and minds to go by. We are ignorant, but have eyes to see with in order to guide ourselves in the ways God wishes us to go" (McCarthy 1923:10).

30. See La Flesche (1930:629; 1932:201).

31. La Flesche (1925:364).

32. La Flesche (1925:267).

33. See La Flesche (1925:66–67, 194, 365).

34. La Flesche (1939:228).

35. La Flesche (1930:570).

36. La Flesche (1925:103).

37. See La Flesche (1925:83).

38. See La Flesche (1921:49; 1925:83, 103–106, 316, 364).

39. La Flesche (1928:296); and see also La Flesche (1921:296; 1925:73).

40. La Flesche (1925:67).

41. These concepts are repeatedly expressed in the rituals.

42. La Flesche (1932:156).

43. La Flesche (1932:167).

44. La Flesche (1932:224). These symbols are also called *wa-zho'-i-ga-the,* "objects of which bodies are made" (La Flesche 1928:84).

45. La Flesche (1921:275; 1932:224).

46. La Flesche (1925:97).

47. Dorsey (1888:396); and see La Flesche (1930:629).

48. La Flesche (1930:682).

49. See La Flesche (1921:51–54).

50. See La Flesche (1928:122–64) for lists of names by clans.

51. See La Flesche (1928:33–75) for two versions of the child naming rite.

52. See La Flesche (1921:51).

53. See La Flesche (1921:69); Fletcher and La Flesche (1911:58); Ponziglione (1889:75); Dorsey (1897:233).

54. See Bailey (1973:19).

55. La Flesche (1921:67–68).

56. La Flesche (1921:68–69); and see also La Flesche (1921:67) for duties of the chiefs.

57. La Flesche (1921:67); and see also McDermott and Salvan (1940:174).

58. The Gentle Sky chief would formally request the priests to perform the new year rite (see La Flesche 1921:146) and undoubtedly was charged with requesting other seasonal rituals as well.

59. La Flesche (1939:3–4).

60. La Flesche (1939:4).

61. Quoted in La Flesche (1921:50).

62. I have assumed that this term was applied to all priests.

63. I have assumed that this term was applied only to clan priests.
64. La Flesche (1939:204).
65. La Flesche (1921:146).
66. See La Flesche (1932:208).
67. La Flesche (1932:194).
68. This distinction is based on my analysis of La Flesche's data.
69. La Flesche (1921:65).
70. See La Flesche (1921:70–71).
71. See La Flesche (1921:69–70).
72. See La Flesche (1925:50; 1930:578).
73. See La Flesche (1932:209).
74. La Flesche (1939:19).
75. La Flesche (1925:91).
76. La Flesche (1930:684).
77. La Flesche (1921:152); for the names and order of degrees for the Puma clan, see La Flesche (1921:153).
78. La Flesche (1921:153).
79. La Flesche (1921:65).
80. La Flesche (1930:682).
81. La Flesche (1930:683).
82. La Flesche (1930:682–83).
83. La Flesche (1925:93).
84. See La Flesche (1925:93; 1930:647).
85. La Flesche (1920:71).
86. La Flesche (1920:71).
87. La Flesche (1921:92).
88. See La Flesche (1921:73; 1939:205–208).
89. See La Flesche (1939:4).
90. La Flesche (1939:204).
91. La Flesche (1932:132).
92. Fletcher and La Flesche Papers, "Notes on the Honor Packs of the Osage, by Wa-shin-ha."
93. La Flesche (1920:73; 1930:578; 1939:4).
94. La Flesche (1920:72).
95. La Flesche (1939:205–208).
96. La Flesche (1939:4).
97. La Flesche (1939:204).
98. Most of the material in this section is based on my analysis of La Flesche's data.
99. La Flesche (1914:66–67; 1930:531).
100. La Flesche (1921:72).
101. Ni'-ka-wa-zhin-ton-ga's wife had the last, and the only known, of these bundles. She gave it to Ni-ka-u-kon-dsi, and it was buried with him (La Flesche 1921:70).
102. La Flesche (1921:70).
103. This is based on my analysis of La Flesche's data.
104. This is based on my analysis of La Flesche's data.
105. This is based on my analysis of La Flesche's data.
106. See the clan order of dwellings for normal village arrangement in Fletcher

and La Flesche (1911:58), and compare with the clan order in the House of Mystery shown by La Flesche (1925:84).
107. La Flesche (1921:62).
108. La Flesche (1921:62).

## CHAPTER 4

1. La Flesche (1930:675).
2. La Flesche (1930:577).
3. La Flesche (1930:533).
4. La Flesche (1930:530).
5. La Flesche (1930:530).
6. La Flesche (1921:59–71).
7. See La Flesche (1921:157–211, 220–37, 254–69, 272–74, 274–85) for the ni'-ki wi'-gi-e of the Puma, Bear, Elder Sky, Wolf, and Gentle Sky clans.
8. See La Flesche (1939:6–7, 12) for the Crawfish wi'-gi-e and the Water wi'-gi-e.
9. Although they speak symbolically of twenty-one bundles, there were actually twenty-four clans with bundles, and each clan had multiple bundles.
10. This is the only reference to the Gentle Sky clan by this name. See clan names in Table 3.1.

## CHAPTER 5

1. See Fletcher and La Flesche Papers, "Abstracts of Letters 1911," letter of May 29, 1911.
2. See La Flesche (1928:30).
3. La Flesche (1930:536).
4. La Flesche (1925:69).
5. La Flesche (1930:727).
6. La Flesche (1930:569).
7. La Flesche (1930:569; 1932:219).
8. La Flesche (1925:70; 1930:569).
9. La Flesche (1930:709). The puma skin was worn by the Xo'-ka in the four initiation rites relating primarily to war: the Songs of the Wa-xo'-be, the rite of vigil, the rite of the "Shooting of a Bird," and the "Ceremonial Distribution of Scalps" (La Flesche 1930:707).
10. La Flesche (1930:709). The buffalo robe was worn by the Xo'-ka in rituals relating primarily to hunting, such as the "Making of the Rush Mat Shrine" (La Flesche 1930:707). It was also worn in the child naming rite (La Flesche 1928:36).
11. La Flesche (1921:74).
12. La Flesche (1925:67, 70).
13. La Flesche (1930:549–550, 557). See La Flesche (1920) for a discussion of the "symbolic man."
14. La Flesche (1930:685).
15. La Flesche (1925:43).
16. La Flesche (1925:46).
17. See La Flesche (1925:42–43; 1930:132, 554; 1932:132).
18. La Flesche (1932:132; 1939:83–84).
19. La Flesche (1925:67–68).
20. See the third o-don' of the "Seven War Honors" (La Flesche (1925:180).

21. La Flesche (1925:53).

22. La Flesche (1925:52). In Fletcher and La Flesche Papers, "Abstract of Letters 1911," Letter of May 11, 1911, he states that other priests may attend initiations but they do not share the "fees" given to the participating priests.

23. La Flesche (1925:54, 238).

24. La Flesche (1925:54).

25. See La Flesche (1925:302; 1930:624).

26. See La Flesche (1925:84, position R in figure).

27. La Flesche (1930:677).

28. La Flesche (1930:563); and see La Flesche (1925:164–70, lines 327–506) for the story of the tally stick.

29. La Flesche (1925:243).

30. See La Flesche (1930:543–44; 1925:46).

31. See La Flesche (1925:84).

32. See La Flesche (1925:114–15; 1930:577–78; 1932:128).

33. See La Flesche (1925:147–48, 179–80).

34. La Flesche (1939:18–19).

35. See La Flesche (1930:652–53; 1925:335–36; 1939:19, 52).

36. La Flesche (1939:14). For the story of the club, see La Flesche (1921:258–61, lines 139–266).

37. La Flesche (1921:261, lines 255–91; 1925:356).

38. La Flesche (1939:15).

39. La Flesche (1925:356). In later years the priests substituted a hatchet (La Flesche (1939:14).

40. La Flesche (1925:234, 364; 1930:675).

41. La Flesche (1925:50).

42. La Flesche (1930:578–79).

43. La Flesche (1921:298).

44. La Flesche (1921:298; 1925:38, 207).

45. La Flesche (1930:577). La Flesche (1932:216) translates the term as "prayer." Although a wi'-gi-e was a request for Wa-kon-da's blessing, this was only one aspect of a wi'-gi-e.

46. This is the ni'-ki wi'-gi-e of the Puma clan; see La Flesche (1921:157–211).

47. See La Flesche (1930:577).

48. La Flesche (1930:535).

49. Saucy Calf did not give La Flesche this part of the Buffalo Bull clan ritual (see La Flesche 1930). La Flesche did, however, record a description for the Puma clan (1925:42–52). The description reproduced here is the one given by Charley Wah-hre-she for the Puma clan. Any differences between what is given here and what would have occurred in the Buffalo Bull clan form would have been minimal.

50. See La Flesche (1930:684).

51. See La Flesche (1930:532).

52. There were actually four principal war clans.

53. This particular version of the Penalty wi'-gi-e was one that could be used by any clan. Many clans had their own versions. See La Flesche (1925:44–46) for the Penalty wi'-gi-e used by the Bear and Puma clans, and La Flesche (1925:51–52) for the Penalty wi'-gi-e of the Men of Mystery clan.

54. This was an archaic word that probably meant "brother." It was used

only in the penalty rite (La Flesche 1932:186). It referred to the supernatural forces that would impose the penalties.

55. The term "grandfather" as used in this and subsequent wi'-gi-e "is not employed in its ordinary meaning but as denoting reverence. The term is applied to things mysterious or of a mysterious nature, such as the sun, the moon, single stars or groups of stars that are particularly conspicuous, and certain forms of animal or plant life" (La Flesche 1925:97).

56. As already mentioned, a number of factors influence the ritual forms in the preliminary ceremonies: which degree the candidate is taking, the clan of the candidate, whether the clan was a peace clan or war clan, and the moiety of the candidate's clan. In his writing, La Flesche gives partial descriptions of the preliminary ceremonies for five different clans or degrees: the Puma for the rite of vigil (La Flesche 1925:52–88); the Gentle Sky for the rite of vigil (La Flesche 1925:242–60), the Elder Sky for the ni'-ki-e rite (La Flesche 1921:238–50), the Gentle Sky for the ni'-ki-e rite (La Flesche 1921:285–92), and those used in the Shrine degree (La Flesche 1930:684–709). La Flesche implies that the ritual forms used in the Shrine degree did not vary with clans. It was a ritual owned by the Water people, and other clans were allowed to use it.

The Gentle Sky was a peace clan of the Sky People. The Elder Sky was a war clan of the Sky People, and the Puma clan was a war clan of the Earth People. Saucy Calf did not give La Flesche the preliminary ceremonies used by the Buffalo Bull clan (a war clan of the Sky People) for the Songs of the Wa-xo'-be. I have attempted to reconstruct these preliminary ceremonies by drawing information from five descriptions given by La Flesche. The difficulty is that not all of the ritual variables are known. If La Flesche did not mention a particular ritual act in one of his descriptions, was it because that clan did not use it for that particular initiation, or did his informant merely forget to mention it?

For this description of the preliminary ceremonies, I have taken the description La Flesche gave for the Puma clan's initiation into the rite of vigil. If not indicated by a footnote, the information is from that description. This description should be basically similar to the one used by the Buffalo Bull clan. All the preliminary ceremonies for an initiation included a formal notice of the initiation, the Moccasin Cutting, the ki'-non, and the Approach to the House. Since the candidate for the Songs of the Wa'-xo-be degree had to acquire the seven animal skins, there had to be a Smoking ritual. Since the description of the seven songs for the Buffalo Bull clan includes a Wa-don'-be, there had to be a selection of the Wa-don'-be. Finally, all the initiation rites except for the ni'-ki-e rite include songs, so there had to be a Night Singing. Although the songs and wi'-gi-e used in these rituals by the Buffalo Bull clan would have differed from those of the Puma clan that I have used, the ideas presented would have been basically the same.

57. The ni'-ki-e degree conferred on the initiate total ritual authority over all of the rites of the wa-xo'-be. These men were, in effect, the heads of the clan priesthood.

58. The statement that only the priests of the three major war clans were present comes from the description for the Gentle Sky. In La Flesche's description of this ritual segment for the Puma clan, he seems to imply that a full representation of all twenty-four clans was present. However, it is clear that this ritual took place in the house of the candidate, and it is doubtful that a

candidate would have had a house large enough to accommodate the priests from all twenty-four clans. Therefore I have substituted the Gentle Sky clan description.

59. The Shrine degree and ni'-ki-e degree did not include a Smoking of the Animal ritual. The only other description of this ritual is the one used by the Gentle Sky clan in its rite of vigil degree (see La Flesche 1925:243–48).

60. This paragraph and the preceding two paragraphs are from La Flesche (1925:243) (Gentle Sky clan).

61. For the Smoking of Seven Animals wi'-gi-e used by the Gentle Sky clan, see La Flesche (1925:245–47).

62. "No explanation could be obtained . . . as to the meaning of this line and the closing line of each of the three following sections. The lines probably refer to the custom of cutting the scalp taken from the foe by a war party into four parts before cutting it into smaller pieces for distribution among the sacred hawks—the wa-xo'-be" (La Flesche 1925:55n).

63. Deer do not have gall bladders (La Flesche 1925:57n).

64. This is the only known version of this wi'-gi-e. It was not mentioned for the Gentle Sky clan, and the Buffalo Bull clan may not have used its equivalent.

65. For a description of the Moccasin Cutting used by the Gentle Sky clan for their version of the rite of vigil, see La Flesche (1925:248–251), and for their version for the Shrine degree, see La Flesche (1930:699–703).

66. La Flesche recorded three other versions of the Moccasin wi'-gi-e: the Elder Sky version, as used in their ni'-ki-e rite (La Flesche 1921:239–241); and the Moccasin wi'-gi-e used by the Gentle Sky clan in their rite of vigil (1925:248–250) and their Shrine degree (La Flesche 1930:700–703). There are some minor differences between these two versions.

67. This sentence and the three preceding sentences are from La Flesche (1930:706).

68. For other discussions of the ki'-non, see La Flesche (1930:703–707 [Gentle Sky, Shrine degree]; 1925:251–57 [Gentle Sky, rite of vigil]; 1921:242–49 [Elder Sky, ni'-ki-e degree]; 1921:285–87 [Gentle Sky, ni'-ki-e degree]; 1928:33–36 [Puma clan, child naming rite]; 1921:74–81 [rite of the chiefs]).

69. The last part of this sentence is from La Flesche (1925:251).

70. This is sometimes called the Wi'-gi-e of the Mussel, in reference to the shell gorget. For other versions of the ki'-non wi'-gi-e and/or songs, see La Flesche (1928:34–35 [Puma clan, child naming rite]; 1921:242–48 [Elder Sky, ni'-ki-e degree]; 1921:286 [Gentle Sky, ni'-ki-e degree]; 1925:252–56 [Gentle Sky, rite of vigil]; 1930:704–705 [Gentle Sky, Shrine degree]; 1921:74–80 [for the version used in the Rite of the Chiefs]; 1939:102–104 [for the version used in the mourning dance]).

71. This sentence is from La Flesche (1930:709). For the symbolism of the puma skin robe, see lines 31–44 of the first Smoking wi'-gi-e.

72. This wi'-gi-e may be considered a continuation of the ki'-non wi'-gi-e. See La Flesche (1925:43).

73. For other discussions and descriptions of the Processional Approach to the House, see La Flesche (1930:707–709 [Gentle Sky, Shrine degree]; 1925:257–60 [Gentle Sky, rite of vigil]; 1928:36–38) [Puma, child naming rite]; 1921:248–51 [Elder Sky, ni'-ki-e degree]; 1921:287–91 [Gentle Sky, ni'-ki-e degree]; 1921:81–83 [rite of the chiefs]).

74. Each clan had its own version of the seven songs. This ritual set was used in the initiation ritual for all of the seven degrees with the exception of the ni'-ki-e degree. However, there are indications that a clan modified its seven songs depending upon which degree was being taken. La Flesche recorded three relatively complete descriptions of the seven songs: those of the Buffalo Bull clan as used in the Songs of the Wa-xo'-be (La Flesche 1930:563–639); those of the Puma clan as used in the rite of vigil (La Flesche 1925:88–205), and those of the Gentle Sky clan as used in the rite of vigil (La Flesche 1925:260–326). Except when noted, what is presented here is his description of the seven songs of the Buffalo Bull clan. In the Buffalo Bull clan version, the seven songs begin with the Songs of Opening of the Wa-xo'-be (see La Flesche 1930:541). The Puma clan began their version of the seven songs with the Song of the Procession to the Sacred House (see La Flesche 1925:78), which I, like the priests of the Buffalo Bull clan, included as part of the preliminary ceremonies.

75. For the war ceremony and the organization of a tribal war party, see La Flesche (1939:3–86).

76. For the Puma version of this song group, see La Flesche (1925:88–99), and for the Gentle Sky clan version, see La Flesche (1925:260–64).

77. Paragraph taken from La Flesche (1925:263).

78. Paragraph taken from La Flesche (1925:89).

79. Sentence taken from La Flesche (1925:90).

80. Sentence taken from La Flesche (1925:91).

81. Paragraph taken from La Flesche (1925:96).

82. Paragraph taken from La Flesche (1925:96).

83. Paragraph taken from La Flesche (1925:9).

84. See La Flesche (1925:99).

85. Neither the Puma nor the Gentle Sky clan had a song set by this name. However, the Puma clan song set called "Sun or Pipe Offering" seems to be addressing a closely related topic (see La Flesche 1925:120–23).

86. Neither the Puma nor the Gentle Sky clan had a song group by this name.

87. For the Puma clan versions of the Wolf Songs, see La Flesche (1925:124–29), and for the Gentle Sky version see La Flesche (1925:290–94). "The Wolf Songs of the Puma clan and also those of the Buffalo Bull clan dwell upon the authority of the eight commanders and upon the mystic traits of the wolf, such as watchfulness, physical endurance, and the ability to resist the longing for home, traits necessary to the officers responsible for the lives of their men. The Wolf Songs belonging to the Gentle Sky clan are supplicatory in character—an appeal to the supernatural to grant to the commanders the same powers bestowed upon the wolf to aid them in overcoming their enemies" (La Flesche 1925:290).

88. These three paragraphs are taken from La Flesche (1925:124).

89. "The word Hon'-ba, day, which is frequently used in the two wolf songs, is not used in its ordinary sense but as an expression of an earnest desire that the commanders shall be made to be as tireless as is the day, in order that they may be able to succeed in their undertaking" (La Flesche 1930:572).

90. Neither the Puma nor the Gentle Sky clan had a song group of this name.

91. For further explanation, see La Flesche (1921:278–79, lines 30–53).

92. See also La Flesche (1921:64–65).

93. La Flesche may have been mistaken in his statement that a hawk was placed on the back of each of the eight commanders. In his writing it is implied that only one hawk, belonging to the Sacred Warrior's clan, was taken with the war party. In his description of the war ceremony, he states that just before the battle the hawk was put on the back of the chief commander only (see La Flesche 1939:79).

94. For the Puma clan version of Songs of Taking the Rattle (a wi'-gi-e and two songs), see La Flesche (1925:114–20), and for the Gentle Sky version (a wi'-gi-e and four songs), see La Flesche (1925:264–71).

95. This paragraph is taken from La Flesche (1925:274), the description of the Gentle Sky clan version of the seven songs. It was stated that the reconsecration of the bird was part of all initiation rituals. However, neither Saucy Calf in his description of the Songs of the Wa-xo'-be nor Charley Wah-hre-she in his description of the rite of vigil mentions this part of the ritual. Thus I am assuming that in the Buffalo Bull clan version of the seven songs, this reconsecration of the hawk was also part of the Songs of Taking the Rattle song group.

96. "The name Hon'-ga U-ta-non-dsi [Isolated Earth] may be interpreted thus: Hon'-ga, a sacred object, or something that occupies the most prominent place among things sacred; U-ta-non-dsi, isolated, or an object that occupies a place that is apart from the other sacred objects. In other words, the name Hon'-ga as here used refers to the earth that occupies a great space by itself and is surrounded by other Hon'-ga that move in the heavens, singly and in groups, as the sun, the moon, the morning and evening stars, and also the various constellations" (La Flesche 1930:576).

97. See the description of the war ceremony (La Flesche 1939:4–5).

98. See the description of the Vigil of the Sacred Warrior (La Flesche 1939:8–11).

99. For the Puma clan version of the Rattle wi'-gi-e (used in the rite of vigil), see La Flesche (1925:115–17); for the Gentle Sky clan version (used in the rite of vigil), see La Flesche (1925:265–67); for the Hon-ga (Land People?) version used in the Shrine degree, see La Flesche (1930:711–13); and for the Wa-zha'-zhe (Water People?) version used in the rite, see La Flesche (1930:713–15). It appears from the versions of the Rattle wi'-gi-e recorded that not only did each clan possibly have its particular version but that there also were still other versions that were the collective property of the Land People, Water People, and Sky People, which were used in some rituals. Although the Puma was a clan of the Land People, the symbolism in its two versions of the Rattle wi'-gi-e is different. In the Puma version, the rattle is the symbol of "the head of a puma and the handle its lower right arm," while in the Land People version it "symbolizes the head of a man, an enemy, and the handle his right forearm" (La Flesche 1930:710).

100. For the Puma clan version, see La Flesche (1925:106–10). La Flesche (1925:275–80) also gave a song group called the rite of vigil for the Gentle Sky. This song group, however, addresses a quite different aspect of the rite of vigil. During the songs, the Singer performs the rite called *wa'-in xa-ge*, wailing while he touches the head of each priest with the pipe and hawk. Earlier we saw this same rite performed in the Smoking of the Animal portion of the preliminary ceremonies. In the seven songs segment of the Buffalo Bull clan version of the Songs of the Wa-xo'-be, this rite is performed in the fourteenth song group, the

Songs of Weeping. With the Puma clan, the wa'-in xa-ge rite is also performed as part of the Songs of Weeping song group (see La Flesche (1925:103–106).

101. See La Flesche (1921:169–72, lines 434–524).

102. These two paragraphs are from La Flesche (1930:107).

103. In his list of song groups, Saucy Calf listed this song as a separate song group (see La Flesche 1930:541).

104. The Xo'-ka in the war ceremony functions differently from the Xo'-ka in the initiation rites. In the war ceremonies, there is no Assisting Xo'-ka, and the Xo'-ka has to recite the wi'-gi-e, sing the songs, and direct the participants himself.

105. For a description of the Sacred Warrior's vigil during the war rites, see La Flesche (1939:8–11).

106. The "head of the order" would have to have been a priest initiated into the ni'-ki-e non-k'on, or Hearing of the Sayings of the Ancient Men, degree. Only men initiated into this degree had total ritual authority (see La Flesche 1921:153).

107. In the Puma clan version of the seven songs, there is nothing comparable to the Making of the Bow Songs. The seven songs of the Gentle Sky contain a song group called "the Making of the Bows" (see La Flesche 1925:271–74); however, "in none of the five songs that compose this group are found any words that suggest the making of a bow" (La Flesche 1925:271).

108. In the Puma clan version, the four songs called the Spirit Songs immediately follow the Opening of the Wa-xo'-be (see La Flesche 1925:78). Only three of these songs were recorded (La Flesche 1925:103–106).

109. Paragraph taken from La Flesche (1925:103).

110. The Gentle Sky clan has a Midday Song group; however, unlike that of the Buffalo Bull clan, it makes no reference to the Sacred Warrior (see La Flesche 1925:318–21). There is no song group of this name in the Puma clan version. There is, however, a group called the Songs of the Sun in which the Sacred Warrior appeals to the rising sun (see La Flesche 1925:120–23).

111. In the Gentle Sky clan version of the Little Songs of the Sun, no mention is made of the hawk. These songs "are appeals for aid from that heavenly body (the Sun) for success in defeating the enemies of the tribe" (La Flesche 1925:280).

112. Neither the Puma nor the Gentle Sky clan has a comparable song group; however, as La Flesche says, this song appears to have been part of the following Wolf Songs group, which the Puma and Gentle Sky clans do have.

113. The Buffalo Bull clan had two separate Wolf Songs groups (three if one includes the Fish-Turtle song) in its version of the seven songs. See note 13, this chapter.

114. In Saucy Calf's original list of song groups for the seven songs of the Buffalo Bull clan, he listed the Weeping Songs and the Song of the Seizing as two separate song groups (see La Flesche 1930:542). Later, however, in La Flesche's discussion of the seven songs, he describes them as one song group (1930:608–21), which he calls wa-thu'-ce wa-thon, or Songs of the Seizing. This discussion in La Flesche is rather confused, and Saucy Calf could not remember part of it. I have reconstructed this part of the ritual by combining information given by Saucy Calf, Charley Wah-hre-she on the Puma clan version, and Shunkahmolah on the Gentle Sky version.

115. The last two sentences are from La Flesche (1925:148).

116. See La Flesche (1925:148) for a similar description in the Puma version.

117. Saucy Calf could not remember the Dream wi'-gi-e used by the Buffalo Bull clan and so I have substituted the Puma clan version (La Flesche 1925:139–44). Although Saucy Calf could not give the wi'-gi-e, he was able to give it in a narrative form (see La Flesche 1930:610–14). In comparing the narrative version of the Buffalo Bull clan's Dream wi'-gi-e and the actual Dream wi'-gi-e of the Puma clan, we find only minor differences.

118. In the Puma clan version the man sleeps facing right, the direction used by the Earth People. I have changed this to read "left," the direction used by the Sky People.

119. These two paragraphs are taken from La Flesche (1925:138–39).

120. La Flesche recorded two sets of the Song of the Seizing, those of the Buffalo Bull clan (1930:608–21) and those of the Puma clan (1925:147–82). With the Gentle Sky clan, the counting by the Wa-don'-be was part of the rite of vigil song group, and La Flesche only briefly mentions this part of the ritual (1925:276).

121. The Gentle Sky clan did not use willow saplings in counting o-don', but a bundle of "of rods permanently kept for ceremonial counting purposes." They avoided using willow saplings "because they were originally dedicated to represent acts of violence and the destruction of human life." This was also true for the other Peace clan, the Gentle Ponca (La Flesche 1925:276).

122. There were two versions of this wi'-gi-e: the complete version, which was used only by the Black Bear clan, the principal war clan of the Earth People (see La Flesche 1925:154–64), and a modified version or versions used by other clans of the Earth People (see La Flesche 1925:148–54 for a version used by the Puma clan).

123. For the version of this wi'-gi-e used by the Elder Water, the principal war clan of the Water People, see La Flesche (1925:164–70). The other clans of the Water People used a modified form of this wi'-gi-e (1925:154), but La Flesche did not record the modified version.

124. For the version of this wi'-gi-e of the Elder Sky, the principal war clan, see La Flesche (1925:170–71).

125. The relationship between this version of the wi'-gi-e of the Beaver and the Thirteen Willow Saplings and the wi'-gi-e of the same name used by the Water People is not clear. It differs from the version recorded for the Elder Water clan (La Flesche 1925:164–70), but whether this is the modified form used by other clans of the Water People or a unique version is not known.

126. In the original publication this was the second song, since the Weeping Song was counted as the first song of the group.

127. This statement and the count that follows were the actual words used by Shunkahmolah when he acted as Wa-don'-be in a ceremony (taken from La Flesche 1925:179–81).

128. La Flesche (1925:180) translated *ga-xthi* as "striking an enemy." The word, however, means "killing an enemy" (see La Flesche 1932:49), and so I have changed the translation.

129. The Osages were well known among the Prairie tribes for cutting off the heads of their enemies.

130. La Flesche (1925:181) translated *u-tsi* as "striking an enemy." The word actually refers to mauling, beating, pounding, or striking (see La Flesche 1932:180). I have chosen to translate it as "hitting."

131. In the Puma version there was a "closing" song that followed the recit-

ing of the wi'-gi-e and the counting of the o-don' by the Wa-don'-be (see La Flesche 1925:181–82). Saucy Calf did not mention such a song for the Buffalo Bull clan.

132. See La Flesche (1925:182–85) for the Puma clan version and La Flesche (1925:316–18) for the Gentle Sky version of the Crow Songs.

133. Paragraph taken from La Flesche (1925:182–83).

134. Paragraph taken from La Flesche (1925:316–17).

135. Saucy Calf did not give the Instructions to the Wife of the Initiate for the Buffalo Bull clan's version of the seven songs. This description is taken from the Puma clan's version in the rite of vigil initiation (La Flesche 1925:192–96). For the Gentle Sky clan version used in the rite of vigil initiation, see La Flesche (1925:284–85). For the Elder Sky clan version used in the Sayings of the Ancient Men initiation rite, see La Flesche (1921:270–72). Although La Flesche states that the Instructions to the Wife used in the rite of the chiefs is the same as the Puma clan version used here, there appear to have been some minor differences (see La Flesche 1921:140–44).

136. In the instructions used by the Gentle Sky clan, there is no direct "reference to the destruction of human life, as the office of this clan is that of the protection of life and the maintenance of peace with all peoples" (La Flesche 1925:285).

137. "[Other Osages] in speaking of this ceremony, said that with the first grain of corn is planted a bit of scalp of the enemy. Also that when the corn ripened, the woman who had ceremonially planted her field gathered the corn from the seven sacred hills, pulling the stalks from these hills and carrying them home. Then she prepares a feast for the priest who had instructed her in the rite and ceremonially presents the sacred corn to him. The priest invites other priests to the feast and shares with them the sacred corn. This ceremony is never again performed by the same woman as it is believed to be efficacious for all her future plantings" (La Flesche 1925:195n).

138. For the Buffalo Songs used by the Puma clan, see La Flesche (1925:196–205), and for those used by the Gentle Sky, see La Flesche (1925:285–90).

139. La Flesche recorded three sets of the six songs: those of the Buffalo Bull clan used in the Songs of the Wa-xo'-be (1930:639–78); those of the Puma Clan used in the rite of vigil (1925:205–37); and those of the Gentle Sky clan (1925:327–70). Although the major features are the same, there are significant differences between the three sets. The Buffalo Bull and Gentle Sky are both Sky clans, while the Puma is an Earth clan. In addition, the Gentle Sky is one of the two peace clans within the tribe, and in contrast to the Buffalo Bull clan, they make few references to bloodletting in their rites. The following descriptions, except when indicated, are from La Flesche's description of the Buffalo Bull clan's six songs.

140. See La Flesche (1925:207).

141. The term *Black Bear* as used here appears to be applied to all seven clans of the Land People.

142. This paragraph and the preceding three paragraphs are from La Flesche (1925:205–206).

143. See La Flesche (1925:206–13) for the Buffalo Songs used by the Puma clan in its six songs. The Gentle Sky clan does not use any Buffalo Songs in its version of the six songs.

144. This paragraph and the two preceding paragraphs are from La Flesche (1925:207).

145. The Omaha version of this Buffalo Song is given in Fletcher and La Flesche (1911:293). The Omaha songs speak of the buffalo's coming from ten different directions.

146. The Puma clan (see La Flesche 1930:129–37) and the Gentle Sky clan (1930:322–26) have the Deer Songs as part of their seven songs.

147. This indicates that there were at least some minor ritual differences between priests even of the same clan.

148. The Black Bear Songs used in the six songs by the Gentle Sky clan differ significantly in content, referring to the four symbolic flint knives in the care of the Black Bear clan and to the Elder Water clan's conferring on the Hon-ga clan(?) authority to organize war parties (see La Flesche 1930:344–47). The Black Bear Songs of the Puma clan are part of their seven songs (1930:185–92).

149. For the Rush for Charcoal Songs of the Puma clan, see La Flesche (1930:213–18), and for those of the Gentle Sky, see La Flesche (1930:327–38). For this ritual's use as part of the war ceremony, see La Flesche (1939:54–59).

150. This paragraph and the preceding paragraph are taken from La Flesche (1925:214). For additional descriptive material, see La Flesche (1930:327, 334, 336). For this ritual as it is used in the war ceremony, see La Flesche (1939:54–59).

151. La Flesche recorded three other versions of the Charcoal wi'gi-e. For that of the Gentle Sky clan, see La Flesche (1925:328–29 [refers to the Black Bear, Swan, and Deer]); for that of the Puma clan, see La Flesche (1925:214–16 [refers to the Puma, Black Bear, Swan, Eagle, and Deer]); and for the one used in the war ceremony, see La Flesche (1939:55–56 [very similar to Puma clan version]).

152. Why the Xo'-ka tosses the standard to the priests of the Deer clan is not clear. The standard is actually made by the priests of the Bow and Black Bear clans. The Deer clan merely supplies the deerskin attached to the standard (see La Flesche 1939:18–19). Although La Flesche does not state why the Deer clan's wi'-gi-e was not included, it was probably because Saucy Calf did not have the authority to give it to La Flesche, if in fact he knew the wi'-gi-e.

153. The Puma clan had a Water Song group as part of its six songs, but Charles Wah-hre-she could not remember them (see La Flesche 1924:218). The Water Songs of the Gentle Sky were part of their seven songs (1925:312–16).

154. There is no comparable song group in the Puma clan's or Gentle Sky clan's versions of either the six songs or the seven songs.

155. There is no comparable song group in the Puma clan's or Gentle Sky clan's versions of either the six songs or the seven songs.

156. The ritual concepts referred to in this song group are found in two different song groups used in the Puma clan's version of the six songs: the Little Evening Song (see La Flesche 1925:220) and the Gray Owl Songs (1925:227–29). This song group is absent from the Gentle Sky clan version.

157. This song group is not found in either the Puma or Gentle Sky clan's version of the rite.

158. Charles Wah-hre-she could not remember the Puma clan Rain Songs or its wi'-gi-e (see La Flesche 1925:230). Also called the Songs of the Clouds by the Gentle Sky clan, this group contained four songs, but no wi'-gi-e (1925:351–55).

159. Whether this was the wi'-gi-e regularly used by the Buffalo Bull clan or

some other version cannot be determined. La Flesche recorded three other versions of the Penalties wi'-gi-e. For that of the Men of Mystery clan, see La Flesche (1925:51–52); for that of the Puma and Black Bear clans, see La Flesche (1925:44–46); and for one that could be used by any clan, see La Flesche (1925:47–49).

160. The ritual forms presented in this song group by the Buffalo Bull clan were divided between two song groups by the Gentle Sky clan: the Songs of the Decorating of the Club and the Songs of the Striking of the Earth (see La Flesche 1925:255–62). Charles Wah-hre-she could not remember this part of the Puma clan's six songs (see La Flesche 1925:230).

161. See La Flesche (1921:261, lines 255–91).

162. Paragraph taken from La Flesche (1925:356).

163. This song group was deleted from the Gentle Sky version of the six songs because of their peaceful nature. For the Puma clan version, see La Flesche (1925:230–32).

164. This paragraph is from La Flesche (1925:230–31), the Puma clan description. It has been changed, however, to fit the Buffalo Bull clan version. In the Puma clan version there is only one song, and the striking takes place during this song. In the Buffalo Bull version, there are three songs, and the striking takes place during the third. In the Puma clan version, the two symbolic birds are the blackbird and the gray hawk; the Buffalo Bull clan used the blackbird and the red hawk.

165. In the Puma clan version this song group is called the Songs of Triumph or the Return of the Bird (see La Flesche 1925:232–36). The Gentle Sky clan called this song group Songs of Drawing the Arrows (see La Flesche 1925:364–69).

166. This paragraph is from La Flesche (1925:364).

167. This paragraph and the preceding two paragraphs are from La Flesche (1925:234).

168. This paragraph is from La Flesche (1925:235).

169. Neither the Puma nor the Gentle Sky clan had a separate Victory Song group in their six songs. It appears that this victory or triumph concept was incorporated into the preceding song group, the Songs of Triumph of the Puma and the Songs of Drawing the Arrows of the Gentle Sky.

170. For the Puma clan closing songs, see La Flesche (1925:236–37), and for the Gentle Sky, see La Flesche (1925:369–70).

171. This paragraph is from La Flesche (1925:237).

172. Reverend Vaill is quoted in Graves (1949:13–15).

## CHAPTER 6

1. La Flesche (1921:73).

2. La Flesche (1921:81).

3. La Flesche (1921:139–40).

4. See La Flesche (1921:144).

f5. La Flesche (1921:139–40).

6. For the description of the ki'-non used in this rite, see La Flesche (1921: 74–81).

7. For a description of the Approach to the House used in this rite, see La Flesche (1921:81–83).

8. The ceremony of the Sending is found in a number of the initiation rituals,

as well as the child naming rite. For other descriptions, see La Flesche (1921:155–56 [ni'-ki-e degree]; 1928:38–40 [child naming rite]; 1930:686–87 [Shrine degree]).

9. In the child naming rite, the Assisting Xo'-ka performs this act.

10. No mention is made of the types of symbolic articles distributed to the clan priests in the rite of the chiefs. The article "sent" in the ni'-ki-e and Shrine degree rites are related to warfare and would not be suitable for this rite. In the child naming rite it is mentioned that grains of corn were given to the priests of the Buffalo Bull clan, cedar fronds to the Gentle Ponca, a red down eagle feather to the Gentle Sky, and a mussel shell to the White Water clan priests (La Flesche 1928:39–40). These items are directly related to the symbols of these clans and are probably the same types of symbolic articles distributed during the rite of the chiefs.

11. See La Flesche (1932:157–58, 376–77).

12. La Flesche called this the wa'-tse-tsi or Star clan in his text, an alternative name for the Gentle Ponca. I have changed this to Gentle Ponca so that it conforms to the standardized list of clans presented in Table 3.1.

13. This clan seems to correspond to the Clear the Way People in the clan list in Table 3.1.

14. La Flesche divided this wi'-gi-e into three parts that he called Red Eagle, the Peaceful Day, and the No Anger. These were three subclans or alternate ways of referring to the Gentle Sky clan. I have made it one wi'-gi-e.

15. This name is also used for the Buffalo Face clan.

16. See La Flesche (1921:140–44) for a description of the ceremony.

17. See La Flesche (1921:84).

## CHAPTER 7

1. The Osages distinguished between true stories and fantasies or fables. A true story was called an u'-tha-ge (see La Flesche 1932:176), while a fantasy or fable was termed hi'-go. "Fables and myths are told only in the wintertime, when the snakes lie frozen underground. They are the guardians of the truth, and an untrue story arouses the anger of a snake" (La Flesche 1932:60).

2. Bailey field notes.

3. Bailey field notes.

4. One story was told of a man who changed himself into a deer just to tease one of his nephews. The nephew, thinking that he was a real deer, shot and wounded him in the leg. Individuals with these abilities did not always control them. Once, before a peyote meeting, one of the men attending told the others that if anything happened to him during the meeting, they were to keep him from leaving the church house. During the meeting the man turned into a snake and started crawling toward the door. The others present didn't stop him. When they saw him the next day he had returned to human form but looked badly shaken by the experience. These were told as true stories (Bailey field notes).

5. See "Superstitious Beliefs," page 2, in Fletcher and La Flesche Papers.

6. See the story of "I-tse-ke and Wa-ho-i-zhi-ge" in Fletcher and La Flesche Papers. La Flesche did not indicate whether this was told as a true story or as a fable.

7. Bailey field notes.

8. La Flesche (1932:90) defined the term as "elf" or "sprite."

9. Bailey field notes.

10. See the story of "Thiu-tsa-zhi-ga" in Fletcher and La Flesche Papers. This was told as a true story.

11. For example, see Gill (1982; 1987); Vecsey (1990); Waugh and Prithipaul (1977).

12. Hultkrantz made little use of La Flesche's Osage work in his comparative studies of American Indian religion. He did not cite La Flesche in either of his more comprehensive studies (1979; 1987), and in his *Prairie and Plains Indians* (1973) he cited only La Flesche's *War Ceremony and Peace Ceremony of the Osage Indians.*

13. See Hultkrantz (1987:20–34).

14. Hultkrantz (1987:14). In an earlier study he defined the difference between Hunting cultures and Agrarian cultures for both North and South America (Hultkrantz 1979:141–49). Hultkrantz was not the first to make this distinction. Earlier, Ruth Underhill (1965:10–19) had noted the distinction between the religions of the "hunter-gatherers" and the "planters."

15. There were places that were sacred, but they were made sacred by human actions, not by supernatural forces. For example, the houses of the chiefs and their fireplaces were sacred and remained sacred as long as they were used. Similarly, in the Osage peyote religion, the sites for church houses, called fireplaces, were ritually consecrated for sacred use. Technically speaking, these sites remain sacred even after they are no longer used and even after their locations are forgotten.

16. See Mooney (1910; 1928).

17. See Dobyns (1966; 1976).

18. See Ubelaker (1976:644).

19. See Dobyns (1976:34–44). The figure of seventeen million is just for the United States and Canada.

20. See Ubelaker (1976:644); Dobyns (1976:34–44).

21. Over the past two decades, academic interest in the Mississippian peoples has increased dramatically, particularly among archaeologists. Most of these studies are highly technical archaeological studies of specific sites or regions. Some recent studies of more general interest are Smith (1990), Galloway (1989), and Peregrine (1992). For the best general overview of these peoples and their historical descendants, see Hudson (1976). James Brown (1991) has an excellent brief overview.

22. See Gregg (1975).

23. To picture the cultural distinctiveness of this region, see the culture trait distribution maps in Driver and Massey (1957) and Driver (1961).

24. Most archaeologists have been cautious in speculating about the historical relationships between the Mississippian peoples of the upper Mississippi Valley and the tribes living there at the time of European contact (see Tanner 1987:25–28). One of the few who has not is Robert Hall (1989), who sees a direct link between the religious symbolism of the Osages and other Siouan, Algonkian, and Caddoan tribes and the Mississippian peoples. See also Carl Chapman's (1980:263) discussion of the Mississippian period in Missouri.

25. For brief descriptions of the Central Algonkian tribes, see Trigger (1978: 610–89); for the Poncas, see Howard (1965); for the Omahas, see Fletcher and La Flesche (1911); for the Winnebagos, see Radin (1923); for the Ioways, see Skinner (1915a; 1926); and for the Kansa, see Skinner (1915b).

26. Why the upper Mississippi, Missouri, and Ohio valley Mississippians were patrilineal but the lower Mississippi valley and Gulf Coast Mississippians were matrilineal involves arguments that go far beyond the scope of this book.

27. For an excellent general discussion of the changes that occurred among these peoples, see Smith (1987).

28. The best general summary of Mississippian religious beliefs appears in Hudson (1976:120–83). Although there is great similarity in the use of religious symbols, the interpretation and general picture presented is very different from that found in La Flesche. Most of these data are drawn from the Creeks and Cherokees. Although particularistic differences would certainly have distinguished the religions of the Osages, Creeks, and Cherokees, I suggest that many of the differences are the result of historical factors. By the time these data were collected, depopulation, dislocation, and European religious influences had blurred the distinction between the formal religious beliefs of the Creeks and Cherokees and their folk beliefs. This problem was further compounded by Europeans and many American Indians who confused children's fables with supernatural beliefs.

# References Cited

MANUSCRIPT COLLECTION

Alice C. Fletcher and Francis La Flesche Papers. National Anthropological Archives, Smithsonian Institution, Washington, D.C.

PUBLISHED SOURCES

Alexander, Hartley B.
1933    Francis La Flesche. *American Anthropologist* 35:328–31.

Bailey, Garrick
1973    *Changes in Osage Social Organization 1673–1906.* University
        of Oregon Anthropological Papers, no. 5. Eugene: Univer-
        sity of Oregon Press.

Baird, David W.
1980    *The Quapaw Indians: A History of the Downstream People.* Nor-
        man: University of Oklahoma Press.

Barnes, R. H.
1984    *Two Crows Denies It: A History of Controversy in Omaha Soci-
        ology.* Lincoln: University of Nebraska Press.

Berkhofer, Robert F.
1978    *The White Man's Indian.* New York: Alfred A. Knopf.

Blaine, Martha Royce
1979    *The Ioway Indians.* Norman: University of Oklahoma Press.

Brown, James A.
1991    The Flason and the Serpent: Life in the Southeastern United
        States at the Time of Columbus. In *Circa 1492,* Jay Levenson,
        ed., pp. 529–34. New Haven: Yale University Press.

Chapman, Berlin Basil
1965    *The Otoes and the Missourias.* Stillwater, Okla.(?): Private
        printing.

Chapman, Carl
1974    *Origins of the Osage Indians.* New York: Garland.
1980    *The Archaeology of Missouri,* vol. 2. Columbia: University of Missouri Press.

Chapman, Carl, and Eleanor Chapman
1964    *Indians and Archaeology of Missouri.* Missouri Book no. 6. Columbia: University of Missouri Press.

Coleman, Michael C.
1986    The Mission Education of Francis La Flesche. *American Studies in Scandinavia* 18:67–82.

Crary, Margaret
1973    *Susette La Flesche: Voice of the Omaha Indians.* New York: Hawthorn.

Din, Gilbert C., and Abraham P. Nasatir
1983    *The Imperial Osages: Spanish-Indian Diplomacy in the Mississippi Valley.* Norman: University of Oklahoma Press.

Dobyns, Henry
1966    Estimating Aboriginal American Population: An Appraisal of Techniques with New Hemisphere Estimates. *Current Anthropology* 7: 395–416.
1976    *Native American Historical Demography: A Critical Bibliography.* Bloomington: University of Indiana Press.

Dorsey, James Owen
1884    An Account of the War Customs of the Osages. *American Naturalist* 18:113–33.
1888    Osage Traditions. *Sixth Annual Report of the Bureau of American Ethnology (1884–85),* pp. 373–97. Washington, D.C.
1897    Siouan Sociology. *Fifteenth Annual Report of the Bureau of American Ethnology (1893–94),* pp. 205–44. Washington, D.C.

Driver, Harold
1961    *Indians of North America.* Chicago: University of Chicago Press.

Driver, Harold, and William C. Massey
1957    Comparative Studies of North American Indians. *Transactions of the American Philosophical Society* 47:165–456.

Eastman, Charles Alexander
1911    *The Soul of the Indian: An Interpretation.* Boston: Houghton Mifflin.

Fletcher, Alice C., and Francis La Flesche
1911    The Omaha Tribe. *Twenty-seventh Annual Report of the Bureau of American Ethnology (1905–1906)*, pp. 15–64. Washington, D.C.

Galloway, Patricia
1989    *The Southeastern Ceremonial Complex: Artifacts and Analysis.* Lincoln: University of Nebraska Press.

Gill, Sam
1982    *Native American Religions: An Introduction.* Belmont, Calif.: Wadsworth Publishing Company.
1987    *Native American Religious Action: A Performance Approach to Religion.* Columbia: University of South Carolina Press.

Graves, William W.
1949    *The First Protestant Osage Missions: 1820–1837.* Oswego, Kans.: The Carpenter Press.

Green, Norma Kidd
1969    *Iron Eye's Family: The Children of Joseph La Flesche.* Lincoln, Nebr.: Johnsen Publishing Company.

Gregg, Michael L.
1975    A Population Estimate for Cahokia. Illinois Archaeological Survey *Bulletin* 10:126–36.

Hall, Robert
1989    The Cultural Background of Mississippian Symbolism. In *The Southeastern Ceremonial Complex: Aritfacts and Analysis,* Patricia Galloway, ed. Lincoln: University of Nebraska Press.

Hallpike, C. R.
1976    *The Foundations of Primitive Thought.* Oxford: Clarendon Press.

Howard, James
1965    *The Ponca Tribe.* Bureau of American Ethnology, Bulletin 195. Washington, D.C.

Hudson, Charles
1976    *The Southeastern Indians.* Knoxville: University of Tennessee Press.

Hultkrantz, Ake
1973    *Prairie and Plains Indians.* Leiden: E. J. Brill.
1979    *The Religions of the American Indians.* Berkeley: University of California Press.

1987    *Native Religions of North America.* San Francisco: Harper and Row.

Jackson, Helen Hunt
1881    *A Century of Dishonor.* New York: Harper.

Kroeber, Alfred
1939    *Cultural and Natural Areas of Native North America.* University of California Publications in American Archaeology and Ethnology, vol. 38. Berkeley: University of California.

La Flesche, Francis
1885    The Sacred Pipes of Friendship. *Proceedings of the American Association for the Advancement of Science* 33:613–15.
1900    *The Middle Five: Indian Boys at School.* Boston: Small, Maynard and Company.
1905    *Who Was the Medicine Man?* Hampton, Va.: Hampton Institute Press.
1914    Ceremonials and Rituals of the Osage. *Smithsonian Miscellaneous Collections* 63:66–69.
1915    Omaha and Osage Traditions of Separation. *Proceedings of the International Congress of Americanists* 19:459–62.
1917    Work Among the Osage Indians. *Smithsonian Miscellaneous Collections* 66:118–121.
1918    Tribal Rites of the Osage Indians. *Smithsonian Miscellaneous Collections* 68:84–90.
1920    The Symbolic Man of the Osage Tribe. *Art and Archaeology* 9:68–72.
1921    The Osage Tribe: Rite of the Chiefs; Sayings of the Ancient Men. *Thirty-sixth Annual Report of the Bureau of American Ethnology (1914–15),* pp. 35–604. Washington, D.C.
1924    Ethnology of the Osage Indians. *Smithsonian Miscellaneous Collections* 76:104–107.
1925    The Osage Tribe: Rite of Vigil. *Forty-fifth Annual Report of the Bureau of American Ethnology (1927–28),* pp. 523–833. Washington, D.C.
1928    The Osage Tribe: Two Versions of the Child Naming Rite. *Forty-third Annual Report of the Bureau of American Ethnology (1925–26),* pp. 29–164. Washington, D.C.
1930    The Osage Tribe: Rite of the Wa-xo'-be. *Forty-fifth Annual Report of the Bureau of American Ethnology (1927–28),* pp. 529–833. Washington, D.C.

1932    *A Dictionary of the Osage Language.* Bureau of American Ethnology, Bulletin 59. Washington, D.C.

1939    *War Ceremony and Peace Ceremony of the Osage Indians.* Bureau of American Ethnology, Bulletin 101. Washington, D.C.

Levy-Bruhl, Lucien
1923    *Primitive Mentality.* New York: Macmillan.
1926    *How Natives Think.* New York: Knopf.

Liberty, Margot
1976    Native American Informants: The Contribution of Francis La Flesche. In *American Anthropology: The Early Years,* John V. Murra, ed., pp. 99–110. St. Paul, Minn.: West Publishing.
1978    Francis La Flesche: The Osage Odyssey. In *American Indian Intellectuals,* Margot Liberty, ed., pp. 44–59. St Paul, Minn.: West Publishing.

Littlefield, Daniel, and James Parins
1981    *A Bibliography of Native American Writers 1772–1924.* Metuchen, N.J.: Scarecrow Press.
1985    *A Bibliography of Native American Writers 1772–1924: Supplement.* Metuchen, N.J.: Scarecrow Press.

McCarthy, Edgar
1923    *Peyote: As Used in Religious Worship by the Indians.* Hominy, Okla.: Private printing.

McDermott, J. R. (ed.), and A. J. Salvan (trans.)
1940    *Tixier's Travels on the Osage Prairies.* Norman: University of Oklahoma Press.

McGee, W. J.
1897    The Siouan Indians. *Fifteenth Annual Report of the Bureau of American Ethnology (1893–94),* pp. 157–204. Washington, D.C.

Mark, Joan
1982    Francis La Flesche: The American Indian as Anthropologist. *Isis* 73:497–510.
1988    *A Stranger in Her Native Land: Alice Fletcher and the American Indians.* Lincoln: University of Nebraska Press.

Mathews, John Joseph
1961    *The Osages: Children of the Middle Waters.* Norman: University of Oklahoma Press.

Mooney, James
1896    The Ghost-Dance Religion and the Sioux Outbreak of 1890.

*Fourteenth Annual Report of the Bureau of American Ethnology (1892–93)*, pt. 2, pp. 641–1136. Washington, D.C.
1910    Population. In *Handbook of American Indians North of Mexico*, vol. 2, Frederick W. Hodge, ed., pp. 286–87. Bureau of American Ethnology, Bulletin 30. Washington, D.C.
1928    The Aboriginal Population of America North of Mexico. *Smithsonian Miscellaneous Collections* 80:1–40. Washington, D.C.

Peregrine, Peter N.
1992    *Mississippian Evolution: A World-Systems Perspective*. Madison, Wis.: Prehistory Press.

Ponziglione, Father Paul M., S.J.
1889    Indian Traditions among the Osage. *Woodstock Letters* 18: 68–76.

Radin, Paul
1923    The Winnebago Tribe. *Thirty-seventh Annual Report of the Bureau of American Ethnology (1916–17)*, pp. 35–550. Washington, D.C.

Ridington, Robin
1992    Introduction. In *The Omaha Tribe*, Alice Fletcher and Francis La Flesche, pp. 1–8. Lincoln: University of Nebraska Press.

Rollings, Willard H.
1992    *The Osage: An Ethnohistorical Study of Hegemony on the Prairie-Plains*. Columbia: University of Missouri Press.

Sebbelov, Gerda
1911    The Osage War Dance. *Museum Journal of the University of Pennsylvannia* 2:71–74.

Skinner, Alanson
1915a    Societies of the Iowa. American Museum of Natural History *Anthropological Papers* 11:679–740.
1915b    Kansa Organizations. American Museum of Natural History *Anthropological Papers* 11:741–75.
1926    Traditions of the Iowa Indians. *Journal of American Folklore* 38: 425–506.

Smith, Bruce D., ed.
1990    *The Mississippian Emergence*. Washington, D.C.: Smithsonian Institution Press.

Smith, Marvin T.
1987    *Archaeology of Aboriginal Culture Change in the Interior Southeast: Depopulation during the Early Historic Period.* Gainesville: University of Florida Press/Florida Museum of Natural History.

Tanner, Helen Hornbeck, ed.
1987    *Atlas of Great Lakes Indian History.* Norman: University of Oklahoma Press.

Tibbles, Henry
1879    *The Ponca Chiefs.* Lincoln: University of Nebraska Press (reprint 1972).

Tinker, Sylvester
1957    *Authentic Osage Indian Roll Book.* Pawhuska, Okla.: Sam McClain.

Trigger, Bruce G., ed.
1978    Northeast. *Handbook of North American Indians,* vol. 15. Washington, D.C.: Smithsonian Institution.

Ubelaker, Douglas
1976    Prehistoric New World Population Size: Historical Review and Current Appraisal of North American Estimates. *American Journal of Physical Anthropology* 45:661–66.

Underhill, Ruth
1965    *Redman's Religion: Beliefs and Practices of the Indians North of Mexico.* Chicago: University of Chicago Press.

Unrau, William E.
1971    *The Kansa Indians: A History of the Wind People, 1673–1873.* Norman: University of Oklahoma Press.

Vecsey, Christopher, ed.
1990    *Religion in Native North America.* Moscow, Idaho: University of Idaho Press.

Waugh, Earle H., and K. Dad Prithipaul, eds.
1977    *Native Religious Traditions.* Waterloo, Ontario: Wilfrid Laurier University Press.

White, Eugene
1965    *Experiences of a Special Indian Agent.* Norman: University of Oklahoma Press.

Wilson, Dorothy Clarke
1974    *Bright Eyes: The Story of Susette La Flesche.* New York: Mc-
        Graw-Hill.
Wilson, Terry P.
1985    *The Underground Reservation: Osage Oil.* Lincoln: University
        of Nebraska Press.

# Index

Act of Slipping Off Wi'-gi-e, 119–20
Aged animal, 271. *See also* Buffalo bull
Aged Eagle Wi'-gi-e, 229–30
Aged Pelican Wi'gi-e, 225–29
A'-ki-da (soldiers), 42, 71
Alexander, Hartley, 3–4, 13–14
Allegorical story of the tribe, 63–73
Ancient priests, 130, 136, 142, 184. *See also* Holy men; Wa-kon-da-gi
Animals, 142
Approach to the House. *See* Processional Approach to the House
Arrow Ceremony. *See* Shooting of the sacred arrows
Assisting singer(s), 79, 135
Assisting Xo'-ka, 78, 85–86, 89, 107, 124, 125, 127, 135, 137, 142, 157, 166, 174–79, 192, 201–202, 212, 213, 217, 218, 273, 274

Bacon Rind (Wa-tse-mon-in), 23–24, 285
Bank-swallow, 89. *See also* Penalty Wi'-gi-e; Swallow
Bean shooters, 279–80
Bear, 32, 80, 176, 203. *See also* Black bear; Male black bear; Red black bear
Bear clan, 23, 35, 41, 52, 58, 65, 69, 71, 74, 75, 81, 88; names and life symbols of, 36; wi'-gi-e of, 243–45
Bearskin robe, 78, 176, 223. *See also* Buffalo robe; Puma robe
Beaver, 38, 203, 238–39
Beaver and the Thirteen Willow Saplings Wi'-gi-e, 167–69, 299n.125
Big Elk, 14
Big Hill band, 18, 26. *See also* Gray Horse
Black. *See* Charcoal; Night
Black bear, 36, 243–44, 246, 269, 301n.148. *See also* Bear; Male black bear; Red black bear

Black Bear clan, 189, 195, 196. *See also* Bear clan
Black bear songs, 195–96, 301n.148
Black bird. *See* Hawk
Black boulder, 36. *See also* Great black boulder
Black clay, 36
Black Dog, 19, 23, 280, 285
Black fish, 38, 238
Black metal, 40, 73, 267
Black snake, 37, 242. *See also* Snakes
Black squash, 270
Black water beetle, 36
Blazing star flower, 40
Blue clay, 36, 254
Blue corn, 39, 264, 270. *See also* Corn
Bonnicastle, Arthur, 26
Boulder. *See* Black boulder; Great black boulder; Great red boulder; Great white boulder; Great yellow boulder; Red boulder
Bow, 38. *See also* Sacred bow and arrows
Bow clan, 41, 54, 81, 216, 240; names and life symbols of, 38; wi'-gi-e of, 237–40
Buffalo, 27, 32, 40, 52, 80, 89, 124, 175, 180–85, 192–94. *See also* Buffalo back; Buffalo bull
Buffalo back, 39, 266. *See also* Buffalo Buffalo Back clan, 232; wi'-gi-e of, 266–67. *See also* Buffalo Face clan
Buffalo bull, 37, 241, 268–73. *See also* Buffalo
Buffalo Bull clan, 19, 20, 41, 47, 49, 52, 54, 66, 68, 71, 74, 75, 79, 89, 123, 127, 134, 155, 167, 180, 189–92, 195, 205, 221; names and life symbols of, 40; wi'-gi-e of, 268–73
Buffalo Face clan, 41, 52, 71, 89, 101, 257, 232; names and life symbols of, 39
Buffalo robe, 78, 92, 108, 177, 179, 292n.10. *See also* Bearskin robe; Puma robe

Buffalo Songs (in Seven Songs), 124, 175, 179–89
Buffalo Songs (in Six Songs), 124, 192–95
Bull snake, 37, 241. *See also* Snakes
Bureau of American Ethnology, 17, 26

Candidate, 77, 84–90, 107, 124, 127, 130, 159, 169, 209, 212, 223. *See also* Singer
Canis Major, 38, 39
Captive, 98, 108, 114, 149. *See also* Sho'-ka
Carrying (a pipe) and Wailing, 94, 159–61, 297n.101
Cattail, 38
Cattail clan, 41, 52, 54, 233, 257; names and life symbols of, 38
Cedar. *See* Female cedar; Red cedar
Central Algonkians, 28–29, 284
Ceremonial Distribution of Scalps degree, 48, 49. *See also* Clan priesthoods
Ceremonial messenger. *See* Sho'-ka
Charcoal, 46, 47, 108, 137, 195, 235–36, 243–45, 259–60, 265. *See also* Fire
Charcoal Wi'-gi-e, 197–200, 301n.151
Chewere Siouans, 28–29, 284
Chiefs, 42–45, 70–71, 221. *See also* Earth chief; Sky chief
Chief's Vigil Wi'-gi-e, 225–31, 275–76
Child naming rite, 23, 42, 46, 48, 57, 59, 65, 74
Choosing the Wa-don'-be, 106–107. *See also* Wa-don'-be
Clan bundles (wa-xo'-be zhin-ga), 28, 45–52, 65–66, 68, 70, 74, 79, 80, 124–27, 190, 212, 215–17, 298n.106
Clan life symbols. *See* Life symbols
Clan names, 35–41
Clan priesthoods, 21, 45, 46, 48–52, 60, 74–75, 78, 298n.106; role in Songs of the Wa-xo'-be, 79; role in Rite of the Chiefs, 223
Clans, 35–42. *See also* Fireplaces
Clan war parties, 46, 68–70, 100, 190
Clear the Way clan, 41, 303n.13; names of, 38. *See also* Ga-Tsiu' clan
Cloud region of the sky, 40. *See also* Sky
Commanders, 123, 124, 132–34, 148–49, 157, 158, 190–92, 200, 215, 220–21, 296nn.87, 89, 297n.93. *See also* Tribal war parties
Cormorant, 54–55. *See also* Great bundles
Corn, 32, 36, 40, 124, 175, 185–86, 188, 192; ceremonial planting of, 177, 179, 180, 300n.137. *See also* Blue corn; Hard corn; Red corn; Speckled corn; Yellow corn

Cornflower. *See* Yellow flower
Cosmos, 29–35, 104–106, 136; as reflected in clan system, 35, 40–42; in ritual, 57–60, 77, 92, 123–24; in the rush mat bag, 51; in village organization, 42–43
Cottonwood, 213–14
Counting sticks (in Rite of the Chiefs), 223–24, 273–74
Crawfish, 36
Crawfish Clan, 41, 54, 223, 253, 274; names and life symbols of, 36; wi'-gi-e of, 253–55
Crisis rituals, 56–57
Crow, 173–74
Crow songs, 124, 173–75

Dark earth (clay), 253
Dark-haired animal, 270
Dark-horned deer, 249. *See also* Elk clan
Day, 31–33, 51, 61, 66, 111–12, 114, 140, 155, 176–78, 182, 207, 214, 216–17, 226–27, 233, 255, 257, 258, 261. *See also* Sun
Deer, 32, 37, 80, 81, 89, 195, 200, 235–37
Deer clan, 41, 52, 54, 71, 81, 202, 240, 301n.152; names and life symbols of, 37; wi'-gi-e of, 235–37
Deer songs, 195
Deer tail headdress, 159
Dhegiha Siouans, 27–29, 284
Dipper, 38
Distribution of Scalps degree. *See* Ceremonial Distribution of Scalps degree; Clan priesthoods
Dog star. *See* Canis Major
Dog Star clan. *See* Wolf clan
Dorsey, James, 16
Double star, 38
Dramatic acts. *See* We'-ga-xe
Dream Wi'-gi-e, 160–66

Eagle, 69, 190, 197, 200. *See also* Golden eagle; Immature golden eagle; Mottled eagle; Red eagle; Sacred eagle; Spotted eagle
Eagle clan, 24, 41, 52, 54, 71, 89; names and life symbols of, 36; wi'-gi-e of, 242–43
Eagle down, 149, 166
Eagle feather, 81
Early Morning Songs, 128–32
Earth, 30–33, 39, 40, 43, 51, 61, 63, 72, 92
Earth Chief (hon-ga ga-hi'-ge), 42, 70–71, 73, 74

Earth division. *See* Earth People
Earth People, 36–38, 40–42, 51, 52, 58, 63, 66, 69, 71, 79, 80, 85, 92, 98, 125, 127, 132, 137, 148, 170, 197, 200. *See also* Moieties
Eastman, Charles, 11–13
E-a'-wa-wom a-ka (Causer of our Being), 31. *See also* Wa-kon-da
Eel, 203
Elderberry, 39
Elder Sky clan, 41, 52, 54, 71, 81, 85, 89, 91, 212, 274, 275; names and life symbols of, 38; wi'-gi-e of, 255–57
Elder Water clan, 41, 47, 52, 54, 81, 85, 89, 91, 138; names and life symbols of, 37; wi'-gi-e of, 232–33
Elk, 36, 80, 89, 247, 250–52
Elk clan, 41, 71; names and life symbols of, 36; wi'-gi-e of, 250–52
Entire earth, 36
Evening star (female star), 38, 39, 247, 256–58

Face painting: of clan priests, 92; of warriors, 197; wife of priest, 176–77. *See also* Charcoal; Symbolic painting
Faw Faw, William, 18
Female cedar, 37
Female star. *See* Evening star
Fire, 32, 43, 72, 80, 114, 136, 137, 195, 197, 221. *See also* Charcoal
Fireplaces, 35, 43, 72, 136, 190. *See also* Clans; Seven fireplaces
Fire ritual, 196–97. *See also* Charcoal
Fish people. *See* Bow clan
Fish-Turtle Song, 157
Fletcher, Alice, 13, 16–17, 26, 288n.13
Flint corn, 40. *See also* Corn; Hard corn
Folk beliefs, 279–81
Footsteps Wi'-gi-e, 117–19

Ga-hi'-ge. *See* Chiefs
Ga-Tsiu' clan, 38, 240. *See also* Clear the Way clan
Gentle Ponca chief. *See* Earth chief
Gentle Ponca clan, 41, 42, 47, 55, 71, 74, 75, 303n.12; names and life symbols of, 37; wi'-gi-e of, 234–35
Gentle Sky (personified), 268
Gentle Sky chief. *See* Sky chief
Gentle Sky clan, 23, 24, 41, 42, 47, 54, 55, 71, 74, 75; names and life symbols of, 39; wi'-gi-e of, 260–64

Ghost Dance, 10, 18
Ghosts, 279, 280
Glycine apios. *See* Prairie potato
Golden eagle, 36, 243. *See also* Eagle
Gray Horse, 19, 26. *See also* Big Hill band
Gray owl, 207
Gray wolf, 80, 89, 132, 203. *See also* Wolf
Great black boulder, 246
Great bundle priests, 46, 48, 52–55, 60, 222. *See also* Rite of the Chiefs
Great bundles (wa-xo'-be ton-ga), 47, 48, 54–55, 73, 75, 222, 223, 275–76
Great butterfly, 88, 209. *See also* Penalty Wi'-gi-e
Great crane, 39
Great dragonfly, 39, 89, 209. *See also* Penalty Wi'-gi-e
Great Evening Songs, 206–207
Great medicine bundle priests, 46, 48, 53, 55, 60
Great medicine bundles (mon-kon ton-ga wa-xo'-be), 45, 47, 48, 72–73, 75, 275–76, 291n.101
Great medicine plant, 269. *See also* Great Medicine Bundles
Great rain songs, 209–11
Great red boulder, 36, 246
Great spotted eagle, 36. *See also* Eagle
Great turtle, 203
Great white boulder, 246–47
Great yellow boulder, 247

Hailstone, 39, 268
Hard corn, 268. *See also* Corn; Flint corn
Hawk Bundles. *See* Clan bundles
Hawks, 32, 50–52, 66–67, 134, 140, 155, 190, 191, 214, 215, 217–19, 302n.164. *See also* Clan bundles
Ho'-e-ga (snare of life), 31, 33, 51, 65, 112, 114, 237. *See also* Snare
Holy men (ni'-ka xo'-be), 45, 47, 152. *See also* Ancient priests; Wa-kon-da-gi
House of Mystery, 46, 57–60, 65, 69, 70, 74, 76–77, 79, 80, 91, 104, 127, 128, 144, 146, 152, 159, 190, 195, 196, 212, 223
House of the Priests, 44
Hultkrantz, Ake, 281–83
Humans, 129, 141, 151–52; existence of, 34–35; place of, 30–31; uniqueness of, 33–34, 142

Immature golden eagle, 36. *See also* Eagle
Indian Service, 16

Initiation rites, 21, 48, 55–56, 59, 62–63, 74–75. *See also* Clan priesthoods; Tribal priesthoods

I'n-lon-schka, 5, 6, 18

Instructions to the wife of the initiate. *See* Wife of the initiate

Invisible world, 30–31, 57, 59–60, 62, 129–31, 141, 142, 180, 222, 276

Iron Eye, 14–16

Isolated Earth clan, 37, 41, 54, 58, 64, 65, 69, 71, 74, 80, 88, 136, 138, 189, 232, 274, 275, 297n.96; name and life symbols of, 37; wi'-gi-e of, 240–42

Isolated Song of the Hawk, 133–35

Jones, William, 11

Kaw, 5, 18, 27

Keeper of the Fireplace, 223, 224; song of, 273–74

Keeper of the Priests, 44

Ki'-non, 91, 145, 175; in Rite of the Chiefs, 224; in Songs of the Wa-xo'-be, 107–16

Ki'-non Song, 108, 110–11

Ki'-non Wi'-gi-e, 108, 110–11, 295n.70

Knowledge, restrictions on, 61–62, 82–83, 192

Kroeber, Alfred, 4

La Flesche, Francis: life of, 10–26; Osage studies, 3–4, 17–26

La Flesche, Joseph, 14, 287n.10. *See also* Iron Eye

La Flesche, Susan, 14, 287n.10

La Flesche, Susette, 14–16, 287n.10, 288n.13

Land People, 36–37, 41, 58, 63–65, 69, 70, 127, 167, 171, 190, 232. *See also* Earth People; Phratries

Large war party, 132. *See also* Tribal war party

Last-to-Come, 40, 41, 58, 68. *See also* Buffalo Bull clan; Men of Mystery clan; Phratries; Sky Peoples, phratries

Last Sky clan, 41; names of, 40; wi'-gi-e of, 264–66

Life symbols, 35–40, 65

Little animal. *See* Deer

Little-earth, 143. *See also* Crawfish Clan

Little Evening Songs, 206–208

Little great medicine plant (poppy mallow), 269

Little Old Men (non-hon'-zhin-ga). *See* Clan priesthoods

Little People (mi'-a-gthu-shka), 279, 280, 303n.8

Little pipe (non-ni'-on-ba zhin-ga), 37, 79, 81, 84, 89, 90, 92, 97, 166, 209, 263. *See also* Pipes

Little Rain Songs, 212–14

Little Songs of the Sun, 66–68, 155–57, 298n.111

Little yellow flower, 263

Logan, Leroy, 5

Logan, Roman, 26

Lookout, Fred, 26

Lookout, Julia, 26

Lookout, Morris, 6

Lungs of the Deer, 235. *See also* Deer clan

Lynx, 80, 89, 97–98

Making the Bow Songs, 148–51, 298n.107

Making of the Rush Mat Shrine degree, 48, 49. *See also* Clan priesthoods; Shrine degree

Male black bear, 80, 89, 197. *See also* Bear

Male puma, 80, 89, 197. *See also* Puma

Male star. *See* Morning star

Man medicine plant, 32, 55, 72–73, 259. *See also* Great medicine bundles

Mark, Joan, 17

Medicine plants, 40

Men of Mystery clan, 41, 47, 50, 68, 71, 74, 89, 92, 127, 134, 135, 140, 167, 171, 189–91; names and life symbols of, 40; wi'-gi-e of, 267–68

Metal. *See* Black metal; Mon'-ce Wi'-gi-e; Red metal; Rough metal; Yellow metal

Metal Bunched clan, 41; names and life symbols of, 36

Mexico, 23

Mississippian peoples, 3, 284, 304n.24, 305nn.26,28

Moccasin Cutting Rite, 91, 101–106, 224, 295n.65. *See also* Symbolic moccasins

Moccasin Wi'-gi-e, 102–104, 295n.65

Moieties, 40–42, 104–105. *See also* Earth People; Sky Peoples, moiety

Mon'-ce (metal) Wi'-gi-e, 230–31

Mon-kon ton-ga wa-xo'-be. *See* Great medicine bundles

Mon-zhon-a'-ki-da, 24

Moon, 30, 33, 36, 38, 39, 66. *See also* Night

Mooney, James, 283

Morning star (male star), 36, 38, 39, 205, 246, 256–58

Mottled eagle, 89. *See also* Eagle; Penalty Wi'-gi-e
Mourning dance, 19, 23
Murie, James, 11
Mussel shell, 37. *See also* Shellfish; Shell gorget
Mysterious Power. *See* Wa-kon-da
Mystic arrows. *See* Sacred bow and arrows

Naming rite. *See* Child naming rite
National Anthropological Archives, 6
Nelumbo lutea. *See* Water lilies
New year rite, 23, 46, 48, 57, 222, 290n.58. *See also* Great bundle priests
Night, 32, 33, 40, 51, 61, 66, 140, 155, 206, 214, 216–17, 246, 256, 257. *See also* Moon
Night clan, 24, 35, 41, 206; names and life symbols of, 40; wi'-gi-e of, 259–60
Nighthawk, 38, 39, 89. *See also* Penalty Wi'-gi-e
Night sing, 77, 91, 107, 224
Ni'-ka don-he (good man). *See* Wa-wathon priests
Ni'-ki-e degree, 90, 294n.57. *See also* Sayings of the Ancient Men degree
No Anger, 39, 253, 303n.14. *See also* Gentle Sky clan
Non-hon'-zhin-ga. *See* Clan priesthoods
Notice to Come and Participate, 90–91. *See also* Preliminary ceremonies

Oak trees, 37
O-don', 23, 78, 80–81, 106–107, 123, 170, 191, 232, 238–39, 256, 259; for seven (Earth) o-don', 171–72; for six (Sky) o-don', 172–73
O-don' counting sticks, 79–81, 166–67, 170, 299n.121
Old Age Bundle, 54–55, 73. *See also* Great bundles
Omaha, 3, 11, 14–19, 27, 45
Opening of the Hawk Bundle, 83
Orion's Belt, 38, 39
Osage history, 18, 21, 27–29. *See also* Allegorical story of the tribe
Otter, 38, 203, 238
Overreaching sky, 39. *See also* Sky

Parker, Arthur, 11
Participants: in Rite of the Chiefs, 222; in Songs of the Wa-xo'-be, 77–79

Pa-thin-wa-we-xta, 24
Peace ceremony. *See* Wa-wathon ceremony
Peaceful Day, 39, 263, 303n.14. *See also* Gentle Sky clan
Peace pipe, 39. *See also* Pipes; Wa-wathon pipes
Pe-dse-mon-i, 24
Pelican, 33, 54–55, 73. *See also* Aged Pelican Wi'-gi-e; Great bundles
Penalty Wi'-gi-e, 86–90, 196, 209–10, 293n.53, 301–302n.159
Personal names, 42. *See also* Child naming rite
Peyote religion, 5, 6, 10, 18–19, 23, 26, 280, 303n.4, 304n.15
Phratries, 40
Pileated woodpecker, 38, 257
Pipes, 28, 46, 53, 63, 64, 65, 74, 78, 81–82, 108, 144, 149, 150, 160. *See also* Little pipe; Peace pipe; Seven sacred pipes; Symbolic man; Wa-wathon pipes
Pleiades, 38–40
Pole star, 38
Ponca, 5, 15, 16, 18, 27
Ponca clan, 71. *See also* Gentle Ponca clan
Prairie potato, 249
Pratt, Richard, 10
Preliminary ceremonies, 294n.56; for Rite of the Chiefs, 224; for Songs of the Wa-xo'-be, 90–123
Priesthoods, 44–45. *See also* Clan priesthoods; Tribal priesthoods
Processional Approach to the House, 83, 116–23, 224, 295n.73. *See also* Preliminary ceremonies
Prophets, 279, 280
Pryor, William, 23
Public rituals, 21, 55–58, 60, 62
Puma, 32, 36, 80, 137, 203, 244, 245, 248, 249, 253. *See also* Male puma
Puma clan, 21, 23, 35, 41, 52, 66, 69, 71, 75, 88, 108, 195, 196; names and life symbols of, 36; wi'-gi-e of, 245–50
Puma robe, 78, 108, 114, 292n.9. *See also* Bearskin robe; Buffalo robe

Quapaws, 27

Rattle(s), 46, 47, 79, 80, 83, 124, 135–38, 166, 174, 202, 215, 217
Rattlesnake, 37, 242. *See also* Snakes
Rattle Wi'-gi-e, 135–40, 297n.99
Red (dawn), 261. *See also* Sun

Red black bear, 40, 265. *See also* Bear;
Black bear
Red boulder, 37. *See also* Great red
boulder
Red cedar, 37, 234–35
Red clay, 36, 254
Red corn, 39, 263, 270. *See also* Corn
Red eagle, 39, 260. *See also* Eagle
Red Eagle, 39, 303n.14. *See also* Gentle
Sky clan
Red Eagle, Paul, 26
Red fish, 38, 238
Red-haired animal, 270
Red metal, 40
Red oak tree, 39. *See also* Oak trees
Red paint, 111–12, 176–77, 179, 216. *See
also* Symbolic painting
Red plume, 268
Red squash, 270
Red star. *See* Pole star
Religion: beliefs and practices, 277–81;
comparison of, 281–85
Religious organization, 45–55
Ripens with the corn plant, 269
Rising Song, 115–16
Rite of the Chiefs, 7, 23, 48, 75, 222–76.
*See also* Great bundles; Great bundle
priests; Tribal priesthoods
Rite of the Shooting of a Bird degree, 48,
49. *See also* Clan priesthoods
Rite of vigil, 23, 45, 48, 75, 76, 160, 165–
66, 173, 177. *See also* Songs of the Rite
of Vigil degree
Rite of Vigil degree. *See* Songs of the
Rite of Vigil degree
Ritual calendar, 56–57
Ritual items: used in Rite of the Chiefs,
223–24; used in Songs of the Wa-xo'-be,
79–82
Rituals: forms of, 294n.56; purpose of,
61–63; structure of, 55–60, 77
Ritual segments: in Rite of the Chiefs,
224–25, 276; in Songs of the Wa'-xo-be,
82–84, 220–21
River, 38. *See also* Rushing waters
Rough metal, 40, 267
Rushing waters, 238–39. *See also* Water(s)
Rush mat bag, 51–52, 54, 190
Rush Mat Shrine degree. *See* Making of
the Rush Mat Shrine degree

Sacred bow and arrows, 47, 79, 81, 216–
18, 223–24, 274–75. *See also* Arrow
Ceremony

Sacred bundles, 5. *See also* Wa-xo'-be
Sacred Burden Strap degee, 48, 49. *See
also* Clan priesthoods
Sacred eagle, 36. *See also* Eagle
Sacred hawk. *See* Clan bundles
Sacred house. *See* House of Mystery
Sacred Warrior, 78–79, 82, 123, 124, 127,
132, 134, 138, 143–45, 148–50, 152–54,
165–66, 191, 192, 206–207, 217, 220, 221,
297n.93. *See also* Tribal war parties
Sacred wood, 200. *See also* Charcoal
Sagitataria latifolia, 248
Saucy Calf, 19–21, 61–62, 129, 134, 155,
170, 174, 181, 182, 189, 192, 195–97, 206,
218, 219, 285, 293n.49, 297n.95, 298n.114,
299n.113, 300nn.131,135, 301n.152
Sayings of the Ancient Men degree, 23, 24,
48–50, 79. *See also* Clan priesthoods
Sedge grass, 37, 235
Sending, ceremony of (Wa-the'-the): 225,
231–32, 273, 302n.8, 303n.10
Seven animals, 79, 80, 89, 166, 195. *See
also* Smoking Wi'-gi-es
Seven fireplaces, 190, 242, 248, 250, 255,
260, 262, 264, 266–68. *See also* Clans;
Fireplaces
Seven o-don'. *See* O-don'
Seven rays, 256, 259
Seven sacred pipes, 53. *See also* Pipes
Seven Songs, 51, 76, 123–24, 190, 192,
296n.74; for song groups of, 123–89.
Shellfish, 234. *See also* Mussel shell
Shell gorget, 108, 112, 114
Sho'-ka, 78, 81, 84–85, 91, 101–102, 104,
107–108, 124, 135, 159, 175, 201, 212, 213,
216–17, 231, 273, 274
Sho'-ka sub-clans, 42, 240, 267
Shooting of a Bird degree. *See* Rite of the
Shooting of a Bird degree
Shooting of the sacred arrows, 83, 216–
18, 225, 274–75. *See also* Sacred bow
and arrows
Shrine degree, 75. *See also* Making of the
Rush Mat Shrine degree
Shunkahmolah, 22, 285, 299n.127
Singer, 77, 79, 80, 107, 135, 159, 161, 192,
218, 219, 222. *See also* Candidate
Sitting Bull, 18, 288n.23
Six animals, 98. *See also* Smoking wi'-gi-
es
Six o-don'. *See* O-don'
Six rays, 39, 256, 259. *See also* Sun's rays
Six rays of the sun. *See* Six rays
Six Songs, 51, 76, 189–92, 219–20,
300n.139; for song groups of, 192–219

Sky, 30–33, 40, 43, 51, 61, 213–14, 233. *See also* Day; Sun
Sky chief (tsi-zhu ga-hi'-ge), 42, 70–71, 73, 74, 275, 277, 279, 290n.58. *See also* Chiefs
Sky clan, 71. *See also* Gentle Sky clan
Sky division. *See* Sky Peoples moiety
Sky Peoples, moiety: 38–42, 51, 52, 58–59, 63–66, 69, 71, 74, 79, 80, 85, 92, 123, 125, 127, 132, 137, 148, 157, 166, 167, 170, 189–91, 200, 218, 232. *See also* moieties
Sky Peoples, phratry: 38–41. *See also* Phratries
Smoking Rite (Non'-ni' A-tha-sho-dse), 91–101, 224, 295n.59
Smoking Wi'-gi-es, 95–100
Snakes, 207–208, 241–42, 303n.1. *See also* Black snakes; Bull snake; Rattlesnake; Spreading adder
Snakes, society, 279–80
Snake Songs, 208–209
Snapping turtle, 37
Snare, 241. *See also* ho'-e-ga
Song of Closing the Ceremony, 218–19
Song groups, 82, 191
Song of Making One Strike the Other, 214–26
Song of the Opening of the Wa-xo'-be, 124–27
Song of Processional Approach to the House, 91, 117–18
Song of Releasing the Arrows, 216–18
Song of the Rush for Charcoal, 196–202
Song of Standing at His Fireplace, 127
Song of Taking the Rattle, 135–43, 297n.95
Song of the Walking Upon the Animal Skins, 121–22
Songs, 61, 75, 82, 83, 191
Songs of the Gray Owl. *See* Little Evening Songs
Songs of the Midday Sun, 152–55, 298n.110
Songs of the Rite of Vigil, 143–48
Songs of the Rite of Vigil degree, 48, 49. *See also* Clan priesthoods
Songs of the Seizing of the Wa-don'-be, 166–73
Songs of the Stars, 205–206
Songs of the Waters, 203–205
Songs of the Wa-xo'-be, 7, 19, 21, 47–49, 66, 75; Buffalo Bull clan version of, 76–221; introduction to, 76–77; structure of, 82–84, 220–21. *See also* Clan priesthoods
Speckled corn, 39, 264, 270. *See also* Corn

Speckled squash, 270. *See also* Squash
Spider, 37, 241
Spirit Songs, 151–52
Spotted eagle, 255. *See also* Eagle
Spreading adder, 37, 241. *See also* Snakes
Spring ritual. *See* New year rite
Squash, 40. *See also* Black squash; Speckled squash; Yellow squash
Standing Bear (Ponca), 15, 16, 287n.11
Sub-clans, 41–42, 244, 263, 303n.14
Sun, 30, 33, 36–39, 43, 64, 66, 72, 77, 92, 104, 108, 111–12, 114, 128–31, 176, 179, 212, 214, 223, 259, 261, 262. *See also* Day
Sun Carrier clan, 41, 71, 89, 91; names and life symbols of, 39; wi'-gi-e of, 258–59
Sun's rays, 38
Swallow, 39, 88–89, 209. *See also* Penalty Wi'-gi-e; Bank-swallow
Swan, 36. *See also* White swan
Swan feather, 223
Swan skin, 81. *See also* War standards
Symbolic animal, 137–38
Symbolic hawk. *See* Clan bundles
Symbolic keepers, of the wa-xo'-be: 47, 68
Symbolic man, 78, 106, 108, 136–38, 223
Symbolic moccasins, 101, 104, 106, 108, 115. *See also* Moccasin Cutting Rite
Symbolic painting, 108, 111–12
Symbolic Painting Wi'-gi-e, 111–15
Symbolic pipes, 138. *See also* Pipes
Symbolic universe, 57–58, 76–77. *See also* Cosmos; House of Mystery

Taking of Seven Animals Wi'-gi-e, 95–98
Taking of Six Animals Wi'-gi-e, 98–100
Tally sticks, 46, 79, 80, 82, 107, 124, 135
Tattooing. *See* Tattooing rite
Tattooing bundle, 54–55. *See also* Great bundles
Tattooing rite, 46, 48, 54, 222, 287n.3. *See also* Tattooing bundle
Thirteen Footprints of the Black Bear Wi'-gi-e, 167
Thirteen Sun-rays Wi'gi-e, 167
Those Last to Come. *See* Last to Come
Three deer. *See* Orion's Belt
Tibbles, Henry, 15, 16, 288n.13
Tobacco, 53, 78, 81, 97, 108
Ton'-won a-don-be. *See* Great bundle priests
Treading Upon Certain Objects Wi'-gi-e. *See* Act of Slipping Off Wi'-gi-e

Tribal bundles, 46, 52–55, 72–74. *See also* Great bundles; Great medicine bundles
Tribal priesthoods, 21, 45, 52–55. *See also* Great bundle priests; Great medicine bundle priests; Wa-wathon priests
Tribal war parties, 65, 74, 98, 123, 143, 148, 190, 220–21. *See also* Allegorical story of the tribe; Commanders; Sacred Warrior
Tsi' wa-kon-da-ge. *See* House of Mystery
Tsi-zhu Wa-bin' I-ta-zhi (Touch no blood), 71. *See also* Gentle Sky clan
Turkey, 249–50

Ursa Major, 39

Vaill, William, 219–20
Vanishing Indian, 10
Victory song, 218
Villages, 42–44
Visible world, 31–34, 57, 59–60, 92, 129–31, 141, 142, 180, 184, 192–93

Wa-don'-be, 23, 78–79, 91, 106–107, 159, 166–67, 169–73, 224
Wah-hre-she, Charles, 21–23, 89, 125, 169, 224, 232, 240, 273, 285, 293n.49, 295n.95, 298n.114, 301nn.153,158, 302n.160
Wah-tian-kah, 23, 279
Wa-kon-da, 9, 30–32, 34–35, 52, 57, 61, 62, 82, 105, 132, 142–44, 160, 166, 184, 192, 211, 226–27, 276–78, 281, 289n.7. *See also* E-a'-wa-wom a-ka
Wa-kon-da-gi (mysterious), 33, 46, 142
Walker, Josephine Claremore, 5
War, 34, 44, 50, 131, 219–21
War ceremony, 23, 46, 48, 59, 65, 74, 98, 123, 138, 195–97
War club, 46, 47, 79, 81, 148, 212, 215–16
Warfare, organization of: 189–91, 220–21. *See also* Allegorical story of the tribe; Clan war parties; Tribal war parties
War honors, 44. *See also* O-don'
War parties, clan. *See* Clan war parties
War parties, tribal. *See* Tribal war parties
War party in great numbers (do-don' hin-ton-ga). *See* Tribal war parties
War party inside the House of Mystery. *See* Tribal war parties
War party outside the House of Mystery. *See* Clan war parties

Warriors, 66, 78, 101–102, 112, 123–24, 134, 137, 138, 148, 158, 159, 166, 173–74, 176, 177, 190, 192, 195, 197, 200, 203–204, 214–21. *See also* Charcoal; O-don'
War ritual. *See* War ceremony
War standards, 46, 47, 79, 81, 148, 197, 200–202
Wa-sho-she, 24
Water lilies, 32, 179
Water Peoples, 37–38, 41, 52, 54, 58, 63–65, 69, 74, 80, 129, 167, 171, 189, 190. *See also* Phratries
Water(s), 37, 203–204. *See also* River
Wa-thi'-gethon (power to search with the mind), 33, 61, 290n.29
Wa-thu-tse-ga-zhi, 21, 23
Wa-thu-xa-ge, 24, 89
Wa-wathon ceremony, 23, 45, 46, 48, 53, 59
Wa-wathon pipes, 48, 53–54. *See also* Pipes
Wa-wathon priests, 46, 48, 52–54. *See also* Tribal priesthoods
Wa-xo'-be (sacred objects), 45–49; interpretations of, 47, 49, 62, 278–79
Wa-xo'-be, clan. *See* Clan bundles
Wa-xo'-be, primary, 46–47
Wa-xo'-be, secondary, 46–47
Wa-xo'-be ton-ga. *See* Great bundles
Wa-xo'-be, tribal. *See* Tribal bundles
Wa-xo'-be zhin-ga. *See* Clan bundles
Wa-zha-we a-thin-bi-kshe, 47
Weeping Song, 159–66
We'-ga-xe (ritual acts), 75, 82, 83, 191, 212, 224, 233
Were animals, 279, 280, 303n.4
White boulder, 36. *See also* Great white boulder
White downy (eagle) plume, 112
White swan, 36, 244–46. *See also* Swan
White Water clan, 41; names and life symbols of, 37; wi'-gi-e of, 233–34
Widows of priests, 79, 160
Wife of the initiate, 79, 175, 223, 224; instructions to, 84, 175–79, 225, 274, 300nn.135,136
Wife of singer. *See* Wife of the initiate
Wi'-gi-e, 61, 64–66, 75, 82, 83, 136, 191, 224, 293n.45
Wild bean, 249–50
Willow, 38, 179, 239–40
Wilson, John (Caddo/Delaware), 18, 280. *See also* Peyote religion
Wind clan, 41; names and life symbols of, 36–37; wi'-gi-e of, 255

Winged Hon-ga clan. *See* Eagle clan
Witches, 279–80
Wolf, 32, 80, 131–32, 158. *See also* Gray wolf
Wolf Clan, 41, 52; names and life symbols of, 39
Wolf Songs, 132–33, 296nn.87,89
Wolf star, 39. *See also* Canis Major
Wolves Wandering the Land Songs, 157–59
Women, 185–86, 188. *See also* Wife of the initiate
Words of the Ancient Men, 75. *See also* Sayings of the Ancient Men degree

Xo'-ka, 9, 22, 77–79, 85–86, 89, 91, 101, 104, 106–108, 111–12, 114–16, 124–27, 130,

142, 159, 175, 192, 201–202, 212–19, 223, 231, 273–75, 298n.104
Xuth-tha'-wa-ton-in, 24

Yellow clay, 36, 254
Yellow corn, 39, 264, 271. *See also* Corn
Yellow flower, 36. *See also* Little yellow flower
Yellow-haired animal, 271
Yellow metal, 40, 268
Yellow squash, 271